ATTENTION

Joshua Cohen was born in 1980 in Atlantic City. He has written novels (*Moving Kings, Book of Numbers*), short fiction (*Four New Messages*), and nonfiction for *The New York Times, Harper's Magazine, n+1, London Review of Books, The New Republic*, and others. From 2001 to 2007, he worked as a journalist throughout Europe. In 2017 he was named one of *Granta*'s Best of Young American Novelists. He lives in New York City.

'Joshua Cohen is one of my favorite nonfiction writers. This book is a cause for celebration.'
— Elif Batuman, author of *The Idiot*

'Cohen, one of our crucial young novelists, has made the non-fiction novel of our moment, formed of a constellation of investigations and inklings. No one's done such a thing so well since George Trow or Joan Didion or Norman Mailer, if ever. It's chasteningly brilliant, and the kind of chastening we unfortunately need.'
— Jonathan Lethem, author of *The Fortress of Solitude*

Praise for *Moving Kings*

'Joshua Cohen is a blacksmith who heats, hammers and molds the language to sharpest, most precise points. Not for the sake of craft, but to tell a troubled story about troubled life in the twenty-first century. This is a dazzling and poignant book.'
— Rachel Kushner, author of *The Flamethrowers*

'Cohen is an extraordinary prose stylist, surely one of the most prodigious in American fiction today.'
— James Wood, *New Yorker*

'Funny, smart, and perfectly addictive, *Moving Kings* is a novel of wonderful scope. It shows Cohen at the top of his powers and is bound to bring him many new readers, hot for a fresh understanding of America.'
— Andrew O'Hagan, author of *The Illuminations*

Praise for *Book of Numbers*

'More impressive than all but a few novels published so far this decade. ... Cohen, all of thirty-four, emerges as a major American writer.'
— Dwight Garner, *New York Times*

Fitzcarraldo Editions

ATTENTION:
DISPATCHES FROM
A LAND OF DISTRACTION

JOSHUA COHEN

'Everyone knows what attention is.'
—— William James, *The Principles of Psychology*,
Volume 1, Chapter XI

CONTENTS

DISTRACTION [19]

—

DISTRACTION

If anything distinguishes my generation of American writers, it's that everyone in my generation became a writer, simply through the act of going online. More words have been written, more words have been read, by my generation than by any other generation in human history. I have to say, as a person who'd always planned on becoming a novelist, as a person who'd always planned on supporting the writing of novels through the writing of nonfiction, I found this daunting. The amount of information and the speed of its dissemination overwhelmed. I'm guessing this was the experience of most Americans born within reach of a midsized untangled extension cord from the year 1980—most Americans who'd grown up with books, only to exchange them for millennial adulthood and screens.

This ever-increasing amount of information coming at us at this ever-increasing speed rendered us unable to adequately attend to our own divided presences, let alone to a world that, though it wasn't united, was suddenly "global." Terrorism in Istanbul, hostages in Afghanistan, shark attacks, lethal mold, a sex scandal involving a missing congressional intern, the Giants v. the Broncos (to mention just a few of the "headlines" of 9/10/2001)—we were utterly incapable of absorbing what was happening. Rather, we were only capable of reacting to it: We scrolled through the plenitude, and clicked "like," and clicked "dislike," and generally ignored anything we weren't able to assimilate efficiently. The dangers of our impatience were obvious: no depth. But considerably less obvious were the dangers involved with a mass culture's rupture into myriad subcultures. Today, our sense of selfhood is undergoing a similar fragmentation. We're all becoming too disparate, too dissociated—searching for porn one moment, searching for genocide the next—leaving behind stray data that cohere only in the mnemotech of our surveillance.

I began writing nonfiction in the wake of 9/11—and was published in print, in hard copy, by newspapers and magazines that would go on to cut pages, wages, and staff, if they didn't fold altogether. Meanwhile, online was busy revising responsibility for the attacks: Bush II ordered them, Cheney let them happen, the American Deep State colluded with the Israelis, the Israelis colluded with the Saudis. I remember enduring explanations about how it was absolutely unthinkable that an explosion of jet fuel would be able to melt that grade and tonnage of steel so quickly and completely as to cause complete collapse. Ergo, the destruction of the WTC had to be a "controlled demolition." Ergo, the destruction of the WTC had to be "an inside job." Here, at the start of my nonfiction career, was the first time I encountered this phenomenon—namely, the violence being done to facticity.

In the years since, the ways in which fact has been under attack have been well documented, in the very venues in which fact has been under attack. Newspapers, magazines—by which I mean, of course, their online successors—are full of much more than information that's true and information that's false. They're also full of true accounts of the dissemination of true information, true accounts of the dissemination of false information, false accounts of the dissemination of true information, and, last but not least, my mind-melting favorite, false accounts of the dissemination of false information. The identity, or identities, of the disseminator, or disseminators, of this information changes frequently. The notions of the degree of culpability to be borne by the organizations that merely disseminate the information that has been leaked, or hacked, or faked, or some combination of leaked and faked, or hacked and faked, changes frequently too. But digital technology is not at fault. Rather, to blame digital technology is to blame ourselves. The average computer user of good faith who seeks regularly to read the news online now has to exercise the type of critical acumen that scholars of literature have always reserved for the analysis of texts: an intense engagement that seeks out secret meanings, hidden biases, hidden agendas. And what's more, our fictional average computer user of good faith who seeks regularly to read the news online has to do so even as the news reads him, or her, and modifies itself accordingly.

I live in a land where the natives don't have to be native and the foreigners don't have to be foreign; a land where everyone's always changing their addresses and switching employers, trading in their old names for new names, and altering their sexual preferences, genders, and fortunes; a land whose peoples have no mutual history, or not much; a land whose peoples have no mutual culture, or not much; a land that lacks any common religious or ethnic or racial identity, along with all reliable markers of education and class, and even a unifying language and consistent ethical and moral principles.

This is where you live too, if you also live online: a land that feels virtual, because everything in it has been reimagined *to distraction*.

In its strictest sense, *to be distracted* means to be

perplexed, confused, bewildered; a *distracted* person is out of touch with the person they used to be; a person "beside themselves," who has to be reminded; a person drawn asunder, pushed away, pulled apart, turned aside; a person "depersonalized," who's lost their grip, their footing, their mind.

Unlike other popular brands of bonkers ("witless," "frantic," "frenzied," "antic"), *distraction* isn't some spontaneous disintegration or unexpected absence of the senses. Instead, it's a gradual disbalancing, which requires only an initial intoxication and then proceeds to intoxicate itself. That's not to say it's a death sentence, however: because, almost uniquely among the mental maladies, *distraction* can be reversed, which explains why it was the term preferred by doctors for one of the earliest certified forms of temporary insanity, and so why it was the term preferred by lawyers for one of the earliest certified forms of the temporary-insanity defense.

Meanwhile, when applied to the crowd, the epithet is declinist: It describes a state that cannot hold; a state diverted.

I considered listing some statistics regarding how many Americans claim they're *distracted*, but while undertaking that research—which I only did because I could do it online—I came into contact not only with how many daily computer users claim they're *distracted*, but also with how many American women aged sixty-five and older, and how many American children who attend public school and have no siblings and reside in nonurban areas, claim *to be distracted* on weekdays v. weekend nights. I was in the midst of compiling all these numbers into a single comprehensive number, but I must've gotten sidetracked, and, anyway, that final sum should be, to quote our Founders, "self-evident": It's everyone. It's

100 percent. And even that figure feels too low by half.

Suffice to say, if you read at the pace of most Americans, which is approximately two hundred words per minute, then you've been reading for approximately six minutes by now, though—if you're like most Americans in another respect—there's also a roughly 50 percent chance you've already taken one break to check your email, and a roughly 75 percent chance you've taken two breaks if you've been reading on your phone.

We click away, but then we return, but then we click away again. We toggle perpetually between our guilt and guilty pleasures.

But though we might experience *distraction* as a shuttling, the shuttling compounds. The ailment tends to multiply itself, to mirror, echo, spin off, and sequelize itself, until the best any of us can do is just acknowledge it: We're spiraling.

You ask: "What was I doing?" You ask: "What was I supposed to be doing?" All you can answer is: *I'm distracted*. It's hard to go any further into it than that.

Especially because what you should be doing is trying to step back. Not to retreat, but to gain another vantage. Stepping back is never a retreat, if you pursue a problem to its origins. We'll only recover if we can find out just how and why this problem of *distraction*—this dim word, this diffuse abstraction—came to so blight us and unravel our brains.

The most venerable of our English words for "losing it" point etymologically to an event that made us that way ("mad"), and to a sad accident that cracked and crushed us ("crazed us"); we have a word that attributes the affliction to the phases of the moon ("lunacy"); we have another that ascribes it to the cycles of the womb ("hysteria"); we have blunt pseudomedical and pseudo-legal jargon ("psychopathic," "sociopathic"), and the inevitable overabundance of mean negations: "insane," "unhinged," "demented," "deranged." All those words, but especially *distraction*, suggest some degree of deviation from a communal standard—some loss of a fundamental collective *traction*, which must immediately be regained.

This was how the Puritans understood the term: denouncing the women at Salem as having been *"Distract'd"* into witchcraft. George III (not the most stable of men himself) was still censuring "the *distracted* colonies" on the brink of independence.

In American life, whenever a governmental or religious entity accused a group of *distraction*, the subtext was that the group (usually of women or minorities) had transgressed a norm or crossed a boundary. If the members didn't course-correct—because, again, *distraction* was correctible—the authorities would have to intervene to restore order.

Likewise, whenever an American politician leveled the *distraction* charge against the country in general, it was typically in the midst of a populist appeal to a base resistant to change: abolition, emancipation, universal suffrage.

"The *distracted* state of the Union" was traditional campaign rhetoric on the march toward Civil War, as antisecessionist candidates in both North and South threatened a turbulent future that would only get worse, unless Americans returned to the ways of the past, as if the past—pre-1812? pre-1783? pre-Revolution? pre-Columbian?—were this bright shining garden of sanity from which they'd fallen.

Given this history, *distraction* grows a great deal thornier than it'd been when it merely delineated the condition of slurping delivery noodles while streaming an Amazon show while holding a ringing phone and trying to remember who you're calling.

The term's past and present usages have a depressing codependency, however: They're like two sides of the same dull blank coin.

When our media fill the air with trashy breaking updates, when our elected officials lie, what they're doing is creating a *distraction*, so as to command our attention for their profit, or to steer our scrutiny away from the more dire of their crimes.

In turn, when we feel overcome by this assault, when the sheer variety of its indecency has worn us into boredom, we withdraw and *distract ourselves*.

And so what had once been a technique for subduing the vulnerable is still with us, but now it's also become the technique by which we subdue our passion and intelligence and keep our vulnerabilities private and intact.

To live in America today is to sit slackjawed at a helpless recline, stuck between the external forces that seek to disempower and control us, and our own internal drives to preserve, protect, and defend our hearts and minds.

In my opinion, there has never been a better time to recall this: the democracy of our *distraction*.

I'm writing it down here, before I forget.

I. HOME

IT'S A CIRCLE: ON THE CLOSING OF THE RINGLING BROS. AND BARNUM & BAILY CIRCUS

JOHNATHAN LEE IVERSON, RINGMASTER

I'm the first person you hear in the circus. I give the circus a language. Nothing happens until I say it. Nothing matters until I say it. I take you in. I bring you across. Because people have to be told, they don't always know how to act in the face of the extraordinary... I don't know what I'm doing next. I mean, I just lost my job and now I'm getting interviewed. I think I'll write a book, not a tell-all. Try and do some hosting, some voicework. People are always bugging me about getting into politics...

The "grandstanding" is over, the "platform" is in splinters, the "bandwagon" has left town. The "tentpole" issues? Forget them. The inclusive "tent"? Without a pole, forget that too. No rings remain into which to throw your hat: The circus is shutting down.

On January 14, 2017, Ringling Bros. and Barnum & Bailey Circus (henceforth RBandB&BC)—America's oldest and best circus, America's last true touring circus—announced that it was closing, and six days later the country mourned, with an exit parade, a grandfinale funeral: the inauguration of Donald J. Trump.

From its very inception, which was coeval with this country's inception, the American circus has been the imaginative grounds of American politics; its touring circuits became campaign circuits; its audiences became constituencies; its capacities for fame became convertible to power. And so the fact of its folding, especially now, can seem like a tragedy: equivalent to the tragedy of Trump, or even entwined.

At the very least, the shuttering of America's top big top represents the shuttering of a substantial American culture: a medium, an aesthetics, a way of life, which has been dragging itself around this country, and around the world, under some merged, acquired, or freestanding variation of RBandB&BC's moniker almost continuously for the last 146 years—ever since the presidency of Ulysses S. Grant.

The circus: No other art form has ever been so vulnerable. No other art form has so swiftly become endangered and gone extinct. You can't, after all, bring about the end of the novel. You can't, try as you might, suspend the poem. But Feld Entertainment (the circus's sole proprietor) can drop and—with a proper display of fanfare, hesitancy, and remorse—has dropped the curtain on the three-ring lions-and-tigers-and-bears-oh-my Greatest Show on Earth®, and ladies, gentlemen, and kids of all ages, the loss feels as fundamental, but also as fundamentally contentious, as the death of jazz, or the death of the blues.

Because just like old black music was "appropriated" into newer, whiter pop, the American circus comes to a close having been gutted of nearly all of its major technical innovations, attractions, and acts, which have since gone on—as if in a descent into an antiseptic afterlife—to become the baseline components of contemporary performance, especially of contemporary recorded or mediated performance.

30

Not to be a joss (circus-people slang for noncircus people) by spelling this out, but: The circus was how acrobatics and juggling got to the Super Bowl halftime show; it was how magic got to Vegas. The circus trained the animals to sit, stay, and roll around for TV and Hollywood, and pioneered the stunt work involved with leaping out of a conflagrant speeding vehicle and landing safely, way back in the dinosaur days before CGI.

The chief genius of the circus, of course, was to have staged all this spectacle and more, always more, all at once, and for one low price of admission—not merely live, but so precariously, proximately live that we the glutted audience were forced to contemplate the mortal risks being undertaken for our entertainment.

The earliest modern "circi" were glorified riding demonstrations, single-ring answers to that most ancient of questions: What do you do with your soldiers in peacetime? In 1768, on the eve of what the British call the American War of Independence, Philip Astley and his fellow cavalrymen of the Fifteenth Light Dragoons opened an outdoor "riding school" at a track outside London. What made their presentation a circus, in the sense that we'd know it, was that it combined the displays of equestrian prowess—including trick-riding, jumping, and military maneuvers in the styles of the Prussians and Hessian hussars—with interludes of clowning that allowed the riders and horses to rest, and were thought to appeal to women and children. Astley's most popular

routine was, at heart, a lampooning of democracy. It involved a clown, cast as the folk hero Billy Buttons, an everyman tailor who keeps trying to mount a horse to ride to the polls to vote in an election, but can't quite get his act together: His saddle slips; his boot becomes stuck in a stirrup and he's dragged; finally, he sits up in the saddle, but in the wrong direction, ass-facing; he spurs the horse into motion, only to fall.

In January 2016, almost exactly a year before RBand-B&BC's end was announced, almost exactly a year before Trump swore his oath, the following exchange occurred on *Meet the Press*:

> CHUCK TODD: As you know, people call you a lot of names. Some of it's positive, some of it's negative. I want to throw some by you. Let's see. Some people are calling you the Music Man of this race. Kim Kardashian. Biff, from Back to the Future. George Costanza. P. T. Barnum. What's—any of those do you consider a compliment? Or do you—
> DONALD TRUMP: P. T. Barnum.
> TODD: You'll take the P. T. Barnum?
> TRUMP: P. T. Barnum. Look, people call you names. We need P. T. Barnum, a little bit, because we have to build up the image of our country.

Racism, misogyny, poor-hating, know-nothingism— by that point in the campaign, Trump had conditioned the public to expect anything, everything, from him, except this: insight. This introspection that most of

America—that most of even Trump's America—had simultaneously been hoping for, yet hoping against. Here was a Trump who not only appeared to understand Barnum, but also appeared to understand himself.

Either that or he was just repeating the last thing he'd heard.

A year later, however, it's tempting to wonder whether now-President Trump has changed his mind—which is to say, with the end of RBandB&BC, might Trump regard its founder as a FAILURE... a LOSER... SAD? Or might he still admire Barnum, because though the business is perished, the name yet survives?

The name or, as Trump put it on *Meet the Press*, the "image": a conceit for which Barnum, who had the benefit of Gilded Age lexical niceties, tended to use terms like "public opinion," "reputation," and "character."

Also "appearance," as in Barnum's nostrum: "Put on the *appearance* of business, and generally the *reality* will follow."

Generally: but not in the case of the circus.

In 1782, one of Astley's former riders, Charles Hughes, founded his own clown-and-pony show, which he called—in a mingling of Roman imperial and British monarchial gravities—the Royal Circus, and, in 1793, one of Hughes's former riders, John Bill Ricketts, brought a rowdier version to America, taking over a hippodrome in Philadelphia, where President Washington was among the first visitors. According to legend, Washington so enjoyed himself that he agreed to sell Ricketts his favorite white battle charger, Old Jack,

for $150, and, in 1797, when Ricketts opened a circus in New York City, Old Jack hobbled along, and spent its retirement on exhibition, being fed lump sugar and petted by patriotic strangers.

On the surface, at least, which is where all vain fame addicts are happiest, Phineas Taylor Barnum (b. 1810) and Donald John Trump (b. 1946) might seem to share some traits in common: obsessions with pachydermatous size and promotional hype, along with a manic drive to project themselves, or their wishful selves, for profit. Both entered politics only later in life, capitalizing on their earlier careers as showmen. Both had lucrative sidelines in land speculation and development and mortifying dalliances with bankruptcy; both married significantly younger women (Trump and Melania Knauss: twenty-four-year age gap; Barnum and Nancy Fish: forty), inveighed against smoking and alcohol, and wrote or "wrote" volumes of self-aggrandizing self-help (*The Art of the Deal* is basically Barnum's *The Art of Money Getting*, just with cruder prose and monetary sums adjusted for inflation by roundabout 200 percent). Both achieved notoriety through making unfulfillable promises to their countrymen who lived in the interior, far from the coasts they called home, and, above all, both amassed their fortunes by lying and then by proprietizing their lies through licensing or "branding," which in Barnum's day was more usually performed upon the bodies of livestock and slaves.

That said, Barnum—who became more liberal as he aged, or just more of a fervent Unionist during the Civil War—never got any further in politics than two terms in the Connecticut General Assembly (where his big issue, as the owner of an itinerant circus, was the breaking of the railroad trusts) and one term as the mayor of Bridgeport (where his big issue, as the head of a circus that wintered in Bridgeport, was utilities modernization). Trump, by contrast, has by the time of this writing already managed (among much else) to drop the largest nonnuclear bomb in the American arsenal on Afghanistan.

That the first hundred days of Trump's presidency coincided with the last hundred days of Barnum's circus seemed a sign. It seemed to represent a final "appropriation"—not of any circus routine this time, but of a basic circus principle: Chaos, or the artful manipulation of the image of chaos, was now being staged not in the center ring but in the Oval Office.

KENNETH FELD, CEO, FELD ENTERTAINMENT, OWNER AND OPERATOR OF RBANDB&BC

The biggest resentment I have is when they say Washington is run like a circus. If only it was so disciplined and organized.

Here's the provenance, the tangled line of succession: In 1870, Barnum and William Cameron Coup established P. T. Barnum's Grand Traveling Museum, Menagerie, Caravan & Hippodrome, which met with great acclaim, and train derailments, collisions, labor disputes, and fires, until, in 1881, it hitched itself to a rival circus run by two Jameses: Bailey and Hutchinson. After Barnum's death in 1891, Bailey — formerly the ringmaster —

assumed control, and after Bailey's death in 1906, five of the seven Ringling Bros. of Baraboo, Wisconsin—the sons of a German immigrant (Rüngeling), who'd been running their own circuses since the 1880s—purchased the remnants of Barnum & Bailey's, and presented it as a separate enterprise until 1919, when they consolidated all their properties into a lone extravaganza.

John Ringling North, a Ringling Bros. nephew, spent most of the '50s partnering with, and in 1967 finally sold his family's show to, a man named Irvin Feld, a son of Russian Jews who'd parlayed the success of his Washington, D.C.–area record emporium into the then-novel field of concert promotion, primarily packaging black artists for majority white audiences: Chuck Berry, Fats Domino, the Platters, the Drifters.

America under Eisenhower was in the midst of a building boom, fueled by its large labor force of veterans. To be considered a city in this country—a true destination city—you had to have an amphitheater: a War Memorial Stadium or Soldiers' Arena. This was the last age in which public buildings were still named after public servants or epochal events, and not yet banks or cable companies. But with only eight teams in the NBA and six teams in the NHL, there wasn't much happening inside them. Irvin Feld, more than anyone else in '50s and '60s America, developed and promoted the "content," whatever would fill the seats.

And so the circus: It was Feld's innovation to ditch the tent and bring the American circus indoors, and he announced this grand-scale relaunch with a purchasing ceremony at the Coliseum: not the one in Nassau County, Long Island, where the circus held its last show on Memorial Day Weekend this year, but the one in Rome.

By promoting a relatively luxurious circus experience—a circus roofed, and amenitized with A/C and upholstered seating—Feld gave RBandB&BC another half century of life, but also changed the nature of the spectacle. The show, now, had to get bigger by the season, not just to impress in bigger surroundings, but also to reimpress itself on younger generations weaned on screens. What followed was an increasingly unsustainable balancing act, between the circus's constant adaptation to impatient if not childish tastes and the maintenance of the slower-paced traditional elements preferred by the paying adults, who yearned for RBandB&BC as it used to be, or as they imagined it used to be: Americana, not America.

But by the time Irvin Feld died, in 1984, and his son, Kenneth, took over, running a circus in this country meant hiring the preponderance of your performers from overseas. The best strongmen were Bulgarian; the best trampolinists were Romanian; the foremost equilibrists were from Russia and Ukraine (often alumni of the USSR Olympic gymnastics program), while most of the horse talent was sourced from Central Asia. In the Soviet sphere, the "circus arts" were always considered official national arts, on par with academic painting and sculpture, and so were supported with state money at state circus schools connected to state circuses. Kenneth Feld would fly behind the Iron Curtain almost annually, seeking performers to sign to twelve-week stints (the maximum that they were permitted to travel and work in America), and though defections were common, his access was never completely curtailed, because the governments—acting as talent agents to Feld's talent scout—would take a percentage on all contracts, and RBandB&BC deals were reliable sources of hard cash.

With the USSR in collapse, RBandB&BC began hiring a rising number of Chinese performers—who, along with the current ample contingent of South and Central American performers, help to put on this most North American, this most proudly American-American, of shows. These immigrant or, more precisely, these wandering-migrant performers are doing the jobs that most natural-born Americans now just can't or won't do: hanging upside-down and executing multiple somersaults between trapezes.

The circus, like the Circus Americanus—aka America at large—is and has always been about foreigners and the otherwise Othered putting themselves in harm's way for the delectation of paying natives. But while both madcap enterprises are decidedly capitalistic, RBandB&BC functions internally like a planned economy, a heterogeneous mobile welfare state governed *in toto* by a single family (Kenneth Feld's three daughters are company executives). Due to the logistics of touring, all circus employees receive, in addition to their salaries, full room and board. They eat with the circus, they sleep with the circus. Most of what they casually wear, at least most of their casual outerwear, appears to be circus-branded. Their children, both the children who perform and the children who don't, learn with circus teachers and go to circus dentists and circus doctors. Their pets, like the animal performers, go to circus veterinarians. This bizarre but constitutive expenditure is one reason, but only one, why the circus is failing.

Barnum's management turned the American circus into the tented embodiment of this country's expansionism: He increased the

38

number and type of its acts and brought on
midway attractions (games of chance, not
games of skill) and sideshows (ranging from
temperance sermonizing to burlesque strip-
tease). Before Barnum's innovations, the
Amerian big top shaded only a single performance area, demarcated from the bleachers by
a single wooden ring, which meant that there
were frequent pauses, to clear the area of
excrement, or prep the apparatuses for
subsequent acts. To rid the circus of such
pauses, and so keep the audience enrapt,
Barnum added a second ring, and then a third,
which he found to be the minimum that
permitted uninterrupted entertainment: In
the event that two rings would have to be
serviced returfed, rerigged, or caged—one
ring would still always be available for performance. This three-ring model ensured that
the show would go on, the circus would never stop, and that the audience was regularly
gavaged with fresh stimuli. It was Barnum's
belief—a belief arrived at on the road, and
through having to advertise and superlativize
his every appearance—that people were never as interested in what was in front of them
as they were in what was in front of others,
and that they were best engaged when being
made actively covetous, concerned with what
other people were engaged with elsewhere.
To be at Barnum's circus—not merely in the
round, but in the tripartite round—was, and
still is, to be trapped in an antique, physical-
ized split screen, tugged perpetually between

39

expectation (the mental chyron of "What comes next?") and neurosis (the mental chyron of "What's going on now in the rings to my left and right?"). Barnum's ideal circus customer has become today's ideal consumer, not least of "breaking news": kept in a state of constant distraction, constantly solicited diversion, suffused not with fear for someone's life, but with what isacronymized online as FOMO: Fear Of Missing Out.

In 1884, Barnum dispatched twenty-one of his elephants across the Brooklyn Bridge as a public-service demonstration of the span's resilience—to verify that it would bear any and all trafficked weight—but obviously too as a publicity ploy, a jumbo lumbering billboard-parade for his circus, whose final incarnation I attended at the newish, mallish Barclays Center six times in one week, walking there across the Brooklyn Bridge from Manhattan.

And the first thing I noticed was: No elephants. Stampeding children, yes. Stampeding parents buying children cotton candy and popcorn and light-up top hats and crowns, yes. Even a sad, tiny gaggle of PETA protesters. And yet: Not a single solitary pachyderm. The GOP's mascot (or its endangered Asian variety) left the circus last year, after a decades-long spate of PETA-filed lawsuits and PETA-backed animal-rights legislation finally succeeded in making their presence too costly, and Feld Entertainment transferred all of their elephants to the Center for Elephant Conservation, a private nonprofit preserve in central Florida about an hour inland from corporate headquarters, where the big gray rugose beasts are cared for, bred, and used for genetic-disease research, and reemployed as "therapy animals" for children with cancer. Nearly every Feld executive I spoke with blamed the precipitousness of RBandB&BC's demise on the elephants' absence—they were surprised when ticket sales declined by roughly 30 percent in the six months since their departure—and, I'll admit, I'm inclined to agree with their conclusion. There at the Barclays, I missed the tuskless wonders myself; not visually or apparitionally, say—not as much their delicate, almost dainty high-stepping, not as much the way they used to chorus-line, linked trunk to tail, mounting each other for the climax of the ménage—but, honestly, as I queued through the metal detector into the concourse, I missed their shit, the reek of it, the warm fecal atmospherics.

The first circuses I ever attended, as a kid in the 1980s, were the Clyde Beatty Cole Bros. circuses, which by their phasing out in the mid-2000s were the last American touring circuses to still be held in the open air, under tattered tents, redolent, in the doldrums of summer, of sawdust and straw and hot piss-puddles of dung. That dung remains my fondest circus memory: its smell so strong that it was also a temperature, a climate, so tropically intense as to transcend the sensory and become, nearly, a philosophical condition. What I mean is: The shit was there, it was plainly there, just where the shitters had dropped it, and I and my siblings and the other children would joke about it, while all the grown-ups around me, including my parents, would ignore it. They'd pretend that it didn't exist.

Now—as a grown-up myself, in a time of streaming media, when no one ever has to leave the couch (except to go to the bathroom)—I can't help but regard the experience of being forced in my youth to sit in public amid the officially unacknowledged fetid stench of the feces and partially digested plant matter of the world's largest land mammal as not merely educational, but morally educational: morally improving, compared to which the Barclays experience seemed fraudulent, weak, and coddled. There was even something evil, something lazy-evil, about showing up to witness scared live animals follow commands and whiplashes delivered by scared live imperiled sweaty humans, and smelling nothing: utter shitlessness, and I had to resist suggesting to the circus's press agent—who'd met me at the box office to conduct me to my roomy ringside seat fitted with two beverage holders and a food ledge—that RBandB&BC ought to sell their elephants' excrement as merch, coprophilic concessions, or else have the odor laboratory-synthesized into a liquid, spray, or gel, so that I might, one day, in the circusless future, use it to anoint the VR headsets of my offspring.

RBandB&BC still tours around by train, not for the romance, but for the efficiency: Even at this late date, rail remains the only way to ensure that all of the nearly three hundred people, five dozen or so animals, and umpteen tons of heavy equipment get exercised, fed, showered, rested, and to the show on time. To perform as many dates as possible, in as many cities as possible, RBandB&BC splits up—into a Red Unit and a Blue Unit. Each unit maintains its own mile-long train—the longest privately owned trains in the world—and each plies its own route across the country, one up north, one down

42

south, because that's the way the train lines are in this country: mostly latitudinally oriented, rarely intersecting along longitude. The circus heads, as the tracks head, as the country spreads, east to west, and so its itineraries can be read as archival maps, drawn by North-South animus, forgotten industrial feuds, and obsolete freight monopolies. Circus acts are so dependent on individual talents that they're essentially unduplicable—you can't just go online and find a substitute family of prestidigitators, plate spinners, or llama wranglers—and so the Red/Blue split requires RBandB&BC to present two different productions, both of which were rejiggered this past year, to compensate for the loss of the elephants. The Red Unit presents Circus XTREME—in which the classic circus arts alternate with extreme-sports demonstrations sourced from a score of other properties owned by Feld Entertainment (Monster Jam, Monster Energy AMA Supercross, Marvel Universe LIVE!): BMX biking, slack-line, parkour. Meanwhile, the Blue Unit, which was the unit that stopped in New York, presents Out of This World, the last production that RBandB&BC will ever put on, yet also the first in all of its history to have a story—as if the circus couldn't bear to leave us without a narrative; it couldn't go gently without a plot.

Once upon a time in faraway deep space (or so this last RBandB&BC production begins) there was a circus

Starseeker named Paulo, who was out canvassing the universe with his Magic Telescope when he spotted two stars, Johnathan and Davis, both of whom he hoped to recruit for his extraterrestrial circus. But—due to union rules, or HR issues, or just the basic ambience of nonsense that pervades every turning point in the circus's script—he was able to pick only one, and he picked Johnathan. The pair flew from planet to planet in a caboose-like spacecraft, scouting out the best circus routines and talent.

That's the backstory. The story itself begins just after the "spec," or opening number, with Davis left behind and feeling (clownishly) dejected. Indeed, he's fallen in with a band of clowns that has the tragicomic luck of becoming imprisoned (not "recruited" but taken hostage and imprisoned) by the evil Intergalactic Circus Queen Tatiana.

Queen Tatiana, then, offers Davis a deal: She'll release him along with the rest of the clowns, but only after he leads them on a mission to find Paulo and Johnathan, steal their Magic Telescope and their roster of performers.

Which is a crazy move on the queen's part, of course: To negotiate with clowns. To trust a clown—even a clown bent on revenge—with anything but clowning.

Queen Tatiana, Davis, and his merry squad pursue Paulo and Johnathan across four planets (two before intermission, two after), each named for an element: Fire, Sand (which I guess is Earth), Water, and Ice (no Gas). On the Sand Planet, Paulo and Johnathan find Alexander Lacey and his tribe of "big cats" (lions, tigers); on the Ice Planet, they find troupes of contortionists and ice skaters and, under the massive Snow Mountain, the Vortex of Ice, which is actually a

44

globe made of steel, in which nine motorcyclists ride simultaneously.

Just then, a moment before intermission, Queen Tatiana, Davis, and his bozo platoon catch up with Paulo and Johnathan, and proceed to hijack their spacecraft, kidnap the talent they've amassed, and rob them of their telescope.

Cue the pyro, smoke, and Queen Tatiana's Russian-inflected cackling.

ALEXANDER LACEY, BIG-CAT TRAINER

I love the circus but I do what I do because I love big cats. And so as long as I can carry on doing that, wherever that may be, then I'll be very happy. Sometimes people say, the animals would be better off in a preserve, where they can relax and do nothing; they can live their lives and be peaceful—but these are working animals, these animals are used to being busy, and you can't expect an animal that's used to being busy six days a week to all of a sudden sit down and do nothing.

ME: You're sure you're not also talking about yourself?

LACEY: Well, yeah.

The second act of the circus feels only slightly shorter than, but just as predictable as, the lines for soft beverages ($8), cheesy nachos ($10), and bathrooms (gratis).

Here, chaser and chased have just been changed around: Now Paulo and Johnathan go after the Queen Tatiana/ Davis/clown troika, who make an escape to the Water Planet (where they conscript the King Charles Troupe, an act that plays slapstick basketball on unicycles), and from there to the Fire Planet (where they impress into their ranks acrobats, hoop divers, and, finally, the Constellation of Cossacks, a pack of daredevil equestrians). With Davis and the clowns busy corralling the acts, and bungling the corralling, Paulo and Johnathan are able to retake the Magic Telescope, though once it's back in their possession, they make the inexplicably generous offer to share it, and Queen Tatiana accepts (how can't she?). As a finale, they announce their intention to join forces and combine all the myriad acts they've been squabbling over into a single mega-circus, and then they take their bows, in an emphatic endorsement of what the souvenir program ($20) describes as "Out of This World Friendship."

KANAK TCHALABAEV, EQUESTRIAN

The horse, I think, is the circus.

ME: Is the circus? Why?

TCHABALAEV: Because it is—versatile? It can be in comedy, or in acts like ours, with a lot of adrenaline and speed. But also there are dancing horses, and the liberty, in which the horses do the tricks on their own, with no rider. The horse has been part of Ringling Bros. for a long time, very long. How did they bring

the circus? The horse. How did the audience go to the circus? The horse. The ringmaster, who does he dress as? He is the man who rides the horse.

ME: How does it feel, then, to not only be in charge of the horses, but also to be married to Tatiana, the Intergalactic Circus Queen?

TCHABALAEV: Not bad, not bad. We don't have to sleep in the stables.

Here are the acts I liked: the spacewalking, in which gymnasts in astronaut suits balance on the rim of a revolving wheel, simulating zero gravity; the silks routine, in which aerialists jump and twirl and unravel themselves to mimic shooting stars; the gradual, measured, concentrated way that three leotarded women twisted themselves into becoming basically balloon animals, or balloon human furniture for one another; the fat/buff husband, fat/buxom wife team who brought out the shivery dogs and prodded a hog over hurdles.

I even liked the circus's theme song:

> *Fast and strong, turbo speed,*
> *they don't need any rest!*
> *We're on fleek, our space fleet,*
> *Paulo knows we're the best...*

But each time I filed out of the Barclays—the aisles clogged by audience members pausing to applaud or clock the Jumbotron, which was scrolling the social-media posts they'd been encouraged to share throughout the show: "dat wuz awesome!!! #ringlingbros," "the sutton and riley families thank u 4 the memories @ringlingbros"—each time I was returned to the street, I had the weird sensation of having missed something.

Not having missed some act, but having missed some deeper message.

There was something odd, something stupid-odd, about this fairy tale/reality show in which all of the characters had the same names as their performers—"Paulo" played by the Brazilian dwarf and capoeira master Paulo dos Santos; "Johnathan" played by the ringmaster, the American Johnathan Lee Iverson; "Davis" played by fourth-generation Italian clown Davis Vassallo; "Queen Tatiana" played by Russian equestrienne Tatiana Tchalabaeva, etc.—and in which each planet seemed to have its own national themes, which were often different from, or just not generally associated with, the nationalities of its resident acts: the Ice Planet, designed to have a Chinese vibe, hosting the Ecuadoran Torres family of motorcyclists yelling in Spanish; the Water Planet, with its Caribbean aesthetics, full of chihuahuas, a kangaroo, and a German dressed in superhero lederhosen.

Was it possible, I wondered, that this ridiculous story I sat through (six times) was actually the story of its performers' own lives—their real true lives—a dramatization of how RBandB&BC had ingathered them all from their respective planet-countries, and in doing so had made them citizens of the mongrel landless circus?

Or, alternatively, was it possible that this story was actually a restaging of American circus history—the account of how rival organizations were always competing to hire, and trying to poach, new performers; how they'd try to filch each other's tricks, and price-fix, poison, injure, arson, and just generally undercut one another until, with the public's interest in circuses dwindling, they finally had to cut their losses and pool their resources—like how Ringling Bros. and Barnum & Bailey together became RBandB&BC?

Or else—in the interpretation most obvious to me—was this story that started touring the country over the course of the last campaign really just a wishful preelection fable, in which an attractive, deep-voiced, red-white-and-blue-attired, undeniably Obamaesque American black man (Johnathan)—the first black ring-master in RBandB&BC history—teams up with his disadvantaged friend, a Latin American dwarf (Paulo), to take on and ultimately tame a megalomaniacal Russian adversary (Tatiana) with a deliciously campy lady-Putin accent and enough compromising or just violent leverage over the Trumpian clowns so as to compel their complicity in her nefarious plans for inter-galactic circus domination?

Of course, when I proposed as much—to the perform-ers I was interviewing, to the Feld Entertainment PR reps who wouldn't leave me alone during the interview-ing—when I suggested to them that their pride-and-joy circus wasn't just a mindless farce, but was in fact a vast geopolitical parable or allegory, consciously/uncon-sciously made out of a mix of current antiisolationist, anti-nativist,be-wary-of-Russia-but-don't-blame-Russia-for-everything-especially-not-the-election imagery and signifiers that it didn't take a Magic Telescope to spot, I got either no response or denials, headshakes of confu-sion, or pity.

DAVIS VASSALLO, CLOWN

I like the fact that it's a little bit of a mystery, the character of the clown. Because a clown is someone that nobody really knows who he is—nobody really knows what's in his head. We call it clown logic—why sometimes does a clown do this? Or that? Or some gesture? Or nothing? I think this is why the clown is the most interesting character in the circus, because you're never sure what to expect...

ME: You're saying you can't tell what's going on, psychologically, behind the makeup, the costume?

VASSALLO: You go to the circus and what? What do you expect? You know that the juggler is going to juggle, the acrobats are going to be doing acrobatics...

ME: But you don't know what—

VASSALLO: You don't know what the clown is going to do. He has to be able to do all of it, but still you're never sure what or why or how he feels about it, ever.

The American circus, like the Circus Americanus, was an exploitative business based mostly on humbug, and given to animal cruelty, blackface minstrelsy, indentured servitude, and slavery—in which dwarves and giants, the hypertrichotic, the "seal-limbed," "the

50

Siamese," and hordes more of the congenitally deformed and disabled were shamelessly presented to the public as "freaks"—but it was also, and sometimes at the same time, something like an aspirational sanctuary, for all the world's discriminated-against, outcast, and shunned, in which they, and the young, and the young at heart, were at liberty to dress and act and perform themselves as they pleased, in the free exercise of their myriad strange talents.

The face of this contradictory nature—the rictus face and embodiment of this democratic paradox—is the clown, who must always remain relatable to his audience, while also serving as an agent of anarchy, the sworn enemy of all continuity and sense.

The clown, then, is the politician of the circus: working both sides of the aisle.

RBandB&BC Clown Alley—which is the traditional name for its battery of clowns—officially recognizes three clown types: the Characters, the Whitefaces, and the Auguste. The Characters are the utility clowns, whose roles find their sources in normal, or occupational, life: They're the clown construction workers and clown car drivers, the clown tramps, clown hobos, clown firefighters, and clown cops. The Whitefaces, by contrast, are the more classical clowns, whose pale-all-over-not-just-on-the-face appearance and demeanor derive from the harlequinade and the *commedia dell'arte*: They're the self-appointed aristocrats of clowning; smart, crafty, clannish joculators, slightly pompous about their heritage.

And then there's the Auguste. There can be any number of Characters and Whitefaces in every Clown Alley, but there can only be one Auguste: He's the sad clown, the tragic clown, the grotesque, whose name betrays him as older or "venerable," with hair typically red and shocked straight out on the sides, and just three ovoids of white around the mouth and eyes, as if to imply an estate—a Whiteface estate—from which he's been excluded. He's the dumb clown, the dim clown, clumsy, klutzy, casually rude, who can never do anything right. That said, the Auguste is the most difficult clown type to play. This is because the Auguste has to be especially good at appearing bad or incompetent, without hurting himself, or hurting others. In the traditional division of labor in Clown Alley, the Whitefaces tell the Auguste what to do, they give him a task, and the Auguste manages— invariably—to screw it up. They order him to reach for a rope, and he reaches, and misses, and takes a tumble. The Character clowns are gathered for a meeting in the center ring, and the Auguste wants to join them; he wants to sit, like they're sitting, in a proper chair, and he goes for the one chair still vacant, but at the last moment the Whitefaces tug it out from under him, and he falls on his ass, and we in the audience can't help but sympathize.

Meanwhile, in the other rings, all of the circus infrastructure—all of the platforms and harnesses, all of the safety nets—are being dismantled.

JOHNATHAN LEE IVERSON, RINGMASTER

And to a large degree the cynical side of me goes, Yeah yeah, America doesn't deserve a Ringling Bros. It really doesn't. Because for 146 years we've been teaching you. Yeah. How we can all live together, how we can all work together, to make something beautiful. How every person matters, every job, and this is

what we're mourning. Not a show but a society. Lots of shows close down but this is a society. Black, white, woman, man, performer, or crew, everyone's equal here, everyone's important. You know, since I've been here I've developed a great affection for animals, but seriously, I'm from New York City, I'm from Harlem; before the circus the most exotic animal I'd ever been around was a squirrel, so I'm not going to get into that cage with the cats, I'm not going to get up on that trapeze bar, but we each have our own role, which gives us dignity. My first dressing roommate, Mark, was as white as day and he wouldn't go on to perform unless this one member of the floor crew, Rafael Suarez, who's Mexican, had rigged his apparatus, and they didn't even speak the same language; they just talked with their hands. But they had this mutual respect. This sense of responsibility for each other. Of all the lessons I've learned in the circus, about humanity, about being an artist, about making art and how to sell art, which is also an art, which the circus did a lot to invent, this was the most profound. That you're responsible. I am. We are. For each other. You understand? And that's what the circus is. Just what its name says it is. What does it mean? From the Latin. From the Greek. It's a circle.

FROM THE DIARIES

Groundhog Day Protests 2017

Stand in the sun in a parkinglot as if to make an antique photo. Daily the sun shines your shadow onto the asphalt. Where it makes no impression. Stand atop this asphalt for a year, you'd feel like you made no impression. Not even a negative. *Washington is not sensitive.*

"Whose streets? His streets. Whose streets? Sour streets."

"No justice! No peace!" The more I yell, the more the threat feels like a description.

"Lock me up! Lock me up!"

A wee pig awoke in our stomachs and jumped out of our mouths. Now let's chant his name.

THE LAST LAST SUMMER:
ON DONALD TRUMP AND THE FALL
OF ATLANTIC CITY

The governments that get themed into casino-hotel-resort properties tend not to be democracies, but oligarchies, aristocracies, monarchies, Africa-and-Asia-devouring empires. Pharaonic Egypt, Doge-age Venice, imperial Rome, Mughal India. Atlantic City has incarnations of the latter two—Caesars Atlantic City and the Trump Taj Mahal—with the Taj being the last property in the city to bear the Republican candidate's name, though it's owned by distressed-asset czar Carl Icahn, who also owns the Tropicana, a crumbling heap styled after the *Casa de Justicia* of some amorphous banana republic. The worse the regime, the better the chance of its simulacrum's survival. Atlantic City's Revel, a hulking fin-like erection of concrete, steel, and glass that cost in the neighborhood of $2.4 billion, opened in 2012 only to close in 2014, which just goes to show that an abstract noun, verb, or imperative in search of punctuation (Revel!) doesn't have quite the same cachet as a lost homicidal culture.

Today, the fake ruins of Rome and India are among the cleanest, safest havens to be found in the real ruins of Atlantic City—a dying city that lives for summer. I was returning there, to my family there, still unsure as to whether this summer would be my last or its last or both.

Now, given the fact that AC's been so perpetually press-maligned that I can remember nearly every summer of the sixteen I spent there being deemed, by someone, "crucial," "decisive," "definitive," or "the last," this suspicion of mine might seem, especially to fellow Jersey Shore natives, irresponsible and even idiotic—so

I will clarify: I don't mean that I thought that after this summer of big media scrutiny but little new money the city would burn, or that the Atlantic Ocean would finally rise up and swallow it. I just thought that, come Labor Day, the city's bad-luck streak would only break for worse and no one would care.

After the legalization of Indian tribal and nontribal casinos in Connecticut in the 1990s and in Pennsylvania in the 2000s; after the legalization of tribal casinos in upstate New York in the '90s and of nontribal casinos in the 2010s; after the damage done to the city by Hurricane Sandy in 2012 and all the myriad, still-ongoing depredations of the global so-called Great Recession that resulted in the closing of four of the city's casinos in 2014 (the Revel, the Showboat, the Atlantic Club, and Trump Plaza), leaving AC with the highest rate of foreclosure of any urban area in the country between fourth-quarter 2014 and the present; this summer—the summer of 2016—already felt like the fall. Maybe this wouldn't be the last summer that White House Subs or Chef Vola's would ever be serving, but it might be the last summer that I, as a sane, unarmed, and relatively pacific human being, would still feel comfortable traveling to them for a cheesesteak or veal parm on foot—taking the stairs down from the overlit Boardwalk to the underlit streets of what's officially become the most dangerous city in Jersey, now that Camden has stopped reporting its crime statistics to the FBI. It occurred to me that if and when AC is ever visitable or enjoyable again, my parents will probably have retired south to Cape May, and the few acquaintances of mine who still live on Absecon Island—the island of which AC is the northernmost town—will probably have left.

But what ultimately had me convinced that AC—

whose historical cycle of boom and bust recapitulates each year in the cycle of "season" and "offseason"— would not be the same, or even recognizable, was the perfect-storm convergence of a few maybe-related, maybe-unrelated events.

First, the budget deadline: If AC couldn't produce a balanced budget for state approval by October 24—and most residents here were convinced that it couldn't, and that Governor Chris Christie wouldn't let it—then the State of New Jersey would assume control of all its offices and operations, commencing with what AC's mayor, Don Guardian (and the ACLU, and the NAACP), regards as an unconstitutional takeover of city government. Should this happen, AC would be the first city in Jersey history to be run from Trenton (besides Trenton). The state would have the power to renegotiate all of AC's contracts, including its union contracts, and to privatize, meaning to peddle, its assets—like the water company, the Atlantic City Municipal Utilities Authority, and the defunct airport, Bader Field—in the hopes of paying off the city's $550 million debt and reducing its $100 million budget deficit.

Second, the ballot referendum: On November 8, two weeks and one day after this likely state takeover, Jersey voters would go to the polls to decide whether or not to approve the New Jersey Casino Expansion Amendment, which seeks to expand casino gaming—until now restricted to Atlantic County—to two other Jersey counties able to provide suitable casino siting at least seventy-two miles from AC. If the amendment is approved—and as of this writing the opinion split appears to be 50/50—get ready for grand-opening celebrations of casinos in the Meadowlands. The logic is that AC has already lost about $2.5 billion in gaming revenue to neighboring states over the past decade, and it's only a matter of time before some enterprising schmuck puts up a betting parlor in Manhattan; the establishment of new casinos up north along the Jersey side of the Hudson might forestall that. Or it might not— but it would certainly ensure that the citizens of the largest city in the country will stop trekking almost two and a half hours on a defunct-bathroom Greyhound, or almost three hours on an Amtrak that because of track deficiencies must be routed through Philly, to lose their shirts.

Of course, November 8 would bring another decision, and not just for Jersey.

I called Mom and Dad, fueled up the car, and left New York, driving Turnpike (Exit 11) to Parkway (Exit 38) to the AC Expressway. There wasn't any traffic.

Back in the (Bill) Clintonian 1990s, when the billboards flanking the Expressway and the Black and White Horse Pikes weren't bared to struts or advertising your ad here, when my father made his money suing the casinos and my mother made hers giving accent-reduction lessons to South Asian immigrants who worked at the casinos, when my parents' friends and professional peers and just about every other adult bowing to my left and right and in front of and behind me in synagogue either regulated the casinos (for the state's Casino Control Commission and Division of Gaming Enforcement), managed the casinos (their gaming floors, food and beverage, and entertainment), or supplied goods and services to and for the casinos (ice, linens, waste management), AC—the city itself—remained a mystery to me, a paradox. It was a place where everyone made a living, and yet where no one liked to live. A place of fantasy (strippers!) and yet of bewildering strictures (you can purchase alcohol 24/7 in stores and bars, but not in strip clubs, though you can BYO alcohol into strip clubs!).

It was, to my teenage self, about a two-dozen-block strip of Boardwalk and two major if seedier streets, Atlantic and Pacific, which I'd visit for fun or trouble before heading out for the less crowded, less polluted beaches or home, making in the course of a single weekend night the same trip that most of the adults I knew made every weekday: between AC (population 39,260) and the whiter, more affluent Downbeach towns of Absecon Island or the whiter, more affluent mainland. The adults were just going to work; their children, or I'll just speak for myself, had drugs to buy and girls to meet.

I also became a casino employee, but only after I was sure I was leaving. The summer of 1998, the summer between high school and college, I worked at Resorts, a casino that lacked an apostrophe so as to appear, I'm guessing, less possessive: of my time, and of the customers' cash. I was a coin cashier, and my job was to stand, fully tuxedoed, inside an excruciatingly bright and noisy barred cell furnished with a tiny surface of faux marble (because marbling camouflages grime, and cash is grimy) and a small round aperture through which slots players handed me their buckets, white plastic troughs emblazoned with the Resorts logo and surfeited with their winnings. I would dump each bucket's lode into the churning maw of my automatic counter, which, while it tallied up the coins, also separated them, shunting the nickels and quarters—the preferred denominations of slots—into vast plastic bags that hung to the floor like the distended gullets of pelicans. I'd read the total from the counter's display and pay the players their rightful take in whichever form they requested it: bills, or—I was supposed to encourage this—chips, which at the time were regarded as the easiest monetary substitutes for players to immediately put back into circulation and thus be parted from. Fiat currencies would soon leave the slot floor altogether, with the introduction of new self-service machines that wouldn't take or pay out with coins at all, but instead took, and paid out to, casino-issued credit cards. At that point, in the mid-2000s, the honorable trade of the coin cashier, like that of the blacksmith (who now only posed for photos at Bally's Wild Wild West Casino) and the riverboat captain (who now only posed for photos at the Showboat), just vanished.

It should be noted, however, that before the casinos phased out coins and we coin cashiers were replaced with self-service machines, we spent all our shifts servicing our lesser machines, trying to declog them—especially on the graveyard shifts, when more and more players came in with buckets they'd use as ashtrays, so that their coinage was interspersed with butts (smoking was banned in 2008), and when more and more players, too late for the dinner buffet but too early for the breakfast buffet, came in with buckets of fast food they reused to hold their jackpots. They'd sit at the slots, pulling the levers or pushing the buttons while poking around in their buckets for fried-chicken drumsticks or BBQ ribs, and shake off the stuck metal before indulging. Coin cashiers were trained to contain these situations, and so were expected to go sifting through the winnings to remove any bones and burnt ends and shreds of skin and breading. Those were the simplest things, the simplest of the foreign objects, to watch out for, mostly because they came in buckets from KFC or in foam clamshell containers from Burger King or McDonald's. Other containers, such as shoeboxes or backpacks, were tougher to monitor, and if I—in the over-air-conditioned heat of the moment, under verbal fire from an interminable line of intoxicated zombies—ended up missing anything, any noncoin article, especially if I ended up missing something sizable buried at the bottom, like a wristwatch or a phone or a med-alert bracelet, it would (usually) announce itself by jamming up the counter, and clearing the jam would (usually) blank the total, in which case I'd have to pay out a quarter-bag's max: $100. Obviously, then, it would be in a slot player's interest, if he or she hadn't won quite $100, to make sure that stray cutlery or a spare key or other sabotage debris were always lurking below the coinage. Obviously too, the casinos knew this trick, and we coin cashiers knew that we were responsible for catching it—that we were being camera-surveilled from every conceivable angle and so might be disciplined, or terminated, for not catching it. But still: I was leaving for college in the fall, and there were midnights, there were dawns, I was finding bloody Band-Aids. Shift after shift, my totals rarely matched up, the amount in coins I'd taken in always considerably less than the amount in bills and chips I'd paid out from my drawers, because I kept having to hand over the $100 black chips or, more often, the crisp, sharp Franklins. Though I hate to credit a Philly boy, it was Franklin who put it best: "Neglect is natural to the man who is not to be benefited by his own care or diligence."

On breaks I ate in the Resorts basement at the employee buffet—which was "free," because it featured leftovers from the customer buffets—and after my shifts I hung out with the only two cashiers around my age, the

only two who after clocking out wouldn't dash for the jitney home. Everyone else I worked with was older—nice
people, family people, immigrant or first-generation
Indians, Pakistanis, Bangladeshis, Vietnamese, and
Thai, who weren't going to squander their precious off-
time arguing with pizza-faced white co-workers over
pizzas at Tony's about what was better, hand jobs or
DIY jerking.

Some nights I'd blow all my earnings at AC Dolls or
Bare Exposure (which enigmatically, or out of legal ex-
igency, once briefly called itself Bare Exposures). Some
nights I'd blow just half my earnings on a room above
the Chelsea or at the El Rancho (the one motel that'd
never carded me and yet is now, deliciously, called the
Passport Inn)—a room from which I'd call a few friends
(males), who'd come and drink and smoke pot with me;
a room from which I'd call a few friends (females), who'd
never come.

Such are my memories, or at least the ones I've offered around like cocktail franks to folks in New
York and other cities I've lived in, whenever someone
asked where I was from and I answered AC and they
said, "Hey, that must've been interesting," or, "Wow,
that must've been nuts." With age, and after becoming assimilated to circumstances I'd never imagined
for myself as a kid from the Shore (in Europe! with a
girlfriend! as a journalist! as a novelist!), I realized that
I'd unintentionally adopted their perspective myself—a
sense of the Shore in general and AC specifically as
strange, even freakish—and so made a habit of sharing,
of performing, only the extremes. I gratified what I perceived to be my more sophisticated audiences with only
the most outlandish anecdotes of my immaturity there,
never mentioning, for example, that I was educated at

the island's particularly good Jewish school and not in its particularly bad, racially tense public school system, and that my parents were—are—kind, pleasant, generous, intellectual people who weren't always 100 percent aware of—because I wasn't always 100 percent transparent about—all the nose-dirtying I got up to after-hours.

Now, having returned to the city—to what AC's Chamber of Commerce used to call "America's Playground" and now calls, with depressing deprecation, "the Entertainment Capital of the Jersey Shore"—I found that my feelings had flipped. What I'd been conditioned to regard as a madcap, hedonistic outlier of a place, an utterly, even excessively incomparable place, now struck me as not exceptional at all, but emblematic, not merely of the rest of the state but of the rest of the country off whose coast it floats. The city of my youth had seemed like a flounder in summer, that bastard flatfish that local fishermen call a fluke. AC 2016, however, was coming to seem like America's bowrider: what captains call the dolphins that swim in front of their boats, riding the wake off their bows as if heralds.

I first noticed this sea change last fall, when a certain type of red-faced, overweight, whatcha-gonna-do-about-it New Jersey/New York male commandeered our national politics. Both Donald Trump and Chris Christie were talked about in my family constantly—Trump since before I was even in utero, and Christie since George W. Bush appointed him U.S. attorney for New Jersey in 2001, and especially since he became governor in 2010. But it was only after suffering through their schoolyard-bully penis contests during the 2016 Republican primaries that I began to recognize how similar they were, how alike in personality and in unctuous, disingenuous style. If I hadn't detected their toxic resemblance before, it was only because they'd been menacing different playgrounds: Trump having always been nominally private sector, brandishing the better, or just more recognizable, brand; Christie having always been nominally public sector, an elected official who must be held to higher standards. The ongoing SEC and congressional and New Jersey state investigations into Christie's alleged misappropriation of Port Authority monies, his allegedly having made federal emergency-relief funds available to Jersey cities affected by Hurricane Sandy contingent on city-government support of unrelated state-government initiatives, and, finally, his allegedly having ordered the George Washington Bridge closed as an act of political retaliation against the mayor of Fort Lee—and so snarling a major artery from Manhattan—will likely continue beyond the conclusion of his term in 2018. Jersey's governor has always been such an unmitigated prick that what stunned me most last spring wasn't Trump's emergence as the GOP front-runner, but Christie's dutiful dropping-out and endorsing him—his assuming a role, even after Trump passed him over for VP, halfway between that of a catamite butler and a henchman capo, the butt of Trump's insulting fat jokes and the fetcher of his milkshakes and fries.

The Republican primary debates marked the televised degeneration of their friendship—or whatever a friendship can mean in politics—which began only in 2002, when Trump's sister, Maryanne Trump Barry, then a Philadelphia-based judge on the U.S. Court of Appeals for the Third Circuit, nominated to that position by Bill Clinton, introduced her brother to the governor. The Christies were invited to Trump's third wedding, to Melania; the Trumps were invited to Christie's first inauguration. A year into Christie's first term, and six years after the State of New Jersey had started to pursue collection of the almost $30 million in back taxes owed by Trump's casinos, the state suddenly reversed course and settled for $5 million. Trump contributed an exceedingly modest share of the money he saved to the restoration of New Jersey's historic gubernatorial residence, Drumthwacket. New Jersey's near-miraculous tax forgiveness must be understood in the same way as its governor's near-miraculous abjection: Neither are demonstrations of Trump's master outmaneuvering, but rather of Christie's cravenness. Christie will do anything to win, or be on the winning team. If he can't be president, or VP, he'll plump for chief of staff, or attorney general, or even just settle for a monogrammed-T swag bag with a Trump hat, Trump Steaks, Trump Wine. Christie's not only inept, he's also running out of options: There isn't much of his party left to knock around. Politics (budget meetings in the statehouse in Trenton) used to be distinct from entertainment (*The Celebrity Apprentice* in syndication), but no more. Christie seems jealous of Trump, not just of his financial success or his nomination but of how well and recklessly Trump, as a former/current reality-TV star, can lie. Christie has always just ignored, withheld, or fastidiously obfuscated. Trump, by contrast, can't afford not to be blatant or audacious in his untruths, so as to keep earning free airtime from the cable networks and radio stations whose ratings and ad revenues increase—blatantly, audaciously—in correspondence.

To me, Trump was always a blusterer, a conniver, a mouth: a cotton-candy-haired clown who crashed the AC party late and left it early and ugly. To my parents and their cadre, the Republican nominee was a more malevolent breed of fraud: a dishonest client and dysfunctional boss. I spent my first weekend in AC persuading my parents to introduce me, or reintroduce me, to their casino friends, acquaintances, and colleagues, and spent my first week explaining my presence to many concerned and baffled adults, to people who didn't recognize me from childhood, to people I didn't recognize from childhood, and to strangers and all and sundry who'd make the time to talk Trump with me. The word I heard most often in reference to the GOP candidate—from Steven Perskie, the former New Jersey assemblyman and state senator whose original gaming referendum brought casinos to AC in 1976; from Nelson Johnson, the New Jersey superior court judge who wrote the book version of *Boardwalk Empire;* from Don Guardian, one of the few AC mayors in my lifetime not to have been charged with corruption; from Ibrahim Abdali and his cousin who'd only identify himself as Mohammed, Afghan refugees who sell pipes and bongs and martial-arts weaponry on the Boardwalk—the word I heard most often was "failure."

Every Trump account I was given in AC described a man so extraordinarily bad at business, or at being anything besides a business celebrity, that he was forced to switch from building casinos to branding casinos with his name, that polysemous pentagrammaton he charged his partners to use and then sued them to remove once the decaying properties became a liability. In the 1980s and '90s, the casinos with which Trump was associated constituted between a third and a quarter of AC's gaming industry. The Playboy Hotel and Casino, which was founded in '81, became the Atlantis in '84, and went bankrupt in '85, was acquired by Trump in

'89 and renamed the Trump Regency; he renamed it again as Trump's World's Fair in '96, and it was closed in '99, and demolished in 2000. Trump Castle, built in cooperation with Hilton in '85, was rebranded as Trump Marina in '97, was sold at a loss to Landry's Inc. in 2011, and is now operated by Landry's as the Golden Nugget. Trump Plaza, built in cooperation with Harrah's in '84, went bankrupt and shuttered in 2014 and now just rots.

And then there's the Trump Taj Mahal, which Trump built with the help of Resorts International in 1990 on financial footings so shaky and negligent that by the end of the decade he'd racked up more than $3.4 billion in debt, including business (mostly high-interest junk-bond) and personal debt, which he handled by conflating them. By lumping them together under the auspices of a publicly traded company, Trump Hotels & Casino Resorts, he dumped all his burdens onto the backs of his shareholders even as he continued to treat his casino receipts as profits, to be raided and reinvested in development in New York. Even while Trump Hotels & Casino Resorts bled an average of $49 million a year into the late '90s, even while its share price plummeted from $35 to $0.17 through the early 2000s, Trump himself continued to receive a salary in the millions, not to mention bonuses and the monies his personally held companies made from his publicly traded company leasing office space in Manhattan's Trump Tower and renting Trump Shuttle helicopters and Trump Airlines airplanes to fly around showroom acts and high rollers. Trump Hotels & Casino Resorts finally went bankrupt in 2004, and in its restructuring became Trump Entertainment Resorts, which itself went bankrupt in 2014 and was fire-sold to Icahn Enterprises, whose subsidiary, Tropicana Entertainment Inc., has run the Taj into a $100 million hole. Carl Icahn, the conglomerate's chairman, was once a wary adversary who now endorses Trump, though he's declined Trump's offer to become the next secretary of the treasury: "I am flattered but do not get up early enough in the morning to accept this opportunity."

On July 1, at the height of the season, the Taj's unionized employees from UNITE HERE Local 54 went on strike, demanding a wage increase and the reinstatement of health and pension benefits suspended in the transfer of ownership. Negotiations were never scheduled; Icahn and the union couldn't agree on a venue, let alone an agenda. In early August, Icahn announced that he'd be closing the Taj after Labor Day. And so the fall forecast kept getting grimmer, with the loss of the city's most prominent casino and more than 2,800 jobs.

The Taj's demise would be chronicled throughout the summer by *The New York Times* and *The Washington Post*, in articles framed as analyses of Trump's finances. These articles, like the leveraged-debt practices they documented, were virtuoso feats, given that they were researched without access to the candidate's tax returns. But reading the articles induced headaches: All those loans and defaults and shell companies shattered, keeping track of them was like counting the beach, grain by grain.

The main issue I had with this out-of-town finance journalism, however, was that it was finance journalism: None of its unbiased sums could account for Trump's meanness—that petty, vile villainy that was being described to me when I was casting around for a place to write.

Because my parents had remodeled my old bedroom into the room of dusty, disused exercise equipment, and because AC has no leisurely cafés or bookshop spaces and its public library is open only 9 to 5, I prevailed on my uncle to make me a key to the office of one of his companies, Fishermen's Energy, a consortium of commercial fishermen who are trying to establish what would be New Jersey's first offshore wind farm, in AC. The building was the Professional Arts Building, which went up in the 1920s and flaunts it; its windows gave onto Resorts. I moved into the conference room, adjacent to the cubicles of my uncle's three employees, who, given Jersey's disinterest in renewable energy, didn't have much work to do—or to put it positively, had the occasional leisure to talk.

The receptionist, Karen Carpinelli, previously worked for a family-run Atlantic County–based neon-sign firm that found itself working for Trump, who preferred to contract with family-run firms because they were easily abused. Trump consistently failed to pay the full amounts he owed, which forced the sign-makers to inflate their prices: Apparently the totals didn't matter, only the discounts did, and if Trump paid at all it was usually half of whatever they billed him. Fishermen's Energy project director Tim Axelsson, who hails from a distinguished fishing family in Cape May, recounted to me how, in 1988, Trump had planned to arrive in AC for the first time in the *Trump Princess*, a $29 million yacht formerly owned by the Sultan of Brunei and, before him, by Saudi arms dealer Adnan Khashoggi. The *Princess*, however, being one of the largest yachts in the world at the time, was too large to navigate the channel, and so Trump paid to have the channel dredged, which it was, without any impact studies conducted or permits obtained (though the N.J. Department of Environmental Protection did issue a belated stop-work order).

69

Fishermen's Energy COO and general counsel Paul Gallagher, who prior to working for my uncle served as AC city solicitor, once served as manager of the Jersey-Atlantic Wind Farm, whose five inshore wind turbines, situated hard by the inlet, help power the city's wastewater-treatment plant. When that project went up, Trump made a call: There were five turbines, he said, as if he were counting up the notoriously short fingers on his notoriously small hands, and there were also five letters in his name—did Paul understand? Would the Jersey-Atlantic people be interested in festooning the poles of their turbines with T R U M P? Apparently, Trump would let them do it free of charge. And this was just the lore to be found in a single office—the lore that was dumped on me about five minutes after moving in.

All along the Boardwalk, the sun-bleached, tattered banners read 'Do AC'—the city's latest marketing catchphrase. The Boardwalk was a scrum of such imperatives, with Trumps on every side issuing edicts and diktats, offering bargains. Trumps in toupees and with their guts hanging over their change belts, out on Steel Pier, out on Central Pier, trying to get me to try the ring toss, though the rubber rings always bounce off the rubber bottles, or to try the beanbag pitch, though the lily pads they're supposed to land on are kept wet and slippery with a shammy. Try Fralinger's Salt Water Taffy, which contains no salt water. Step right up and I'll guess your weight, or at least I'll make your wallet lighter. What American literature taught me—what Melville taught me in *The Confidence-Man*, what Poe taught me in "Diddling," that imagination or fantasy can be a form of greed, even a uniquely American form—the shills and

70

carny barkers taught me first, at $2 a lesson: I would never win that stuffed elephant.

The Boardwalk's kitsch, the kitsch of Trump's former properties along the Boardwalk, merely reinforces how retro a mogul the candidate is: a throwback who doesn't care he's a throwback, who's barely aware he is, dressed to impress in a padded Brioni suit and a tie with a scrotum-size knot. After a sham career spent endlessly lauding himself as the last great product of the last great era when our country still made things, when our country still built, he now spends what's basically his retirement—which he considers America's retirement, his and its mutual licensing age—wallowing in sentimentality and goading with nostalgia. He's a magnate brat who in an age of rapid computerized transactions and exponentially unaccountable ethereality didn't make his name, such as it is, or his fortune, such as it is, on Wall Street, but rather in the old-school outer boroughs, and later in schmancier Midtown, developing what he'd inherited. He deceitfully prides himself on having employed real, tangible workers (including illegal immigrants and Mafia contractors) to build real, tangible things (which tend to have structural insufficiencies and the same black glass that's used in TV/movie evil-overlord compounds and fascist government architecture throughout the Middle East and Central Asia). Not for Trump any bundling, derivatives, or microtrades—just the anachronistic micromanaging of flamboyant chandeliers and ornate door handles. He's the steak-n-taters CEO, not an asexual vegan baby of the algorithm revolution.

Making my rounds of the Boardwalk bars, it was eerie: how every person's take on Trump was the same, or was so precisely contradictory. Locals—especially those who knew the candidate's business history—vigorously loathed him, while visitors—especially those who knew nothing of that history—were equally passionate in their admiration and praise. "He's just another billionaire." "He's one of us." "He's a liar." "He's so honest." Common to the heated speeches of both were the apparent influences of alcohol and fear. Everyone I was meeting seemed drunk on fear: of the candidate, of their country, of themselves.

The ambient scare that Trump has put into the populace, and the way his calculated swoops through the news cycle moderate or exacerbate this emotionalism, regulating it like a professional thrill, reminds me more than anything of gaming: of what it feels like to put my money on the line. It's as if Trump—this vanity candidate, famous beyond law—is offering all of us a wager: that he can inflame his rhetoric and press his luck without ever pressing it too far—without alienating all women and black and Hispanic voters, and without getting too many Mexicans, or too many Muslims, or even just some white Democrats, beaten up or killed.

This, of course, is the only type of wager that Trump can ever make: a bet against America, counting on our dumbness, counting on our hate. He'd never take a turn at one of the properties he's owned; he'd never belly up to one of the voting-booth-like slot devices on which his AC businesses were based. Trump, a man addicted to success, and—if his oration is any indication—a man with extremely limited reserves of self-control, can't ever gamble, because he can't ever lose. I'd bet that Trump is barely even familiar with the table rules, for the simple reason that he doesn't have to be; all he has to know are the odds to know that he can't beat them. Having owned the house, he'll never tempt the house. All he can do is torch it. Which is why Trump won't lose the election, at least not in the reckoning of his supporters. Even if Clinton is declared the winner, most likely even before Clinton is declared the winner, he'll allege some sort of conspiracy; he'll blame someone else; no failure can be his fault. He'll accuse the game of being rigged—he already has. He'll indict the nature of the game itself, calling the political process both overregulated and underregulated, prohibitive in cost, inefficient, and just plain evil, and the sad thing is, he's not wrong.

The saddest thing, though, is that the only place in AC—the only place in America, it seems—where you can go to escape his sped-up diet-pill tics and wiggy tirades is one of his former casinos. Two weeks into its union strike, two weeks before the announcement of its closing, the Taj was a mess of stained carpet, moldy walls, leaky ceilings. Regular maintenance personnel had been replaced by skeleton crews of temp labor, but since the dealers aren't unionized, the casino was open, and remained so locked down, so focused on keeping me unfocused and yet maximizing my TOD (German for "death," but also casinoese for "time on device"), that none of its screens carried anything but ads for inoperative buffets and upcoming circus extravaganzas that would have to be canceled. No CNN, not even Fox.

The Taj, like most casinos, has primarily always been a slot palace, and any square footage given over to table games has to favor those that most favor the house: roulette, where the house edge is 5.26 percent, and craps, where the house edge is 1.4 percent, over the easier-to-understand and easier-to-play blackjack, where the house edge is .5 percent (slots are allotted a house edge of up to 15 percent). To put these numbers into words: You done never had a chance. But as long as your pleasure quanta (booze, food, shows, and carnal atmospherics) outweigh your pain quanta (your losses), research has demonstrated that you'll keep playing along, encouraged through every bad roll or spin or card by PR exhortations, or by the living example of Trump—whose image used to be everywhere in his former casinos; whose image is now everywhere except in his former casinos—telling average citizens that they too can beat the odds and become winners, the ultimate avatars of American exceptionalism.

This type of self-empowering yet self-sabotaging, ignore-all-the-facts-and-go-for-broke gaming faded from fashion through the '90s with the spread of numeracy online. Data was suddenly determining, because it had suddenly numerated, everything, and I can recall how by the time I was working at Resorts it already felt ridiculous that anyone would go to a casino to play any game besides poker, a game in which players compete not against the house for its money, but against one another, for one another's money, with the house taking only a tiny percentage of each pot—the vigorish or rake (typically 10 percent, up to $4). It follows that casinos don't make much money on poker, and so the few AC casinos that still provide a room for it do so begrudgingly, with the hope that the players' companions—their angry spouses and nursing attendants—will find their ways elsewhere in the casino, to the slots.

Of course, one of the beauties of poker is that it doesn't have to be played in a casino—it can be played anywhere, for cheaper. The first and last semiregular private game I ever participated in began at the Broadway Suites on W. 101st Street and Broadway in New York on some weekday in 1998—just after my summer at Resorts—and ended on that hungover, smoke-fogged day after Election

Day 2000, when an art-history student left the table to hyperventilate on the floor by the poky Zenith TV and an ethnomusicology student went to find a dictionary—a paper dictionary—to check the definition of "chad."

After the stolen election of *Bush v. Gore*, which was the first election I and all the other players in that game were eligible to vote in, it became normal for people of my generation—kinda-sorta millennials immersed in the mathematics of poker, who followed the Texas hold 'em tournaments just then being televised and played in online games between IRL games and participated in online poker tutorials—to also immerse themselves in all manner of election-relevant math, to memorize and rattle off how many electoral votes each state had, and to argue about which were the decisive counties or districts or, as in the case of Florida, precincts in each state, which percentage of overvotes or undervotes would have to be counted as legal votes for which outcome to occur, and, of course, how the outcome would've been different if all the states, or if certain states, had split their electoral votes along the lines of their popular votes as opposed to awarding them winner-take-all—all of which were topics too specialized for, because too inaccessible to, prior generations of American voters, which kept up with the elections through the morning paper and evening news, without any interactive maps or regression analyses or aggregated (ranked and weighted) polling.

Of course, whenever you're reading a poll, what you're reading are odds, which you can convert yourself by flipping each percentage into a fraction, subtracting the numerator from the denominator, and dividing the difference by the numerator. For instance, if Clinton is leading Trump in the popular vote 48 percent to 42 percent, as she seemed to be throughout much of the summer, her odds of winning are 1.083:1 and Trump's are 1.38:1. However, with the electoral vote determining the presidency, each online bookmaking site projects its own 270/538 split to calculate its odds (for parimutuel betting, meaning, say, a bet that Clinton will beat Trump by any margin; and for betting the spread, meaning, say, a bet that Clinton will beat Trump by the exact margin of 330–208). Ironically enough, most of the more reliable sites that'll trade U.S. election action for cash are registered in the U.K., the Bahamas, or elsewhere abroad, because America doesn't quite approve of betting on politics—not because betting on politics is cynical, but because it's considered a variety of sports betting, which is illegal in all but four of the states.

America: a country in which even a noble law has to be justified through the drudgery of precedent and stupid technicality.

Wednesday night, the Local 54 picket crowd chanting and waving placards outside the Taj was just about as sparse as its poker-room crowd and equally gloomy: "No contract, no peace!" "All day, all night, Taj Mahal is out on strike!" The poker room was all chairs, stacked and overturned and empty chairs, and two tables of half bachelor-party fools, half "grinders": pseudo-pros who if they'd been playing just against one another would've played tight, would've folded and waited, "grinded" in the interest of making a slow, steady profit. But tonight they were staggered between the bachelor-party fools, so the strategy was different, the tactics were looser. The old hands were taking advantage.

Out of shape, insomniac, amphetamined sharks, not circling, just sitting, around the circular tables, sniffing for blood or for related signs of weakness. They were waiting for a player—for a neophyte, a tourist in murky waters—to lose patience and bet, or to match or raise a bet of theirs or another's, not out of any discernible logic or psychology, but because discipline is boring, and no one comes to a casino to be bored.

That's the moment the bullying sets in—the daring, the teasing and taunting, which is often unvoiced, and often merely imaginary.

This was how it kept going down: An older, more experienced player would, after a period of concentrated play, without warning go all-in, which gambit the bachelor-party rubes would alternately take as a temptation and a test, a measure of their capacities and so of their manhoods: whether they had the balls to accept the challenge—because if they'd had the intellect, they might've declined it—or whether they were too cowardly, too womanly, too whipped. And so they'd let themselves go; they'd let themselves react—they'd become, I guess, reactionaries.

This whole circumaggravating and cumulatively gross situation of being provoked, or feeling like you're being provoked, and then having to resist responding to the provocation, and then not being able to resist responding because you're convinced that it's all just a bluff, seems to me quintessentially male. It forces its victims to choose—quickly, and in a sensory-overloaded, blinking, chirping environment—between the logical brain and the lower instincts, between getting out and getting even. Now, project all this parasexual, paraviolent incitement from the ludic, monetized poker table to the shouldn't-be-ludic, shouldn't-be-monetized political stage, and what becomes discernible is the liberal-conservative dilemma, in which the societal demands of social responsibility (folding) vie against the ego demands of animal appetite (staying in play and even raising the stakes), and reveal themselves to be zero-sum irreconcilable. This, I've decided, is Trump's technique: not numerically probabilistic or predictive (and so of limited use against the experienced), but a crude psychologizing that seizes on every weakness at the American table—all the poverty, ignorance, bigotry, and pride—and squeezes, until the electorate mans up and loses everything.

I tried bringing this up at the table, which consisted— at this ungodly and incalculable fluorescent hour of night/morning—of two grinders; two superdelegates, let's call them, who'd broken away from their bachelor party; and one guy who could've been anybody, in short-sleeved hoodie, board shorts, flip-flops, and wraparound sunglasses, who kept complaining about how difficult it was to get a proper martini during a labor dispute.

Grinder 1, Ricky from Philly, was annoyed and snapped at me: "No talking politics." Grinder 2, Bill from Bridgeton, said, rather mysteriously, "That stuff don't throw me none." Bachelor 1 said, "Fuck Trump, but fuck Hillary harder." Bachelor 2: "Bitch hasn't gotten it in a while—you can tell."

I left the table about $100 up after ten or so hours—$10 an hour being just about what I'd been paid nearly a decade ago at Resorts. I stumbled out onto the Boardwalk, into wan sunshine and mist, and found myself recalled to AC's marquee agon: what you're supposed to do with yourself once you're finished gambling. The only movie theaters left on the island were an IMAX, which was only showing *Warcraft*, and a filthy handful of XXX stroke rooms. The live-music scene is now dominated by dinosaur acts (Vanilla Ice appearing with Salt-N-Pepa and Color Me Badd; Rod Stewart: The Hits), and the art scene, which used to feature the paintings of Sylvester Stallone, has since been demoted to displaying the paintings of Burt Young (who played Uncle Paulie in the *Rocky* franchise). Also: It wasn't a beach day.

I got some (expired) yogurt and (unripe) plums from the Save-A-Lot, AC's only remaining supermarket, crawled back to the Professional Arts Building, and clicked through the news. There he was: Trump, the constant companion, the always-on, always-up-for-anything enabler. A link on the homepage of *The Press of Atlantic City* brought me to a better-funded paper's lead item about Trump's campaign chest: Trump's campaign, it was being reported, had basically nothing left in the bank, and yet had paid out more than $1 million for each of the past few months to Trump's companies, for use of Trump Tower office space and Trump-owned transportation—this was the Taj scam 2.0. In an accompanying clip, Trump was asked for comment, and answered in incoherent banalities before swerving into remarks about terrorism—or what he always refers to as "Islamic terrorism." Unwilling to go to my parents' house and unable to sleep in the office tilt-and-swivel chair, I picked up the book I'd brought from New York: *The Theory of Poker,* a how-to classic of 1987 written by David Sklansky, a native of Teaneck, dropout from UPenn's Wharton School of Business (where he just missed overlapping with Trump), winner of three World Series of Poker bracelets, and arguably the greatest draw and hold 'em player of all time. In the very first pages of his book—which I must've read a dozen times before, for a reliable soporific—Sklansky lays out his Fundamental Theorem, which in my amped-up wakefulness now hit me like a law on the level of gravity's: "Every time you play a hand differently from the way you would have played it if you could see all your opponents' cards, they gain; and every time you play your hand the same way you would have played it if you could see all their cards, they lose."

Here, presented in sane, rationalist fashion, was the insane truth behind this race: that if Trump just keeps on being Trump, and if Clinton keeps pivoting and responding to his every move, he wins. The only way that Clinton can win, according to Sklansky's schema, is to force Trump to become inconsistent, but since Trump is already inconsistent—since he's consistently inconsistent—that's impossible.

As my uncle's employees dragged in for the day, I formulated what I'll call Cohen's Hypothesis, or the Cohen-Clinton Lemma: "If the game you're playing becomes impossible to win, then your main opponent is probably yourself."

A table, where anyone can sit, where fortunes are exchanged: This was America, at least the East Coast white-folks version after the Civil War, when a limitless sense of economic growth seemed to derive not only from the Union's victory but also from the untrammeled expanses of the Western frontier and the prodigious influx of young single European males who kept washing up on the New York shore, including, in 1885, a sixteen-year-old from Kallstadt, Germany, named Friedrich Trumpf, who came here, as many have, and many will always, not to worship freely or speak freely, but to avoid his homeland's compulsory military service and try to make some dollars. Trumpf—father of

Fred, grandfather of Donald—landed at Castle Garden, New York, America's first immigration depot, which processed more than eight million people over its four-decade career. By the time Friedrich Trumpf had become Frederick Trump—by the time he'd become not just a U.S. citizen but a prominent hotelier and brothel owner catering to gold rush prospectors and an elected justice of the peace—Ellis Island was open and processing about five thousand immigrants a day, not a few of whom would spend their dotages in the nearly thirty thousand low-income residential units that Frederick's son, Fred, would put up throughout the New York outer boroughs with the aid of state and federal subsidies and tax abatement. Fred's son, then, came of age at a time in which about one-third of the country—over a hundred million "ethnic whites"—had a parent or grandparent who'd entered this country through Ellis Island. These were Donald's people, well before he ever leveraged them into a voting bloc. After all, these were his tenants; he was their landlord. The Trump family's low-income, multifamily "projects"—in Flushing, Jamaica Estates, Bensonhurst, Sheepshead Bay, and Brighton Beach—were intended to be, and remain, substantially whiter than the projects of any other city developer.

Today, a hundred years after the peak of white ethnic pilgrimage to America, go to those projects—to those white ethnic enclaves that still exist in New York—and ask the people you meet where they're from. Poland, Ukraine, Russia, etc.: The post-Soviets constitute the latest and perhaps last wave of Caucasian "pilgrims" whose acculturation and class ascension has been the dominant narrative in modern American life, until recently suppressing the narratives of forced immigration (black slavery) and genocide (Native Americans).

I tried a version of this interview method at the Irish Pub on St. James Place in AC—one of the city's best, and only, noncasino bars—and about half of the people I asked said things like, "AC," or "Brigantine," which is the next barrier island to the north, or else they just named the last bar they'd come from: the Chelsea, or the Ducktown Tavern. But the other half of the people— say ten or so—without any prompting answered my purposefully vague question of "Where are you from?" by offering, "I'm half Irish, a quarter German, and a quarter French," or, the arithmetic be damned, "I'm half Dutch and two-thirds Italian." The people who gave me those answers were male and, respectively, twenty-six and twenty-eight years old. In AC, the Irish Pub is festooned with Irish flags; the Italian restaurants and bakeries in Ducktown, the historic Italian neighborhood, are hung with Italian flags; and next to both the Irish and the Italian standards there's always the Stars and Stripes. In the Northside, which is the historically black side—AC is so confused that it's flipped the compass, so that the Northside is, in terms of true cardinality, the western-bay-facing side of the island—I didn't notice many flags at all.

These white ethnic roots—of "Italians" who don't'a speak'a Italian, of "Irish" who grew up in the Pine Barrens or on the Delaware River—creep into every element of Jersey life, even East Coast life, and if you try to resist their stifling, a gang of wifebeater-and-tracksuit-pants-wearing thugs always drives up to intimidate you with baseball bats and tells you to "suck it," in that rough, tough, I'm-from-a-cop-family-that's-also-a-crime-family accent that doesn't derive from any specific language or identity anymore, but rather from TV and movies and mongrel desperation. The sheer, shrill insistence on the continued relevance of these identities strikes me as a valid if annoying reaction to the fact that their progenitors—the immigrants themselves—have all just passed away. But with grandparents and parents gone, the identities they bequeath are perverted, which explains why first- and second-generation American ethnic whites have abandoned their forebears' traditionally pro-union, pro-welfare liberal Democratic politics, which were formed by the Great Depression, and amid the privations of the Great Recession found solace in the more medieval aspects of their Catholicism: social conservatism and racism. The result is a Republican Party that's a caricature of the Republican Party, in the same way that Jersey Irishness is a caricature of Irish Irishness, and Jersey Italianness a caricature of Italian Italianness (don't even get me started on the Jews). With this swift deracination of ethnic whites, America will lose its last sense of white authenticity, of genuine white culture—of a whiteness that's always opposed and been opposed by the whiteness of the WASPs, the Puritans who once were this country's elite—and a massive segment of the populace will have to resign itself to an undifferentiated paleness: a whitehood-as-nonidentity, that of a people from nothing, from nowhere, denied grievance. Ethnic whites are a dying breed, who've understood only just recently—historically speaking—that all they can be now is American whites, in an identity loss that they regard in their trauma as an identity theft—perpetrated by "minorities" and "illegals," and aided and abetted by that African Muslim Obama.

It's no coincidence, then, that rage has become the prime political motivator of the white electorate today—given that theirs is both the last generation able to remember any ethnic white grandparents and the first generation whose standard of living has not appreciably improved on their parents'. Trump's supporters resent this so vociferously, it's as if a birthright's been revoked: This was not the country that "they," meaning "their ancestors," had been sold when they bought the boat ticket over. This was not what being white was supposed to be like, scrapping for the same scarce jobs with diversity-hire blacks and Hispanics and, worse, refugee Middle Easterners. Feeling wronged, feeling disillusioned, they retreat into mendacity and yearning—though because they have no faith in an economy that's betrayed them and have lost all belief in what their forebears called the American Dream, they yearn not for a better future, but a better past. This is what Trump means by promising to "Make America Great Again": promising to return us to a time that never once existed.

Call it the American Daydream, an idyll that's intimated and hinted at everywhere in AC: on billboards, on postcards, in the lobby of the Professional Arts Building, which is festooned with giant photomurals of all the old, since-demolished, European-style grand hotels that lined the Boardwalk at its bustling heyday, the totality of the scene captured in a black-and-white that's been touched up, that's been rosied, with pastels. Every day, taking the elevator up and down for cig breaks, I'd study these murals—I'd try to resist their calliope charms. Put starkly, the danger at the heart of sentimentality or nostalgia is how directly it's predicated on racism. That Great America that will be Made Again and the politics of racial oppression are, like the ingredients of any decent melting pot, inseparable.

AC was founded in 1854, just a year before Castle Garden opened in New York. Before then, Absecon Island was just a desolate sandspit that had been fishing-and-hunting grounds to the Lenni Lenape, and then a farmstead to the Quakers, and finally a minuscule, ramshackle village inhabited by the family of Revolutionary War veteran Jeremiah Leeds, whose cousin, "Mother Leeds," was said to have spawned the Jersey Devil.

The idea to turn the island into a faddish summer health resort on the Victorian British model belonged to Dr. Jonathan Pitney, a physician, while the financial support and practical infrastructure were supplied by Samuel Richards—the scion of a rich South Jersey bog-iron and glass dynasty—who built the Camden-Atlantic line, a railroad that connected AC with the cross-Delaware cities of Camden and Philadelphia. The railroad's engineer was Richard Osborne, who named the city after its ocean, and predicted that it'd become "the first, most popular, most health giving and most inviting watering place" in America.

But the city's first megahotel, the United States Hotel—in the mid-1850s the largest in the nation, with more than six hundred rooms—was initially mostly vacant. The Philadelphia elite balked at the rude accommodations, the grime and smoke of the open-air train, and the rapacious swarms of greenheads and mosquitoes. However, the main reason that the moneyed set wasn't overwhelmingly attracted to AC seems to have been tradition: The good old families tended to already own good old second homes, to which they'd repair not for a weekend—because weekends, then, didn't exist—but for the duration of the summer. To give further context: Beachgoing and ocean swimming didn't become established forms of recreation in America until well after the Civil War, and at the time of AC's founding, the coastal towns that later became famous as resorts—the closest to AC being Cape May, but also Rehoboth, Delaware; Newport, Rhode Island; and Cape Cod, Massachusetts—were still significantly active as ports.

AC's regular clientele, then, turned out to be regular people, "red-bloods" with "blue collars": people, usually of recent immigrant stock, who couldn't afford second summer homes and typically had short vacations, or just a short single day—Sunday, God's day—to profane with their pleasure. The first time a Camden or Philadelphia carpenter and his family could afford to pay another person to cook for them; the first time a Newark/Elizabeth or New York longshoreman and his family could afford to pay another person to eat and sleep in their house—to room and board in their rooming house or boarding-house—they went to AC: the only vacation destination on the East Coast to which there was direct rail service; a city clapped together out of water and sand and dedicated almost exclusively to making the Irish, Italian, and Jewish urban poor feel rich, or richer. This is the process that created the American middle class, which in America—unlike in Europe, where the middle class had always been a feudal characterization of artisans and merchants—became more of an ideology, or more of a delusion.

For nearly a century—the 1850s through the 1950s—new immigrants and their native-born children would come down to AC, dress in their finery, and stroll along the Boardwalk, which was invented to keep sand out of the hotels but became a lucrative commercial property that was also publicized as an education and an exercise.

This raised wooden and later wood-and-metal midway featured displays of America's emergent production power (exhibitions of Edison's innovations stretching out over the piers) along with ample opportunities to consume (branches of the most fashionable Philly and New York boutiques selling ready-to-wear clothing at the very advent of mass tailoring), establishing in the imaginations of promenaders the commensality of industrial progress and personal, familial, and even ethnic progress. At its height—say, the turn of the century—at the height of the day—say, once the sun had tipped toward the bay—this grand boulevard took on the aspect of a nonstop parade route, a pageant of freshly minted Americans floating by, all showing off and being shown off to, mutually reveling in having "arrived," in having "made it."

Of course, this sense of success was premised on a fundamental injustice. Check out any of the old photographs, any of the old film reels, and note the rolling chairs—AC's signature white, wheeled wicker chairs that were first introduced for the use of the disabled back when the city was still being touted as a retreat for the infirm, but later adopted by able-bodied patrons. The people pushing those chairs are black—the only black people on the Boardwalk. In the surviving images of nearly all the early hotels, restaurants, and bars, it's the same: blacks in white uniform, their faces almost always averted from the camera.

At the turn of the twentieth century, one out of four AC residents was black, a ratio that gave the city the highest per capita black population of any city above the Mason-Dixon Line—which, if it didn't take a sharp turn to form the Delaware border, would overlay the county line between Atlantic and Cape May counties.

Much of this porter and kitchen and laundry workforce was made up of freed slaves and their descendants, who came north because the hospitality industry was more profitable, and had more opportunities for promotion, than, for instance, sharecropping. What this meant was that black AC was occupied with its own—more precarious, more constrained—attempts at achieving upward mobility: Compared with black communities elsewhere in America, black AC was prosperous.

These symbiotic or parasitic middle-class fantasies based on racial oppression were the great sustainers of AC—along with vice, which unites people of all colors. An economy reliant on seasonal tourism wouldn't countenance Prohibition, and from 1920 to 1933 the city just outright ignored the Eighteenth Amendment. Forget speakeasies and clubs: Alcohol was sold out in the open in the city, whose wharves had ample docking space for bootleggers' ships. Opium dens and brothels were tolerated, but the numbers games were more popular, as were more formal card parlors. All this vice was allowed to flourish under the dispensation of the local machine, which was nominally Republican but operationally total: It had no opposition, and it even handpicked which Democrats would lose to it. The first boss of this machine was Louis "Commodore" Kuehnle, owner of Kuehnle's Hotel, and its most infamous was Enoch "Nucky" Johnson, who spent three decades remuneratively installed in the nothing position of Atlantic County treasurer. Kuehnle and especially Johnson exacted money from the rackets in exchange for police protection—turning the police into a mercenary force for the rackets—and after pocketing shares for themselves, invested the rest into purchasing peace from the state and federal authorities, and in acts of patronage both major (building Boardwalk Hall) and minor (charities for orphans and widows). This unlawful but effective arrangement wouldn't just grow in scale, it also served as blueprint for allied endeavors. In May 1929, the summer before the stock-market crash, Johnson assembled a conference in AC—the prototype convention of this convention town—that attracted the emissaries of organized crime from Philadelphia, New York, Kansas City, Detroit, Chicago, Cleveland, Boston: Al Capone, Lucky Luciano, Meyer Lansky, Dutch Schultz, et al. This was the founding of America's first national crime syndicate, and it was Capone who—in a late-life interview he granted the FBI from Alcatraz—most succinctly summarized their agenda: "I told them [in AC] there was business enough to make us all rich and it was time to stop all the killings and look on our business as other men look on theirs, as something to work at and forget when we go home."

Capone's statement was prophetic—just not for the gangsters, or the "illegal" gangsters at least. Hard times came to AC with Prohibition's repeal, and were compounded amid post-WWII prosperity—under the machine of state senator Frank "Hap" Farley, and the more independent and so less effectually venal city governments that followed—with the gradual nationwide legalization of nearly every vice that previously had been most safely and most dependably available within the city limits. More than the rise of air travel or the proliferation of private car ownership and the interstate system—more than the miracle of air-conditioning—this was the greatest threat to AC: permissiveness abroad, as municipalities throughout the States became more accepting of sin, or just more interested in taxing it.

Nevada approved gaming in 1931 in response to the

crash. By the end of the '50s, Las Vegas had emerged as the gaming capital of America, and by the end of the '70s—when New Jersey finally caught up and officially approved gaming in AC—the precedents were already in place for the rash of both tribal and nontribal approvals that followed.

And so the continued expansion of casinos, and the continued extrapolation of casino principles into governmental policy—into the scaffolding of a state that can deny its citizens all but the barest amenities of welfare and health care, only because it sanctions their conviction that they're all just one bet, one lever tug, away from becoming rich, chosen, elect, the American their ancestors had aspired to be, the American that God had intended.

I found myself—America finds itself now—at the very end of the Boardwalk. The very end of this immigrant's midway lined with cheap thrills and junk concessions, pulsating with tawdry neon and clamoring moronically. The end of this corny, schmaltzy Trumpian thoroughfare that entertains us with its patter and enthralls us with its lies.

And yet we stay here, on the Boardwalk, because it's safer than stepping down. Because we trust the Boardwalk, at least we trust that it can't be trusted, and so we're reassured by how straight it seems, how direct it seems, the way it lulls us back and forth. We're threatened by the pavement, by the city that we might find there. The ghost streets off Pacific Avenue and Atlantic Avenue, off Arctic and Baltic—all the broken roads and dead-end alleys left behind by Wall Street, which underlies every street of the Monopoly board.

Here, unlike on the Boardwalk, everything is real. Here everything is both ghostly and real. Vacant houses. Apartments boarded up to protect against squatters. Eviction and foreclosure papers flap from the doors like tongues. NOTICE TO CEASE, NOTICE TO QUIT, papers keeping the sun out of the windows. The apartment houses rubble away into empty lots pierced by wind and drowned in the shadows cast by shuttered penthouses. Empty lots spontaneously converted for parking, a sign in the windshield of a Saturn: pleese dont take me. Walking between the Boardwalk and the Professional Arts Building, walking between the Professional Arts Building and my car spontaneously parked in a dirt and, after the rain, mud lot, meant passing the porn store, which, especially if I was making the trip after sunset, meant getting accosted. By men who slept on the beach and spent their waking lives on the street, where there were fewer police and more chances to hustle. Corner of Pacific and MLK Jr. Boulevard. Guy trying to bum cigarettes. Guy trying to bum a dollar for booze. Guy trying to deal to me. "Yo, got coke, yo." "Molly, molly." "Got syrup." Taking my money and not coming back. Trying it all over again the next day unabashed, and then when I told him I'd rather just talk, he got in my face, called me gay, called me a cop. A woman telling me how the check-cashing place would only cash checks made out to people with addresses in Atlantic County by people or businesses with addresses in Atlantic County. Telling me she lived in Georgia, or had once lived in Georgia, and her only hope of returning was this check from her cousin in Camden. "Ain't Camden Atlantic County?" "No." "What Camden then?" "Camden County." "Goddamn."

Another woman giving me some woe chronicle of

how she was running to catch a jitney and fucked up her knee, and how with this one knee blown and all the weight on the other, the other got fucked up too, and how she got laid off, either because of the injury or unrelated to the injury, and was homeless now, and how every time she went to the doctor's office she just got a referral to another office that was never open, and no lawyer would take the case and sue the jitneys. Man standing in the midst of the lot holding up either a raincoat or construction tarp, screening a woman squatting pissing or shitting.

Down at the Boardwalk's terminus, by Oriental Avenue, by night, the seagulls keep flying into the Revel and dying. Or they flap and limp around a bit before dying. You never see or hear the impact, you just get what happens after. Immense white gulls, flapping, limping, expiring. They fly into the Revel's giant vacant tower of panes and break their necks, because without any lights on, the glass is indistinguishable from the sky.

P.S., Offseason

On November 1, the New Jersey State Department of Community Affairs rejected Atlantic City's budget and rescue plan. On November 8, Election Day, the New Jersey Casino Expansion Amendment failed. New Jersey itself went for Clinton, but the country went for Trump. The morning after, while Clinton delivered her concession speech, New Jersey's Local Finance Board voted 5–0 to approve Governor Christie's immediate takeover of Atlantic City. I am writing this on that morning—it is November 9. A gray day, humid and rainy. My parents called to say that it was the anniversary of *Kristallnacht*.

NOTES ON THE CONCESSION

In writing the Constitution, America's Founders privileged the electoral vote over the popular vote both to protect states' rights—to ensure that each state had a proportional voice in its federal governance—and to mitigate the passions of populism. Here's Alexander Hamilton: "A small number of persons, selected by their fellow-citizens from the general mass, will be most likely to possess the information and discernment requisite to such complicated investigations." So, the way it was supposed to work, the way it used to work, was that people didn't vote for a candidate directly, but for an (elite, educated) elector—one per district—who would evaluate the nominated candidates and vote on the people's behalf. After the Civil War, however, all that changed, as the party apparatuses went about choosing their own electors, who weren't free agents, then, but prepledged—meaning they weren't expected to "deliberate" (Hamilton's term), they merely had to certify: They rubberstamped the popular will. And so Trump has just won the highest office in this country, the highest office in the world, by the very mechanism intended to squash his type of candidacy—a candidacy based not on policy, but on destruction. By electing Trump, by not electing Clinton, the folks the Founders never trusted have gotten their revenge: "Deliberate" liberalism has once again been circumvented and the tyranny of Obamaera "discernment" overturned.

This must be said: Nothing in this election was rigged. Sure, there was external meddling (Russia, WikiLeaks), and, sure, the FBI's pursuit of Clinton for keeping her secret public emails on her secret private server was unfair (and rendered moot by the external meddling of Russia, WikiLeaks), but no one has yet argued that the voting machines were tampered with, or that the totals were altered. Everyone seems to be in agreement (perhaps because everyone seems scared not to be in agreement): The system worked. That is, the system worked by failing—the evidence that it worked is that it failed, and it appears that it will continue to fail as long as the citizenry remains so divided, which is to say as long as opportunistic and conscienceless demagogues are able to muster Christian whites from the middle of the country (most of them working-class and male) and "identify," or, as they say online, "identitarize," them into a reliable voting bloc—indeed, into America's first majoritarian voting bloc. Never have so many people of the same race all voted the same—rather, never have so many people of the same race all been manipulated into voting the same, in a brazen campaign that re-cast their unreconstructed fear of the Other (blacks, Hispanics, Muslims, empowered women) as a modern fear of empowered robots and globalism's exportation of American jobs.

As a journalist who covered Trump's campaign, I daily experienced the effects of this manipulation, in the form of his supporters' rabid opposition to nearly everything I was: journalist, Jew, New York. I was routinely accused of conspiring with fellow members of "the tribe" and the "shady" global capital "cabals" that finance "the media" to deprive nonurban Christian White America of its economic supremacy, by transferring the resources that'd enabled that supremacy (college admissions, financial aid, insurance, jobs) to urban minorities, in order to purchase their votes for Clinton and to forestall their (innate, biologically innate) violence. The bulk of the swastikas I encountered at the rallies were backward: rightfacing. I laughed then, out of pity, out of angst. I laughed until I was told: Backward was on purpose; rightfacing was the point.

But the fundamental divide in this election has been nondemographic and off the map—it's not the rift between races or ethnicities or genders, or the gap between the interior and the coasts, but the gulf that's been opened up between Actions and Words. Trump, who's been repeatedly accused of sexual harassment, sexual assault, attempted rape, and rape, has suffered more for what he's said—for his hot-mic comments about grabbing women "by the pussy." While both facts—the accusations and the comments—have astounded me as a man, the theoretical distinction, or the practical distinction in their consequences, has astounded me as a writer. My own words, during this election, have been pointless. Inconsequential. They've changed nothing. They've swayed no one.

Trump supporters believe they've elected a man of Action, so as to purge a man of Words: Obama. Of course, the utter reverse of that formula is true: Obama did things (including the wrong things), Obama made things (including mistakes), but Trump, in all his biblical attainment of seventy years, has merely bloviated. It occurs to me that nearly all of the beliefs most dear, or most publicly dear, to Trump supporters have been like their swastikas: true only in their opposite, their counterpole inversion. Rarely has a mass delusion been so complementary or symmetrizing. Trump is a friend of the working class? No: He's an exploiter whose businesses have consistently cut employee benefits and pay, refused to employ union labor, and stiffed contractors. Trump is a self-made success? No: The bulk of his businesses have failed, and his net worth—which can only be estimated, because he never released his tax returns—would almost certainly have been higher had he never gone into real estate and casinos (and airlines and golf courses and universities and vodka) at all and just taken the money (about $40 million) he'd inherited from his father and invested it conservatively, Standard & Poorly, in mutual funds.

The most dangerous rhetorical shift comes only now: It came earlier this morning, actually, when a man who's spent the last year, if not the last few decades, bullying and lying stepped into the victory-speech spotlight, smirked into the cameras, and delivered a halting attempt at helium-pitched, hifalutinal prose-poetry—congratulating his rival (whom he'd threatened to jail as recently as yesterday), and avidly promising, as all successful candidates avidly promise, to be a president for "all Americans." This magnanimity he displayed wasn't sincere, or even pseudosincere—an actorly invocation of a stabilizing tradition. Instead, because it was so uncharacteristic, and yet so self-amused, it struck me as nothing more than gloating: Here was a man not only proud of his win, but also proud of what he thinks is his ability to conceal his pride, which he's deluded enough to think he's doing competently. Trump is a man who can be inclusive only in triumph, because inclusiveness can only increase that triumph—it can only increase him. After his remarks, the "normalization" commenced. Mainstream TV personalities (who in this election emerged as anything but mainstream: as fringe) piled on the praise, and speculated as to how the candidate might change once in office, or be changed by the office. Correction: not the candidate, the president-elect. Later in the day, with the markets holding steady, Clinton gave her concession speech, and Obama spoke too—just now. Everything is being done to restore some sense of national self-respect, some smidge of international dignity, in the face of a fascism of vanity, because a fascism without convictions.

FROM THE DIARIES

Lecture Review

"[...] no truer synthesis of anachronism and incongruity [...]"

Memoir

The genre of an age that's lost all hope of a biographer.

EXIT BERNIE

New York's Town Hall is a janky half-decrepit theater founded by suffragists in 1921, famous for hosting Charlie Parker, Dizzy Gillespie, and, more recently, *A Prairie Home Companion*, coming to you live from the tourist-scrum of Midtown Manhattan. I was here in January, to get talked at by Senator Bernie Sanders, democratic socialist, ranking minority member of the Senate Budget Committee, former Vermont representative in the House, former mayor of Burlington, civil rights activist, husband, grandfather, Jew, and, at the time of this writing, contender for the Democratic nomination for president of the United States.

Settling into my seat, I was panicked. I'd received an email from the campaign's communications staff indicating that today's speech was going to be the senator's yuge (huge) speech on the economy—a subject I've always found so abstract, so speculatively mad, determined by so many numbers and percentages and decimal points, bound by so many holding companies and corporate ties, that it seemed to hop, skip, and jump over the human and dwell instead amid the empyrean of the unmentionable, or at least undiscussable, alongside such topics as comparative eschatology and the relationship between free will and the godhead. To speak about the economy with any efficacy, or so as to provide any entertainment, the senator would have to take all the ugly, corrupt, almost animal malfeasance that lurks below the shiny machined surfaces of terminology like "mortgage-backed securities" and "predatory lending," and breathe it into life, into *lives*, into real-seeming sagas of real people who'd been duped, indebted, and dispossessed—hardworking, American, etc., people who'd lost their savings, and lost their homes, in a tragic confrontation with a cipher.

And frankly, I didn't think the senator had that in him. Sanders, at least the Sanders I'd been tuned to, cannot tell a story. Though he's always invoking regular folks, he never names them, and in fact the only folks he ever names are far from regular and are entered into the record strictly for the purposes of citation, or indictment: politicians, military personnel, academics, business executives, and bankers. Sanders has none of (Bill) Clinton's charm, and regardless of his reluctance to be a deficit spender, less than none of (Hillary) Clinton's faux charm—that ability, or willingness, shared by Obama and even George W., to give a State of the Union in which the tale is told of a Mr. X who'd worked for X number of years at X type of job, only to get laid off when his employer moved to Mexico or China. And then suddenly, as if by magic, the camera pans to the balcony... and there's Mr. X, beaming along with Mrs. X, and the X children, who have all miraculously benefited from Y and Z policies.

I hate that cornpone crap—but not like Sanders hates it. And his inability, or unwillingness, to crassify like that seems to derive from some deep inner trust in the logical, some sense that if a policy is honest and intelligent enough, it doesn't need to be justified by a name or face—it doesn't need to be sold to you. And while this might never be a feasible way to publicize a movie or TV show, let alone a novel or even a work of election journalism, just such an approach might be the only way to get a socialist elected to the presidency.

¶ White Balance

A lot of things have to happen to ensure the successful filming and broadcast of a major address: Electricity has to be adequate; coverage angles and obstructions must be negotiated. There are sound checks. And finally, once all that's been put to bed, the last thing that has to be attended to goes by the wonderfully polysemic term "white balance." Now, it's important to remember not to trust everything we see, or hear, or read. Perception is relative, as the Sophists and Roger Ailes have always told us; observation skews. Color temperatures, or intensities, are never absolute, but depend on the device sensing them: the rods and cones of eyes, and cameras. This means that they have to be transformed, or, in film terms, "corrected," into new intensities appropriate to the display medium—say, the sRGB computer monitor standard, or the HD of cable news. The color white, that reflector of light, is the simultaneous combination of all colors. This makes white the standard by which all other colors are judged. To "white balance" an image is to ensure that its white looks white. If that's the case, then all the other colors will look like themselves too. This, at least in film, generally is regarded as positive.

A man mounted the stage, stood between five American flags and a podium, and held a slab of white card stock aloft. He yelled, "White balance." The camera people, up on risers behind me, adjusted accordingly. Most of the camera people were white. The man holding the card stock was black. Most of the journalists and the volunteers stalking the aisles issuing hashtag instructions were white. The 1,500-member capacity audience included many people holding their own "white balance"-type signs, card stock scrawled with Sharpie proclaiming their debt, their dispossessions. They were a gender-balanced mix of white, black, Hispanic, South Asian, and Arab. They were waiting for a Jew.

¶¶ Doing Jewish

He just comes out, no-nonsense. His suit rumpled, his tie stupid. He barely acknowledges the applause. His hands are up and waving hello but in that don't-make-a-fuss, don't-get-up-on-my-account gesture. *Sit down already, will you?!* The clapping exists in another universe, inaccessible to him, like the laugh track on *Seinfeld*. Apropos of that Show about Nothing, it makes sense that the great Sanders impersonator has turned out to be Larry David: Sanders's fellow Brooklynite, who, before he played the senator on *Saturday Night Live*, was a writer on the show who got only one skit produced and a stand-up comic who so notoriously feared and loathed audiences that he used to bail on club dates that were going poorly. Like David, Sanders is a man who came to the front of the camera reluctantly and who always somewhat resents it, or seems to. The front of the camera is where the idiocy lies.

Sanders is not a fluent speaker, and his formulations grate. His speech is barely paragraph-worthy, barely sentence-worthy; its closest model would be the text of a PowerPoint, delivered with a Yiddish *krechts*. It's the speech of a Bernie or Bern, never a Bernard. This unrelenting seriousness is embodied by his hair, which is the same white, hot mess it always is and always will be. It's not merely that Sanders is unconcerned with appearance, it's that he's consistently unconcerned, and that consistency reinforces the consistent emphases of his voice, which, in turn, reinforce the consistent phrases he voices. This is a man who doesn't just stay "regular," but stays "identical"; whose superficial shambles belie a formidable resolve. He has the fastidiousness of most post–New Deal *alter kockers* who lay out copies of the *Daily News* beneath them on the subway, to preserve their pants; he has the rhetorical range of a CPA who spends his lunch break counting heart pills or jelly beans. How many jelly beans, Bernie? Sixty jelly beans! And by the way, the six largest banks in this country, which "issue two-thirds of all credit cards and more than 35 percent of all mortgages," also control "more than 95 percent of all financial derivatives and hold more than 40 percent of all bank deposits." And if that's not enough, try this: "Their assets are equivalent to nearly 60 percent of our GDP," Bernie says. "Enough is enough," and the crowd howls.

That last line is classic, in affect: the way he pronounces it with equal parts rage ("Enough") and resignation ("is enough"). This is a man resigned to his rage, a put-upon, artless, gray-flannelized man whose single-minded fixation on domestic income inequality and financial reform is every bit as enervating and drudgey as it is practical and admirable.

This dichotomy is what makes Sanders fascinating, though it's not why millions of people, not just Larry David, but millions of Larry Davids in kitchens throughout America, take pleasure in doing impressions of him, or in doing what I'm going to call ostensible, or displaced, impressions. Because despite any exactitude of gesture and phonation—the open-hanging mouth, the tongue thrust, the accent's glides, the nonrhotics, the shrugging and grimacing, the peeved shaken fist and wag of the finger—the true thing being impersonated goes unsaid. Larry David does not "do" Bernie Sanders; Stephen Colbert, Jimmy Fallon, and Seth Meyers do not "do"

103

Bernie Sanders; neither do they "do" "pregentrification Brooklyn," nor do they "do" "old man." Instead, what they "do," and what they're relishing "doing," is "Jew," and it's been surprising to me that no one has had the Trumpian schlong to admit this, or to call anyone out on it. Jews know it, and none of them are offended, because Jews embrace Bernie for the same reason that everyone else does; they're magnetized by one of the only things that America today seems to lack: genuine political conviction, founded in an authentic ethnic identity that can be read as white, but that isn't racist.

¶ The Racial Politics of Yuge

It's become fairly clear, and I hope not just to me, that white people in this country have gone crazy. Granted, an apocalyptic belief in the final, definitive loss of four hundred or so years of economic and cultural supremacy will do that to you—the fall has been long in coming; masters of the universe should've been better prepared. Instead, they act stunned. And to cope with that loss, as well as to cope with the fearmongering of Fox News and right-wing talk radio, which promises them Muslim terrorists in every closet and under every bed, they— or an insanely significant cohort—seem to have given themselves over to the worst sort of race-baiting and antiimmigrant nativism, under the guise of making or keeping America "great," which is to say, making or keeping America "white."

What this requires, besides bigotry, is the valorization of a white identity that seems strong enough to counteract the deracinating and emasculating forces of capitalism and what bigots take to be the outrageous sense of entitlement, propensity for violence and crime, and the outsized sexual appetites, of Mexicans (by which they mean all Latinos) and blacks. What I'm talking about, of course, is Trumpism: a cult led by a racist, or a man who plays a racist on TV, who also revels in emphasizing his outtaborough tough-guy cred, though the truth is he's neither a Belfast brawler nor a Neapolitan mafioso, but the rich-kid scion of a millionaire family of German descent from so far out and leafy in Queens that it's basically Nassau County, Lawn Guyland. Still, he talks trash like a corner guy. A hood.

It stands to reason, then, that liberals become yugely pleased when they encounter a white liberal in whom they can deduce an equivalent or, honestly, more genuine and utterly sane version of that same authenticity. Sanders knows this, or at least his advisers do, and in the address produced for Town Hall they have advantaged this asset by interlarding slogans from the Occupy Wall Street Slogan Generator, verbal barrages in a style I can only call Aaron Sorkin joins the IRS, with myriad opportunities for Sanders to use, abuse, and redefine Trump's favorite pet verbiage:

> Wall Street executives still receive yuge compensation packages... Wall Street cannot continue to be an island unto itself, gambling trillions in risky financial instruments, making yuge profits... A handful of yuge financial institutions simply have too much economic and political power over this country... Unlike big banks, credit unions did not receive a yuge bailout... Wall Street makes yuge campaign contributions...

The substance of Sanders's remarks is lost in these moments. All anyone hears is a yawp truer to the idealized New York street than Trump's. Instead, what they hear is that word used negatively: With Sanders, huge is bad. Enormous bank, bad. Huge deficit, bad. The word has become so big that it must fail. A person in front of me—a black person—leans over to another black person and whispers the word in her ear. They turn to face each other and grin. This is *nachas*.

¶ Jewish Power

Everything I've written so far is predicated on two assumptions I'm not sure I want to defend: One is that Jews in the American context both are and aren't white people; the other is that I have some understanding of what Jewishness means, or is signified by, in the mind of Bernie Sanders, who was born on September 8, 1941—aka the day that Hitler began the disastrous encirclement of Leningrad—and who grew up in a three-and-a-half-room, rent-controlled tenement apartment off Kings Highway, in Brooklyn, the second and youngest son of a Yiddish-speaking traveling paint-salesman father, who'd emigrated from Poland and lost most of his family to the Nazis, and of a first-generation American Jewish homemaker mother, who'd spent her childhood afflicted with rheumatic fever and who died during a heart operation at the age of forty-six.

To be sure, the senator himself, whose formal involvement with Judaism began with Hebrew school and a bar mitzvah in the '50s and appears to have faded after a '60s stint in Israel picking apples on a kibbutz, hardly wants to talk about that heritage. Neither in speeches, nor in interviews. When I ask about this reticence—not to Bernie directly, but his support staff—I get nothing, except the sense that about half the staff I've met is Jewish. Sanders's 1997 memoir, *Outsider in the House*, mentions his Judaism only twice, once to characterize the ethnicity of his childhood neighborhood and once to characterize the ethnicity of his parents.

When Sanders was confronted with the evangelical Zionophiles of Liberty University, whom he addressed on Rosh Hashanah last year, he gave brief bland quotes pertaining to spiritual beliefs and to the social-welfare-and-justice philosophies of Judaism. However, more frequently, when pressed about his faith—or what he would do to combat Islamophobia, as he was at George Mason University a month later—he brings up the Holocaust, and the importance of elections, noting that Hitler was elected, after all. Neither of those approaches holds much meaning for American Jews, who, like most Americans, are more concerned with this country's ghettos, and the concentration camps it's running in Guantanamo Bay and on the Mexican border, than with rehashing any foreign martyrdom. To date, Sanders's most public, but also most parlous, statements on his own Semitism occurred in the first two of his two-person debates with Hillary. In early February, in Durham, New Hampshire, he delivered what was received as an atypically personal closing statement that referred to his father as a Polish (i.e., not a Jewish) immigrant, a descriptor that the Nazis, to say nothing of coeval Poles, would have disputed. A couple of weeks later, at another debate in Milwaukee, Sanders was asked whether he was worried about becoming "the instrument of thwarting history" (Hillary's ponderous, self-thwarting, self-fulfilling prophecy-phrase), by postponing the election of America's first female president. Sanders responded: "From a historical point of view, somebody with my background, somebody with my views, somebody who has spent his entire life taking on the big money interests, I think a Sanders victory would be of some historical accomplishment as well."

It takes a village, but a village of rabbis, to interpret this statement, given its semantic sleight—its impersonality ("somebody"), ambiguity ("my background," "my views"), and utter alienation from the self (the climactic third-person "Sanders victory"). Who wouldn't be confused as to whether a Sanders victory would be of "some historical accomplishment" as the triumph of an ideology, or of a Jew? Which is to ask, cynically, which Sanders is the more electable: the Eurocratic redistributionist, or the Ashkenazi son of the commandments? Which revolution was Sanders promising, the one that takes on Wall Street, or the one that takes on prejudice? Was he demanding Jews be counted among minorities in America, or was he tacitly acknowledging that his white maleness was costuming for his ethnic status and so offering a sly critique of our culture of superficial tokenism?

The ambivalence of this statement marks the man who made it, and not, ironically, President Obama, as the commanding code switcher in chief of contemporary politics. I'd argue that Obama never has delivered a statement to the American public intended to be received one way by whites and another by blacks. Hillary never has and never would deliver a statement that meant one thing to women and a whole entire other thing to men. However, Sanders's "historical accomplishment" was taken to mean "the first Jewish president" by Jews and "the first Democratic Socialist president" by the 97.8 percent of the American populace that isn't Jewish. I'd even hazard that this was how Sanders intended it to be interpreted, and that this double meaning encrypts a private as much as historical truth that for modern Jewry the left may be the mightier birthright, its social-policy compassion and antidiscrimination imperatives constellating an identity that supersedes any other—a replacement for Judaism even more Christian than Christianity.

As Sanders surely knows but would never discuss, socialism—and its legislation at the national, or universal, level as communism—represented the most provocative and ultimately most poignant attempt by Jews to integrate into Christian society since the emancipations of the Enlightenment. Throughout the Middle Ages, Jewish political involvement was limited to what amounted to extortion: Confined to ghettos, confined to certain occupations, forced to dress according to the sumptuary laws, and perpetually vulnerable to the depredations of hostile populaces, Jews were organized into communities, which were permitted a token degree of autonomy, and forced to pay for protection. They were compelled to lend, or give, money to benevolent regents, who sometimes spared and sometimes slaughtered them. That's why the republican revolutions of Enlightenment Europe impacted the Jews more culturally, or commercially, than politically: Their upheavals meant that more sons of moneylenders were allowed into schools and allowed to ply other trades, though justice, as always, was gradual, and far from global. It fell to socialism, then, to fire the Jewish political imagination, with Marx declaring, in his 1844 review of Bruno Bauer's *The Jewish Question*, "The question of the relation of political emancipation to religion becomes for us the question of the relation of political emancipation to human emancipation." In other words, the true struggle didn't consist of persuading a certain government to let a certain citizen-race freely practice its religion;

109

it consisted of persuading all citizen-races to surrender their religions and join together to freely practice universal governance. It was Marx's conceit that under capitalism all peoples had become "Jews": forced by dint of social, but predominantly economic, inequalities to act entirely out of what he characterized as "practical need" and "self-interest." Marx's money lines: "What is the worldly religion of the Jew? *Huckstering*. What is his worldly God? *Money*." He concludes: "Emancipation from *huckstering* and *money*, consequently from practical, real Judaism, would be the self-emancipation of our time."

Now, it's all too familiar, and all too cheap, to mention how that hope died: in Sovietism, amid the show trials and gulags. Even as the Holocaust's carnage factories were starting to churn, an exiled Trotsky continued to censure Zionism, declaring, "Never was it so clear as it is today that the salvation of the Jewish people is bound up inseparably with the overthrow of the capitalist system." To summarize the Jewish anti-Semitism lurking behind nascent socialism, just apply Marx's description to Trotsky's prescription: To Marx, to live under "capitalism" was to become "a Jew"; while to Trotsky, "Jews" could only be saved by destroying "capitalism," which is to say, they could only be saved by destroying themselves.

What both Marx and Trotsky, not to mention Lenin and Stalin, were proposing was that Judeo-capitalism must evolve into revolutionary socialism—or into communism, as a successor to the dream of Jewish autonomy-oligarchy-kleptocracy. What would redeem this self-hating morass of identity synecdoche and self-eradicating metonymy was America, a country ripe for personal or racial or religious reinvention, in which

110

the transformational procedures that caused European Jews to de-Judaize themselves into "socialists" and separate themselves from their co-religionists by branding them "capitalists" was reproduced by nearly every immigrant ethnicity: Italians, Irish, Russians, etc., and eventually by the nation's disenfranchised—blacks—who recognized that socialism had been crusading for emancipation and desegregation well before those most basic civil rights had been enshrined as American law.

Nearly all of the major figures who enabled this integration through reidentification, who went down like Moses into the rail yards, packing plants, and sweatshops, and brought socialism to America, were Jews: Daniel De Leon (1852–1914), a Sephardic immigrant from Curaçao and the forefather of industrial unionism, became the leader of the Socialist Labor Party of America and a three-time failed candidate for governor of New York; Samuel Gompers (1850–1924), an immigrant Jew from England who was the first president of the American Federation of Labor; Victor L. Berger (1860–1929), an immigrant Jew from Austro-Hungary, who founded the Social Democratic Party of America, converted Eugene V. Debs, who had been a Democratic member of the Indiana General Assembly, to socialism, and became the first socialist elected to the House; Morris Hillquit (1869–1933), a Jewish immigrant from the Baltics, who co-founded the Socialist Party of America and was a two-time failed candidate for the mayor of New York City and representative of New York's ninth congressional district—Sanders's birth district; and Saul Alinsky, the Chicago-born codifier of community organizing, who influenced Sanders's grassroots-collectivization campaigning (and, parenthetically, served as the subject of Hillary Clinton's undergrad thesis). These Jews, who established American socialism, did so in an adopted language. Their main rhetorical twist was to insist that "democracy"—lowercase "democracy"—didn't exist, except as a lexical superstition that meant "capitalism."

¶ Money Libel

This revalencing, however, regardless of its aspiringly assimilated American socialist pedigree, might still serve as yet another explanation for why Sanders is loath to discuss his Judaism: Money is at the center of his platform. He stood onstage in New York, three blocks from the Bank of America building, seven blocks from Morgan Stanley headquarters, eight blocks from JPMorgan Chase, eleven blocks from Citigroup, and accused those and other banks, and the credit-rating agencies, and the regulatory agencies, not just of criminal negligence but of having done deliberate harm:

> Greed, fraud, dishonesty, and arrogance, these are the
> words that best describe the reality of Wall Street today.

The entirety of the formula reminded me of the High Holiday liturgy, when Jews stand in front of one another, and in front of God, to enumerate their sins and repent for them: "greed" (beat your breast), "fraud" (beat it), "dishonesty" (beat it), and "arrogance" (beat it). I understand this characterization betrays my own sensitivities more than Sanders's, but still I couldn't avoid the association, or the suspicion that even while he was accusing, he was also atoning. But for whom? And for what?

A confession: The fact that there were no pogroms in this country after the 2008 financial collapse still astounds me, and almost had me convinced that anti-Semitism was on the wane in America, until I was reminded of the equally astounding fact that no goyish bank CEOs were shot or stabbed or beaten or kidnapped in the aftermath. And though Jewish men are seen as disproportionately represented in bank boardrooms, at least as disproportionately as they're represented on bookstore shelves, and in pairings of non-Asian men with Asian women, the truth remains that the vast majority of bank CEOs are goyim, not to mention that the largest bankruptcy to result from the crisis—indeed, the largest in American history—was perhaps Wall Street's most historically Jewish firm, Lehman Brothers, which went to its grave with $613 billion in debt.

Still, pockets—empty pockets—of anti-Semitic tropes still fester: websites dedicated to the kabbalistic significance of the number 613 (the number of *mitzvot*, or commandments, in the Torah), and to the Zionist Occupied Government perpetrated by Lloyd Blankfein at Goldman Sachs; Ben Bernanke was chair of the Fed; Robert Zoellick, also at Goldman, headed the World Bank. Sheldon Adelson ran, and still runs... Sheldon Adelson. Jews comprise around 2 percent of the U.S. population, yet over 40 percent of U.S. billionaires...

This money libel, in which Jews are accused of draining money from world coffers, is the modern version of the blood libel, in which Jews were accused of draining the blood of Christian babies for ritual use, which itself was a medieval renewal of the ancient accusation that Jews were the killers of Christ. The metaphoric equivalencies, between blood and money, money and Jews, coruscate from under the slander: Jews, who murdered the child of God, were punished and condemned to wander, or rather, they were forced to "circulate," and so to conceal their identities, to "convert" or "exchange" their identities; in every situation, they had to remain "fungible." In sum, Jews move like money moves, and their Judaism, like all valuta, is an arbitrary principle, both race and religion yet neither—always in transit, always redefining its worth, capable of taking on all forms and no forms, like their God.

The thing is, while I'm quite certain that Jews don't hold Easter-time baby-murdering ceremonies, nor do they control all world events, I'm not sure that the poetry—the metaphors, again—behind the money libel is unfair, or wrong. Jews have always been mutable, and made trades. They've always passed, or tried to pass—as Christians, as socialists, as white. Some of us even broke out of Brooklyn poverty, sat in to integrate the University of Chicago, marched with Martin Luther King, Jr., moved to Vermont to dabble in the counter-culture, and convinced a bunch of libertarians with guns that we were enough like them to elect us mayor of the state's largest city, and then to send us to Congress and even, who knows, beyond.

¶ Deflation

Here's Sanders's chief speech technique: He puffs the audience up into a frenzy with all variety of denunciations, and then—he lets the air out... whoosh. So many of his policies seem like deflations—reductions of banking influence, sure, but also letdowns, paltry punch lines to elaborately set up jokes.

For example, after railing against the banks for a few impassioned minutes, he says that under his administration, he's going to go all (Teddy) Roosevelt and bust them up. How's he going to do it? Are you ready?

114

Within the first one hundred days of my administration, I will require the secretary of the Treasury Department to establish a "too big to fail" list of commercial banks, shadow banks, and insurance companies whose failure would pose a catastrophic risk to the United States economy without a taxpayer bailout.

A list! Note where the stress lies: not on the breaking, the bashing, the smashing, the pleasure of revenge, but... on a piece of paper! As Spielberg might remind us, "The list is life."

Another few impassioned minutes are spent lamenting the repeal of the Glass-Steagall Act, which, as Sanders explains, disentangled the activities of commercial and investment banks. What's he going to do it about? He'll reinstate it, with new provisions!

But instead of outlining what those new provisions might be, he instead credits Elizabeth Warren with having conceived them, or introduced them, and then delves into a history lesson on how the original act was passed under (Franklin) Roosevelt but repealed under (Bill) Clinton. He concludes the non sequitur by quoting former secretary of labor Robert Reich at length, and in doing so once again demonstrates his penchant for referring to himself in the third person:

Bernie Sanders says break them up and resurrect the Glass-Steagall Act that once separated investment from commercial banking. Hillary Clinton says charge them a bit more and oversee them more carefully... Hillary Clinton's proposals would only invite more dilution and finagle.

Yes, "finagle." Which, though it's technically derived from Old English, has never sounded more Yiddish.

More? Sanders goes on a rant about interest rates, about bank fees, the rape of the middle class. To quote Chernyshevsky, "What is to be done?" Sanders says he's going to order a cap on ATM fees at $2! Or, to be precise, "two dollas"!

One last? Like an amateur observational comic, he asks the audience if they've noticed that banks are making more money than ever, but when you need a bank in your neighborhood, you can never find one. What. Is. Up. With. That? If you want a loan, you have to go to a payday lender, who entraps you in a debt cycle. So, *nu*? Sanders would empower all U.S. post offices to offer essential banking services.

This was the most intricately signifying stretch of his performance, as he seemed to be doing Larry David doing him, but doing the material Seinfeld might try out in a guest appearance at a civics class on his child's Take Your Father to Work Day. Of course, he wasn't. Sanders wasn't doing anyone, not even himself. This wasn't about him, because nothing is.

This is about how lists and ATMs in the post office are going to save America.

¶ Usury

Nothing could've prepared me for what came next—the ultimate complication of my emotions, and the one statement that will forever prevent me, who makes judgments about everything, from ever being able to decide whether Bernie Sanders doesn't care about his lack of polish, or doesn't even recognize his lack of polish:

> If we are going to create a financial system that works for
> all Americans, we have got to stop financial institutions
> from ripping off the American people by charging sky-
> high interest rates and outrageous fees... The Bible has a
> term for this practice. It's called usury. And in *The Divine
> Comedy*, Dante reserved a special place in the Seventh
> Circle of Hell for those who charged people
> usurious interest rates... Today, we don't need the hellfire
> and the pitchforks, we don't need the rivers of boiling
> blood, but we do need a national usury law.

OK, then. Usury. The derivation is Latin, *usuria*, from *usus*, past participle of *uti*, "to use." Usury means demanding compensation for the "use" of money. It means, in contemporary terms, "charging interest."

Sanders has the literature correct: The Bible pro-scribes usury, but what he failed to mention—what he doesn't seem, again, to either care about or recognize— is the fact that this proscription allowed the Roman Catholic curia's various inquisitions to prosecute it as a heresy, punishable by death. Of course, moneylending was one of a handful of occupations that Jews were per-mitted to engage in, or, in not a few cases, coerced into engaging in, during the Middle Ages, which makes it understandable why noblemen and merchant borrowers would be interested in criminalizing interest. This made the money they were borrowing essentially free, and the moneylender would have to lend on the black market to turn a profit. Dante condemns this practice, that's true, and relegates usurers not just to the Seventh Circle, but to a subcircle of the Seventh Circle, the lowest of the low: to be harried by the monster Geryon and tortured below the suicides and murderers, amid the sodomists and blasphemers. I wonder whether Sanders would agree with the Florentine poet's stance on men who have sex with other men, men who use the name of God in vain, and men who off themselves. (To be fair, I presume he's on board with being antimurder.) I also wonder whether Sanders shouldn't have chosen a less-charged, less-invested-with-peril name for his proposed legislation—a name that wasn't used as a virtual synonym for crafty Jewish malice for over a millennium and a half. What about the No Outrageous Fees Act (NOFA)? Or the Lower Interest Rates Regulation (LIRR)? I mean, couldn't one of his volunteer redshirts from Harvard/Yale/Sarah Lawrence have googled "usury," just to gauge how fraught that term might be, especially from the mouth of a Jew? Or maybe the requisite googling was done, and Sanders intends to provoke, or just can't be bothered?

The great artwork concerning usury Sanders leaves unquoted: Shakespeare's *The Merchant of Venice*. And it was at the moment that he pronounced the word again that I had the sense of being present at a new and very skewed production.

Sanders stood ragged on the creaky stage of Town Hall, in the heart of not Venice but another water-bound Serene Republic. He spoke with the same zeal we expect from Shylock, had the same demands for justice, the same ludicrous faith in the judiciary, and even—I swear—some of the same desires.

Here's the plot: This country's middle class, represented by Sanders/Shylock, has given a loan, is coerced into giving a loan, to Antonio, who for the purposes of this version will be played by the banks. This loan is in the form of a bailout. When it comes time to repay the loan, the banks refuse, claiming that they can't, which only means that they won't, and so Sanders/Shylock hauls them to court and demands repayment of his bond. That bond, though it's merely symbolic, is also human flesh, and so it's deemed too much—too beyond the pale—not just against the law, but also against natural law. The banks claim that to deprive them of their flesh would be to deprive them, and so the republic, of life: Shylock, in his bloodlust, must be a savage. The play ends—Shakespeare's original play ends—with Shylock on the skids, condemned to wander, without a family, a business, a home.

Exit Bernie, taking no questions:

Follow not;
I'll have no speaking: I will have my bond.

FROM THE DIARIES

New York Signs: Last Exist for the Verrazano-Narrows Bridge

Still following the coast, which veered to the north, we
reached, after fifty leagues, another land, which was much
more beautiful and full of forests. There we anchored, and
with twenty men penetrated about two leagues inland,
only to find that the people there had fled to the woods.
Searching around, we found a very old woman and a
young girl of eighteen to twenty, who were crouching
amid the grasses in fear. The old woman had two little
girls carried up on her shoulders, and clinging to her neck
was a boy—they were all about eight years old. The young
woman also had three children, all girls. When we came
upon them, they began to shriek. The old woman made
signs to us that the men had fled to the woods. We gave
her food, which she accepted with pleasure, but the young
woman refused us and angrily threw whatever we offered
to the ground. We took the boy from the old woman
to carry back to France, and wished to take the young
woman too, because she was very beautiful and tall [*di
molta bellezza, e d'alta statura*], but it was impossible to lead
her away because of her crying [*non fu mai possibile per i
grandissimi gridi*]. And so, as we were far from the ship and
still had to pass through the woods, we decided to leave
her behind.

A letter from Giovanni da Verrazano to King Francis
of France, describing his first encounter—as the first
European to enter the Narrows—with the native
Lenape, 1524. Every Sunday I drive H's parents' car
over the Narrows to Staten Island for pizza. I want
Denino's. Though H thinks Totonno's is better, because

120

of its crust. Da Verrazano thought the Hudson River
was a lake.

New York Signs: Yield

A transitive verb, from Old English's *gieldan,* akin to
Old High German's *geltan,* "to pay," dating from before
the twelfth century: recompense, reward; to give or
render as rightfully owed, or required; to give up,
or give in, to die; to surrender, submit, or relinquish
oneself, another, or an object, to another, to an inclina-
tion, or temptation; to bear, or bring forth; to produce,
or furnish; to give revenue as return from investment;
to give up a hit or run, in baseball; an intransitive verb:
to be fruitful; to cease resistance, or contention; to give
way to pressure, or influence; to give way under physical force; to give place, or precedence; to be inferior;
to be succeeded by another; to relinquish the floor of
a legislative assembly; a noun: something yielded; the
capacity of yielding. Famous usages: "To yelde Jesu
Christ his proper rent," Chaucer; "What say ye,
countrymen? will ye relent, / And yield to mercy
whilst 'tis offer'd you," Shakespeare.

New York Signs: Siamese Connection

Get used to parking elsewhere and saying "conjoined."

New York Signs: LIRR

A German friend of H's who lived in New York while
pursuing an indistinct business degree would, every
summer, find a very pretty boyfriend who had, or
whose family had, a beach house in the Hamptons.

Every Friday, she'd go out there, taking the Long Island Railroad, the LIRR, which she'd pronounce in its fullness, not as an acronym but as a guttural word: "I'll be back on Monday, I'm taking *the Ler*." "No to the car, no to the jitney, *die Ler* is faster—*tschüss!*"

New York Signs: R Trains Run Express

Until they don't.

New York Signs: Stop

The German friend told H and H told me: What TV and movies call a "restraining order," real courts in real life call an "order of protection."

LETTER TO RUTH MAY RIVERS

(*Still from footage shot of Boyd and Ruth May Rivers*)

Dear Ruth May Rivers,
   *There aren't many great moments of film related to blues
music and, of those, there are precious few that are performances: The better musicians tend to stiffen up when not just
heard but seen. Two moments that come to mind have to do
with Robert Johnson (of whom only* two photographs *are
extant). In the late 2000s, friends of a Memphis businessman
named Leo "Tater Red" Allred bought a dilapidated movie
palace in Ruleville, Mississippi, which had formerly belonged
to a man named Bill Jackson. These friends found a cache of
old film canisters on the premises and, knowing Allred to be
something of a local historian, duly passed them along. They
turned out to be reels filmed by Jackson himself: footage of
football games and parades. But two of the reels were out-
liers: One showed the day-to-day life of white inhabitants
of Ruleville; the other showed the day-to-day to life of black
inhabitants of Ruleville. Apparently, Jackson got the notion to
drum up community interest in his theater by using it to show*

the community to itself. He'd screen these hometown movies during the breaks in double features—screening the white reel at the white showtimes and the black reel at the black showtimes. In both the white and black versions, citizens of Ruleville relax on a weekend noon: They mug for the camera, they socialize, they shop. But a curious figure was discernible in the black version: a behatted busker strumming his guitar, with a harmonica braced near his mouth. He's playing his heart out, it seems. He's playing soundlessly. The man appears to be, or bears an eerie resemblance to, Robert Johnson. Once this suspicion was announced, the press and experts swarmed like weevils: Jimmy Page and Robert Plant were convinced, but Robert Lockwood—the only guitarist to have studied with Johnson—claimed it wasn't him; cineastes noted that one of the reel's wide shots had caught a glimpse of the theater's marquee, which advertised Blues in the Night, *a noir musical directed by Anatole Litvak. That movie premiered in December 1941. Johnson, of course, died in August 1938, but still—the Johnson estate ignored this debunking; some wishful academics accused the skeptics of sabotage; some self-appointed researchers online even suggested that, if the man in the film wasn't the blues master himself, it might be the devil that owned his soul.*

The second Johnson moment is also marked by absence. John Hammond, Jr., a formidable white blues musician and the son of the record producer, talent scout, and civil rights activist John H. Hammond, served as the producer and Delta drag- oman to a 1991 U.K. Channel 4 documentary entitled The Search for Robert Johnson. *In it, Hammond managed to track down a woman named Willie Mae Powell, a permed, prim geriatric in oversize oval glasses and floral prints who, in the flower of her youth, had dated Johnson briefly. Though Johnson might've dated half of black female Mississippi in the 1930s, only "Willie Mae" was immortalized in song—Johnson sings her name twice, as the only words of the fourth and final*

124

verse of "Love in Vain"; the remainder of the verse is just howls and meows, yearning vowels sung in a train whistle's falsetto. Powell had not seen Johnson in over half a century and had never before heard the song—not in the decent Rolling Stones cover, not in the execrable Todd Rundgren cover, and, most pertinently, not even in the glorious Johnson original, which Hammond proceeded to play for her on-camera. Upon hearing her name sung for the first time, Powell cried. I cried too—I cry every time I reload the clip.

I should say, Ruth May, that my concern is not to resurrect the women who were the subject and the object of the famous blues. Women certainly don't need that advocacy from me: At least, Bessie Smith and Ma Rainey don't need it, and neither, for that matter, do you. Instead, I mention these instances of celluloid Johnsoniana because the mere potential of their existence appears to make a human out of a legend. Whereas the stunning video clips—six of them—that the Lomax Collection produced of you singing along with the singing and guitar-playing of your late husband, Boyd Rivers, at your home in Canton, Mississippi, in 1978, do the very opposite: They appear to make a legend out of a human. Out of the approximately six thousand films and video clips and approximately ten thousand audio recordings that archivist and ethnomusicologist Alan Lomax and his father, John Lomax, made throughout the American South for the Library of Congress, for themselves, and for posterity, between 1933 and 1996, yours are among the very few to accomplish this: They make two legends out of two humans.

To be sure, the Lomaxes had made their share of stars before, but this had much to do with timing. Lead Belly's Lomax recordings (done at Angola Prison Farm in Louisiana, 1933–34) and Son House's Lomax recordings (done at Clack's Grocery in Lake Cormorant, Mississippi, 1941–42) were released to the public coincident with the folk revival and were

125

championed, and plagiarized, by the likes of Bob Dylan and other avatars of the acoustic white counterculture. To put it plainly, then, Alan Lomax got to your husband too late—in the disco era—which is why even now, twenty-five years after your husband died in 1993, his talent remains unrecognized. Boyd Rivers was—as I'm sure you've always known—the most commanding(-sounding) and yet most vulnerable(-sounding) blues artist of the second half of the twentieth century. That this accolade is earnable by an oeuvre of just the six videos for the Lomax collection and eight audio recordings (done for an enterprising German record label in 1980) is not unprecedented. Henry Sloan—who was, according to lore, the éminence grise and griot of Dockery Plantation in Dockery, Mississippi (which spawned Charlie Patton, Willie Brown, and Tommy Johnson, among others)—left no recordings; Robert Petway left only sixteen tracks; William Harris and Dan Pickett left only fourteen apiece; Luke Jordan and Buddy Boy Hawkins left only twelve apiece; King Solomon Hill's awesome immortality rests on eight, four of which are alternate takes; Geeshie Wiley and Elvie Thomas cut six (two of which are classics: "Motherless Child Blues" and "Last Kind Words Blues"); Cecil Augusta played a single song for Alan Lomax's recorders ("Stop All the Buses"), then vanished.

Enough. I want to explain what I got from your and your husband's recordings and I hope you will forgive me. Blues music, to my mind, is not just dangerous to all law-abiding, churchgoing folk, but dangerous to man in general—to men, and especially to white men. There is something attractive, almost demonically attractive, about that slough of self-pity and lament—all that woe-is-me-poor-boy-long-ways-from-home lugubriousness can lead, in my experience, to the imputation of a certain romance or even heroism to bad-feeling. There is a sense in the blues—more than that, there is lyrical confirmation—that music is a man's sole comfort and

126

consolation, that music is all that a man has left to turn to, once a woman does him wrong. This is pigheaded, obviously. It is isolating and chauvinistic and dumb. But it is also the truth. Or it can be. Gospel music is sung with a choir, a congregation. Whereas the blues are sung when you have no congregation and your family's dead and your lover's gone skipped town with your best friend—the blues are sung when you have nothing else to say or even live for.

This, I'm confessing, was my own immature take, until I saw—until I heard—your performances. All of the other clips in the voluminous Lomax archive of "field" recordings feature men, solo men, or men in duo, buddies bucking each other up, but yours present a couple. Your husband introduces: "My name is Boyd Hillard Rivers. This is my wife, Ruth May Rivers. We've been married fifteen years and ever since we've been together we've been trying to sang." And you did, the two of you in your livingroom with imitation-wood paneling and zebra-hide-patterned carpet; you dressed up in a vest, slightly shy about opening wide to show your gold teeth, until the spirit took over and reassured you; your husband massy and booming, as he stomped his feet in time with his thumb-picked downstroke and shook an organ-like storm surge out of his Gibson SG. As you two went at it in harmony, in octaves, and then with you going low and him going high to meet in unison, I had my epiphany: The blues can also be shared. It can also be sung together. Sadness doesn't have to be solitary or solitarizing: There is a way of making it mutual, even mutual between husband and wife.

I realized: The two individuals who comprise a couple must try to make each other feel less alone and it might be that the best way to do that is to join voices against that common condition—to mourn that common condition in such a way as to reinforce each other's strength. Boyd Rivers: "Tell me how do you feel when you come out?" You: "Come out the wilderness?"

127

BR: "When you come out?" You: "Come out the wilderness?"
BR: "When you come out?" You: "Come out the wilderness?"
BR: "Tell me how do you feel when you come out?" You:
"Come out the wilderness?" Together: "Leaning on the Lord?"

*What is truly evil and bluesing in this world is not what
one individual does to another, but what the world does to all
of us: It makes us die. Your accompaniment of your husband,
your husband's accompaniment of you, showed me the power
that comes from having made a deal with a solid partner—
not by midnight at the crossroads, but in broad daylight in a
quaint tidy livingroom—a deal to resist despair.*

I send you my very best wishes,

Joshua Cohen

FIRST FAMILY, SECOND LIFE:
ON THOMAS PYNCHON

Pinco de Normandie sailed to England with William the Conqueror. His son, Hugh, held seven "knights' fees in Lincolnshire" and four "bovates in Friskney." Four centuries later, his descendant Edward Pynchon was ennobled and granted a coat of arms "per bend argent and sable, three roundles with a bordure engrailed, counterchanged." By then the Pincheuns had settled snugly into gentry life in Essex. Nicholas Pinchon became high sheriff of London in 1533, and his son, or nephew, John married Jane Empson, daughter of Sir Richard Empson, a minister to, and casualty of, the doomed regime of Henry VII. John's son was also John, and his son was William Pynchon, who in 1630 sailed with John Winthrop to found the Massachusetts Bay Colony, of which he was elected treasurer. He established the towns of Roxbury and, while pursuing the fur trade, Springfield, where he deposed the accused witches in the trial preceding Salem. He served as model for Colonel Pyncheon in Hawthorne's *The House of the Seven Gables*, and in 1650 wrote *The Meritorious Price of Our Redemption*, whose critique of Puritan Calvinism caused it to be burned in Boston and to become the New World's first banned book, though only nine copies survived the pyre. (Among those who voted against the censure was William Hauthorne, Hawthorne's first colonist ancestor.) This was the proto-American literary debut of a family that later included the Reverend Thomas Ruggles Pynchon (1823–1904), president of Trinity College, Hartford, and author of *The Chemical Forces: Heat–Light–Electricity... An Introduction to Chemical Physics*; Dr. Edwin Pynchon (1856–1914), author of "Surgical Correction of

Deformities of the Nasal Septum"; and Thomas Ruggles Pynchon, Jr., born in 1937, in Glen Cove, Long Island, author of *V.*, *The Crying of Lot 49*, *Gravity's Rainbow*, *Slow Learner*, *Vineland*, *Mason & Dixon*, *Against the Day*, *Inherent Vice*, and now *Bleeding Edge*.

Anyone who's written at the end of so long and distinguished a line has been faced with a choice: either embrace the legacy or attempt to disassociate from it. (Hawthorne added the "w" to distance himself from John Hathorne, cruelest of the Salem magistrates.) This, of course, is merely a more public version of the decision of whether, and how, to transmute individual experience into prose. Thomas Pynchon—the most private, or publicly private, of American novelists—has been considering such disclosures for half a century now, in the way he's handled both his famous family in his work and his own fame in life. The single overtly autobiographical statement he has provided to date appears in the introduction to a collection of his early and only short fiction, *Slow Learner:*

> Somewhere I had come up with the notion that one's personal life had nothing to do with fiction, when the truth, as everyone knows, is nearly the direct opposite... [F]or in fact the fiction both published and unpublished that moved and pleased me then as now was precisely that which had been made luminous, undeniably authentic by having been found and taken up, always at a cost, from deeper, more shared levels of the life we all really live.

I've read that introduction a dozen times, and most of Pynchon's novels at least twice, yet I'm still not sure what to make of this assertion. I'm still not sure whether *V.* (1963)—which takes as its premise the search for a mysterious, free-floating signifier that might be a woman named Victoria, and/or Veronica, and/or an incarnation of the goddess Venus, and/or the city of Valletta, and/or Victory in WWI and/or WWII—becomes any clearer with the knowledge that Pynchon wrote it after serving in the Navy and attending Cornell, where he audited lectures by that shapeshifter Nabokov (Vèra handled correspondence and gave the grades). Nor am I sure whether *The Crying of Lot 49* (1966)—which concerns the machinations of a certain Yoyodyne, "one of the giants of the aerospace industry"—is enriched by the information that between 1960 and 1962 Pynchon lived in Seattle and worked for Boeing as a technical writer for the Bomarc interceptor-missile project. Then again, it strikes me that Pynchon's defense-contracting stint finds direct expression in *Gravity's Rainbow* (1973), that treatment of the Third Reich's V-2 rocket program. But I'm still confused as to whether I should read the hero of that novel—Tyrone Slothrop, an American G.I. whose erections foretell the ground-zero impacts of V-2s in London—as an embodiment of John Winthrop or, because Slothrop's ancestor William Slothrop is portrayed as having published a controversial theological treatise called *On Preterition*, as a surrogate for the author himself.

Gravity's Rainbow was written by hand on quadrille engineering paper, and on Kool cigarettes, coffee, and cheeseburgers (to name just the legal substances), in Mexico City and in a whitewashed bungalow on 33rd Street in Manhattan Beach, California. The 1974 Pulitzer Prize committee refused to honor the novel, despite the jurors' unanimous recommendation (the committee called it "turgid" and "overwritten," "obscene" and "unreadable"). But it went on to win the

National Book Award in 1974, for which ceremony Pynchon dispatched a comedian, "Professor" Irwin Corey, to deliver a nonsensical speech: "[I] accept this financial stipulation, ah, stipend on behalf of, uh, Richard Python for the great contribution and to quote from some of the missiles which he has contributed [...]" In the '80s, Pynchon left his agent, Candida Donadio, to be represented by Melanie Jackson, great-granddaughter of Theodore Roosevelt and granddaughter of Robert H. Jackson, the Supreme Court justice and Nuremberg prosecutor. The two married in the '90s and had a son, Jackson, who was such a fan of *The Simpsons* that Pynchon made a cameo (his animation was drawn with a paper bag instead of a head). Only ten images of Pynchon are publicly available, including a video captured by CNN in 1997 that occasioned this rebuke from his agent/wife by fax: " 'Recluse' is a code word generated by journalists ... meaning 'doesn't like to talk to reporters.' " Then there's the photo published by the *Times* of London in 1997, which provoked legal threats from Henry Holt, Pynchon's publisher at the time.

What else? Pynchon was raised Catholic and attended mass. He was the best friend of Richard Fariña (author of *Been Down So Long It Looks Like Up to Me*) and the best man at Fariña's wedding to Mimi Baez (Joan's sister). He was reportedly so ashamed of his Bugs Bunny teeth that he underwent extensive cosmetic dental surgery....

All this information came to me via the web, which has established Pynchon as its literary divinity. Not Philip K. Dick, not William Gibson—it's Pynchon who commands the largest and loudest community online. It's a congregation of fanboys, academics, techno-anarchists, wannabe fictioneers, parents' basement—dwellers, and burnouts—some using real names, some using fake names, many anonymous—who analyze and squabble over every scrap of the Shroud and splinter of the Cross, in search of the Message.

In the early days of home-use internet, back when the first major e-marketer appeared under the sobriquet Yoyodyne (sold to Yahoo in 1998 for $30 million in stock), users of Yahoo and AOL messageboards and chatrooms asserted that Pynchon was J. D. Salinger or the Unabomber, a Branch Davidian or "Wanda Tinasky," who in witty mock-Pynchonian letters to the editors of the Anderson Valley Advertiser identified "herself" as a bag lady living under a bridge in northern California. With the gradual uploading of scholarship in the form of journal PDFs and dissertation .docs, the digital Pynchonverse got its act together, and by the mid-'90s had become a halfway-disciplined research collective of amateurs and professionals, though one that took a break every toke or two to speculate wildly. Hey, get a load of this—Pynchon's working on a novel about Lewis & Clark (rather, Mason & Dixon); Michael Naumann, past publisher of Henry Holt and former German minister of culture, helped Pynchon gather materials concerning the David Hilbert circle in Göttingen, and went on the record as saying the author's next book would trace the amours of the Russian mathematician Sofia Kovalevskaya (material appearing in *Against the Day*). Pynchon himself never participated in any of this, of course, though there were at least a dozen contributors I can remember who claimed to be him, or were suspected of being him. My favorite posted under the webonym Martin Scribler, and if you're bored already: waste.org.

Serious literary discussion on the internet began with Pynchon fans—which is just the type of generalization to spark a flame war with the science-fiction freaks, who'd claim that the Pynchonites showed up late to the party. I certainly did. It was 1994, and I was thirteen or fourteen when I found the *Playboys* in the basement and the Pynchon novels on a shelf in my father's office. On the floor between was the new computer, the family's first, a Gateway. Porn was difficult to find and slow to load, but the Pynchon guides, being text-based, were instantly gratifying. I read the threads—the rumor and gossip arbitrage, conspiracy swaps and paranoia—as if they were stray strands of Pynchon's own narratology. I had a 28.8k dial-up modem and, despite all Pynchon's warnings about technocracy's incursions, no notion of what surveillance and social control lay ahead.

It was the web that educated me about contemporary literature, not through any primary or even secondary texts that were published there, but through its use. To go online was to experience in life what Pynchon—and his heirs closer to my own generation, like William T. Vollmann and David Foster Wallace—were working toward in fiction: a plot that proceeded not by the relationships developed by the characters ("people") but by the relationships to be discerned among institutions (businesses, governments), objects (missiles, erections), and concepts (hippie-dippie Free Love and the German *Liebestod*). I read about Modernism—big "M"—and post-modernism—small "p"—thanks to links sent to me by strange anagrammatic screen names, and if I couldn't get through Fredric Jameson yet, I could get through a GeoCities site that summarized his work. Modernism was something made by and intended for a limited but discerning audience; postmodernism, by contrast, had popular or populist aspirations—it wanted to be famous, *and complex*! It wanted money, *and respect*! The two movements connected in the "systems novel," a phrase minted by the critic Tom LeClair to describe the complicative methods of John Barth, Robert Coover, Don DeLillo, William Gaddis, Joseph Heller, Ursula Le Guin, Joseph McElroy—and Pynchon.

Before these writers, books deployed closed systems of symbols that, if untangled, provided a substrate of meaning separate from, but communicating with, the action and dialogue (think of Fitzgerald's ad for Dr. T. J. Eckleburg or Hemingway's bullfighting). But these new writers favored books that operated on open systems, that treated the entire world symbolically, and that were inextricably enmeshed with the literary whole (think of the contrast between twentieth-century sensibility and eighteenth-century language in *Mason & Dixon*, or the palimpsest of genres—scientific, spy thriller, teen adventure, western—in *Against the Day*). Perhaps the paragon of the systems novel's associative processes is the "Byron the Bulb" episode of *Gravity's Rainbow*. An ostensibly immortal lightbulb named Byron illuminates, among other places, "an all-girl opium den" and "the home of a glass-blower who is afraid of the night" in Weimar Berlin, the brothel of a Hamburg prostitute whose "customer tonight is a cost-accountant who likes to have bulbs *screwed into his asshole*," and the bunk of a Nazi scientist in a subterranean rocket factory in Nordhausen. It's a section whose fifteen-year time-frame also accommodates examinations of " 'Phoebus,' the international light-bulb cartel, headquartered in Switzerland"; the mutual business interests of General Electric and Krupp; the production of filaments; and the synthesis of tungsten carbide.

Fiction has long been described in the terms of a coeval technology, at least since the fade of the vacuum tube, but it was the genius of the systems novelists to produce fiction expressly along the same schematics. In the '70s their novels could be said to function like transistors, while in the '80s they could be said to function like integrated circuits. By the '90s, however, systems technique had been usurped online: the internet replicated its protocols, while the web replicated its surface-shifting—the rapidly changing scenes, the characters introduced, developed, then dropped.

Back when I frequented Amazon—before my favorite independent bookstores began closing and I quit the site, cold turkey, in 2006—I was fascinated by how much it resembled the novels I was buying on it: I'd click on a book by Pynchon, and then lower down or on a sidebar of the page I'd find other titles to add to my cart, suggestions generated by the site's algorithms, but also supplied by other users. People who bought *Mason & Dixon* also bought *Vineland;* if I clicked, I found that people who bought *Vineland* also bought books about the history of the FBI, the CIA, and the War on Drugs, and from there I'd be just a click or two away from the people who also bought fallout-shelter survival kits, pallets of canned meat, bottled water, and tinfoil. Wikipedia's debut reinforced this organizational lesson. As of the date of this writing, the voluminous Thomas Pynchon wiki—which if printed out would surely eclipse the oeuvre of its subject—links to a list of American tax resisters (Pynchon refused to pay any war-designated tax increase in 1968); the American tax resisters' wiki links to the Redemption Movement (a group maintaining that when America abandoned the gold standard, in 1933, it continued to back its debts by pledging its citizens' lives to foreign governments as collateral); which in turn links to the wiki for *The Matrix* (1999); linking to Laurence Fishburne; linking, no doubt, to Kevin Bacon.

When news of the publication of *Bleeding Edge* went around Twitter in spring 2013, it set off a surge of chatter on the usual sites, but not for the usual reasons. This wasn't just another Pynchon book; this wasn't even just another Pynchon book with the internet in the margins (ARPANET, which was developed in the '60s and '70s by an arm of the American military, had a cameo in Pynchon's *Inherent Vice*). Rather, this would be a book dramatizing it all front and center, "a historical romance of New York in the early days of the internet," according to the P.R. copy. I was excited, but also wary. As a reader I was hoping for Pynchon's ultimate reckoning with the surveillance state he'd been railing against since the reign of J. Edgar Hoover—a culminant tilt at an institution of spying and mass mind-manipulation more powerful, and more voluntarily submitted to, than anything ever dreamed up by Reagan, Nixon, the KGB, the Stasi, or the Nazi SS. But as a novelist I also worried about how Pynchon would write about the very technology that has plagiarized his methods and that has made the sporadic lapses of fact in his meticulous research—indeed, that has made his face—a matter of public record.[1]

1. The day after the book's galley was delivered to me—this was just after the NSA Prism scandal broke—I took it along to a dermatology appointment and started reading it on the subway. Immediately a man stomped across the car and without saying anything stuck out his iPhone and snapped a shot of the cover. He was white, stocky, about five foot six, and jumped out at West 4th Street—in other words, demographically representative. Later that evening I found the pic posted online. It had

Ahem, ahem: The novel was also about 9/11.

"Bleeding edge" is a techie phrase meaning beyond even the "cutting edge"—so new that it hurts. The irony of this as a title is that the novel is set mostly in the spring and summer of 2001. Pynchon offers such nostalgic references as Beanie Babies, Furbys, Pokémon, Razor scooters, and Jennifer Aniston still in Rachel mode alongside a presidency just stolen and a tech bubble just burst. Downtown, the towers of the World Trade Center throw their foreshadows over Wall Street. A stretch farther north, between TriBeCa and the Flatiron, lies Silicon Alley, a New York tech district that actually existed, or that was actually hyped to have existed—a real estate figment like NoHo or SoHa or even the West and East Villages (originally the Village and the Lower East Side).

Here, in Pynchon's telling, two types prevailed. One consisted of generic deracinated White People who'd gone out West like the prospectors of yore, but who when they bottomed out amid the Bay's Zen gardens and organic-smoothie chains found themselves yearning for real urban grit—or at least for the really yuppified grit of gentrifying Giulianiville. The other was made up of city lifers, the ethnically identifying—or not yet post-identity—strivers who've always served as New York's color: the wise black bike messenger, the Irish cop and fireman, the social-club Italian, the backroom-fixer Jew; the "genuine," the "authentic," the huddled masses yearning for cash.

Meanwhile, "on the Yupper West Side"—Pynchon's own neighborhood—Maxine Tarnow is just trying to

... already received a few hundred likes. In the weeks that followed, *Bleeding Edge* galleys appeared on eBay, being auctioned—being purchased—for upward of $1,500.

get her life back together. She's a gun-toting fraud investigator who's recently had her certification revoked for unwittingly abetting an embezzlement, and a doting single mother of two precocious young boys, Ziggy and Otis, whose stock-trader father, Horst Loeffler, keeps offices in the World Trade Center and casual mistresses throughout the boroughs. Filmmaker Reg Despard, hired by a computer-security firm called hashslingrz to make an in-house documentary, retains Maxine to background-check his employer's finances once his access is curtailed by CEO Gabriel Ice, "One of the boy billionaires who walked away in one piece when the dotcom fever broke." This would be the same Ice who's after the source code for a clandestine second-life website called DeepArcher (pronounced "departure"), developed by Maxine's acquaintances Lucas and Justin, two Valley vets out to raise a ruckus, and capital, in the Alley.

Maxine's inquiries into DeepArcher and hashslingrz serve as the book's basic binary. The former gets her caught up in an insomniac second life in which she wanders through an unregulated cyberniche, a "framed lucid dream," that morphs in appearance and purpose according to user input—mediascapes of ghetto squalor one moment and pristine desert the next, all "in shadow-modulated 256-color daylight, no titles, no music," untainted by advertising. The latter entangles her in the physical world, what Pynchon calls "meatspace," investigating a host of sketchy (in every sense) personalities: Nicholas Windust, a federal agent whose first job was "spotting for the planes that bombed the presidential palace and killed Salvador Allende" on 9/11/73, and who went on to run "interrogation enhancement" and "noncompliant-subject relocation" squads in South and Central America; Avi, Maxine's brother-in-law, a recovering Mossad agent; Rocky, a fugazi Cosa Nostra venture capitalist; Igor and his stooges Misha and Grisha, Russian gangsters who've invested with Bernie Madoff. All or some of these characters point to the idea that the U.S. government, or rogue elements within it, was aware of and maybe even plotted—perhaps in league with Ice—the 9/11 attacks (for which readers will have to wait until page 316).

Obviously, the opposite might also be the truth. Ice, through his partners in the Middle East and shell companies in the Emirates, might be a hero, if not of America then of the right—laundering money for the undisclosed locations of the "war on terror," coming soon to a screen near you.

But wait, there's more—if you enjoyed 9/11, you might also enjoy red herring, which aren't native to the coast of Long Island, unlike the Montauk Project. This actual paranormal conspiracy theory—regarded as the successor to the Philadelphia Experiment—is, in Pynchon's telling, "a kind of boot camp for military time travelers" that kidnaps, starves, beats, and sodomizes American preadolescents. They—"Boys, typically"—are trained to become the agents of tomorrow, or yesterday, "Assigned to secret cadres to be sent on government missions back and forth in Time, under orders to create alternative histories which will benefit higher levels of command who have sent them out." Now, keep in mind that this explanation of the Montauk Project, which is supposedly accessible by a tunnel under Ice's vacation property, comes to Maxine not in meatspace but in DeepArcher, from an Adderall-addled "IT samurai" named Eric Outfield, or rather from his avatar, whose "soul patch pulses incandescent green."

Page 316:

> Maxine heads for work, puts her head in a local smoke
> shop to grab a newspaper, and finds everybody freaking
> out and depressed at the same time. Something bad is
> going on downtown. "A plane just crashed into the World
> Trade Center," according to the Indian guy behind the
> counter.
>
> "What, like a private plane?"
>
> "A commercial jet."
>
> Uh-oh. Maxine goes home and pops on CNN. And
> there it all is. Bad turns to worse. All day long. At around
> noon the school calls and says they're shutting down for
> the day, could she please come and collect her kids.
>
> Everybody's on edge. Nods, headshakes, not a lot of
> social conversation.
>
> "Mom, was Dad down there at his office today?"
>
> "He was staying over at Jake's last night, but I think
> he's mostly been working from his computer. So chances
> are he didn't even go in."
>
> "But you haven't heard from him?"
>
> "Everybody's been trying to get through to everybody,
> lines are swamped, he'll call, I'm not worrying, don't you
> guys, OK?"

Maxine—part JAP, part MILF—tries to buck up her
guys, as does Pynchon's flattest style in what's inevitably the book's roughest stretch (roughest to read and
to write, I'd imagine). The novel's zany tangents and
waves of punning fall away for a spell. We're left with a
possibly husbandless woman on the couch alongside her
possibly fatherless children, who've temporarily forgotten their game cartridges because the onscreen carnage
is so compellingly uncontrollable. That excerpt's last

quoted line and its implications are key to every family's sense of frustrated codependence. Sometimes the phones work and sometimes they don't, leaving Dad—Horst—in limbo incommunicado, his fate in the hands of God, or Wolf Blitzer.

The attacks of 9/11 gave rise to bad invasions, bad occupations, and bad laws, but one of their least-noted but most-consequential impacts on the homefront was how they encouraged a society of total contact with a furious and mortal urgency (which Pynchon reinforces by using the present tense). Nowadays, to lose touch is to die; if you're ever buried by rubble, the first thing you do is call and pray that the signal's strong enough to let your last words live at least on voicemail. Before 9/11, the online world was engaged with at home, in a chair, at a desk. Having a cellphone—Pynchon prefers "mobile phone"—wasn't a social norm, let alone a requirement akin to having a heart, or a brain, or lungs. In *Bleeding Edge*, cellphones ring fewer than a dozen times, and their occasional presence merely accentuates their absence.

If one of the barest necessities of fiction is keeping two characters apart for enough time for a misunderstanding to ensue—a misunderstanding that can be resolved only by the protagonists individually moving toward each other, and toward the book's conclusion—cellphones, now "smartphones," have become the chief antagonists of fiction. Today, we're rarely denied the opportunity of contact, and all contacts—phone numbers and email addresses—can be digitally exhumed. Pynchon, by setting his novel on the cusp of the attacks, makes desperate comedy out of this last chance at inaccessibility, this final dark and silent millennial moment. He does so by exaggerating all the improbabilities and coincidence tricks of a previous information revolution—that of the Victorian novel, whose outlandishness was later called realism.

In the Victorian novel, chance is a mechanism of resolution: Two characters, separated for a bit, "suddenly" meet in a street, or at the theater. In Pynchon's books, chance is a religious or spiritual mechanism. Meetings must have "meanings," mysteries. In *V.*, graffiti in a toilet stall spurs an electricity seminar when the image turns out to be a diagram for a band-pass filter. In *Lot 49*, the recurring doodle of a muted postal horn leads to the exposure of an underground mail network that has been passing correspondence via trash cans since the French Revolution. *Bleeding Edge* has a cruder approach, familiar from Pynchon's other historical novels (*Gravity's Rainbow*, *Mason & Dixon*, and *Against the Day*), in which happenstance provides the pretext for information exchange: Maxine is lazing by her office window when she notices Igor's limousine (its Cyrillic bumper sticker translates as my other limo is a Maybach); she gets in, only to find March Kelleher, a renegade lefty blogger who just happens to be Ice's mother-in-law. March has to courier Igor's Madoff money (thanks to Maxine's tip, Igor cashed out just in time) to Sid, March's ex-husband and a drug runner, up at "a dance club near Vermilyea." Why not, Maxine goes along; once the deal is done, Sid offers to return them to the 79th Street Boat Basin in his antique motorboat, but the DEA gives chase and the trio flee down the Hudson, losing their pursuers by the Island of Meadows, a wetlands preserve just off the coast of Staten Island's Fresh Kills landfill. This boat ride is merely an excuse for March and Sid to discuss their daughter, Tallis, and their son-in-law, Ice, which itself is merely an excuse to dump tons of data on Maxine and the reader both. But the indulgences are justified by

Pynchon's beautiful way with the trash:

> This little island reminds [Maxine] of something, and it
> takes her a minute to see what. As if you could reach into
> the looming and prophetic landfill, that perfect negative
> of the city in its seething foul incoherence, and find a set
> of invisible links to click on and be crossfaded at last to
> unexpected refuge, a piece of the ancient estuary exempt
> from what happened, what has gone on happening, to
> the rest of it. Like the Island of Meadows, DeepArcher
> also has developers after it. Whatever migratory visitors
> are still down there trusting in its inviolability will some
> morning all too soon be rudely surprised by the
> whispering descent of corporate Web crawlers itching to
> index and corrupt another patch of sanctuary for their
> own far-from-selfless ends.

All the events described above occur in Pynchon's
shortest sentences and shortest paragraphs to date,
in fewer than a dozen pages. The result is a breathless
major bandwidth rush and a dizzily profound book
about the internet that accomplishes something of which
the internet has rarely been capable. It doesn't quite
make the reader believe that American Flight 11 and
United Flight 175 were brought down by Stinger missiles launched from a rooftop in Hell's Kitchen, but it
does make the reader believe why and how someone else
might believe this—why and how March Kelleher might
believe this—and that, fellow citizens, is sympathy, or
empathy, or literature.

Here's another intrigue from online, though this one is
verifiable: William Pynchon's magistrate son, John, was

a friend of the colony's road surveyor, Miles Morgan, "the hero of Springfield," who in 1675 defended the town against the Wampanoag tribe and was the forefather of J. P. Morgan (Pynchon was the presiding official at Miles Morgan's wedding). The Pynchon and Morgan families would go on to maintain business ties for the next three hundred years, until the stock market crashed the country into Depression. By that time, Pynchon & Co. had become one of America's most prominent brokerages (and the publisher of pamphlets surveying investment prospects, including "Electric Light and Power: A Survey of World Development"). According to Charles Hollander, writing in the journal *Pynchon Notes*, Pynchon & Co. was destroyed by its brief liaison with Chase Bank—the Rockefeller bank—in what might've been a speculation trap aimed at damaging this close associate of the Morgans. The Pynchon family had to auction off their property and furniture and, in debt from a reclamatory lawsuit, senior partner George M. Pynchon, Jr., committed suicide. In Hollander's reading, much of Pynchon's fiction plays out as revenge against the Rockefellers and their dismantling of the Morgan economy of steel, coal, and railroads in favor of an economy of plastics, oil, and weaponry.

Bleeding Edge, appearing after 2008's Depression Redux, deals with the next economy—the virtual—in which the Rockefellers aren't the born elite but the products of meritocracy. Zuckerberg, Brin, Page, Bezos, Jobs, Gates: six sons of American sprawl, three of whom are Jews, one of whom is also a Soviet émigré; one born to a teenage mother and adopted by a Cuban immigrant stepfather; another given up for adoption at birth by his Syrian father and American mother. They are us and we are them, not just biographically but in that we help create what they sell us and improve their services—along with their fortunes—all just by our use.

It follows that the old Pynchonite dichotomy of Us v. Them doesn't apply anymore. In canonical Pynchon, when the military police closed in, when the *federales* swooped down, there was always a stained mattress to crash on in the Village, or a band of pot growers in Mendocino County who'd stash you. You'd be safe there, in whichever countercultural cult—the Whole Sick Crew (*V.*), or the People's Republic of Rock and Roll (*Vineland*); you'd be safe, that is, until your friends got bought out, or sold themselves, and became agents too, or at least collaborating adults who read nonfiction or nothing at all. If Pynchon's characters were left behind by America, they denied that America and terrorized only themselves. They regarded any America that would reject them as fake, and only their own inner America as real—a country not of grandly insistent progress and Horatio Alger success, but of Henry Adams regret and failure. A country of the "preterite"—a characterization Pynchon attributed to William Slothrop in *Gravity's Rainbow*—meaning the passed-over, the neglected, the abandoned; the Melvilles, not the Hawthornes.

Bleeding Edge, however, offers an indication that Pynchon has finally given up on seeking the soul of the nation his family helped found. For Pynchon—the embattled bard of the counterculture, disabused of all allegiance—the last redoubt has become the family, and the last war to be waged is between our virtual identities and the bonds of blood; a war to keep the Virtual from corrupting the Blood, if not forever, then for time enough to let the lil' Ziggy and Otis Tarnow-Loefflers of this world live with the merest pretense of freedom (childhood). Pynchon understands that in the future there will be no secrets, no hidden complots—everything will be aired and any second life, whether in the cloud or in the firmament, will be despoiled or denied us. Adult sanity, then, must depend not on the lives we make online, but on the lives we make off it—our kids—on how we love them, and how we raise them, and the virtues and good-taste imperatives we pass on to them from our progenitors. Smirk if you're a smirker and claim this as the conclusion of an embourgeoised aging-hippie novelist gone soft (or of the Mafia and the Jews), but I'm not sure whether Pynchon means this emphasis on consanguinity in the spirit of salvation or of damnation. It is, regardless, sweetly sad. Sweet and lowdown sad. The online moguls have tried to persuade us that we're not losing a nation, we're gaining a world. Pynchon proposes that both are mere second lives, fakes. Only family is real.

LETTERFORM, ISLANDFORM

The letter I'd like to describe did not exist, it seemed, except in the dream I dreamt for three consecutive nights, December 2009. Coleridge smoked opium and hallucinated an entire poem, "In Xanadu did Kubla Khan / A stately pleasure-dome decree": whereas I, not a poet and trying to wean myself off Xanax and Vicodin and Percocet, had difficulty retrieving from my rest even a coherent letter. I went to bed early all three evenings at my parents' in Jersey, the anti-Xanadu. Three evenings of uneasy slumber and yet upon waking this was all I could recall: an elongated Hebrew *lamed* (ל), a distended Arabic *lam* (ل), the rough form of a fishing hook (lengthened, stretched; though the Semitic Ur letterform is thought to derive from the shape of a shepherd's staff or cattleprod), a finger curled to beckon, a kinked tongue, a carpet hung from the railing of a balcony and beaten of its dust until the remnant's pattern was pure black outline (but this is embellishment now)... the dream was of this letter only, without color, just a character inked or perhaps even incised in black upon the nothingness that is not black itself, just sleep.

To describe a letter that *already exists*—the letter "j," say—without writing it or saying it, is as difficult as describing a piece of music or plastic art: Rather, how to form the lines and how to pronounce the sound and name of that letter can be described without being demonstrated just as accurately, or just as inaccurately, as can the melodies, harmonies, and timbres of a symphony, or the shapes of a nonfigurative sculpture or painting. But to describe a letter that *doesn't exist* is a task seemingly more difficult than describing fake music, which Thomas Mann did well in not a few of his books, or describing fake art, which Marcel Proust, who regularly went to bed early, excelled at. I know of no writer who has, even unsuccessfully, described an imaginary letter whether in sound or image. However, I emphasize that my own experience was visual only. Before proceeding I have to admit I have no idea how my dreamletter would sound if pronounced (though something tells me it would be closer to a vowel than a consonant, and certainly it lacks the "lateral approximant" "l" sound of the *lamed/lam*).

In thinking of my dreamletter on the mornings after, I thought not of its identity as a letter (it couldn't have "an identity"), but about its "meaning": the meaning of its appearance. Dreams can be interpreted as representations of fears, but dreamletters cannot represent fear or any other emotion or thing—only letters and words actually existing can function in that way as symbols. Indeed, the only content of my recurrent dream besides the shape of the letter—pineally burning, nearly gashed into my forehead, that's how close it felt in retrospect, how deeply substantial—can be said to be the thought, the feverishly intellectual thought, that "this is a false letter, without significance, at most it's a self-reference, at most it's a picture of a picture," and so my dream announced, silently, its own meaninglessness, interpreting itself as unfit for interpretation.

First thing upon waking after the second night's dream I tried drawing the letter, but never captured what I could so clearly remember envisioning (which is not the same as being able to clearly envision it, to recall it "photographically").

My first attempt has a strange spermy loop at bottom that my hand forced me into but that was not in my dream. Also, I find it all too sinuous (I should mention that half of my failure is due to haziness; the other half is that I can't draw).

My second attempt, after the third night, locates that loop at the top of the shape, not the bottom. Unlike the previous day's, this sketch's lines are too rigid, too severe: squared off.

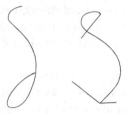

I'd been exploring toponyms—specifically, how islands came to be named after their shapes in the days before dirigible, helicopter, and airplane flyovers: aerial photography. How did the premodern inhabitants of an island called Snake Island know that it was shaped like a snake without being able to fly above it, or without seeing pictures taken from altitude? Perhaps they stood on mountains, but not every island named for its shape has a mountain peak at center from which the entirety of the land can be surveyed. Is it possible that one of the skills possessed by earlier man was the ability to walk the perimeter of a landmass and, from that walk alone, to develop a mental picture of the total form of his route? If so, then this pedocartography is a talent since lost and remains unrecorded in every language. There are many Snake Islands: a curl off Boston Harbor, a straighter Snake Island of the Philippines. Other Snake Islands are named Snake Island because there are snakes there, but these two, and a few others, are said to be named for their islandform: their serpentine coasts. The Dry Tortugas of the Florida Keys were named for the many turtles sighted there by Ponce de Leon, but history has it that Columbus called the Caribbean island of Tortuga what he called it because it was shaped like a turtle, or tortoise—humpbacked. Yuantouzhu means Turtle Head Isle. Kelyfos Island also translates to Turtle Island. Crocodile Island, off Boracay, also of the Philippines, is shaped like a crocodile. Muuido, of South Korea, means dancer's dress and looks like a dancer's dress. Shark Island, offering views of the Sydney Opera House, resembles a shark (there's at least one other Shark Island, in Thailand). Elephantine, in the Nile, looks like an elephant's tusk. Gato Island, a cat (skeptical tourists are told, "A sitting cat"). Tongpan Island, a barrel. Udo Island is a cow lying down or, in an alternate account, the head of a cow. Tobago exports tobacco, but is also said to be shaped like the smoke from Trinidad's pipe (though Columbus named Trinidad for the Trinity). Anguilla is a slippery eel. Dolphin's Nose, of India, is not an island but a massive jutting rock. Naming islands strikes me as different from naming rock formations after what they resemble—e.g., the Mitten Buttes, Horseshoe Mesa—because while it seems a natural imaginative leap to imbue giant risen inanimate stone with animate qualities, it seems quite unnatural to imbue the earth underfoot, the native earth, with equivalent personality. Rather, I have the sense that indigenous peoples can never regard their own land as, for example, a llama or tree, whereas a distant hill or another tribe's islet, precisely because it is conceivable as external, might be so understood. Conquistadors experienced not just geography but whole cultures at a similar remove and so named what they saw without attempting to understand it. Sighted from the safety of a crow's nest or prow, the foreign was always one thing—"the foreign"—not many things; the exotic is singular for a reason: ignorance. The New World was really, in terms of enduring civilizations, older than the Old; each India has its Indians. There is no Native American word for "America" *in toto*.

The first aerial photograph was taken in 1858; the Frenchman's name was Gaspard-Felix Tournachon, aka "Nadar." The image was a view of the village of Petit-Bicetre, taken from the basket of a hot-air balloon tethered to float at an altitude of eighty meters. The balloon's basket contained a darkroom. Tournachon's pictures haven't survived, however, so the oldest extant aerial photographs are James Wallace Black's of Boston from 1860, also taken from a balloon roped to earth. Images captured by automatically timed exposures from rockets, kites, and carrier pigeons—"bird's-eye views"—were popular throughout the 1880s and '90s, while the first widely publicized images taken from an aircraft were (silent) movies courtesy of Wilbur Wright, captured on an exhibition trip to Rome in 1909 (European governments were quick to grasp the military promise of flight photography and cinema). Sherman Fairchild of Oneonta, New York, invented the flash camera in 1915, and five years later pioneered the aerial imaging of Manhattan, creating the most perfect map of that borough's imperfect grid by assembling a series of overlapping photos (Manhattan's earliest substantive aerial imaging had been accomplished by British photojournalist James Hare, 1906). *Mannahatta*, in Lenape dialect, was most likely pure description: "many hills." The island has since been described, by a Victorian travel guide, as a "sole-fish"; paintings of the

Depression depicted it as an ironing board and a trowel; not a few poems have transmuted it into a sweat drop or tear. Sitting on the subway one afternoon, I looked up from my book to the system map and saw it—I saw my letter. The lower bulge of the Battery, the upper winnow of Harlems and Inwood. Manhattan, incognoscible first letter of an alphabet dreamt but as yet undiscovered.

FROM THE DIARIES

Meditations

From my literature professors I learned that conviction can substitute for truth. From my history professors I learned to confuse the details for the spirit. From my parents I learned what debt was. From my employers I learned that honor must be its own reward.

Consider the relationship between depression and taste, or discernment. Both lead to exclusion. Soon you can't stand any TV or movie or even any book. Soon nothing can satisfy. But while the depressed person encounters everything with a sense of pointlessness, what ultimately alienates the person of taste is the feeling of compromise, or of being compromised.

Art is capable of eliciting—that is "eliciting," not "expressing"—every emotion but sadness. Because the art with which sadness is expressed is itself the consolation and cure. This is a very basic premise. Sadness.

Act always in accordance with your own contradictions, and in the absence of contradictions, act against yourself.

9/11 BLUE

Just as democracy might be antibiological, blue—democracy's color, demoted from royalty's purple—is rarely found in nature. Ultramarine, extracted from the blue stone called lapis lazuli, was once more expensive than silver and gold, and Renaissance artists had to negotiate with their patrons for individual drops of the stuff upon receiving their commissions (ultramarine means, literally, "over the sea," because most lapis was imported from Afghanistan). Indigo, derived from plants of the Indigofera genus, tended to blacken, and was not lightfast, while azurite, derived from the mineral of the same name, turned green when mixed with water. Smalt, a ground glass colored with cobalt, would fade, and the chemical properties of copper were not yet understood, even as late as the Enlightenment. "Prussian blue" was the palette's first synthesized color: $Fe^7(CN)^{18}(H^2O)x$, where $14 \leq x \leq 16$... This was the color the Prussian army was uniformed in, on their marches to vanquish Denmark, Austria, France... The sky that September day should not be aestheticized. It should only be remembered. After all, what we intemperate strollers of Broadway might call clear and beautiful is only the result of a daily collision: sunlight crashes into our atmosphere, constantly crashes and shatters the spectrum, of which we perceive only a minuscule portion. Like safety, like security, a clear blue sky is a sensory fact that's fundamentally an illusion.

FROM THE DIARIES

Hat Lessons Gleaned from Attending a Film Noir Marathon with a Nonagenarian Ex-Milliner Who Never Stops Talking

"Twentieth-century men can be divvied up chronologically into two groups: those who wore hats and those who didn't. Conventional wisdom has it that hats went out of fashion with JFK, who was the first president not to wear a hat to his inauguration. But the truth is that hats were already on their way out under Ike. This was when you had the creation of the interstate system. When Americans started driving lots of cars. You ever try to wear a hat in a car? I mean a hat-hat? There's not enough room. It's like trying to keep a penguin inside your refrigerator."

"You can tell when a film was made by how its hero handles a hat. The actors from a hat generation tend to take off their hats on the appropriate occasions and if they don't, there's usually an implication, like an implication of purpose. Whenever an actor from a hat generation sets his hat on a table or chair, he does so with the crown facing down, so as not to bend the brim. Whenever an actor sets his hat brim-down, crown-up, I can tell he's from a no-hat generation, I can tell he's young, and I get depressed. I don't like being reminded that an actor's an actor."

"Guys on the East Coast called the two frontal concavities of a fedora 'the pinches.' Guys on the West Coast called them 'the dents.' My brother, my eldest brother, who lived in Chicago, he called them 'dimples.'"

"Fedoras for the good guys. Derbies for the bad guys and comedians. Though comedians wore porkpies too.

156

As did blacks. Homburgs were worn by the other ethnics, mafiosi, and Jews. Cowboys for the cowboys."

"I don't know anything about women's hats. All I know is, any woman wearing a fascinator is guilty of the crime of redundancy."

"The wind would've blown that straight off."

LETTER TO STEPHEN SHORE

(*U.S. 22, Union, New Jersey, April 24, 1974*)

Dear Stephen Shore,
My first experience interacting with photographers who weren't my relatives and who weren't always yelling at me to "smile"—who weren't even shooting me at all—was back in the early 2000s, when I was in my early twenties and working as a journalist throughout the former Eastern Bloc. This was also my first experience with the hopeless prospect—rather, with the ideal—of being "unbiased." The photographers I was working with were older Germans, Czechs, Slovaks, and Poles—"photojournalists" is the journalist's word—who would either follow me around on stories or read my stories after I wrote them and then go to the same locations and/ or visit the same people I'd interviewed and shoot them. I knew all too well what was missing from my writing—what I'd had to leave out due to journalism's stylistic conventions and standards of facticity. I knew all too well the confusions between what I saw and what I thought (not to mention the disjunctions between what I heard from the people I was interviewing and what they thought), just as I knew all too well

the difficulties in distinguishing between my private desires to define "the truth" and my professional responsibilities to protect a more public notion of "the verifiable truth," which was, I was realizing, ultimately too culturally specific to America to be trusted by most of the people I was living among and "reporting on"—the Ukrainians and Russians in particular. To be sure, the photographs that accompanied my writing would leave out many things too, but then, to my mind, they were primarily scrutinized for their aesthetics: An image didn't always have to be "correct," it merely had to be "compelling," which is an artistic type of "accuracy." Needless to say, I was envious of these photographers—I envied them even after they were forced out of journalism, when the news business went online and started expecting writers to take photos for themselves. A few of these old photographer friends are still in touch, through the very technology that ended their careers.

I'll return to that technology in a moment, but for now I'm trying to trace a certain growth—a certain education. Writers of your generation generally eschewed writing about the word—about literature—for writing about the image. This shift can be attributed to market forces or just to a bid for relevance in a culture whose imagination was becoming increasingly pictorial. Regardless, this writing was on my shelves (in books), and in my mailbox (in magazines and newspapers), and what struck me the most about reading it (besides the glibness of its popular incarnation in film and TV reviews, and the pretentiousness of its academic incarnation in the field of "media studies") was the feeling that most of it was already historical, if not already obsolete—the feeling that the philosophical concerns that the writers of your generation had framed around the image had become, for everyone of my generation, all of whom were becoming writers and image-makers, real and actual problems. The debate about whether depictions of things were, or could be considered, or

159

should be considered, things; the debate about whether a repro-ducible work would ever be capable of critiquing the culture of reproducibility, without becoming complicit in it—what had once been the abstruse or at best theoretical speculations of a minuscule elite were now practical matters online, practical anxieties afflicting everyone with a Facebook account, or everyone who had a friend with a Facebook account. As digital technology diffused faster and wider than even photographic technology had during the century before, there was a sense among millennials that if we didn't assert our individualities online, we'd be left behind and lost. We'd become the new philo-sophical concerns—strictly theoretical.

I admit to feeling this way myself, and it was because I felt this way that I wanted to become a writer: I wanted to write books. To identify with the word under the sign of the image was my rebellion. I wasn't quite sure how to do it, however. I wasn't quite sure what writing had to be done. None of my reading gave me any guidance or model. None of the writers I was reading, whether in fiction or nonfiction or even in any genre-hybridity, was dealing with digital culture—which was presenting itself as the apotheosis of literary culture—in any way that appeared recognizable, let alone sustainable. All of them were either panicking or complaining or trying to ignore it or just waving the white flag of the page, surrendering, and going under.

That's when I returned to photography, Stephen—to your photography. I found your work, I admit it, online. In your photographs, and in the photographs of a few of your cohort, I found a "language" or "voice" that seemed both personal and impersonal at once—the sincerest simulation I've ever encoun-tered of what it might mean to be "unbiased." I wondered how you did that, how you seemed to sidestep judgment by standing still—I wondered, to get to the heart of my curiosity, why certain interstates and suburban intersections and diner

160

sandwiches and motor-inn toilets that American literature,
along with my own American life, had always instructed me
to regard as lonely or bereft, appeared, through the steadiness
of your hand and eye, almost noble. Uncowed. Unashamed.
Proud and yet serene. The answer (I can hear you saying
it under your breath) is "form." The answer (obviously) is
"structure."

Your work takes the detritus of our American surround-
ings—our powerlines and telephonepoles and advertising
signage and the shadows they all cast—and returns it, through
neutral observation, to its fundamental existence as geometry:
lines and angles, planes and solids. You look at a curb, a bag,
a bed, a plate and cutlery, and, in time, they become what
they've always been, or what they always might have been
if anyone had looked before: a horizon, a vanishing point, a
frame. The result, for the viewer, or for this viewer, is para-
doxical: Instead of being estranged from my environment, I'm
brought closer. Instead of being defamiliarized, I'm empow-
ered. This, then, is the lesson I owe you for: that the mass chaos
I perceive all around me is merely a choice of my perception,
and that it doesn't have to be a burden but a challenge, as to
whether I myself am able to derive from it its inherent usable
form—its inherently humanizing, logical, even beautiful form,
which is only to be found through engagement, not reaction.

I thank you for that, Stephen.

Have a happy happy seventieth birthday.

Yours,
Joshua Cohen

DOWNTOWN UNDERGROUND:
ON JOHN ZORN

*Sheriff Zornson rode into the canyon on a dusty buckskin.
A Colt was on his hip and a hot wind was at his back. /
"Detective O'Zorn?" The voice came across the office cool
and high from a trenchcoated blonde with a mouth as plump
and red as the center banquette at the Stardust. / Captain
JZ10003 stood on the deck of the IND-Stillwell trying to
slow his breath. There, onscreen, out in the circumambient
void, spun the last jagged fragment of the planet he'd been
sent here to save.*

Corny parodies of pop tropes might be as close as lowly
prose can get to describing, or embodying, the deliriously
acquisitive music of John Zorn. The western dime, the
detective pulp, the space opera; not to mention their
more recent incarnations on TV, in movies, and online—Zorn samples, then reshapes, the equivalent chaos
of the musical world, both with the improvisations of
his own bands, in which he's played alto saxophone,
and in his formally notated compositions.

But we'll stick with writing for a moment. In order to
reproduce Zorn's musical process in a piece of criticism
about that process, one is thrown back not only on the
hoary surface surfeit of postmodernism, especially on
the Beat-era cutups of William S. Burroughs, but even
further into the ludic realm of surrealist parlor pastimes.
To demonstrate, you can take the words of any sentence
in this essay, cut them out of the page, and redistribute
however you want—"and want you redistribute however"—intending the loss of sense to be literature, not
senselessness.

But musical notes do not have meanings like words

162

do. This lack of meaning has allowed Zorn to rewrite Arnold Schoenberg's *Serenade* in his own *Chimeras* for flute, clarinet, piano, violin, cello, soprano, and percussion; it has allowed him to redo Anton Webern's *String Trio* in his own string trio, *Walpurgisnacht*; to redo Alban Berg's *Lyric Suite* in his string quartet *Memento Mori*; and to refashion Pierre Boulez's *Le Marteau sans maître* for a similar ensemble plus turntables in *Elegy*. These appropriations cannot be heard, however, because the pitch sequence, the musical equivalent of narrative, has been disrupted, rearranged. One would not know it without studying the scores, but Zorn's *Cat o'Nine Tails* scrambles blocks of quotations from quartets by Elliott Carter, Iannis Xenakis, Schoenberg, and Berg; his *Aporia* for piano and orchestra appropriates, on the most fundamental technical level, the *Requiem Canticles* of Igor Stravinsky.

The note "C" should not be looked up in the dictionary under "C"; the note itself signifies nothing, functioning only with regard to whatever note comes before it and whatever note comes after. Instead of literary meanings, then, musical notes have relationships. And what's most important to the reception, to the hearing, of a musical note is that relationship or context. These contexts are resolvable into systems, and these systems dominated Western music for centuries. In the system known as tonality—the system of Mozart, the system of Lou Reed—the scale has seven notes, with seven relationships per octave known as intervals. In the dodecaphony pioneered by Schoenberg, all twelve notes of Western tuning were used, with twelve relationships per octave, in a system described by Schoenberg as being made of "twelve tones related only to one another."

The primary innovation of American popular music

was to transcend such relationships. Within two decades of pop music's post–WWII ascendancy, the first generation of critics for magazines like *Creem* and *Rolling Stone* began naming, if not describing, new genres unconcerned with the interactions of tones: "hard rock," "glam rock," "prog rock," "punk," "postpunk," "New Wave," "No Wave," "metal," "heavy metal," "death metal," "thrash," "skronk," "avant-skronk." A century after the demise of Western classical tonality, the notated language of music had become a mediated language of styles, of sensibilities—racial, sexual, political. Before the culture of celebrity transcended practice and every recording artist suddenly was also an actor and memoirist with a line of sneakers and perfumes, the ancient technical systems of music would be replicated by a greater system or organizing principle—a music business in which forms of music were related to one another only by genres and anyone who transgressed a given genre was said to be, in the clichés of criticism, "pushing boundaries" or "crossing over."

The record-company boardrooms are located floors above the asphalt's grit and blocks north too, in Midtown: Warner Music Group at Rockefeller Center, EMI at 150 Fifth Avenue, Sony/BMG Music Entertainment at 550 Madison Avenue, Universal Music Group at 1755 Broadway, near Carnegie Hall (these companies are known as the Big Four; the Big Five included an independent BMG, bought by Sony in 2004; the Big Six also included Polygram, bought by Universal in 1998). But Manhattan's music is south, and began south, where the city itself began—"Downtown," a subjectively delimited district that spawned the music known even

164

outside of New York as "Downtown Music."

Accounting for what made Downtown "Downtown" can easily bring us deep into the past, and deep into folly. Suffice to say, Downtown, for our purposes, must be considered a city in itself, which was staged between Union Square's politics and Wall Street's money just at the moment that industry was leaving Manhattan and sweatshop factories and port warehouses were being converted into lofts. Zorn's Downtown, however, can be said to have started with the movement known as Fluxus, a concatenation of plastic artists, poets, and musicians centered around George Maciunas, whose 1963 manifesto announced that his group would "Promote living art, anti-art, promote NON ART REALITY to be grasped by all peoples, not only critics, dilettantes, and professionals." Early Fluxus concerts were held at 112 Chambers Street, in a loft occupied by Yoko Ono half a decade before she met John Lennon and, later, moved Uptown to the plush fixtures of the Dakota. (Regular audience members included Marcel Duchamp and the inventor of the silent concert, John Cage.) It was the intermedia and collaborative community spirit of Fluxus—its "living art"—united with its subversively accidental perspectives—"anti-art"—that found its most explicit expression with Zorn, whose interests assimilate a scene of dozens into the praxis of a single musician.

Fluxus performances of the music of La Monte Young (whose composition *$50* featured him getting paid $50) and Terry Riley (whose *In C* featured the note "C" repeated indefinitely) were taken as models by two younger musicians who drove taxis and ran a moving company together: Philip Glass and Steve Reich. Their performances of a minimalist, partially notated, partially improvised music closed the gap between

165

Downtown's experimentation and classical music culture, which lived at Lincoln Center, an arts complex opened in the mid-1960s, many subway stops Uptown, where the grid, and gridlike decorum, reigns supreme. Glass's and Reich's own ensembles—the Philip Glass Ensemble, Steve Reich and Musicians, each dedicated to presenting the work of their respective composer-conductor—were influential for Zorn, who would perform his own music live with his bands, Naked City and Masada particularly. As for performance venues, Downtown's "Lincoln Center" was diffuse: The Kitchen, opened in 1971, was a major Downtown stage—among the first in an unheated, and un-air-conditioned, line that involved the Experimental Intermedia Foundation, Roulette, the Alternative Museum, Dia Art Foundation, and Artists Space, and continued through the opening of the Knitting Factory in 1987, Tonic in 1998, and Zorn's club, the Stone, in 2005, located on 2nd Street and Avenue C in a former Chinese restaurant.

Obviously, throughout this period a more official culture kept on keeping on. The #1 album of 1976 was Frampton Comes Alive; disco's ball twirled over the dance floors; while Uptown, for the formal-dress folks, it was Mozart and Beethoven as usual. When the 1980s arrived, representing for the majority of Americans an MTV/VH1 homogenization of culture, Downtown proved the infamous exception: genre distinctions, in the mean streets, were meaningless, as a mess of loud, angry music rose up amid the squalor, IV-drug addiction, and AIDS suffering of the administration of Mayor Ed Koch. The conversion of New York from cacophonous wasteland to bougie functionality began with Rudolph Giuliani, who as a young federal prosecutor led a landmark police action in 1984 that cleared Tompkins Square Park—Zorn's immediate neighborhood—of its narcotics trade. By the time Giuliani became mayor ten years later, "gentrification" was not just a buzzword they taught at university but a program that expanded New York University, while spattering Downtown with luxury boutiques.

CBGB, the punk club that debuted the Ramones, lost its lease in 2006 and is now a men's fashion store selling $130 T-shirts and $800 pants. The Knitting Factory and Tonic, two clubs whose schedules Zorn frequently curated, were forced to close due to rent increases. Downtown jazz clubs now cater almost exclusively to European and Asian tourists who pay inflated prices to sip watery alcohol and not smoke in the most illustrious bastions of American music. In November 2008, Christie's held its inaugural auction of punk memorabilia. A Patti Smith poem sold for $375; a poster advertising a concert by Television, signed by Richard Hell, "realized" a price of $313. In December 2008, the Rock and Roll Hall of Fame Annex NYC opened Downtown. Its collection contains the ultimate ready-made relic: a urinal from CBGB.

Zorn's career is a parallel street to Downtown's decline—one-way, but in the opposite direction. He was born in Queens on September 2, 1953, making him a Virgo, making him gifted at languages and attracted to the foreign; that his moon is in Cancer makes him ingenious and likable, but also overly sensitive and petty; all of this might make him the sort of person who believes in astrology. Zorn has always existed on this knife-edge: He's sincere but defensive, a wiseass but also a mystic.

These opposites collided on the corner of 175th Street and Jewel Avenue in the Utopia section of Fresh Meadows, between Jamaica and Flushing. Zorn's subway, his umbilicus to Manhattan, was the F train, which brought in the bridge-and-tunnelers for their weekend doses of kulcha. Utopia/Fresh Meadows was Jewish; the Zorn family was Jewish; but John, the youngest of two, was sent to a church's Sunday school, and the family celebrated Christmas (Zorn's mother was an education professor at NYU; his father, who emigrated from Ukraine at age six, a hairdresser). After graduating from the United Nations High School, Zorn went on to Webster College in St. Louis, where he studied music for three semesters. The piano, guitar, flute, and clarinet he'd tinkered with as a teenager were gradually supplanted by the saxophone, and, after a float to the West Coast, Zorn returned to New York in 1975, ensconcing himself in the Colonnades Building on Lafayette Street. The apartment he slept in by day moonlighted as the Theater of Musical Optics, a prime setting for concerts of improvised music whose attendance seldom exceeded four.

Zorn's next decade was spent composing "improvisational frameworks" (which his bands would read off blackboards and index cards), while personalizing an approach to his instrument, negotiating between the black vernacular of jazz "sax" and the extended techniques of contemporary-classical woodwinds (blowing through the mouthpiece without fingering the keys, fingering the keys without blowing through the mouthpiece, slap-tonguing, multiphonics). In 1985, Zorn signed with the label Nonesuch and recorded *The Big Gundown*, his arrangements of the music that Ennio Morricone wrote for director Sergio Leone's 1960s spaghetti westerns. A recording of *Spillane* followed, Zorn's noirish homage to the Mike Hammer detective novels.

But in 1987, after initial success, a restless Zorn moved to Tokyo, where he spent the next six years steeping himself in its hardcore and noise circles, playing the troublemaker role of *gaijin* guru while also managing to master Japanese. At the time, his chief project was the band Naked City—named after the 1958 TV show, itself named after the 1948 film—featuring Bill Frisell on guitar, Wayne Horvitz on keyboards, Fred Frith on bass, and Joey Baron on drums. In 1993, however, the grind of bicontinental life, along with the death of his father, returned Zorn to New York, and to Judaism—homecomings that informed his founding of "Radical Jewish Culture," a mid-'90s movement that marked a retaking of Downtown aesthetics, and their intermingling with Downtown ethnicity, by the secularly Jewish generation born in America after the war.

Two projects emerged from Zorn's relocation: Masada, an acoustic quartet named after the Judean mountain where, in 73 C.E., an army of Jews martyred themselves instead of surrendering to the Romans; and Tzadik, Zorn's own record label, whose name is the Hebrew word for "righteous." Subsequently, definitive marks of Uptown approval began arriving for Zorn's compositions: a MacArthur "Genius Grant" in 2006, and Columbia University's William Schuman Award in 2007. With the Stone programming six nights a week and Tzadik releasing almost fifty albums per year, many of its owner's own music, Zorn had become Downtown's premier impresario, a DIY success story and so both a vindication and betrayal of antiestablishmentarianism.

Zorn's first compositional innovations were evident

169

with his *Game Pieces*, structured improvisations in which the composer acted as conductor, cuing musicians through gestures and signs (including doffed baseball caps and holding up a prearranged number of fingers). Happily, maximally, Zorn used improvisation to guide his composing just as a rare coterie of daring conservatory-grade musicians were starting to gig and make their bones: the denizens of Naked City and Masada, and peers like pianist-composer Uri Caine, guitarist-composers Marc Ribot and Elliot Sharp, and conductor-cornetist Lawrence D. "Butch" Morris—all hyphenated performer-composers who could not only read music but also improvise their own improved versions of it on the spot. Although once established as the first-call saxophonist of this scene that was, on street level, ten scenes or more, each with its own ephemeral cults, Zorn again adlibbed a dance on the outer rings of counterintuition: At the turn of last century, he relinquished his reeds, abandoning nightly performance to focus on composing.

From the beginning, Zorn's compositional systems were always his own, not just personal but hermetic. While his *Game Pieces* rewrote avant-garde aesthetics through a new skill set, Zorn's take on popular music was belated yet total. Naked City audaciously defined the popular as a certain intensity or energy, and proceeded to gather under that insatiable rubric of Zorn's private invention a host of related sonics: blues, jazz, cartoon music via Warner Bros. composer Carl Stalling (*Looney Tunes*) and MGM composer Scott Bradley (*Tom and Jerry*), both kinds of cowboy music (country *and* western), and all those old/new varieties of rocks and metals. Throughout this madcap amassing of repertoire that could be played only by ensembles of close friends and neighbors, Zorn was also composing scores for export and for traditional reproduction—thoroughly notated pieces orchestrated for classical instrumentation.

There has not yet been a complete catalog made of Zorn's compositions, or a compiled discography, and such a task can seem beyond the ambitions of even the most ardent Zornithologist. Since there are over a hundred albums, and thousands of compositions (Masada alone boasts a book of 613 "tunes," reflecting the number of mitzvot, or commandments, in the Torah), it might be better to just account for their highlights with one of Zorn's signature forms, the list: There are the soloist showcases (*Aporias* and *Contes de Fées*, a de facto violin concerto); string quartets (*Cat o'Nine Tails*, *Memento Mori*, *Kol Nidre*, *The Dead Man*, *Necronomicon*); piano trios (*Amour Fou*); sonatas (*Le Mômo* for violin and piano); solo music, whose extremes are exemplified by the stridencies of *Goetia* for violin and the antic *Carny* for piano; vocal music, notably *Rituals*, for mezzo-soprano with "wind machines, wooden gears, gravedigging, bull roarers, bird squeakers"; and then there's the film music, including soundtracks for TV commercials by David Cronenberg and Jean-Luc Godard, Japanese anime, a documentary about Yiddish writer Sholem Aleichem, and a gay porno entitled *Latin Boys Go to Hell*.

Zorn, then, might be the most we can ask of a modern artist: prolific. In an age of excess, the more excessive the artist, the more important he seems. In an earlier age, when composers accepted musical systems without question, creating their works within not only a single system but also a single style, Zorn might have been accused of exploitation, of thinking too big with too little.

This accusation would still ring true if Zorn were

171

actually a creator, or foremost a creator, a composer in the olden mode: piano, pen, paper, five-lines-to-a-staff. But he's not. He's something newer—an artist as browser, as curator, an amasser of references, a filcher of licks and riffs, a relentlessly curious collector of kitsch.

Here would be the place for the diligent writer to perform an online search for "collecting," then to collect those results into a paragraph, copy-'n'-pasting quotations from (in alphabetical order) philosophers Giorgio Agamben, Jean Baudrillard, and Walter Benjamin. The lattermost was the first to consider seriously the activities of the Collector, whom he established as an emblematic urban personality, flâneuring through a rush hour's undifferentiated mass in desperate search of only one thing—whatever other people miss. This person used to be Benjamin himself, and it used to be Marcel Proust, who collated and rewrote easily ignored, easily forgotten observations and overheard remarks into a novel that provided the deepest literary engagement with the social reality of his time. But when, through technology, that reality became overwhelming in its stimuli, this person—this, as Saul Bellow would have put it, "first-class noticer"—went from being a participant or social commentator to a sort of attending trashman, a searcher through the detritus that an accelerant culture had left behind. The refined collector of the bourgeois nineteenth century was to be recycled as me, as you, and, iconically, as disposaphobic Zorn.

With the advent of online, the accumulation of dreck finally fits everyone's budget. In an era in which culture is becoming ever more free—people expect free music in these downloading days, as concert attendance perceptibly wanes—everyone becomes their own archivist, their own immediate memorializer. Just as Zorn pieces together with saxophone spittle the shards of pop and unpopular records, we too, from the laziness of our livingrooms, customize our lists of Top 10s and rotating Favorites; we've become DJs of the self, montagemakers or editors of the films that are our lives.

But when we select and shuffle music, we are seeking the familiar, whereas Zorn—working with musicians and not computers, sampling not through clicks but by transcription—is determined to defamiliarize us through challenge. His goal seems to be the imprinting of a local sensibility on an unprecedented wealth of source material, giving both a flippant finger to skyscraper corporatism and a human face to technological perfection. This means that his music is both open and parochial—while listening, it helps to have a sense of humor, preferably Zorn's sense of humor—and driven by giddy outrage (*Zorn*, in German, means "rage"). This split is most enjoyably evinced when Naked City improvises on traditional jazz and blues forms at outlandish volumes and speedfreak tempi, debanalizing the chord changes of Tin Pan Alley through visceral force; or else when Masada pursues its brand of klezmer and transitions from Eastern European cantorial kitsch—a snaky synagogue melody—into a variant of "free jazz," as the tightly spaced Oriental intervals are expanded into yelps, the disconsolate howls by which multiculturalism mourns Culture.

Essentially, Zorn's provocative brilliance lies in this: For all that he encompasses every distorted barre chord and hiphop break, the way that showtunes swoon and ragtime syncopates, he persists in turning that plenitude inward, encoding his own experience of influence.

173

When we listen to his transformations of canonical classical music especially, we are listening to music by listening to listening, as what has to be called Zorn's music, and nothing but Zorn's music, is amplified in both its newness and historicity. In the same way, the New York—the Downtown—that sounds the grounding bass of his biography is not the city that is or was, but a city of Zorn's own composition.

The New York I live in is lately, like all megalopoleis, also located on the cloud, and the effects of its having gone virtual have not been virtual. Online's intensification of New York's socioeconomic shockwave that historically located arts neighborhoods concentrically farther from Midtown's concentrated power, and in my own lifetime from what became Ground Zero, has ensured that Downtown can now be anywhere—that the underground has, finally, moved. But where to? Brooklyn or brooklyn.com? The most notable new music after Zorn's might be the whirring hum of the fan that cools a computer's circuits from fevered searching.

FROM THE DIARIES

Meditations from the Gym

Smoke and drink in moderation, but define that moderation not by the practices of others, but by your own appetites' extremes. Sleep like it's practice for death.

Judge your friends and lose them. Hate everything that lacks the ambition of estrangement.

Avoid imagination. It is merely the plagiarism of your inexperience or ignorance.

What in school was true in life is false and in death will be meaningless.

In the office, work. Outside the office, work to forget.

Love only he or she who feeds you. And love yourself least of all.

Take not a taxi, because were you to be murdered, or were you to kill yourself—by jumping in front of a bus or train—your money would still be useful to others.

Without pain, there is no gain. But with pain, there is no gain either. There is never any gain. Pain, therefore, is meaningless.

EDITING THE I:
ON GORDON LISH

So here I am at midnight, sitting in a Barcalounger, reading the *Collected Fictions* of Gordon Lish while idly masturbating. Idly, that is, not idolly, because Lish is no god of mine so much as he is a lazy indulgence. And if what comes of this is merely tedium with the occasional spasm of delight, so be it. Nearly all of these one hundred *Collected Fictions* are written in the first person—no other people exist for Lish—which will explain this guilty pleasure: me speaking as me, but imitating him.

Perversion, awareness of language, a perverted awareness of language, brevity, comedy, stock phrases— these mark the fictions of Gordon Lish. Not the stories of Lish, *the fictions* (Lish enjoys italics too). Over the past three decades, Lish has published five collections of them, which have now, on the occasion of his seventy-fifth birthday, been bound into a single volume that either reliably diverts or dulls with its obsessions: men and women, literature, sex and the self.

I'm of both minds, then, here in my Barca. Lish so obviously knows what he wants out of writing: a single voice singularly voicing, a monologue that pleads but does not please. And yet it's not what I want out of writing—which is to say utter immersion within the tale, not just facile sentences comprising facile clauses, rhetoric-schmetoric, the cant that ultimately can't. Reading prose like "Shun negativity. Eschew negativity. Send down negativity. Turn a cold shoulder to negativity. Never know the name of negativity. Make yourself the assassin of negativity," all I want to do is play Mad Libs, negating each instance of negation with a scatological noun.

Sitting here in my Barca, reading with one hand, it's

difficult not to pronounce the pained and painful line, the line that will make me seem even more ridiculous than any public whacking: Lish, editor extraordinaire—reviser of Don DeLillo, Barry Hannah, Harold Brodkey, and Cynthia Ozick—needs an editor. Less collecting, more selecting—there it is. I'm mortified. One of us has no clothes on.

In the twentieth century, editors, who are supposed to sublimate their egos, instead developed them to match writer with market: Think of Maxwell Perkins, editor at Charles Scribner's Sons, fleshing out F. Scott Fitzgerald's books while trimming Thomas Wolfe's; think of Lish at Alfred A. Knopf, similarly editing—minimizing—Raymond Carver. Whereas Perkins worried over Wolfe's pacing, and worried about keeping Fitzgerald sober and solvent, Lish's editorial interventions went beyond deletion and reordering, into changing the surface of the prose itself, and so changing the very intentions of Carver's corpus—their collaboration less amity than an agon. As Carver, a Fitzgeraldian figure, drank himself away, Lish kept busy by stripping his author's fiction of everything he considered extraneous—the padding, the stuffing, the interiority between the incidents—with a violence that communicated a concomitant violence of mood underlying Carver's domestic exchanges. Since the originals of Carver's stories are often two or three times longer than the canonical versions, what Lish did to them (and gloated about doing to them) requires another verb. Not "edit" but "traduce," "violate," "molest."

By contrast, the techniques that Lish imposed on his own fiction, and that he advocated for decades in the notorious non-MFA writing workshops he ran after leaving Knopf (workshops in which he mentored, among others, Amy Hempel, Christine Schutt, and Diane Williams), are considerably simpler to articulate. "Recursion" is Lish's fancy term for unfancy "repetition"; "consecution" is a catch-all concept for the ways in which the grammatical or phonic qualities of a word, or the structure of a sentence, can be brought to bear on the choice of the word or the structure of the sentence that follows; "swerve," meanwhile, is Lish's method for frustrating "recursion" and "consecution," by introducing into the body of a fiction a theme, or narrative vantage, which hadn't been used before, and is not logically, structurally, or phonically expected. This trinity of techniques is so prevalent in Lish's work as to read like a trinity of tics. Take the fiction entitled "The Practice of Everyday Life," in which the recursion abounds, the consecution hinges on the polysemy of "come" and the opposition of "out loud" and "aloud," while the swerve is accomplished with the belated identification of the narrator's audience or occasion:

> What is it? You think it's me? If it's me, then, okay, then
> I'm not arguing, then it's me. But what I mean is am I
> just being too stippy-minded all of the time? Because
> some of the time I think I am all of the time being just
> too stippy-minded for my own good. Like take this word
> come which they use. How come it's come? Didn't you
> ever stop to think I don't get it how come it's come? How
> come people don't say go? You know, I'm going, I'm going,
> I'm going! I just for once in my life would like to hear
> somebody screaming my God, my God, I'm going! Oh,
> but they can't, can they? They say they're going and you
> think they're making a peepee. You say to somebody I'm
> going, the first thing they're going to think about you is

what are you doing, are you making a peepee? Remember when your mother said to you will you please for godsakes go already? Remember when your mother would stand outside the door and say to you I don't have all day, so for godsakes will you please go already? My mother used to do that. My mother used to say make and go. Make was to, you know, make was for you to make a number two, whereas go, go meant do the other one. It was like make was like this productive thing, wasn't it? You make and, presto, if you did it, you made something. There was like this poiesis involved. It was like taking a dump was like having this poiesis which was involved. Okay, I am just thinking my thoughts out loud. Or how about this—how about aloud? You don't hear people saying aloud anymore. Who says aloud anymore? But so who's in charge of these things like this—humanity saying out loud instead of saying aloud? Remember when everybody used to call it a Coney Island Red Hot? There were these places that sold you these frankfurters and they called them Coney Island Red Hots. Forget it. You're not interested. I was just over at my friend Krupp's.

Etc., etc., etc.—for another two pages.

Gary Lutz, a fiction writer and another of Lish's former students, once described his teacher's verbally verberating aesthetic as one "in which virtually every sentence had the force and feel of a climax." He was particularly taken with Lish's idea of consecution, while I myself am particularly taken with Lutz's description of the idea of consecution as a "procedure by which one word pursues itself into its successor *by discharging something from deep within itself into what follows*" (italics mine).

Sitting here in my Barca, reading the *Collected Fictions* of Gordon Lish, I could be doing anything else. I could be describing my Barca, for one, the color and texture of its upholstery; I could be describing the room surrounding my Barca, for another; the room's shelves and what is on them and how the items got there—but that would be literature and so a betrayal of Lish, for whom even furniture is made of language, and who would be more interested in whether I called the room's other seating element a "sofa" or "couch" ("davenport"? "chesterfield"?) than in telling the tales of the people who have sat there.

But while Lish's work can always be likened to self-pleasure, self-pleasure—mine and yours—cannot always be likened to Lish's work. It is the person, however, the singular first person, that makes Lish's inky spurting truly seminal. The first person, the ascendant voice of the past two centuries—from Dostoyevsky's underground origins to Beckett's authorial endgame—is today the shrillest voice of daily expression: the online overshare, the chat-window confessional. What once was literature—revelatory direct address—has become blogorrhea: the timestamped account of what happened this morning, of what our peeves and attractions are, of what we do to ourselves and one another by night. Lish was former laureate of that plaint, of its degrees of self-knowledge, its valences of tone. If Lish's soliloquies have any counsel for today's solipsistic culture it's this: Every "I" will always be a fiction; every first person is the last person you were.

FROM THE DIARIES

Four Facts I Learned in a Bar on Staten Island

In 1992, tuition at NYU was $15,620/year. In 1996, the
starting salary of an associate at Lehman Brothers was
$72,580/year. Since 2008, Budweiser has been owned
by the Belgians. No one hires bankers over forty.

A Successful Man in Chicago is Complimented on His Suit

"This thing? This is the seventeenth suit I've ever
owned!"

LIP SERVICE:
ON ARETHA AND BEYONCÉ

To begin with, two very different women sang two very different songs. At Obama's first inauguration, in 2009, Aretha Franklin sang "America," aka "My Country 'Tis of Thee." In 2013, at Obama's second inauguration, Beyoncé sang "The Star-Spangled Banner." Or did she? Which is to wonder, does lip-synching to your own recorded track (or, as the cable babblers put it, "prerecorded track") really count as singing?

And so the controversy swelled, like horns through a swirling string section.

Let's do away with the stupidities: Lip-synching to someone else's recorded track is crazy fraud or inept karaoke; lip-synching to your own recorded track, which is what Beyoncé did, makes sober professional sense, especially if you're the opening act for one of the most widely broadcast events on the planet. Especially too if you're performing outside, where it's hard to hear your live backing band and the January temperature is just north of freezing—voices chap and crack before the skin does.

About Aretha's performance, I have nothing bad to say. It's true that she's older than she used to be (who isn't?) and that she lacks the energy she used to have (who doesn't?), but she's still as brilliant as it gets, the best American singer since, at least, the invention of the wax cylinder phonograph. Most critics attribute Aretha's preeminence to a combination of her voice's natural flexibility and her mastery of tonal inflection (the smoky turning sweet, the sweet turning tart and ironic); others cite her sensitivity to "word-painting" (to making "sound-pictures" of the lyrics, as in when she extends the word "freedom" into *"free—freedom—freeeedom,"* or the phrase "let it ring" into *"let it ree-ee-ee-ee-ee-ee-reeng,"* tolling out the blue notes). All of this is true. But what's incredible is how she's been able to maintain that preeminence, namely by ensuring that she keeps the essence of her voice the same even as her range—her vocal register, once gigantic—has diminished. Singers tend to find their tension toward the upper echelons of their registers, and many like to pretend that they're having difficulties hitting a high note that they can confidently hit, in order to bring a sense of drama to the proceedings—to turn the song into a struggle. Aretha never used to do that too much—perhaps out of pride or perhaps because, like Annie Oakley, she could hit anything. But now that she can't, the difficulties are apparent—the difficulties are real, and so the drama's real too. The notes might be lower but the stakes are higher.

Beyoncé's performance held its own fascinations. I'm sure it would've sounded just as engineered and glossy if she'd been singing live. She is that type of professional. She has managed her life. Not for her (or not yet) Aretha's multiple bad marriages, bad record deals, weight issues, and alcoholism. That said, even with all her diva-control, Beyoncé definitely ended up with the worse song. "America" is a regal hymn, whose tune derives from the Commonwealth anthem "God Save the Queen," or "King," depending on who's reigning. "The Star-Spangled Banner," by contrast, is bombastic anacreontic macaronic pseudomartial beer hall music.

Beyoncé loosened up midway, after "the bombs bursting in air," when she abruptly tugged out her in-ear monitor, which apparently was giving her problems. This, I have to say, took a brass vagina, or whatever the female equivalent is of burnished metal balls. It also made her more casual and you could tell from her face, or I convinced myself I could tell, that, having given herself a taste of *"free—freedom—freeeedom,"* she wanted more. She wanted to be able to embellish on the spot and let the moment guide her glissandi. Instead, out of respect for the presidency or for the 20.6 million who were spectating, she was condemned to sing along to the recording exactly as she'd made it, in a session with the Marine Band the night before. What this was, then, was a lesson not just in the glories of spontaneity, but in the ways in which one can become locked into certain ways of performing, which is to say, locked into certain ways of being, which might appear more safe or reassuring initially, but are actually more dangerous and limiting when put into practice. It's a lesson that Obama himself might've benefitted from, when considering the national security policies of his second term.

WIKI: WHAT I KNOW IS

W. I. K. I.

What. I. Know. Is.

What I Know Is: I would like to address the topic of knowledge in the novel.

What I Know Is: That to address the topic of knowledge in the novel is also to address the topic of knowledge outside the novel.

What I Know Is: This is inevitable, going outside.

What I Know Is: The seasons are changing to fall.

What I Know Is: A "wiki" is a site that is collaboratively created by its users.

What I Know Is: I found this out online.

What I Know Is: My search for the definition of the word "wiki" took all of .54 of a second, though my reading of the search results took longer (took so much longer that it's still ongoing).

There is a lesson to be derived from this.

Now more than ever we must insist on differentiating between *being able to know something* and *actually knowing it*.

This difference can be calculated in time.

But not only *in time*. And the difference doesn't have to be *calculated*.

What I Know Is: Some time in the spring of 2007, a friend of mine was traveling in Germany and, after visiting me in Berlin, made a pilgrimage—as is customary for Americans, and for Jews, and I'm sure for many other types of people—to the site of the former Buchenwald concentration camp, near Weimar. Writing me about the experience once he'd returned to the

States, he said he'd found the exhibitions at Buchenwald to be "painstakingly accurate and tasteful."

What I Know Is: About a decade later I was back in the States myself and found myself sleepless and struggling to write an obituary of Imre Kertész, the Hungarian-language, Germany-residing Nobelist, and a survivor of the Buchenwald camp. In the course of my research I made a pilgrimage—as is customary for journalists on deadline—to the Buchenwald wiki, which described the postwar renovation of the camp into a memorial and museum as having been "painstakingly accurate and tasteful." In other words, the wiki for Buchenwald—in the edit by a user named Redactosaurus—described Buchenwald in the very same words as did my friend.

What I Know Is: There are only four conclusions to come to: 1) Either my friend read the wiki and unconsciously plagiarized its description, or 2) my friend read the wiki and consciously plagiarized its description, or 3) my friend *wrote* the wiki and so was merely plagiarizing himself, under the username Redactosaurus, or—the last conclusion—4) given the ten-year gap between identical quotations, this was all just a very strange coincidence.

What I Know Is: "Painstakingly accurate and tasteful."

What I Know Is: Strange.

I never know whom to trust.

And I can't help but wonder whether you trust any of what I've just told you.

What I Know Is: I now have the same mistrust for news that I used to have for novels.

186

What I Know Is: Technology has made both more "unreliable."

All books today are digitized—at least all books that are written today are digitized, novels very much included. They're lumped into the matrices with all the other content. "A piece of prose is a piece of prose is a piece of prose," as Gertrude Stein might, or might not, have written, depending on what site you read.

Contemporary scholars, then, with just the click of a key, can tell you which German or Hungarian or Holocaust survivor or YA author uses the most adjectives, or adverbs, per sentence, per paragraph, on average, or when split infinitives were a thing, or not a thing, in Anglo-American prose (by women of color, whose first editions sold over ten thousand copies). The study of novels, especially, is becoming, or has already become, the study of data. Every Dickens novel has been mined. Every Dickens character described as having a very short nose, or a very long nose, or a very twisted nose, has been tagged. Deconstruction—unconscious betrayal, or betrayal by the unconscious—is for the microchips now.

That said, it's also a fact that novelists have access to the same tools as do the academics, and can act preemptively in their own defense. Novelists can search through their own texts and eliminate repetitions, fixations, manias—they, we, can obliterate our own subliminal thoughts in the hopes of forestalling the psychologizing of readers intent not on pleasure but on profiling.

This double act—the academic or critic using technology to drill into the psyche of the writer, the writer using the same technology to frustrate that drilling—results in a curious double bind: Who, here, is doing the censoring?

If I know that all of my words might one day not be read consecutively, or even read at all, but merely treated as an etymological, or grammatical, tranche, to be analyzed and monetized by search algorithms, wouldn't the honorable response be to try to sabotage that system and write against its parameters—which is to say, to plagiarize, or not to write at all?

BOUNDLESS INFORMANT:
ON GREENWALD'S SNOWDEN

First, collect all the details you can on everyone you've ever encountered—this will serve to "alienate" or "dehumanize" them, and turn them into "characters." Second, search this trove for connections among the characters—links of behavior, temperament, ideology, vocabulary—because it's the connections that make a plot. Third, settle on the character with the most or just most interesting of those links to narrate the plot, or to be narrated through it by an omniscient third person. This is how you write a novel. This is also how you operate an intelligence agency.

The NSA is a thoroughly modern organization. Its techniques are those of Kafka—who anonymized his suspects under the alias "K" and extended to them only the presumption of guilt—and of Nabokov, who venerated artifice, loathed psychology, and insisted that the role of the novelist was that of a "wizard" or "puppet-master," tugging the strings and making the characters dance. A more direct association might be made with Joyce's *Ulysses*, which so intensely monitors Leopold Bloom that he seems less a person than a welter of metadata about Dublin, June 16, 1904.

Modernism has always sought to impose form and structure—and so fate—on a character, as opposed to letting it arise out of a character's essential "nature." Today we are nothing if not characters acting out the roles of our lives for the reading and rewriting of our intelligence minders, but what makes our predicament postmodern is that *we know it*. Confirmation has come courtesy of the journalist Glenn Greenwald and his source, the NSA contractor of conscience Edward

Snowden, a character so decent that John le Carré or Frederick Forsyth would've blushed before conceiving him.

Greenwald's *No Place to Hide* is a hybrid, beginning as an airport thriller recounting the author's contact with Snowden and ending as a course text on the global amassment of digital communication. Like many thrillers, and like many course texts, it seems to be the work of a committee. Though Greenwald's is the only name on the cover, the NSA deserves its credit too. Almost the entire latter half of the book consists of charts and graphs made by that agency and obtained by Snowden; when it comes to PowerPoint presentations, America remains second to none.

Throughout both halves, Greenwald, a civil rights lawyer by training, invokes the First Amendment as a guarantee of his right to interpret the Fourth—the Constitution's protection against warrantless search and seizure, adopted in response to the writs of assistance, which licensed the British to occupy and confiscate the property of colonists. A cloud born of server clusters, traffic through underwater cables and satellites in orbit—such is the contemporary condition of what that amendment so quaintly calls our "houses, papers, and effects."

In December 2012, Greenwald—who has lived in Brazil with his partner, David Miranda, since 2004, in protest of U.S. antipathy toward same-sex marriage—receives an email from "Cincinnatus," a cybernym that promises vague disclosures; all Greenwald has to do is install the encryption software PGP (Pretty Good Privacy) on his laptop. But Greenwald, perpetually on deadline, blows him off.

Flash forward six months: The documentary film

maker Laura Poitras (who was then finishing her movie trilogy about abuses of power in post-9/11 America) conscripts Greenwald to meet an NSA leaker in Hong Kong. Together, they follow the slapstick tradecraft instructions: Go to the Mira Hotel, locate a conference room festooned with a green plastic alligator, and ask a staff member the pass-question "Is there a restaurant open?"

Et voilà—a gawky postadolescent materializes, fussing with a Rubik's Cube, the identifying prop.

Up in Snowden's room—where noodle containers have mounted and pillows are pressed against the underdoor draft—Greenwald vets Snowden and goes through the exfiltrated files. He returns to his own room at the nearby W Hotel only to summarize the files in dispatches sent to *The Guardian* (the U.S. *Guardian*, as the British *Guardian* is constrained from publishing material deemed vital to U.K. security—later, in an attempt at intimidation, Government Communications Headquarters forced the British paper's editors to destroy their own hard drives). While still in Hong Kong, Greenwald exposes a series of orders by the U.S. Foreign Intelligence Surveillance Court compelling telecoms to turn over call logs; PRISM, a program for the bulk collection of all email, voice, text, and video-chat communications routed through the servers of Google, Microsoft, Apple, Yahoo, et al.; and BOUNDLESS INFORMANT, a tool that generates "heatmaps" of the metadata captured by PRISM.

Finally—Greenwald breathes:

After the "BOUNDLESS INFORMANT" article was published, Laura and I planned to meet at Snowden's hotel. But before leaving my room, out of nowhere, as I sat on my hotel bed, I remembered Cincinnatus, my anonymous email correspondent from six months earlier, who had bombarded me with requests to install PGP so that he could provide me with important information.

Amid the excitement of everything that was happening, I thought that perhaps he, too, had an important story to give me. Unable to remember his email name, I finally located one of his old messages by searching for keywords.

"Hey: good news," I wrote to him. "I know it took me a while, but I'm finally using PGP email. So I'm ready to talk any time if you're still interested."

I hit "send."

Soon after I arrived at his room, Snowden said, with more than a small trace of mockery, "By the way, that Cincinnatus you just emailed, that's me."

This is a humorous and humanizing update of a James Bond bromance. And, like the best of those, it imparts a sense of the relationship's cultural disparity—between the intelligence analyst and the civilian citizen, between the Fifth Estate of tech and the Fourth Estate of journalism. In every instance, the side with more intel can't help but treat the other with "more than a small trace of mockery."

After describing Greenwald's return to Brazil, and the online debut of the Poitras-filmed clip in which Snowden outed himself to the world—incriminating himself in a bid to explain and to obtain public support—the book turns to slides of the spying programs and protocols. Someone in Fort Meade has caps lock stuck. PROJECT BULLRUN, EGOTISTICALGIRAFFE, MUSCULAR, OAKSTAR, STEELKNIGHT, SILVERZEPHYR—they're like the names of losing racehorses, or midlife-crisis yachts. The point is this:

Everything we say on phones and write in emails is being monitored, stored, and parsed. Though that power has been abused in approximately 3,000 cases per year—often by NSA employees gathering LOVEINT on their exes—it's not the capacity for abuse as much as it is the NSA's exemption from reporting it and immunity from being prosecuted for it that constitute the greatest argument against bulk collection. The greatest argument, that is, after the Constitution.

Snowden could easily have set up his own WikiLeaks-style site. Instead, he has chosen to hold our free-speech institutions to account. *The Guardian*, *The New York Times*, and *The Washington Post*—all have reported on Snowden's cache and in consultation with the NSA redacted specifics that could endanger active agents. The highest task of the critic is not to condemn but to correct, and this is what Snowden has done. He has excoriated the surveillance state, and in doing so has elevated journalism.

FROM THE DIARIES

Salt and Pepper Shakers

To survive as a couple you have to stand by each other,
no matter what, inanimately.

*When We Stopped Saying We Were Going to Move Out of the
City*

When we stopped saying we were going to move out
of the city, we had: nothing to talk about at parties,
nothing to talk about on the Q/N/R trains, nothing
to talk about to my aunt, her mom, the pizza guy, over
decent but insufferable sushi, in the movie line. When
the bun place closed. The midnight-movie theater in
Midtown. When the deli that did its own pastramitizing
shut down too. I'd always liked that bun place. When
we stopped saying we were going to move out of the
city, we became more bearable. We broke up and stayed
the children we'd never have.

DATASEXUAL: ON MOROZOV, LANIER, JOHNSON AND GOOGLE

Datasexuals are to Silicon Valley what hipsters are to Brooklyn: both are ubiquitous and, after a certain point, annoying. These days, one has to search really hard to find daily activities that are not being tracked and recorded; now that everyone carries a smartphone, all walks of human existence are subject to measurement, analysis, and sharing. [...] Alexandra Carmichael, a health entrepreneur and one keen devotee of the datasexual lifestyle, records forty things about her daily life, from sleep and morning weight to caloric intake and mood, not to mention sex, exercise, and day of menstrual cycle. [...] The most impressive feat of self-measurement comes from Larry Smarr, a computer scientist recently profiled in *The Atlantic*. Smarr is in a different league from most self-trackers; he tracks everything they track—and more. For example, he collects and analyzes his poop. As *The Atlantic* puts it, "He is deep into the biochemistry of his feces, keeping detailed charts of their microbial content. Larry has even been known to haul carefully boxed samples out of his kitchen refrigerator to show incautious visitors."

— *To Save Everything, Click Here*, Evgeny Morozov

# of books read for this review: 4.
# of pages total: 1,424.
List price of books, total: $104.
List price of ebook versions, total: $51.96.
Best book because of its thoughtful resistance to utopian technological dogma: *To Save Everything, Click Here*, Evgeny Morozov.
Worst book because of its thoughtless embodiment of utopian technological dogma: *Future Perfect*, Steven

Johnson.

Other books: *Who Owns the Future?*, Jaron Lanier; *The New Digital Age*, Eric Schmidt and Jared Cohen.

Most notable achievements of Evgeny Morozov: Editor at *Foreign Policy*; writer of *Net Effect*, a popular blog whose "aim is to help you navigate the dense world of technology news and understand the impact that technology has on foreign affairs"; author of *The Net Delusion* (2011).

Most notable achievements of Eric Schmidt and Jared Cohen: Chairman of Google and director of Google Ideas, respectively.

Jaron Lanier: Digital media designer, VR innovator, self-styled anarcho-consultant to the likes of "Walmart, Fannie Mae, major banks, and hedge funds."

Steven Johnson: Media theorist, TV guest, radio personality, college-circuit lecturer; "I'm a father of three boys, husband of one wife, and author of eight books, and co-founder of three websites."

Relationship between Jared Cohen and Joshua Cohen, the author of this review: None.

Relationship between Joshua Cohen and Google: Use of Google search, Gmail account.

# of books published about the internet/web since the start of 2013: 10,668, according to Amazon.

Significance of 2013: Fortieth anniversary of the internet's protocols being developed by the United States Department of Defense (1973, Robert Kahn and Vint Cerf presented their TCP/IP design at the University of Sussex in Brighton, U.K.); thirtieth anniversary of that protocol's implementation (1983, the Defense Department required all computers that hosted its internal network, or intranet, to conform to TCP/IP).

Date of last celebration of the birth of online

connectivity: 2009, the fortieth anniversary of the Defense Department's original network, ARPANET (Advanced Research Projects Agency Network, 1969); and the twentieth anniversary of the web, invented by Tim Berners-Lee, working out of the European Organization for Nuclear Research, or CERN (originally the Conseil Européen pour la Recherche Nucléaire, 1989).

Chance of getting disparate governments, research institutions, multinational conglomerates, and authors just trying to sell their books to agree to a firm standard date on which to celebrate the birth of online connectivity: 0 percent.

Subtitles of the books under review, with no attempt to link them to their titles proper: *Technology, Solutionism, and the Urge to Fix Problems that Don't Exist; The Case for Progress in a Networked Age; Reshaping the Future of People, Nations, and Business.*

Reason why publishers and maybe now even authors are convinced that subtitles help sell books: Inconceivable.

The only book under review without a subtitle: *Who Owns the Future?*

That book's answer to the question of its title: You.

That book's answer to the question of who owns the present: Global "Siren Servers" like Facebook and Google, which have managed to take control of the internet, concentrating in a few hyperdactylic hands vast reserves of material wealth derived directly from the information you provide them.

What "your information" is, according to Lanier: Your identity on social media and networking sites, your purchasing profile and browsing history, that of others who are socially networked with you, emails, chats, etc.

What else "your information" is, according to Lanier: An asset.

What you get in return for giving this asset away, according to Lanier: "reputation," "karma," and "free services" like Facebook, Google search, and Gmail, which depend upon your data to better calibrate how to sell you goods and services (i.e., through ads based on keywords).

What Lanier proposes instead: "Two-way transactions," which will finally turn you "the used" into you "the user," the beneficiary of your own information.

How many times this reviewer was reminded of drugs while reading Lanier's perseverating, palilaliac evocations of "use": 12.

How many times this reviewer did drugs in the same period: 1.

How this proposal to cut you in on the profits generated by the monetizing of your online identity is a betrayal of Lanier's previous book, *You Are Not a Gadget* (2010): That previous book was more of a philosophical or spiritual manifesto—indeed, *A Manifesto* was its subtitle—whose wariness of technological promise was premised on the conviction that collaborative or interactive cultures deincentivized originality and were prone to commercialization; this new book, however, overturns that individualist caution by casting you the human—a term this reviewer prefers to "user"—as nothing more than the overworked sales rep of your own enumerated "self."

Representative passage: "Here's a simple example of how you might make money from the cloud in a humanistic future of more complete accounting. It's based on the kind of dubious calculation that's typical of cloud entrepreneurship today. You meet a future spouse on an online dating service. The algorithms that implement that service take note of your marriage. As the years go by, and you're still together, the algorithms increasingly apply what seemed to be the correlations between you and your spouse to matching other prospective couples. When some of them also get married, it is automatically calculated that the correlations from your case were particularly relevant to the recommendations. You get extra nanopayments as a result."

What Lanier calls this type of redistribution: "The humanistic information economy."

How disappointed is this reviewer in Lanier: Enough to end our relationship, despite forfeiture of any future "nanopayments."

What better suggestions this reviewer has to more equitably redistribute the profits generated by the monetizing of your online identity: A hypothecated federal tax on all social-media and search-engine advertising profits, the revenue from which would be spent directly on job creation (i.e., finding new work for people—book reviewers, for example—whose occupations have been technologically peripheralized or obsolesced); an online social movement calling for all "two-way transactions" to disburse a fixed percentage of profits to charity, including but in no way limited to nonprofit groups advocating "net neutrality."

Replacement of social norms by commodity exchange: Bad.

Replacement of social activities by commodity exchange: Bad.

Obfuscatory term for both: "Gamification."

Other examples of gamification: Quitting smoking or drinking by depositing money in an online escrow account that is lost to you if you lapse, but will accrue interest if you do not; keeping fit by walking or running a certain distance within a certain time, distance and time to be measured by your smartphone whose WiFi function cannot be activated until the quota has been met.

Evgeny Morozov's term for treating social norms and/or activities as unexploited opportunities for commodity exchange: "Solutionism."

Other vocab from Morozov's book: "Bouncing" ("whenever information collected for one purpose [e.g., campaign contributions] is used for another purpose on another site"); "highlighting and shading" ("whereby some pieces of the disclosed information take on unintended, disproportionate roles in defining the person's reputation").

Morozov's problem with "solutionism": "Recasting all complex social situations either as neatly defined problems with definite, computable solutions or as transparent and self-evident processes that can be easily optimized—if only the right algorithms are in place!—this quest is likely to have unexpected consequences that could eventually cause more damage than the problems they seek to address."

Examples he details: Loss of sense of adventure by driving under the influence of GPS; loss of moral or ethical sense developed in the discharge of petty chores by automating them/contracting them to machines.

Place of Morozov's birth: Belarus.

Saliency to this review: Belarusians spend a lot of time waiting in lines.

More important issues addressed: "Algorithmic gatekeeping," in which computers do their own censoring, flagging so-called "pornography" and "hatespeech"; how "closed" web policies restrict public speech in totalitarian regimes (Belarus, China, etc.) while "open" web policies erode privacy in democracies.

Google's politics of "open" and "closed," according to Schmidt and Cohen: America will remain fairly stable insofar as it continues to remake online in its own image; i.e., as a space for developing and testing the products by which more-closed societies will open themselves to democratization and so to capital.

Translation: Americans will use Twitter to get famous; Arabs and Iranians will use it to compete with, and counteract, theofascist governance.

How life will be for Americans, according to Schmidt and Cohen: "Entertainment will become a more immersive and personalized experience in the future. Integrated tie-ins will make today's product placements seem passive and even clumsy. If while watching a television show you spot a sweater you want or a dish you think you'd like to cook, information including recipes or purchasing details will be readily available, as will every other fact about the show, its story lines, actors, and locations. If you're feeling bored and want to take an hour-long holiday, why not visit carnival in Rio? Stressed? Go spend some time on a beach in the Maldives. Worried your kids are becoming spoiled? Have them spend some time wandering around the Dharavi slum in Mumbai."

How this tourism will be accomplished, according to Schmidt and Cohen: By hologram, projected into your home.

How life will be for everyone under less stable regimes, according to Schmidt and Cohen: "In the coming decades, we'll see the world's first 'smart' rebel movement. [...] Before even announcing their campaign they could target the government's communications network, knowing it constitutes the real (if not official) backbone of the state's defense. They might covertly reach out to sympathetic governments to acquire the necessary technical components—worms, viruses, biometric information—to disable it, from within or without. A digital strike against the communications infrastructure would catch the government off guard, and as long as the rebels didn't 'sign' their attack, the government would be left wondering where it came from and who was behind it. The rebels might leave false clues as to the origin, perhaps pointing to one of the state's external enemies, to confuse things further."

How many of the tactics described above have already been undertaken not just by Arab and Iranian dissidents but by the hacker collective Anonymous against American police departments, military and intelligence infrastructure, and, if you can believe it, NASA: roughly 50 percent.

# of times this is acknowledged in this book: 0.

How much Steven Johnson believes in collaboration: 100 percent.

# of authors of this book by Steven Johnson: 1.

# of times Johnson acknowledges that the type of decentered data-sharing he advocates might result in a massive uptick in data theft: 2.

Terms coined by Johnson in his previous book, *Where Good Ideas Come From* (2010): "The adjacent possible" (inventors use old inventions to make news ones), "exaptation" (inventors developing technology for one application only for it to be used in another).

Terms coined in his new book: "Peer progressives" (members of decentralized cooperative movements, whether cultural like Wikipedia, economic like Kickstarter, or political like Occupy Wall Street), "pothole paradox" (that a pothole outside your house is about to be fixed by the city is the single most important news item in your life and yet the least likely to be reported upon by traditional media, which paradox is used by Johnson to advocate for greater online customization of journalism).

\# of times "hive mind" is defined as "a dense network of human intelligence": 1.

\# of times Renaissance Venice and Genoa, and Ottoman Istanbul, are described as "peer networks": 1.

This reviewer's incredulity that people can be paid to come up with this crap: Total.

This reviewer's naïveté: Boundless.

Requisite Marshall McLuhan concept that Johnson "appropriates": "Affordances," or the tendency of each new medium to shape the message it communicates (e.g., movies and TV prioritizing the auditory and visual over the textual).

Application of McLuhan's "affordances" to all the books under review: The new type of text property, whether book or ebook, regarding technology, is intended to appear quickly and disappear quickly and probably even in the best of cases should not be reviewed; the obvious speed of its composition, and the brief sales window in which it is expected to perform, all form the velocity of its "sending," and too its method of "reception": rush through; do not pay attention; things are changing fast.

Malcolm Gladwell: Blurber of the Johnson book, thanked in the Acknowledgments section of the Schmidt and Cohen.

Also thanked in the Acknowledgments section of the Schmidt and Cohen: WikiLeaks founder Julian Assange, *New York Times* book critic Michiko Kakutani, former secretary of state Henry Kissinger, Evgeny Morozov.

Takeaway scores on scale of 10: Morozov 6, Schmidt and Cohen 4, Lanier 2, Johnson 1.

Other new books this reviewer considered reading: *Big Data: A Revolution that Will Transform How We Live, Work, and Think*, Viktor Mayer-Schönberger, Kenneth Cukier; *Automate This: How Algorithms Came to Rule Our World*, Christopher Steiner; a stack of Mexican novels; friends' poetry.

# of hours spent on this review, including reading: 80.

Monies earned: $800.

Hourly rate: $10/hour.

Word count: 2,382.

Rate per word: $0.33585222502/word.

What $800 can buy at Ibrahim's cart just outside the building this reviewer was writing in on Van Brunt Street in "hipster" Brooklyn: 400 hotdogs, 266.666 hamburgers, 800 sodas.

# of times Google was consulted for this review: 82.

FROM THE DIARIES

Navajo Reservation

A portrait of a horse painted on horsehide with a horsehair brush. I'd like to write a book like that, but where—or what—or who—is my horse?

Medium Thoreau

"One generation abandons the enterprises of another like stranded vessels," Thoreau, *Walden*.

"There is an incessant influx of novelty in the world, and yet we tolerate incredible dullness," Thoreau, *Walden*.

Medium: One generation abandons novelty, another enterprises the dullness of vessels. Tolerate the incessant yet stranded world.

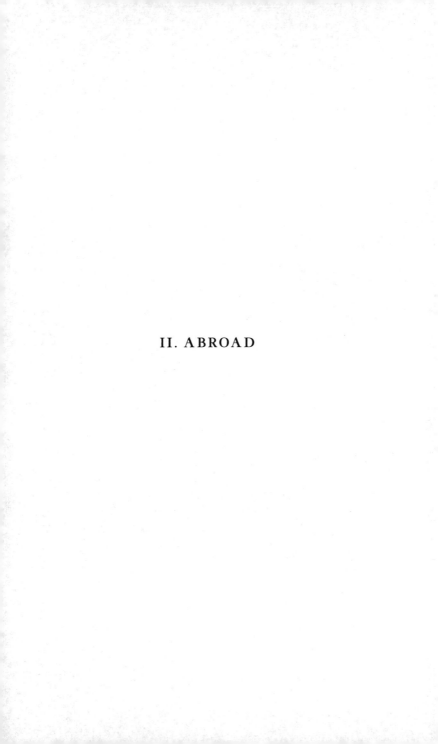

II. ABROAD

WRITING ABOUT THE PRESENT:
MIRROR, BODY, SHADOW

¶ Mirror

It was Stendhal writing under the protective guise of a bogus epigraph (attributed to historian "Saint-Réal") who decided it was the novelist's job to hold up a mirror at the side of the road to catch everything that passed. This would remain the prescription for description in what would later be called the realist novel for the next century and a half. Today, however, everyone is followed down every road by mirrors: We're tracked by these mirrors to the office and to lunch and through all the rooms of our homes, and though surely we've sped up our pace of life in order to evade them, they're becoming cheaper and cheaper to produce and install, and even lighter and less conspicuous for our family and friends and stalky strangers to carry with them, in the forms of computers in their bags and phones in their pockets. And beyond even that—these mirrors don't merely reflect momentarily anymore, no—now they also record, and so make all our moments eternal. The final change will come when these mirrors stop following us, and we start following them—seeking out their surveillance, and so seeking out their immortality, becoming so involved in our pursuit of them that we'll forget what type of machines they truly are, and all we'll be able to sense are these strange people coming at us at top speed—just "people," because we won't be able to recognize our own shrieking selves, and so we'll inevitably either crash into our own representations, or just swerve at the ultimate moment toward the precipice instead, from which we'll fall—we'll fall—which is the sole process by which realism becomes reality.

¶ Body

Stendhal proposed the novel as a mirror held up to the side of the road for a single purpose: to make the political/aesthetic argument that if a novel was concerned with the immoral or ugly it wasn't the fault of the novel or author but of the thing/situation it was reflecting. Don't blame the mirror for the puddles in the road, Stendhal was saying, blame the road-surveyor or -inspector. In the nearly two centuries since *Le Rouge et le Noir*, however, Stendhal's intent has been distorted or downplayed, and what literature has been left with is the image of the novel as image, a reproduction not of a consensus or objective "reality," but of one author's subjective experience.

Zola born in 1840, two years before Stendhal died, and one year after the appearance of the daguerreotype—the first commercially practical photographic process—referred to this impossible reproduction of a consensus reality as "idealism," and opposed it with "naturalism," which characterized novels that sought to expose the forces that produced that consensus. The naturalist novel, from its birth in the late nineteenth century through its disguised heyday in the twentieth, has been precisely about how reality is "made," as distinct from what reality "is."

Zola defined this naturalistic approach in an essay that responded to a medical text by a contemporary, the physiologist Claude Bernard, which attempted to transfer the scientific method governing experimentation in chemistry to the precincts of biology—the treatment of disease. It was Zola's goal to diagnose French society as a doctor would a patient's body: by analyzing its comorbid maladies one at a time, with a nib as sharp as a scalpel. Only after this diagnosis would treatment—extraliterary,

210

political treatment—be possible.

Zola titled his essay "The Experimental Novel," and inasmuch as that epithet "experimental" has plagued the careers of countless modern writers, its original context must be recalled: "The experimental novelist," Zola writes, "is therefore the one who accepts proven facts, who points out in man and in society the mechanism of the phenomena over which science is mistress, and who does not interpose his personal sentiments, except in the phenomena whose determinism is not yet settled, and who tries to test, as much as he can, this personal sentiment, this idea *a priori*, by observation and experiment." After a paragraph break, though, Zola hazards a "personal sentiment," but only in terms of his own incomprehension: "I cannot understand how our naturalistic literature can mean anything else. I have only spoken of the experimental novel, but I am fairly convinced that the same method, after having triumphed in history and in criticism, will triumph everywhere, on the stage and in poetry even. It is an inevitable evolution." Zola's hope, which he outlines in this essay and realizes in his Rougon-Macquart series, was to show how characters, and how the characters of nations and classes, etc., could all be taxonomized in a vast social hierarchy, and so how their development could be portrayed as methodical as well, through the inheritance and acquisition of physical, mental, emotional, and psychological traits, in a process whose guiding intelligence wasn't Darwin or Lamarck or even God, but the Novelist-Scientist, who was bound to natural law as strictly as any of his fictional animals.

Zola, early in his essay-experiment, invokes the authority of Balzac (born 1799, and so a generation younger
than Stendhal and perhaps two or three generations
older than Zola) as a herald of this new literature of
process:

> The novelist starts out in search of a truth. I will take as
> an example the character of the Baron Hulot in *Cousine
> Bette*, by Balzac. The general fact observed by Balzac
> is the ravages that the amorous temperament of a man
> makes in his home, in his family, and in society. As soon
> as he has chosen his subject he starts from known facts;
> then he makes his experiment, and exposes Hulot to a
> series of trials, placing him amid certain surroundings
> in order to exhibit how the complicated machinery of his
> passions works. It is then evident that there is not only
> observation there, but that there is also experiment; as
> Balzac does not remain satisfied with photographing the
> facts collected by him, but interferes in a direct way to
> place his character in certain conditions, and of these he
> remains the master.

A dozen pages later Zola quotes Claude Bernard's
medical-metaphoric conception of the "vital 'circulus'":
"The muscular and nervous organs preserve the activity of the organs which make the blood; but the blood, in
its turn, nourishes the organs which produce it." Then,
Zola writes:

> Go back once more to the example of Baron Hulot in
> *Cousine Bette*. See the final result, the denouement of the
> novel: an entire family is destroyed, all sorts of secondary
> dramas are produced, under the action of Hulot's amorous

temperament. It is there, in this temperament, that the initial cause is found. One member, Hulot, becomes rotten, and immediately all around him are tainted, the social circulus is interrupted, the health of that society is compromised. [...] Suppose that Hulot is cured, or at least restrained and rendered inoffensive, immediately the drama ceases to have any longer any *raison d'être*; the equilibrium, or more truly the health, of the social body is again established. Thus the naturalistic novelists are really experimental moralists.

Engels once said that he learned more about France from Balzac than from "all the professed historians, economists, and statisticians of the period together." Paul Lafargue, in his *Reminiscences of Marx*, writes that Marx—who was born in 1818, the year Balzac decided to dedicate his life to writing—so deeply loved *La Comédie humaine* that if he ever finished with economics he intended to write a study of it. Though not even a sentence of that study ever appeared (rather, Marx borrowed a few of Balzac's sentences for *The Eighteenth Brumaire of Louis Bonaparte*), it seems that what Marx most appreciated in Balzac's sequence was the way in which it illustrated the processes by which an individual, while operating under the delusion that he or she was forming society, was instead being formed by it. Marx transferred the personalities and struggles of Balzac's characters—their struggles with spouses, lovers, employers, employees, clergy, and the chaos of the Restoration and July Monarchy—to entire social classes: the newly individuated bloc of the working proletariat, which (I nearly wrote "who") fomented a failed revolution and was left to suffer under the repressions of Napoleon III.

It doesn't take a Žižek to point out that identifying a

213

social problem in fiction doesn't solve that problem in life, and that while a book can describe the processes that create a problem, that description itself becomes an integral component of the problem's irresolution. The writer is never exempt from, or outside of, the writing, then, but remains as much a product of ideology as any of his or her characters.

The selves that all true writers must recognize and acknowledge in the ideological mirror—the selves that are most fully created by the writer becoming aware of his or her emplacement in multiple simultaneous identity-continua (economic, gender, sexual, racial, etc.)—feel so supernatural that, paradoxically, they seem to render even the most fantastical fictions "natural." Marx referred to these selves, these negative images of the faces that a writer presents to the world, as "shadows."

For many of my peers, to write about the present is to search for a mirror that will show only shadows.

FROM THE DIARIES

Brows

"Why is the brow so devilishly vital to the *fin de siècle* novel?" Sven asked in iffy translation while furrowing his brow.

Freckles

The maid's freckles were like the use of French in a Russian novel: distracting, excessive—*imbécile*.

8/20/2013

So here it is, the *Zibaldone*, one of the greatest blogs of the nineteenth century, of any century, for that matter—and what matter it is! 2,584 pages! Translated, edited, printed, bound, shipped, and received from the tattooed hands of my Monday/Wednesday/Friday UPS guy, Phil—a process that required seven years and the efforts of seven translators, two editors, more than two dozen "specialist consultants," in German, French, Hebrew, Mongolian/Tibetan, philosophy, the history of science, etc., a partridge, a pear tree, and Phil, not to mention *Il Cavaliere* himself, Silvio Berlusconi, who took a break from his women and media companies and the media company that is Italy to arrange partial funding and take a tax break on art. Then there were also the daily emails and phone calls from Important Editors to get Farrar, Straus and Giroux to send the galleys to me. Unpacking the paperback stack, I understood FSG's hesitation. Sending out copies, even review copies, of Leopardi's masterwork must get expensive—sort of like sending out review models of the Roman Coliseum—but still, why invest what must've been hundreds of thousands of strong euros or weak dollars to prepare a book for publication only to stint on crucial freebies? Why work so intensely to put together a diary so intensely of and about the page, and then try to placate a critic—who, in order to read the entirety and write anything even remotely coherent by deadline, will have to put off all other paying assignments, sex assignations, sleep, and laundry—with an ebook version? These, rather similar concerns about human folly, are Leopardi's subjects.

Online time is comprised of all the times of all the texts we click. Each session, then, is a history of sessions, a temporality salad, a chronological *Zibaldone*, which is apparently a slang term for a meal or dish slapped together out of available ingredients. I'm downtown, at a café featuring B&W photos of Naples on the walls and accordion renditions of "'*O Sole Mio*" on the stereo and a menu that insists on the proper adjective, "Italian," before every section heading—Italian Appetizers, Italian Sandwiches, Italian Coffee—the list of Italian Desserts lacking for nothing but zabaglione, that concoction of egg yolks, sugar, and sweet wine, intended to be scooped or sipped, or both.

The time of print is different—if I have to continue the metaphor, print is best read like a recipe: one line, then another, unidirectionally, in order. Reading backward is like using flour as garnish.

Online reading becomes writing with interactivity: Social media feeds compel constant update and continuous response. Leopardi was faithful to his journals, but he was never their slave. He wrote only when he had something to write about (no deadlines!), and only for himself (no editors!). As for me, I'm trying to remember—since I don't have a smartphone, just a stupidphone, I still have to remember—which author it was who once claimed that, regardless of how blasphemous a book might appear, all books were essentially moral, because while reading and writing you're not doing anything active, like looting, or bombmaking. When I first read that sentiment I was impressed, but now—in this break from a dead poet's prose in the middle of a Wednesday—I'm not. Passivity has its morality too: While reading and writing I'm not, for example, calling my uncle in the hospital, or my sister in L.A., both of which I have to do before the weekend. Leopardi, who was an ugly hunchback, lived at his family's estate in Recanati for much of his life, and hardly ever left its library, which was stocked with anthologies, dictionaries, encyclopedias, and manuscripts in every major and a few minor and even defunct languages, many of which he mastered. The first page of the *Zibaldone* bears the nondate "July or August 1817," which captures his spirit exactly, especially because, according to the editors' introduction, it was appended to the work in 1820. The last entries arrive in 1832, written in Rome, and Florence, to which Leopardi, age thirty-four, had fled to experience the world unprinted. He died at thirty-eight, of cholera, in Naples.

The tables all around me are full of laptops, which should be called "I'm a freelancer with a studio apartment and don't have anywhere else to work but heretops." The marble is fake, but in the context of that fakeness the veins might be "real." I should've gone to the library. The line to order ends where the line for the bathroom begins.

8/23

Zibaldone #3: "A plant or animal seen in real life should give us more delight than when it is painted or imitated in some other way, because it is impossible for an imitation not to leave something to be desired. But the contrary is clearly true: from which it appears that the source of delight in the arts is not beauty but imitation."

I'm not sure—though maybe this only applies to plants and animals. What about literature—the differences between an original and a translation? What about experience? Because if I had the choice between another

218

day in this café or going on an all-expenses trip to Italy, I'd take the ticket, no question.

#29: "Everything is or can be happy, except man, which goes to show that his existence is not limited to this world, as is that of other things."

Another grumble. I can imagine inverting, or negating, that statement: "Everything is or can be happy, except man, which goes to show that his existence IS limited to this world, UNLIKE that of other things." Which is to say, I'm fairly convinced it's our consciousness (of death) that prevents our happiness. But what's especially troubling about that statement is "everything"—"other things." What does Leopardi mean? What else does he regard as not just being capable of happiness, but actually seriously happy? Animals? Can animals be happy? Maybe. But, come on, plants? How can a brainless root be called "happy," as opposed to just "alive"? Maybe Leopardi's point is that for some things, for some dimidiate things, "happiness" is plain "living"? What then to make of this cheap ceramic cup and saucer and this cheap metal spoon I can twist and bend without it shrieking? Leopardi must've been insane, not least because he expected a next life, and expected it to be glad. I'd settle for a $4 latte.

8/24

"Boredom." Leopardi uses the word a lot—*noia*, apparently—which doesn't seem bored in italics. Baudelaire has his *ennui* (1857); Durkheim, his *anomie* (1893); but before them both, Leopardi—who has the concern for the individuality of spirit of a Baudelaire, and the concern for the social body of a Durkheim—is predisposed to *noia*, "the passion most contrary to and farthest from nature," "the feeling of nothingness, and of the nullity of what exists, and of the very one who conceives and feels it, and in whom it *subsists*" (Leopardi's italics). Nonetheless the translators of this volume have decided to keep *noia* out of the text, and rely, instead, on "boredom."

The repetitions. Again.

#2: "Passions, deaths, storms, etc., give us great pleasure in spite of their ugliness for the simple reason that they are well imitated, and if what Parini says in his Oration on poetry is true, this is because man hates nothing more than he does boredom, and therefore he enjoys seeing something new, however ugly."

#s 89–90: "Rather, I would say that the unknown gives us more pain than the known and, since that object frightens us or saddens us or makes us shudder, we do not know how to leave it alone. And even if it disgusts us, we still find a certain desire to put it into some perspective so that we can understand it better. Perhaps also, and so I believe, it comes from a love of the extraordinary, and the natural hatred of monotony and boredom that is innate in all men, and if an object presents itself that breaks this monotony and steps out of the common run of things, however much more burdensome it seems to us than boredom (but perhaps, at that moment, we do not notice or think about this), we still find a certain pleasure in the shock and agitation that the fleeting glimpse of that object produces in us."

#239: "Hatred of boredom is the only reason that today we see gatherings of people eager to watch bloody spectacles, such as public executions and the like, which have nothing pleasurable in themselves (unlike the contest, display, etc., of gladiators and wild animals in the circus) but only insofar as they provide a vivid contrast

220

with the monotony of living. The same is true of anything that appeals simply by being extraordinary, even though, far from being pleasurable, it is in itself deeply unpleasurable."

#s 345–346: "When a person proposes purpose to himself either for action or indeed for inaction, he will find delight in things that are not delightful, even in things that are unpleasant, almost indeed in boredom itself."

Leopardi, official interpreter of Leopardi.

9/1

So, experiencing the emptiness of the world (*noia*) leads us to seek the nearest salvation, which is, expectedly, the ugliest. What are we to do? What salvation should we seek? Not the easiest, but the simplest, the apt. We should become a bit like a child. Or like "the ancients," who had "negligence, certainty, carelessness, and I would even say ignorant confidence." What happened to us that we're so careful now? What defeat made us this timid, and witting? Naturalness—an "illusion" last sustainable during the reign of Augustus—crumbled when the imperium crumbled, into barbarity, modernity. We were left to the void, and denatured by *noia*. Unable to return to our illusion, we engineered "reason," and followed its dictates to corruption. Philosophies, religions—artificialities perpetrated by system.

Leopardi regards paganism's lapses as purer than Christianity's because at least pagans who act unethically are acting naturally, not contradictorily. At least the Greek and Roman gods were humane, he maintains, in that they felt human passions, even to the point of meddling in our affairs; they patronized, and were influenced by, our art. If you died as a Greek or Roman you took your memories and emotions with you into a sort of exile. This was infinitely preferable to the Christian heaven, which cast life on earth as the exile, from which redemption was a calculation, or a transaction. In the Roman Catholic rite hell became avoidable via a formalized penance, the sacrament of confession. Each dead person's soul, however, had to be judged for assignation—this suggested a purgatory: an amorphous transitional state, until the Medieval Church deemed it a locatable space or place because the fate of dead unbaptized newborns required the accommodation of a limbo, located adjacent. The next logical provision was time, and though each sin earned its sinner a designated wait, the popes offered swifter passage for a price: indulgences. To Leopardi, each innovation merely distanced humanity further from the true religion, which wasn't the one Constantine adopted, or the one Jesus bled for, or even Olympus's—but "certainty," "negligence," unicity.

Leopardi's lifetime was marked by a great Europewide cyclicity; a return to Vico and his *Scienza Nuova*: the idea of history as recurrent. Political history organized into a cycle, from an age of myth to an age of epic heroes or iconic rule, to an age of egalitarian populism destroying itself into myth again. Later, biogenetics—via Lamarck, Haeckel—would conform: Embryos matured into adulthood through a recapitulation of the evolutionary progressions of their ancestors. Both ideas were clever—writerly clever—but wrong. Leopardi was never wrong. He couldn't be; not with a talent that transmuted every theme to literature. The ultimate in circuitousness: addressing the world as a way of addressing style.

Culture's martyrdom was congruent with religion's,

but later—coinciding with Spanish-Habsburg rule (1559–1713). The *Seicento* (as Italy would call the 1600s) wasn't quite the *Quattrocento*, but still: the piano, invented in Florence, the violin, perfected in Cremona; Monteverdi, Vivaldi; Caravaggio, Tiepolo, Bernini, Borromini. Not to mention Galileo. What about its literature? Gabriello Chiabrera, anyone? Fulvio Testi, yes/no? Manfredi? Zappi? Filicaia? Guidi? Leopardi praises their originality, only to qualify that originality as "small in scale"; he allies them and groups them into schools, then assails them as imitators of Dante and Petrarch; Guidi can never be called "inconsistent," because his every poem demonstrates a "formal mediocrity and frigidity." "Most of Chiabrera's finest *canzoni* are no more than very beautiful sketches." Boccaccio wouldn't have written any better about this lot: sentimentalists, hyperbolists, academicians peddling sham erudition. Their refinements were technicalities: Latin and Greek borrowings, compoundwords, confounding puns, resulting in a verse that read like zealous Bible commentaries not to circulate outside the cloister; an abstruse fanatic math. Leopardi's just recording what he's seen and heard, of course, which is his inheritance of a tradition that's forgotten how to see and hear for itself. Italy's near past fashioned poems out of its far past, but its future will source them from feeling directly. The only way to share a feeling is to share how it was evoked (the sight and sound): the lesson Leopardi found in Homer. This can still be done, if not "effortlessly," then with "concealment": the lesson Leopardi found in Virgil. His emotions will be his senses. His self will be his nature.

Homer and Virgil both practiced "prosopopoeia": inventing voices for objects and landscapes; But Leopardi provides "his own" voice. To skies, celestial bodies, Italy, friends, above all "to himself." With it, he addresses a you, singular, plural, specific, ambiguous, everything, nothing. Personality, the birth of fallacies.

Leopardi's prose personifies nature, though it does so chiefly by personifying its indifference.

What is a rhyme? The illusion of reason. What is an image? "A part of the world oppressed by fog / and sullen Jupiter."

9/6

Happy/sad birthday to me. One year younger than Leopardi was when he'd finish with this book. When he'd leave it unfinished. Completion, being the hope, being impossible. To Leopardi, the struggle is to keep proportional, balanced. Another issue of translation. The translators admit that "translating *noia* by 'boredom' is a kind of reverse anachronism," but claim that "the concept is addressed continuously in the *Zibaldone*, and to avoid confusion can only be translated by a single word, even if *noia* and 'boredom' are not exactly the same thing." They go on to note the challenge they faced with *convenienza* and its adjective *conveniente*: "There is a sense of *convenienza* that has to do with wholeness, or the perceived relation between the whole and the parts, or the parts with each other (proportion, harmony, agreement), and another that has to do with belonging (appropriateness, fitness, rightness, suitability, becomingness, and so on). In the end, the English 'propriety' and 'proper' seem to fit both semantic areas best, as well as having a certain *gravitas* about them, and in spite of their linkage to 'proper behavior,' which is not usually the issue in the *Zibaldone*."

I hate the word "gravitas." It reminds me of testicles—it's a term for "balls," which has "no balls"—I'm aware that recording this isn't proper behavior. But I'd like to imagine that the ancients, whoever they are, would've mentioned it. Only because to refrain from doing so would've felt, meaning "been," unnatural. This is my problem. This is our problem, today. To restrain, or not to restrain—we're not sure what feels unnatural; I'm not even sure what "is."

9/8

#1,307: "If I may be permitted an observation regarding a trifling matter that might seem ridiculous to spell out, and hardly deserving of being written down. There are some really minute parts of the human body that man is only able to observe with difficulty, very rarely, and only by chance, in others, and which he is only used to observing in himself."

9/10

But is *convenienza* naturally derived? Or just our own artificial construction? I thought about this, then realized I wouldn't be able to think about it. We/I believe in wholes, but live in parts. Not even in parts (fragments, shards), but in the nullities between them, the cracks that comprise our shattering.

Proportion, harmony—to be relevated, or yearned for. Who doesn't want repletion, completion—Concinnity Now? But who wants the culture that is its complement?

Total Leopardian roundedness of character requires total consciousness: of self-frustration, self-sabotage, perversion. Leopardi wants me to be aware of my failings; I want that too, but I also want to hang on to my cigs, my rye, my humor.

For Leopardi, "weakness" evokes a "compassion," which he calls "the only human quality or passion that has nothing to do with self-love. The only one because even self-sacrifice for heroism, patriotism, virtue, or a beloved [...] always comes about because on that occasion the sacrifice is more satisfying to our mind than anything we might gain." The implication being that "weakness" can't be beneficiated, or changed into strength; it can only be made mutual. I just wish that Leopardi would be more explicit about the form of pity he preferred: an eye, an ear, a word, a heart, a sack of *scudi;* an insomniac reader nearly two hundred years after his death. He died a virgin (according to his friend and unrequited gay crush, the writer and statesman Antonio Ranieri).

9/12
#1,979: "There's nothing to be said. Man's present condition, in obliging him to live and think and act according to reason, and in forbidding him to kill himself, is contradictory. Either suicide is not against morality, though it is against nature, or our life, being against nature, is against morality. Since the latter is not so, neither is the former."

9/14
I've been skipping the philology. But I stop at #2,053: "The vast has to be distinguished from the vague or indefinite. They please the mind for the same reasons, or for reasons of the same type. But the vast is not necessarily vague, and the vague is not necessarily vast.

Nonetheless, these qualities are always similar in terms of the effect they have on the mind."

9/16

It's back again, the we-like-that-which-destroys-us thing, #2,118: "It is pleasurable to be the spectator of vigorous, etc. etc., actions of any sort, not only those relative to man. Thunder, storm, hail, a strong wind, seen or heard, and its effects, etc. Every keen sensation in man brings with it a vein of pleasure, however unpleasurable it is in itself, however terrible, or painful, etc. I heard a farmer whose land was often severely damaged by a nearby river say that nonetheless the sight of the flood was a pleasure as it advanced, rushing swiftly toward his fields, with a thunderous noise, and carrying with it a great mass of rocks, mud, etc. And such images, while ugly in themselves, always turn out to be beautiful in poetry, in painting, in eloquence, etc."

Entries on politics (nations evolve along with their citizens), and on the politics of language: All contemporaries of Hegel were Hegelian, it seems, whether they liked it or not (Leopardi didn't). He criticizes German—for lack of rigor?—and criticizes French—for being incapable of the sublime? Languages evolve too, I guess. Which means there's still a chance for the Italian novel.

From #2,136: "What is the derivation of the verb *aptare* [to adapt], from which our *attare, adattare,* and the French, etc.? From *aptus.* And what do we think this is? A participle of the very old verb *apere.* And what is the original meaning of *aptare*? That of the verb *apere,* that is, to bind."

As poets to meter, mortals to death. And prosateurs to pretension.

On a bus to Atlantic City, to my family—unflushable shit in the chemical toilet, piss in the aisle, expired buffet vouchers wedged between seats. Leopardi says that every living being loves itself equally, because it loves itself infinitely. Regard is comparable only in degree, and only in infinity. Absolute. I Heart New York. Jersey Strong. I want to copy down another quotation about "boredom," but then I want to copy down so much, so many contradictions: #4,175. "Not only individual men, but the whole human race was and always will be necessarily unhappy. Not only the human race but the whole animal world. Not only animals but all other beings in their way. Not only individuals, but species, genera, realms, spheres, systems, worlds. Go into a garden of plants, grass, flowers. No matter how lovely it seems. Even in the mildest season of the year. You will not be able to look anywhere and not find suffering."

Changing trains, for home, at Trenton. Leopardi in accidental palinode-mode: bestowing the unhappiness he'd already ordained for humanity on the rest of the biota. But not just that: He's also asserting that each weed and seed and class of beast feels its own despair, as if despair were the substance of diversity. What about #29, though, "Everything is or can be happy"? What's become of the diarist who damned himself, and yet remained sanguine about the prospects for joy among "other things"? The world's suddenly suffering, "evil." Leopardi is, in our lexicon, "depressed." This is because of a frustrated love (for Ranieri? for his cousin Geltrude Cassi?), or infirmity: biography.

A purposeful contradiction is not a contradiction. It's change. An accidental contradiction is not a contradiction. It's growth. Still. There is such a thing as a contradiction.

"*Perversato* for *perverso*": Leopardi notes the substitution of "raging," or "fury," for "perverse," or "depraved"—a word must have a body, a motion, emotion, intelligence. The world's monstrous incoherence demands a victim but will get a witness.

"These are things that we do not know, nor can we know; that none of those that we do know make even likely, still less do they authorize us to believe them. Let us therefore admire this order, this universe. I admire it more than anyone. I admire it for its perversity and deformity, which seem to me extreme. But before praising it, let us at least wait until we know with certainty that it is not the worst of all possible worlds."

Tu dormi: Io questo ciel, che sì benigno
    Yes, you sleep, while I come to my window
appare in vista, a salutary m'affaccio,
    to salute this sky that seems so kind,
e l'antica natura onnipossente,
    and eternal, all-commanding nature
che mi fece all'affanno.
    who created me for suffering.

International jet-set philosopher Slavoj Žižek—a Rasputin beard, a bundle of somatic motor tics and twitches including nose rubbing, mouth rubbing, bad-dad-jeans smoothing, and clutching at the black T-shirt that bears his monogram, "Ž"—wasn't just staying at the Strand Hotel; he was bunkering there. Not only was he refusing to leave the hotel for our talk, he was insisting on meeting in what had to be its single least interesting room: a windowless conference box in the basement, furnished with an ovular cherryish table and faux-Bauhaus swivelers, each place set with Strand leather blotter, Strand stationery, Strand pen. Between us was a bottle of tepid Strand water.

This served to make an already fake situation even faker, by which, of course, I mean "Real"—this was Žižek, after all, the Yugoslav-born, Ljubljana-based academic and Hegelian/mock-Hegelian; mascot of the Occupy movement, critic of the Occupy movement; and former Slovenian presidential candidate, whose prime contribution to intellectual history remains his redefinition of ideology from a Marxist false consciousness to a Freudian-Lacanian projection of the unconscious.

Translation: To Žižek, all politics are formed not by deliberate principles of freedom or equality, but by expressions of repressed desires—shame, guilt, sexual insecurity, you name it. According to Žižek, we're all cönvinced we're drawing conclusions from an interpretable world when we're actually just suffering involuntary psychic fantasies.

Žižek was spending the day in wall-to-wall promotion mode, talking up his new movie *The Pervert's Guide to Ideology* (described in the press materials as "a lecture

on film, in film"), while his new wife, Slovenian journalist Jela Krečič, three decades younger and twenty
floors upstairs, chain-smoked on her balcony (junkets
make cheap honeymoons). Krečič is Žižek's third wife,
The Pervert's Guide to Ideology the sequel to 2006's *The
Pervert's Guide to Cinema*—I wondered how he felt about
franchises: What would be different this time around?

"I can't see the future," he said. "And I haven't seen
the movie."

So I told him about it. In the sequel, as in its predecessor, he stands around on the recreated sets of Hollywood
classics and, between concussively edited clips, proceeds
to desublimate their meanings: the shark in *Jaws* is not a
shark but a semantic void, much like the Mitteleuropean
conception of "Jewry"; it's lucky that the *Titanic* hit the
iceberg, because if it hadn't, Kate would've left her rich
fiancé for penniless Leo—death, then, spared her the fate
of living poor.

Žižek, listening for the exact amount of time it took
to de-recline his chair and cross his legs out of their
manspread, exploded—with memories of the earliest
foreign media he consumed, Perry Mason novels and
Columbo in Slovene and Serbo-Croatian, which led,
obviously, to a seminar on Hitchcock's TV show and
movies: "a true work of art, the definition of it is that
it survives decontextualization." About to make another jump, he stopped. A photographer had entered the
room, then left. "How do you call this rule that the actor
shouldn't look directly into the camera?"

"The fourth wall," I said. "Don't break the fourth
wall."

"Yes. Yes. But what interests me is that there is one
genre where it breaks—hardcore pornography."

He tore away the page he'd been scribbling on—stacked

231

squares—and began scribbling triangles on the next.

"Friends told me that the latest trend, at least in Europe, is public sex. They showed me some clips, and they're terrifying. A couple enters a streetcar, half-full, simply takes a seat, undresses, and starts to do it. You can see from surprised faces that it's not staged. It's pure working-class suburb. But what's fascinating is that the people all look, and then they politely ignore it."

Žižek's style in person is the same as in his *Guides*: verbose, associative, dissociative, obscene ("Fuck realism!"), anecdotal ("I was just in Istanbul..."), enjargoned (*"jouissance"*). He went on to analyze Angela Merkel, Joschka Fischer, Robert Redford and *The Company You Keep*, then transitioned to recaps of the dialectic and the Kantian categoricals: Government surveillance was "private," Žižek insisted, not "public," "precisely in the sense that we're all embarrassed by it when it goes public."

He flung his pen to the blotter and gripped his beard. "It's bad if we're controlled, but if we're not, it can be even worse." A theory of religions followed; Malevich and formalism; why Prokofiev was better than Shostakovich; Platonov, Shklovsky, Brecht; the importance of racism to foreign relations. The closest analogue to Žižek's indefatigable critique is the very subject he's always critiquing: global capital. It didn't matter whether any of his "product" or "programming" was consistent or cohered; it didn't even matter whether any of the thoughts he spewed for this interview—let alone the thoughts of his approximately fifty books to date—would ever be consumed: Instead, all that concerned him was production.

"What do others see in me?" Žižek finally asked, though it was unclear whether he was summarizing

Freud, or summarizing Lacan summarizing Freud, or asking me—the last journalist of his junket's day—my opinion.

"You say you love me, but why?"

But I'd never said that, so it had to be rhetorical.

"It's absolutely my idea that the state is an agent of what Lacan called 'the gaze of the Other.' The gaze is always minimally erotic."

This was the first moment he looked me in the eye. Then he went on to explain something else.

FROM THE DIARIES

Conversation Summary (Next Table)

A woman recounts a dream in which she had sex with
a celebrity. Her boyfriend, or husband, gets angry. The
woman says it was only a dream. Her boyfriend, or
husband, gets up from the table. The woman, getting
up too and following him, says it means nothing not
just because it was only a dream, but also because the
celebrity was dead. (As for me, my Polish is so bad I
wasn't quite able to determine whether the celebrity
had been alive in her dream or she'd been dreaming
of necrophilia.) (Another shameful admission: I still
can't quite accept the existence of such things as Polish
celebrities.)

Why I've Never Had Sex in Hungary

Mom calls me in Budapest: "Bring me back that papri-
ka paste... the kind in the squeeze tube... Aren't all the
women beautiful...? Don't they all look like me?"

NO ONE HATES HIM MORE:
ON FRANZEN'S KRAUS

What's the German for a writer who resurrects a writer who would have hated him? Until a word is coined, I'm going to go with "Franzen"—after the most famous American novelist of the moment, whose commercial and critical success has brought him, if his public statements are any indication, nothing but misery. His new book, *The Kraus Project*, returns him to the early 1980s, before he wrote *The Corrections* and *Freedom*—two internationally bestselling epics of middle-class white America struggling with marriage, parenthood, illness, and climate change—and his two earlier, somewhat disavowed systems novels. Thirty years ago he was just a Swarthmore student abroad in what was still West Berlin, exploring his vices and discovering, and tentatively translating, the great Viennese "antijournalist" Karl Kraus.

The Kraus Project is Franzen's reckoning with his undergraduate self; with his ambitions and frustrations; with his completist tendencies to let no juvenilia go to waste and no headline go unremarked; and with the publishing legacy of the generation of the 1960s and 1970s. That was the era when Pynchon, Barth, and Coover were embarking on a counterculturally charged reassessment of the symbolic and structural principles of the novel, and when Kraus's virtuosic, vitriolic style—halfway between Karl and Groucho—was being introduced to Anglophone readers, in translations by the Viennese refugee and Brandeis professor Harry Zohn[1]:

1. The previous Kraus renaissance was just a minor part of the Americanization of Jewish-European literature, which began immediately after the Holocaust, with émigré translations of

Many share my views with me. But I don't share them with them.

To have talent, to be a talent: the two are always confused.

Why should one artist grasp another? Does Mount Vesuvius appreciate Mount Etna? At most, a feminine relationship of jealous comparison might develop: Who spits better?

To write a novel may be pure pleasure. To live a novel presents certain difficulties. As for reading a novel, I do my best to get out of it.

I no longer have collaborators. I used to be envious of them. They repel those readers whom I want to lose myself.

From a torch something drops occasionally. A little lump of pitch.

Die Fackel ("The Torch") was Kraus's magazine. It was the smoky, scalding, staplebound enemy of mixed metaphors, pan-Germanism, the House of Habsburg, everything French, pro-Semites and anti-Semites, and the popular press, especially Vienna's paper of record, the *Neue Freie Presse*. In 1899, the twenty-four-year-old Kraus—the son of a wealthy paper manufacturer from Gitschin in Bohemia, now Jičín in the Czech Republic—renounced Judaism and converted to Catholicism

... Arendt, Benjamin, Buber, Kafka, Scholem, and of the Yiddish tradition, published in affordable trade editions by Schocken Verlag, which, after being closed by the Nazis in 1939, left Berlin for Mandate Palestine, en route to New York. That period ended definitively in 1987, with Schocken's acquisition by Random House, which in 1998 was acquired by Bertelsmann, a Germany media firm that during the war was the single largest publisher of Third Reich propaganda.

(either as a social expedient, or a perverse justification for his already developed self-loathing), and published the first issue of *Die Fackel*. He reported the news by what's now called aggregation, offering commentary and emendation. He inspected Austria-Hungary's unconscious just as the empire was splitting up. Not that Kraus had any time for psychoanalysis: If his most private thoughts were to be disclosed, it was not because the process would benefit him, but because it would benefit the public; Kraus confessed not just to Vienna's sins, but for them.

As is common with cult journals, *Die Fackel*'s subscribers were as illustrious as its contributors: Peter Altenberg, Oskar Kokoschka, Adolf Loos, Heinrich Mann, Arnold Schoenberg, August Strindberg, Georg Trakl, and Frank Wedekind (whose play *Spring Awakening* Franzen translated in 1986 and published in 2007). Kafka was a loyal reader, as was Benjamin, who regarded *Die Fackel* as the literary fulfillment of Trotsky's permanent revolution—"an eternally new newspaper." Gershom (then Gerhard) Scholem turned the noun *Fackel* into a verb, *fackeln*, "to torch on": This wasn't necessarily flattering but did back Kraus's assertion that anyone who criticized him became more popular than he was. *Die Fackel* appeared whenever its editor pleased: quarterly, monthly, weekly, even daily. After 1911, until the end of Kraus's life in 1936, he was its sole contributor.

He wrote essays, which today, in English and even in German, are read in excerpted sentences and paragraphs: in aphorism. The works of Hermann Broch, Robert Musil, Arthur Schnitzler, and Stefan Zweig are intact because their preoccupation with Vienna was merely prologue, material for extrapolation. Kraus was too honest, or too impatient, to try his hand at fiction, and instead got directly at the facts and his opinions: He attacked the liberal "Jewish press"—by which he meant the secular *Neue Freie Presse*—for spilling too much intellectual "blood" in defense of Leopold Hilsner, a Jewish cobbler from Polná wrongly convicted of the ritual murder of two Christian girls (i.e., the blood libel), and attacked the conservative "Jewish press"—by which he meant the secular *Die Zukunft*—for outing Prince Philip Friedrich Alexander of Eulenburg-Hertefeld as a homosexual. For Kraus, all Germanophone media were a cabal, in which Jewish editors on the left displayed a pathetic sense of solidarity with their co-religionists, and Jewish editors on the right sought a pathetic normalization through knee-jerk patriotism. Kraus proclaimed himself the final incarnation of the Wandering Jew, and pitched camp in the extreme middle: the only position from which to survey the shifts between the collapsing official censorship bureaus, the internal censorship that editors practiced to influence politics and game the property and stock markets, and the way the resultant liberty to scandalize increased circulation, which increased the appetite for scandal, which was itself scandalous. It all engendered a pervasive sensationalism: the true "news cycle" of every empire in decline.

The Kraus Project is Franzen's bid to force an equation: Vienna a century ago = America today. To prove it Franzen has translated a handful of essays in their entirety, and subjected them to an approximation of Kraus's technique, by writing footnotes so extensive that they dominate every page and turn the annotated text into the subsidiary: Kraus's essays become the headnotes to Franzen's angst. Interspersed are glosses by the American scholar Paul Reitter, who has the thankless job of historically contextualizing Kraus's grievances, and the German-Austrian writer Daniel Kehlmann, whose interpretations can be divided into the four categories that Freud apportioned for jokes: the obscene, the aggressive, the cynical, and the absurd. Franzen insists on a connection between Kraus—who was misunderstood by Viennese Jews of his era, and who frequently misunderstood himself—and Kehlmann, a twenty-first-century Viennese goy who writes novels and, what's worse, was born in Munich. Despite the timidity implied by his enlisting of collaborators, Franzen offers Kraus's original German on the verso of each leaf, as if he wants to be caught in infelicity or error—or in a desperate attempt to bulk out to three hundred pages what might have been a *Die Fackel*–sized pamphlet.

The essays Franzen has translated are "Heine and the Consequences" (1910), "Afterword to 'Heine and the Consequences'" (1911), and "Nestroy and Posterity" (1912), all three from Kraus's most energetic period; "Between Two Strains of Life: Final Word" (1917), essentially an after-afterword to the third printing of his Heine essay; and the sub-Brechtian poem "Let No One Ask..." (1934). Kehlmann calls the last "a masterpiece of brevity and despair," and "one of the most important short poems of the twentieth century," but really it's Kraus's wan excuse for not addressing Hitler's seizure of the chancellorship: "It passes; and later/it didn't matter." But it did matter, only not to Kraus, who was ailing and depressed.

Kraus wrote about Heine for the usual reasons young critics write about older authors: to kill the father, sleep with the mother muse, and be reborn. He linked Heine's most limpid and lazy style—developed, in Kraus's telling,

239

during Heine's precious self-imposed exile in Parisian salons—with the style of the feuilleton, the pastel postcard of gossip and apolitical arts criticism that began appearing in French newspapers in 1800, as if to provide a pleasant distraction from Napoleon's centralization of power, and then spread throughout Europe, taking on, according to Kraus, each language's, and country's, worst attributes. In Germany it became pedantic and moralizing; in Austria-Hungary melodramatically moody and snobbishly refined. Kraus compared the sentimentality of Heine, a Jew from Düsseldorf, with the farce of Nestroy, the Catholic dramatist from Vienna, and it's no surprise which of the two he found lacking. Kraus was a lifelong frustrated poet and playwright, and though his translations of Shakespeare are entertainingly strange, it comes as a relief that most of his major play, *The Last Days of Mankind* (1930), is appropriated street-speech, and quotation from press and radio.

"The masses" are the byproduct of the mass production of language: The linotype machine—the internet of the *fin de siècle*—ensured the fast and cheap dissemination of more periodicals, and so of more fast and cheap rhetoric, than ever before. In the first Heine essay, Kraus fixates on the industrial capacities of the logos, in a German masterly in its truncations: *"Glaubt mir, ihr Farbenfrohen, in Kulturen, in denen jeder Trottel Individualität besitzt, vertrotteln die Individualitäten."* A version of this characteristically untranslatable sentence might be: "Believe me, you multicolored multiculturalists, turning every idiot into an individual turns individuality itself idiotic." Franzen has: "Believe me, you color-happy people, in cultures where every blockhead has individuality,

individuality becomes a thing for blockheads." He skips the neurotic beauty of *Farbenfrohen*, and the economical swerve of the noun *Trottel* becoming the verb *vertrotteln*; and though both omissions are forgivable, a culture where prominent American novelists can use the word "blockhead" will itself become a blockheaded culture. But the most important element lost in this passage, which follows a condemnation of the Frenchification of German, is Kraus's paradoxical use of *Individualität*, a noun that had come to German from the French only a half century earlier. In the 1760s Rousseau redefined *individuel* from meaning "indivisible," or "numerically distinct," to meaning "a single person," but it was only with the second volume of de Tocqueville's *De la démocratie en Amérique* in 1840 that *individualisme* took on the positive connotation of a heroic severance of personality from the herd, and was opposed by negative, greedy *égoïsme*; both terms were soon shepherded into German.

Instead of elucidating this paradox, and inquiring whether Kraus was aware of it, Franzen writes the following note:

> You're not allowed to say things like this in America nowadays, no matter how much the billion (or is it two billion now?) "individualized" Facebook pages may make you want to say them. Kraus was known, in his day, to his many enemies, as the Great Hater. By most accounts he was a tender and generous man in his private life, with many loyal friends. But once he starts winding the stem of his polemical rhetoric, it carries him into extremely harsh registers.
>
> ("Harsh," incidentally, is a fun word to say with a slacker inflection. To be harsh is to be uncool; and in the world

of coolness and uncoolness—the high-school-cafeteria
social scene of Gawker takedowns and Twitter popularity
contests—the highest register that cultural criticism can
safely reach is snark. Snark, indeed, is cool's twin sibling.)

Any resemblance to real snark, living or dead, is
purely coincidental. Franzen goes on to spank Salman
Rushdie (for joining Twitter); *n+1*, "a politically committed print magazine that I respect" (for praising the
internet while not addressing its impoverishment of
writers); and the liberal professoriat (for savaging capitalism in contemporary feuilletons written on Apple
computers). The footnote is scattershot, but not exceptional. Just as Kraus's densely argued texts deplore the
mechanization of verse, so Franzen's unstructured
exegeses attempt to summon a similar abhorrence of
the digitization of the novel. He never considers that
if German poetry was able to survive the German-
language press (and two wars, and communism), the
odds are that American fiction will survive Google.

Kraus proceeds to assault Heine for favoring surface
over depth, citing everything from Heine's excessive
punning to his insistence on referring to his poems
as "songs," in effect inviting composers to set them to
music: call it incentivization, in a viral campaign
involving spinets. Franzen might not have written *The
Corrections* to be optioned by HBO—the chamber music
of our time, with David Simon our Mendelssohn—but
he agreed to the option, and so the only thing that pre-
vented his book's debasement was an inept script that
died in development. Kraus writes in Franzen's translation: "To be responsive to literature, you cannot be
responsive to music, otherwise the melody and rhythm
of music will suffice to create a mood." A cursory dig into

242

the Grimms' dictionary will uncover that *Stimmungsreiz* (Franzen's "mood") is a misty German word meaning "charming atmosphere" or "delightful ambience," which Kraus is deploying sardonically ("mood" is plain *Stimmung*). Franzen writes: "To this line my friend Daniel Kehlmann, who is an actual Viennese and a deep student of Kraus, offers the comment: 'Who the hell knows what Kraus is really saying here.'"

I do, for one, and all novelists should: Kraus is saying that the more care a writer takes with the surface sound of a sentence, the more the sentence can stray from sense. But he's also slyly contradicting himself by coding that statement in a prose of remarkable phonic intricacy. Self-conscious style, though, isn't something Franzen worries about anymore. In 2010 he told the *Paris Review:*

> And, by a wide margin, I've never felt less self-consciously preoccupied with language than I did when I was writing *Freedom*. Over and over again, as I was producing chapters, I said to myself, "This feels nothing like the writing I did for twenty years—this just feels transparent." I wasn't seeing in the pages any of the signs I'd taken as encouraging when I was writing *The Corrections*. The sentences back then had had a pop. They were, you know, serious prose sentences, and I was able to vanquish my doubts simply by rereading them.

If Kehlmann's contributions are shameful, Reitter's are dutiful and smart, and those reassuring initials "PR" attached to his notes were the only thing that kept me reading. Franzen's *Project* might be redeemed if it attracts readers to Reitter's two vital books: *The Anti-Journalist: Karl Kraus and Jewish Self-Fashioning in Fin-de-Siècle Europe* (2008) and *On the Origins of Jewish Self-Hatred* (2012). A snippet from the former is wiser on Kraus than all of Franzen's equivocations combined:

> Kraus operated in a medium in which, to a particularly
> extreme degree, literary language was made exchange-
> able and consumable and was assimilated into various
> projects of social advancement. His project of internecine
> resistance took him, correlatively, particularly far in the
> direction of developing a style that would not be easy to
> assimilate—that would not have "consequences" in the
> way he believed Heine's literary journalism had.

But of all the presences in *The Kraus Project*, it's not Reitter, Kehlmann, or Kraus who proves to be Franzen's most dangerous interlocutor: It's Franzen himself. He writes about his loneliness on his Fulbright trip to Germany; about his relationships with women, and with the specters of Harold Bloom and Pynchon. He writes about envy, and how it encourages productivity, and how it limits productivity, and about the folly of the very notion of artistic productivity. He writes against blogs, yet allows a comparison between *Die Fackel* and blogs; he writes about the way websites disturb the reading experience, but does it in pages bracketed into German and English sections and in notes that confuse me more than anything I read online—that confuse me more than the Talmud. He writes about competition and the work ethic, but never mentions his own Heine: David Foster Wallace, a master of the nuanced citation who managed to be both smarter and more casual, crazier and kinder.

"My explicitly stated goal," Franzen writes of himself in 1980s Berlin, "was to save the American novel—from social one-dimensionality, from critical preoccupation with the prison-house of language, from the off-putting avant-gardism of Pynchon and his kind." Apparently, he stayed inside and smoked cigarettes and typed for twelve hours a day, and it was in reading this autobiographical stretch—in breaks from my own smoking and typing—that I came to recognize a landsman. It seemed that we were both involved in *Bildung*, or "cultivation," the German-Jewish discipline that shaped my grandparents, from Cologne, and the method by which German Jewry sought to become not just accepted by an adopted homeland, but to embody its quintessence. I realized that Franzen—perhaps more than any other American novelist, and certainly more than anyone else ever raised in the Congregational Church in the Midwest—felt like a guest fighting to be loved by a host culture, yet conscious that such love can never be fought for, and that the struggle was in equal parts futile and imaginary. He let his origins oppress him, just enough for him to know how to oppress himself in the event that America didn't exile him, or have him executed.

I've come to regard this as Franzen's Jewish Problem: Denise's overrelished Judeophilia in *The Corrections*, blatantly counterpointed with her mother Enid's overrelished Judeophobia; the depiction in *Freedom* of Jewish neocons rallying around the Iraq War, and its ridiculous portrayal of a New York diamond-district salesman dealing rings while wearing phylacteries—which the religious wear only during prayer; and the way this book treats Kraus's *Jüdische Selbsthaß* (Jewish self-hate) by the trick of letting Reitter sort it out, and the way it treats the Holocaust, by letting Kehlmann apostrophize it, leaving Franzen himself free to pontificate about Israel/Palestine with a sophistication that would barely pass muster on a local network affiliate, let alone on CNN. But I'm prepared to forgive him all this, as readers have to forgive Franzen everything, only because no one can ever hate him as much as he already hates himself. Franzen must know that he will never receive any review as cruel as the ones that, with each book and media appearance, he gives himself. It's his awareness of all this, and his inability to restrain himself from betraying that awareness, that puts America's foremost novelist in contention to become the world's foremost Jewish novelist *tout court*—the inheritor of the crown of feathers. If only he were funnier, or cared a bit more about sex.

RECOGNIZED WITNESS:
ON H.G. ADLER

On May 18, 1961, toward the end of Session 45 of the Eichmann trial, Judge Halevi asked State Prosecutor Bar-Or if he'd finished submitting into evidence all the documents relevant to the Theresienstadt camp. Bar-Or said he had, though of course there was also "the well-known book by Dr. John Adler": "This is the outstanding book about Theresienstadt, and it is called *Theresienstadt*."

> JUDGE HALEVI: Was he there?
> STATE PROSECUTOR BAR-OR: He himself was in Theresienstadt. I simply hesitate to burden the court with material. This is an excellent, authentic book. It is based on impeccable sources. It is a thick volume, and it is at the disposal of the court. I simply hesitate to submit it. Much has been written about Theresienstadt. I try to submit material which refers to the Accused, without impairing the general picture. We are faced with the difficult problem that one has somehow to compromise and to select, otherwise there is no end to it.

In *Eichmann in Jerusalem*, Hannah Arendt seized on the mention of this book by H. G. Adler as a rare moment of nuance in the trial:

> The reason for the omission was clear. [Adler's book] describes in detail how the feared "transport lists" were put together by the Jewish Council of Theresienstadt after the SS had given some general directives, stipulating how many should be sent away, and of what age, sex, profession and country of origin. The prosecution's case would

have been weakened if it had been forced to admit that the naming of individuals who were sent to their doom had been, with few exceptions, the job of the Jewish administration... The picture would indeed have been greatly damaged by the inclusion of Adler's book, since it would have contradicted testimony given by the chief witness on Theresienstadt, who claimed that Eichmann himself had made these individual selections. Even more important, the prosecution's general picture of a clear-cut division between persecutors and victims would have suffered greatly.

Arendt's point is that no prosecution would have wanted, and no defense would have dared, to address the forced collaboration of Jews in their own extermination. No instance of a Jew unloading the cattle-cars could be allowed to mitigate the guilt of the Accused. But Arendt failed to state the obvious: that being forced to participate in another's death while waiting for your own was victimization at its most perverse. What the Jerusalem judiciary didn't trust the world to comprehend was something that was already being taught in Israeli schools, and for survivors was a basic fact.

Hans Gunther Adler arrived in London in 1947, and wrote his nearly thousand-page book in feverish haste. He recorded the activities of the Judenrat alongside how many grams of food each inmate received each day, and how many hours they were allowed to sleep each night.

Over the next three decades he became the survivor who wrote the most but was read the least, producing more than thirty books of history (*The Administered Man*, a study of the deportations of German Jewry), sociology

(*The Experience of Powerlessness,* a study of camp organization), poetry, and fiction, all published on a shoestring in West Germany and not translated into English until now. The revival of interest in him began, in the English-speaking world, in 2001, when W. G. Sebald's *Austerlitz* was published. *Austerlitz*'s protagonist is obsessed with Theresienstadt and regrets that "now it is too late for me to seek out Adler, who had lived in London until his death in the summer of 1988." In 2002, after Sebald's death, the translator Peter Filkins came across a copy of the German original of *The Journey,* the middle novel of a trilogy by Adler, in Schoenhof's Foreign Books in Cambridge, Massachusetts. Filkins found a very different Adler from the chronicler who had inspired Sebald. Adler's subject remains the same whether he's writing fiction or nonfiction—the events between his deportation in February 1942 and liberation in April 1945—but whereas the style of his nonfiction is conventionally academic, the style of his fiction embodies the trauma: Internal monologues turn out to have been spoken aloud; dialogue is exposed as two sides of a psychic break; events are given out of sequence; each passage's vocabulary is determined by its theme—biblical, technological, legalistic, medical—rather than by its characters.

Panorama, the first volume, was written in 1948 but not published until twenty years later. It's a third-person *Bildungsroman* about a character called Josef Kramer—a Josef K with his name made explicitly Jewish. When WWI breaks out, Josef is sent away from an unnamed city that resembles Prague to live with the Neumann family in provincial Umlowitz. Later, he attends boarding school and joins a scouting group on a trip to Landstein Castle. From here, the biographical correspondences can be confirmed: Adler was born to

249

German-speaking Jews in Prague in 1910, studied musicology at its German University, and worked as secretary of the Urania, an educational association that hosted popular talks by the likes of Einstein and Thomas Mann; Josef follows a similar track. Adler was pressed into slave labor to help lay a railway line between Prague and Brno, then he was sent to Theresienstadt, Auschwitz, and two subcamps of Buchenwald, Niederorschel and Langenstein. He puts Josef through all of that except Theresienstadt, which is reserved for the second novel in the sequence. In confinement Josef comes to realize that his life so far—from the Neumanns' dry goods store to his education and employment—has been preparing him for the camps, where "everything is a useless nightmare, no one able to think beyond the day itself, the panorama narrow and closed in."

The Journey, written in 1950-51 and published in 1962, adapts the deportation and internment experiences into an entire book that details in a mix of third-, second-, and first-person narration the destruction of the Lustig family—a doctor, his wife, their two adult children, and the wife's sister. At Ruhenthal, which is Theresienstadt, they reenact Adler's ordeal. Adler arrived in Theresienstadt with his wife, Gertrud Klepetar, in 1942; his parents, who arrived separately, died in the camp that year. Gertrud's father died in 1943, and in 1944 her mother was deported to Auschwitz. Gertrud insisted on following, and Adler followed his wife. Both mother and daughter were murdered on arrival. Filkins, in his introduction to *The Journey*, writes that of all the German-language novels about the Holocaust, only three besides Adler's have been written by Jews with direct experience of the camps: Fred Wander's *The Seventh Well*, Jurek Becker's *Jacob the Liar* and *Night*—not the book by Elie Wiesel, who wrote in French, but a vengeful novel by Edgar Hilsenrath. Filkins's point about the anti-Semitism of postwar German-language publishing would have been stronger if he'd noted that only one of his Germans, Hilsenrath, was born in the Reich. Becker was born in Poland, Wander in Austria, and Adler in what, at the time, was the third city of Austro-Hungary. Adler is the only member of this group whose books risk aestheticizing the killing, which he describes in a range of metaphors: The Lustig women are portrayed as rabbits; the crematorium is a zoo, a terrarium, a cinema, and an "ash factory"; the act itself is an efficient performance spoiled only by the victims, who "neglected at the end of the execution to step out from behind the curtain and acknowledge the cheers of those left behind."

The final volume of the trilogy, *The Wall*, was written between 1956 and 1961 and published posthumously in 1989. Its narrator, Arthur Landau, remembers the immediate aftermath of the war in "the city," which is still Prague, and his émigré life in "the metropolis," which is London. Arthur is a freelance scholar immersed in an interminable manuscript with the working title *Sociology of Oppressed People*. He's writing that book, and presumably this book too, in a drab flat on the fictional West Park Row, which he shares with his second wife, Johanna, and their two children, Eva and Michael. Arthur's first wife, Franziska, was killed at Auschwitz, but his memories of her are so vivid that he is able to project images from their past together onto the wall of the title, a symbol, for him, of both the limits of meaning and of his salvation: "Before it I can exist and rise to become a figure that is visible and casts a shadow, though within myself I remain an indeterminate entity." In German this final volume of the trilogy was published, against Adler's wishes, as *Die unsichtbare Wand* (*The Invisible Wall*), to avoid confusion with the host of other books that appeared as the Berlin Wall came down.

Every writer on the Holocaust is faced with an absurdity: that the most thorough chroniclers of the tragedy remain the Nazis themselves, who left a long paper trail of censuses, genealogies, banking records, transportation manifests, and matériel requisitions, a body of evidence accessible to anyone who understands German and euphemism (*arisieren*, "to Aryanize," meaning to expropriate a Jewish-owned business; *liquidieren*, "to liquidate," transferred from the lexicon of commerce to death). Holocaust survivor writers have had to become editors or translators of the Reich's first draft, and none understood this better than Adler. Obfuscation through defamiliarization (describing Jews as "animals" and "units"), the revalencing of rhetoric ("reclaiming" the Slavic countries for the "*Großgermanisches Reich*"), the subordination of individual autonomy to archetype and allegory, the force of repetition: Adler may have been introduced to these techniques by Kafka, Hermann Broch, Robert Musil, or Alfred Döblin, but he mastered them by studying Goebbels and Eichmann and his clerks, whom Adorno called *Schreibtischmörder*, "desk-murderers."

The Nazi bureaucrats were responsible for two of the most malevolent fictionalizing experiments of the twentieth century, both of which Adler experienced and wrote about. The first was Theresienstadt itself. In 1940, the Nazis converted the Czech garrison town into a camp for nearly 150,000 Czech, German, Austrian, and Polish Jews, a quarter of whom died of starvation, dehydration, or typhus. Most of the remainder were moved to Auschwitz and Treblinka. In the summer of 1944, with Denmark protesting against the deportation of its Jews to Theresienstadt, Germany capitulated to diplomatic pressure and allowed the International Red Cross to visit the camp to prove that no exterminations were being carried out on site. The Reich Security Main Office, sniffing a P.R. opportunity, ordered the Gestapo to implement Operation Beautification (*Verschönerungsaktion*), which would transform the camp temporarily into a picture-postcard hamlet.

Sebald describes it accurately in *Austerlitz*, because he relied on Adler's account. "It was decided," Sebald writes, "to organize the ghetto inmates under the command of the SS for the purpose of a vast cleaning-up program: pathways and a grove with a columbarium were laid out, park benches and signposts were set up, the latter adorned in the German fashion with jolly carvings and floral decoration, over one thousand rosebushes were planted." Food rations were increased; new clothes—not just uniforms—were sewn. Conditions in the barracks improved, especially after seven thousand prisoners were dispatched to Auschwitz a month before the inspectors' arrival. Dr. Paul Eppstein, president of the Judenrat, was appointed mayor for the day, and tasked with leading the Red Cross contingent on a tour; *Brundibár*, a subversive children's opera whose villain resembled Hitler, was performed; a football game was played, and there was a show trial in which Jewish lawyers, judges, and jurors tried another inmate for "theft." The Red Cross report, made public only in 1992, might as well have been ghostwritten by the Reich: "The SS police gives the Jews the freedom to organize their administration as they see fit." A later propaganda

253

film presented the camp as a spa town for the Jewish elite, which explains Adler's name for it in *The Journey:* Ruhenthal means "Valley of Rest." The novel depicts it as a sanatorium with an identity problem: Sometimes the Jews are the patients and the Nazis are the benevolent physicians pursuing their "cure"; at other times the Nazis are "the diseased," armed lunatics bent on eradicating their Jewish caretakers.

Adler encountered the second fictionalizing experiment only after liberation, when he returned to Prague as an orphan and widower. The city's Jewry had been almost wiped out, but Josefov, the medieval Jewish quarter, had been preserved intact. Under the supervision of Reinhard Heydrich and Karl Rahm, the commandant of Theresienstadt, its synagogues, meeting halls, and burial society buildings had been turned into repositories of Judaica: prayerbooks, Torah scrolls, gold and silver religious paraphernalia, and textiles seized from across Czechoslovakia. These were to comprise the collection of a clandestine Jüdisches Zentralmuseum, accessible only to Nazi officers and researchers who required accurate, not anti-Semitic, information on an extinct race. The wartime museum held just four exhibits—among them a display of Hebrew manuscripts and an installation illustrating the Jewish lifecycle that featured a circumcision knife and a shroud—and was curated by Czechoslovakian Jewish specialists. The museum, reclaimed by the remnants of Prague Jewry in 1945, hired Adler to catalog its library of roughly one hundred thousand volumes. But then the new regime began clamping down on Jewish institutions, and by the end of the decade had effectively closed the museum by nationalizing it. Adler, however, was in London by then, and the only books in his cramped flat were the ones he was writing and the ones he'd smuggled out.

Cultural continuity; collective memory; the conflation of "belonging" and "belongings"; the assuaging power of art: These are all humanist concerns that after the Holocaust were less acceptable than ever to Adler's London cohort of displaced Germanophones, who held with Adorno's dictum that "to write poetry after Auschwitz is barbaric."

The essay the line is from, "Cultural Criticism and Society," was written in 1949, just as Adler, who'd written poetry throughout his time in the camps, was trying to publish his first novel. The next year he reviewed Adorno's *Philosophy of Modern Music* for the BBC Third Programme, and used the opportunity to initiate a correspondence with his fellow musicologist. Several meetings ensued, alternately fraternal and fraught. In 1956 Adorno invited Adler to lecture on Theresienstadt at the Institute for Social Research in Frankfurt. In 1957 Adler was invited to give another talk, this time to a private circle. The title was "Ideologies under Slavery." Adler interpreted the title socially and psychologically: Ideologies are imposed on a people until a people imposes them on itself. Adorno's interpretation was political and economic: Ideologies are the result of systems that determine the identities and actions of everyone, both oppressors and oppressed. A rift ensued, which Adorno exacerbated in the essay "Negative Dialectics" in 1966, in a passage that unmistakably attacks his former friend:

> Perennial suffering has as much right to expression as a tortured man has to scream; hence it may have been wrong to say that after Auschwitz you could no longer write poems... But it is not wrong to raise the less cultural question whether after Auschwitz you can go on

living—especially whether one who escaped by accident, one who by rights should have been killed, may go on living. His mere survival calls for the coldness, the basic principle of bourgeois subjectivity, without which there could have been no Auschwitz; this is the drastic guilt of him who was spared.

Or of him, perhaps, who spent the war in Pacific Palisades, California?

The Wall travesties Adorno in the person of Professor Kratzenstein, a man convinced that all miseries are "the result of economic conditions." He is the head of the International Society of Sociologists, which is the Institute for Social Research done up in clown make-up and fancy dress. Bereft in London, his English still shaky, Arthur seeks the support of the society for his *Sociology of Oppressed Peoples*, but all he gets are "platitudes" and "dogmatic declarations." The émigré intelligentsia are no help either: Leonard Kauders (based on Franz Baermann Steiner) and Oswald and Inge Bergmann (based on Elias and Veza Canetti) refer him to a philanthropist who doesn't offer any money, just a job at a wallpaper factory. Arthur is going broke for writing a book about deception, self-deception, and persecution, while professional Marxists brand him a schnorrer and advise him to return to Soviet Czechoslovakia. The absurdities of Theresienstadt and the museum recur in Hampstead, not quite as tragedy, but not quite as farce either.

It was Adorno's idea that capitalism had stripped philosophy of its revolutionary capacities. What was left was art, the last emancipator and partisan of truth. But

Adorno was using the word "truth" (or *Wahrheitsgehalt,* "truth-value") in a way that was already becoming outmoded. His "truth" always gestured toward an "essence," a below-the-surface system of pitches, colors, or symbols that would organize an artwork and instantiate its worth; but contemporary usage was returning the word to its Enlightenment definition—quasi-scientific "factuality." This is the position we're in today, when most writers invoke "truth" only as a pre-emptive defense against those whose primary impulse is to fact-check and accuse.

It's perverse that the closer a writer is to the Holocaust the more closely their work is scrutinized and questioned. In the 1990s the old news reemerged online that Elie Wiesel's most famous Holocaust book was a revision of an earlier, fiercer Yiddish version. The French text, written under the spell of Sartre and Camus, sublimates the parochial appetite for revenge into a universalist obligation to testify. Wiesel's revision was ammunition to denialists. He had already proclaimed, decades before he won the Nobel Prize, decades before he took Oprah to Poland, that "some events do take place but are not true; others are—although they never occurred." Along with Primo Levi, Tadeusz Borowski, Aharon Appelfeld, Piotr Rawicz, Jakov Lind, and Jerzy Kosinski, he elided events and fashioned composite characters to attain a sense of realism—but that doesn't mean that Auschwitz was a hoax, or that Israel is illegitimate. Writers who survived don't seem to be allowed the same license as Cynthia Ozick or Martin Amis, who've imagined their Shoahs in comparative peace.

The lasting legacy of Holocaust literature seems to be its utility as a template for contemporary sagas of victimization, be they memoirs of child soldiers in Africa, or of women throughout the ummah. These books are re-garded as proof of adversity conquered: They dramatize all powerlessness or blunted will into martyrdom; their characters endure on heart alone, in scenes arranged with Hollywood cunning; their authors treat their grief as an imperative not just to write but for readers to read them. But Adler warily wrote the truth, and he did so by the Adorno method, even if Adorno never certified it: His fiction individuated the nonfiction he wrote, in forms that adapted, and realigned, the grotesque "non-fiction" he experienced. Between the two genres was a wall, perhaps "invisible," perhaps imaginary—a mental fence between allied integrities.

Arthur concludes *The Wall* with a fantasy in which Kratzenstein offers him an apology, and celebrates his work at a sociology gathering on Shepherd's Field—Hampstead Heath—which resembles a carnival, complete with bumper cars and a shooting gallery. As the festivities dwindle, and Arthur stalks back alone to West Park Row, he prepares himself to face the fact that not only was it all just a dream, but that its recording and even its dreaming have consequences: "Thus I have robbed myself of the last opportunity to find a place among my contemporaries, to feel that I have a function as a member of society, even if it is only that of being a recognized witness to what I have lived through."

FROM THE DIARIES

What Kind of Neighborhood is Palilula (Belgrade)

The kind of neighborhood where people think it's fun
to put stolen disarticulated decapitated mannequins out
on their balconies.

The Hague

The General answered the Examining Magistrate:
"But how can it be genocide, if we killed them individually? Because we hated them individually—I did,
separately—each and every one."

CONDUCTING MORTALITY:
ON HENRY-LOUIS DE LA GRANGE'S
MAHLER

Playbills are necessary only insofar as the art they describe is not; it is as if listeners have to be distracted from the music they're supposed to be listening to. These programs tell us that the slow drag we're about to hear is no ordinary funeral procession but a Trauermarsch, composed in the dying days of the Austro-Hungarian Empire, under conditions of, usually, unremitting misery. Fill in the blank: The composer of this work suffered from insanity, tuberculosis, syphilis, or suicide. Go on any night to any concert hall: You will see people looking and seeing, not hearing, and the sound they make riffling pages is often louder than the pianissimos of the slowest slow movements. These notes, so opposed to musical notation, tell us the sequence of the evening's entertainments and their stories as well, in the tradition of nineteenth-century "program music"— music that seeks associations outside of itself, aerating aural experience through reference to nature or philosophy, to literature or the visual arts. Although some metaphors provided by these notes reflect a composer's intention, all insist on refusing music its abstraction, on transforming its absolute, mathematical quality into the emotionally relatable, the familiarly human. The New York Philharmonic's most recent note for a "symphonic poem," *Eine Alpensinfonie* by Richard Strauss, succinctly outlines, away from the five lines of the staff, its composer's extramusical program:

The action takes place in the space of twenty-four hours, from predawn through the late night. Over the course of

260

twenty-two discrete episodes (one is bipartite, so we may identify twenty-three events), the listener goes up the mountain and down again, encountering along the way a catalog of natural features one might expect to find on such a journey—forests, streams, meadows, and so on—as well as a hunting party (in the Sunrise), some close calls (slippery Dangerous moments and a violent Tempest), a spectacular view from the summit, and a post-sunset return home where our mountaineer(s) must surely sit back and contemplate what has been a most excellent excursion.

Among those who ventured a less excellent excursion into program music was Strauss's friend and rival Gustav Mahler, who would write a program for his first symphony, which debuted in Budapest in 1889 as *A Symphonic Poem in Two Parts*. For its Hamburg revival of 1893, Mahler divided the work into *Memories of Youth*, describing movements one through three, and *Commedia Humana*, describing movements four and five; the untitled first and third movements were originally divided by an andante entitled *Blumine*, a flowery term for "flowers." Unsatisfied in more than just his professional life, young Mahler was an inveterate revisionist: The first movement was said to represent spring, which "goes on and on," followed by *Blumine*, then a scherzo entitled *Full Sail*; the second half of the symphony began with *Aground*, which was also the Trauermarsch, followed by the finale of *Dall'Inferno al Paradiso*, "the sudden outburst of despair from a deeply wounded heart." The Hamburg performance also found Mahler appending to this symphony the subtitle *Titan*, even while denying that this had anything to do with the novel of the same name by Jean Paul Richter.

No poet and decidedly no impresario, he eventually

dropped the programmatic pretense and entitled his first symphony First Symphony, keyed in D major. As both a worshipper of Bach's counterpoint and a director of opera, which was an art that preceded program music with story or dramatized plot, Mahler concluded that pure expression, or music qua music, was the higher calling. Leaving behind Strauss's Alpine fantasies, and even Wagner's rewriting of the *Nibelungenlied*, music in Mahler's hands became abstract if not in sound then in inspiration, based on a literature of the soul whose only reader was himself. Mahler's disavowal of musical narrative was the first display of the egotism that would keep audiences at arm's length, not only from his compositions but from his conducting as well. With this denial Mahler promoted himself to genius, which he perceived sardonically as a sort of godhood—a position just superior to that of director of the Vienna State Opera.

Mahler was always an absolutist, a purist of the self. Henry-Louis de La Grange, the most Mahlerian of Mahler's biographers, brands his subject with the following purist innovations: As a conductor, Mahler was the first to prohibit seating after the beginning of an opera, at least until the end of the first act, a practice that disturbed Hapsburg higher society, who loved, above all, making an entrance; he was also the first to dismantle "the claque," those purveyors of false applause who would provide singers with enthusiastic and enthusiastically remunerated audiences (he hired private detectives to shadow the wings). The first to value talent in acting as much as in singing, Mahler was a pioneer of opera staging, collaborating with production designer Alfred Roller on sets and costumes that sought unity with the music and not mere accompaniment. Mahler, in turn, was the only batonist outside of Bayreuth who would realize Wagner's dream of the total theater, the Gesamtkunstwerk, "the total artwork"; even though this musician was himself fractured, thrice estranged, and homeless—not only as a conductor who'd rather compose but, by his own admission, as "a Bohemian among Austrians, an Austrian among Germans, and a Jew among all the peoples of the world."

Here is the program behind the program. He was born in 1860 in the kingdom of Bohemia, raised in the margravate of Moravia; his family, as Jews, had been granted freedom of movement by the ruler of those lands, Emperor Franz Josef. The Ausgleich of 1867 created the dual monarchy of Austro-Hungary, serving to grant equal rights to Austrian Jews (but not their Hungarian brethren), with the emperor finally giving constitutional credence to the ecumenical reforms of his predecessor, Josef II. Mahler studied in Vienna, lost a composition competition, and embarked on a career as conductor in the provinces (Ljubljana, Olomouc, Prague, Leipzig, Budapest, Hamburg). After converting not to Protestantism, which attracted many Jews of his generation, but to Austria's more reactionary Catholicism, Mahler was appointed director of the Vienna State Opera, or Hofoper—the most prestigious position in the musical empire, and thus in the musical world.

Between conducting few worthwhile premieres and many revolutionary productions of Mozart, Beethoven, and Wagner, Mahler wrote lieder, nine of his own symphonies, and left a tenth unfinished. He married Alma Schindler, "the most beautiful girl in Vienna," according to Bruno Walter, Mahler's conducting protégé, who was always ready to please. (Alma would sleep with the following personalities: architect Walter Gropius, painter Oskar Kokoschka, and writer Franz Werfel. She died a lionized drunk in New York a half century after the death of her first husband, whose memory she zealously cherished.)

The year 1907 was the family's *annus horribilis:* their eldest daughter, Maria Anna, known as Putzi, had scarlet fever, then died of diphtheria at the age of four; Mahler was diagnosed with the weak heart that would kill him (his susceptibility to bacterial infection of the heart was probably caused by rheumatic fever); and, with an anti-Semitic campaign in the Viennese press setting the backstage for power plays over musicians' pensions and repertoire that can only be described as operatic, Mahler quit the Hofoper to conduct in New York, at the Metropolitan Opera and, later, with the Philharmonic. Following his second Philharmonic season, just a week after the lunching ladies who administered the orchestra confronted him with outrageous contractual terms, Mahler incurred another heart infection. He died three months after that, in 1911 in Vienna, of endocarditis. De La Grange, not only a French baron but a fussy exquisitist, fawner, and manic completist, calls Mahler's congenital disease a "mitral incompetence"; in the appendix of his four-volume, five-thousand-page biography, he gives Alma Mahler's recipe for her husband's favorite dessert, Marillenknödel, or apricot dumplings.

In the summer of 1910, Mahler rushed on a depressed whim to Leiden, the Netherlands, for an informal consultation with a vacationing Sigmund Freud (it should be remembered that the name of that city, in German, means "pain"). There, during an extended stroll, Mahler apparently unburdened his soul to his fellow dreamer and Moravian Jew. In the absence of their session's transcription, we're forced to settle for the work of de La Grange, who mistrusts the psychological and focuses instead on the facts, refusing to interpret. As the founding president of the Gustav Mahler Musical Library in Paris, a city that never particularly enjoyed his beloved composer, de La Grange has written a biography that tells us how Mahler made himself, and then how, like a god, he tried to remake the world in his image.

It would seem that de La Grange has done all this Freudian-unconsciously, believing he was confining himself to the essentials, even as the scope of his ambition betrays him as a man seeking to outbombast the best, obscuring the exigencies of Mahler's life with hundreds of names and dates, musical analyses, and extended quotations of period journalism. Mahler is accorded so much biography—more than Thayer's Beethoven (three volumes), more than Jahn's Mozart (four volumes) and Newman's Wagner (five short volumes)—because he came of age coevally with daily arts journalism (Mahler was both the most badly and well-reviewed conductor of his day, because he was the most reviewed), and because, as a conductor, he was a kind of celebrity. Just as an exorcism of Mahler's art might require multiple soloists and choruses, redoubled strings, triple winds, and offstage ensembles, an organ, and a percussion battery that includes cowbells, an account of Mahler's life requires similar resources in literature: over a million words, multiple languages, and thirty years of writing (finished this spring, de La Grange began research in the mid-1950s). Conversely, giving a summary of these books is like producing a Mahler medley, condensing periphrastic brass into a brief fanfare, followed by thematic catalogs played in unrelenting succession. De La Grange's first English volume follows Mahler from birth through his engagement at the Hofoper in 1897; Volume Two covers the beginning of that ten-year affair, through 1904; and Volume Three, which concludes with Mahler's leaving Vienna in 1907, focuses on his personal and conducting travails, even while it chronicles his composing success: The Third and Fourth symphonies are played more widely; the Fifth is premiered; in only three summers off from the Hofoper, the "tragic" Sixth, the Nachtmusik Seventh, and the "Symphony of a Thousand" Eighth are composed. Volume Four is a translated, graphomaniacally expanded version of the French edition of Volume Three, *La génie foudroyé* (the bibliographic history of de La Grange's project would require a biography of its own); it opens with Mahler's first visit to America, the conductor "yearning," as the poem says on Liberty's pedestal in New York Harbor, "to breathe free."

Like an actor, who in terms of fame is the true operatic diva of today, or a director, who's nothing but a remade conductor, Mahler, too, split his time, living bicoastally between the Blue Danube and the Hudson. In American winters he noised famously from the podium, and in European summers he quietly wrote, alternating seasons leading the Metropolitan Opera and the newly professionalized New York Philharmonic with vacations spent in Toblach in the Tyrol (today Dobbiaco, in Italy), feverishly avoiding old friends, jealous of his wife's love affairs, and working on the last two of his symphonies and the song cycle on Chinese poetry, *Das*

Lied von der Erde.

American critics, though cautious not to appear too Europhilic, generally warmed to Mahler's conducting while remaining ignorant of his own compositions. At least popular taste would've had a better incentive to appreciate the symphonies: Mahler's occasional quotations were accessible to Europeans and Americans both (many of whom, after all, were Americans of only the first or second generation), and his music's dance forms and folk tunes, even if invented, his *ländler* and *hatscho*, were in their blood, their mothers' milk. And knowingly sophisticated city audiences in New York as much as in Vienna could have responded to, and so would have been satirized and flattered by, the music's excesses, its proudly demonstrative kitsch.

Indeed it was in America that coexistence—Old World repertoire, New World scene-set—became crosspollination: Downtown Manhattan, which held thousands of Mahler's co-religionists, was a raucously simmering "melting pot," and although the man who came through Ellis Island for the first time in 1907 was certainly different from those rag-peddlers and rabbis in steerage, he was still party to their mess—a massive influx of Slavs and Mitteleuropeans, from the most talented, which would be him, down to the talentless, with the barrel organist who'd play outside Mahler's window at the Hotel Majestic on Central Park West situated somewhere in between.

Outside the bounds of biography, these busy American intersections would inspire a reception of Mahler's compositions that continues to this day. In Mahler's time, juxtaposing popular music with classical repertory was not new, but regarding the popular as "banal" was, and so Mahler, writing at the very recognizance of kitsch—and at the invention of a strain of European irony more immediately apparent, perhaps, in the journalistic feuilleton—can be heard as the first musical postmodernist, juxtaposing and deconstructing historical periods and historicized qualities: projecting, as Arnold Schoenberg's friend and Austrian musicologist Hans Keller wrote, "a crucial space of historical time against a musical plane." Keller was citing Mahler's Third Symphony, which contrasts its scherzo with the scherzo's historical forerunner, the courtly minuet.

After Classical melody was advanced, next came Romantic harmony, and finally, Mahler's music seemed to say, the modern superimposition of styles. This phenomenon was only a self-conscious version of what could be found freely in the American streets. Neighbors cramped in tenements spoke different languages, and Mahler's Jews, mostly Hasidic *Ostjude*, were living on the same Manhattan island, just blocks south, but they in sumptuary garb, practicing traditions from centuries past. Meanwhile, America, the democracy in which Mahler marveled that if you wished to say hello to President Roosevelt you could, and if you didn't, you didn't have to, already represented the capitalist endgame of the turmoil stirring in revolutionary Russia. The Church had supported Bach, Maria Theresa supported Gluck, Esterházy supported Haydn, Josef II supported Mozart; Ferdinand II, Leopold I, and Charles VI were all patron musicians themselves; Beethoven, to a lesser extent, exploited his various princes and counts, his Waldsteins, Lichnowskys, and Razumovskys; but then patronage faded like gilding, and Wagner had to go begging in support of sartorials and gourmandizing before mad Ludwig II and the luxuries of Bayreuth. Who would support Mahler, or those like him, if any were to follow? Socialism would not. And America's answer then is America's answer now, which shocked Mahler's Europe, used to censors and bursaries, state subsidies and aristocratic meddling. The Invisible Hand of the Market would prove a fickle conductor, impossible to follow.

Just as one sits with a program when faced with an hours-long concert of Mahler's music, when faced with such a titanic biography there's nothing to do but first look through the pictures. In the late nineteenth century, Mahler's parents, Bernhard and Marie, are posed separately in a provincial photography studio; in another shot, their six-year-old son, Gustav, hat in hand, stares off into the distance, *molto misterioso*. His white lace collar is perfectly in place; his other hand gestures to an ornate ironwork chair, on which rests a folder of sheet music. Following the official press photographs of Mahler's fame, with their suits, black cravats, and pince-nez, come the candids, the snapshots: Mahler, informally lounging. As if our paparazzi had taken an interest in German opera, the autocrat of the Hofoper is to be seen letting it all hang out: calm at his cottage at Toblach, with his daughter Anna on a rare morning spent outside his *Häuschen*, or composition hut. Family picnic at the Pragser Wildsee, 1910: Mahler and Alma alongside Oskar Fried, the first conductor to record Mahler's music, who would commit the Second Symphony to disc more than a decade later. Then, the couple onboard the *Amerika*, the boat that was bringing Mahler home to die, 1911. In these photos, the tie is no longer immaculate; the hairline has receded, the locks themselves are tangled; the shirt is a touch untucked, and the belly pouches;

there is often a hand—the conducting hand, the composing hand—reposing in a pocket.

As technology becomes more familiar, we become more familiar to ourselves. Whereas paintings aggrandize their subjects, photography has a way of scything even a genius down to size. As they enter the twentieth century, Mahler's symphonies, like the latter images of their composer, become less fit for public consumption. In a Vienna in decline as in an America ascendant, social mores relax like waistbands; we kick off our shoes and, with them, our pretense. From the cracks between empire formality and global informality, neuroses bloom, best described by another Germanic Jew estranged in Bohemia, Kafka, to whom Mahler would be compared by Adorno. Critical theory as pioneered by Adorno would tell us that Mahler's formal, stylized portraits represent preference as opposed to reality; they show us how Mahler wanted to be seen as opposed to how he actually was, or how he was seen by his contemporaries. Like an antique idea of musical appreciation, the ideal photograph of the old style would confirm nothing more than class or good breeding, not necessarily taste, and certainly not individuality.

Such picture-perfect respectability would be destroyed by WWI, after which Mahler's disciple Schoenberg would aver that an art that had been popular could not, by definition, be an art that was good, and any music that was hated by the old order was destined to be loved not only by the new but by posterity. The Romantic would birth the revolutionary, then, and times would change, not cyclically but forever; generations would no longer be reactionary toward one another—as the generation that enjoyed Beethoven did not enjoy Wagner, and the generation that enjoyed Wagner did not enjoy Mahler—but instead would become consolidated into a single mass, no longer stratified. Karl Marx described such a revolution against history in political terms; Walter Benjamin, in messianic terms; Mahler's music provides anthems for both.

It's telling to remember, amid the twilight of Romanticism and the rise of what Benjamin called "mechanical reproduction," that no recordings or films of Mahler exist. Neither radio, on which music was first broadcast in 1906, nor audio recording, which didn't become feasible for orchestras until after WWI, ever captured the maestro conducting—not opera, not any of his own compositions. His absence here speaks every cliché in the world: "louder than words," certainly louder than de La Grange's logorrhea. All that exists of a biographical Mahler outside the many pages of his many biographies are four Welte-Mignon pianola rolls of him playing his own lieder and movements from two symphonies. They are, and the response they engender is, ghostly automatic.

Ultimately, asking how our time is different from Mahler's is to ask whether history repeats, and whether yesterday, even if unrecorded, can communicate to the present and future. That history cannot repeat, which is an idea infused with both European Weltschmerz and hopeful American gusto, finds resonance in Mahler's greatest contribution to compositional technique—what has been called "progressive tonality."

In this technique, a work begins in one tonality and ends in another, unlike the symphonies of Beethoven, which tend to end in the keys in which they begin: Even a movement of a late Beethoven string quartet begins in A minor and ends in A minor, despite what middle modulations transpire. If Mahler were to have scored history itself, then that music, like the music he actually lived to compose, would grow to oppose sonata form, in which an exposition is always, after a development, brought back to itself with a recapitulation. The philosophical program for this most generative of musical forms is that of dialectics as defined by Fichte, but popularly attributed to Hegel, who was born in the same year as Beethoven, the foremost innovator of the nineteenth-century sonata. In a classic dialectic, a thesis (exposition), followed by an antithesis (development), leads to a final synthesis (recapitulation), which, as a consonance of thought, has more in common with the initial thesis movement than does dissonance, which was always thought antithetical to philosophy and especially religion.[1]

Such a pattern played out in Mahler's milieu of Germanic Jews. Mahler, like Kafka, like Karl Marx a generation before, was born into the bourgeoisie, then became an artistic "Bohemian," if only to redeem himself from guilt, before he was expected to be reabsorbed by the bourgeoisie, in a classical resolution, as if the key of home and hearth were a sunny C major. Except it wasn't, and the basses surged beneath on a soured tone. Kafka left his parents' house in Prague for a young Polish girlfriend and Berlin; Marx abroad

1. Although Bach and Mozart both ended compositions in different keys than they began them (as did Schubert, Schumann, and numerous opera composers), Mahler applied this practice to pure music, establishing it not as a dramatic conceit but as an analogue, or technique, for transcendence. The term "progressive tonality" was first used by Dika Newlin, a student of Schoenberg's at UCLA and, later, a punk-rock musician.

in Paris abandoned verse and metaphysics, entering politics to effect not art but change. Revolution is just that, an inability to be reintegrated, and, unlike his life, Mahler's music cannot be reintegrated. Forsaking the sonata's inevitable resolution, his compositions can lead only to discord, in a progressive development with no recapitulation save death. The ultimate modern depressive, Mahler fell in love with his death as the final finale, and this love, a one-man version of Wagner's *Liebestod*, is what elicits our empathy today. The soundtrack of this death, because so much about Mahler's life is cinematic, has become the soundtrack to all death, even to the death of music, and the fact that Mahler's symphonies lack a certain program or biography for whatever degenerescence has been scored allows us to impute sufferings of our own, to become, in them, acting conductors of our personal mortalities.

It's reductive but romantic to say that as Mahler dies, the uppercase Artist goes thanatopsical too. As Karlheinz Stockhausen wrote in his Age of Aquarius introduction to de La Grange's first volume (1973): "This is one of the first monuments of the new world-era, in which Mahlers will become scarcer while biography upon biography will be written." After Mahler, Schoenberg's dodecaphonic disciples equalized dissonance and consonance, then retreated to the academy, where composed music subsists on charity and tenure; with the spread of record and radio, pop repertoire began to trump the classics, and radio began to sell advertising time (it's advertising that allowed our playbills, the name since trademarked, to be printed and distributed for free from 1884, the year Mahler scored his First Symphony);

moving pictures with sound were only a war away, and television would later serve to further moot the visual allure of live music.

The individual genius, like any individual, becomes devalued by a mass market; and an insistence on perpetual revisionism has saved our age both from false artistic gods and from the seriousness necessary to make godlike art. Furthermore, any true biography or program intending to describe Mahler's "world-era" should engage with the Holocaust, which sounded the last discordant cadence of Mitteleuropean culture. It was the death camps of the east that not only killed but further decontextualized its victims, among them, in American hagiography, Mahler himself. Although the composer could not have been personally martyred in that tragedy, his posterity was—his symphonies said, by the Mahler-maniacal Leonard Bernstein, to have prefigured the terrors of Auschwitz. Hitler was present along with Mahler at the premiere of Strauss's *Salome* and even heard the director of the Hofoper himself conduct *Tristan und Isolde* in May 1906. But Hitler did not kill Mahler, and contrary to myth, America didn't either; it advertised and paid well for his talent. Mahler made many times over in New York salary whatever he lost of Vienna's showy but disingenuous obeisance.

In the end, however, none of these programs work. Mahler supposedly said, "My time will come," and Bernstein, kitschmeister extraordinaire, did much to make that utterance public. But Mahler, referring to Strauss, had actually written: "My time will come when his is over." Enter confusion, center stage: Sometimes it's better to know everything; other times it's better to know nothing. Between the acts, we can talk, though music is allowed.

FENCING FOR HITLER:
ON HELENE MAYER

If sport is a surrogate for war, fencing comes a touch too close to the real—ninety centimeters to be exact— though swords, like lives, were shorter in the Middle Ages. What is athletic now was once practical training for knights: Swords—later "foiled," beaten not quite into plowshares but into foils, sabres, épées—were only permitted to noblemen, who often got themselves into duels. A man insulted you or your lady and you challenged him to fight. There were rules. There was death.

By the early Renaissance, students too were allowed to carry swords, and a culture of rapier practice emerged that would gradually be officialized, in the German-speaking countries, as *Mensur*, or "academic fencing"—an extracurricular pastime, organized by university administrations, intended not to settle scores or provide exercise but instead to build character through doing both. Bloody swordplay became ludic fencing— as in the Anglo-Saxon "defense"—a sublimation game without winner or loser.

By the turn of the nineteenth century, Jews had joined the sport through fraternities that provided protection along with a formal, relatively nonviolent way to respond to anti-Semitic provocations and defend honor. Fencing matches between Jewish and non-Jewish clubs to settle individual disputes drew capacity crowds, with the result that the Jewish physique—so subject to stereotype, eugenics, phrenology, Mendelization—was normalized through scars, or "smites," proud badges of the *Kaiserreich*-educated. Jewish and non-Jewish women, in turn, formed their own clubs, and the best clubs of both sexes were religiously and ethnically integrated by

275

WWI. In 1924, women's fencing became an Olympic event (men's fencing had been admitted to the first modern Games, of 1896). And in 1936, the épée was first fitted with an electrical sensor, meaning a hit, or touch, became pure data, no longer left to a judge's call. Nazi predilections for technology and taxonomy were about to mark the Berlin Olympics.

The two most compelling competitors were *"der Neger,"* the American track star Jesse Owens, with his four gold medals, and the German-Jewish fencing goddess Helene Mayer. Born in Offenbach-am-Main in 1910, she was only bat mitzvah age—though she never had a bat mitzvah—when she gave up ballet and won her first German women's fencing championship. She might have gone to the Olympics that year—1924, the year after Hitler's unsuccessful coup in Munich—if Germany, still suffering the Treaty of Versailles, had been allowed to compete. By 1930, she'd won six German championships. Germany was readmitted to the International Olympic Committee in time for the 1928 Amsterdam Games. Mayer won gold.

In the 1930s, Mayer was presented, she self-presented, as an Aryan heroine, a pinup Valkyrie—five foot ten, 150 pounds. As an anonymous scrap of German newspaper doggerel put it:

> *A female creature of modern times,*
> *she wins handily in her fencing costume,*
> *and behold, she has blond braids,*
> *and ties around them a white band.*
> *A blue eye, a German skull,*
> *youth's grace in her countenance,*
> *a well-built girl from the Rhineland—*
> *but she fences like the devil.*

276

Plaster-of-Paris statuettes of her, Greco-Roman in modeling, sold wildly. *Heil He*—pronounced "hey"—was her cheer.

Mayer arrived at the 1932 Los Angeles Games as excited to tour Hollywood as to repeat victory, but she lost, placing fifth. Just two hours before the final matches, she'd been informed that a German team ship, the *Niobe*, had sunk, drowning all sixty passengers, including her boyfriend, Dr. Alexander Gelhar. Disconsolate and contemplating retirement, Mayer made the lucky choice to stay in Southern California, enrolling at Scripps College, where she founded a fencing program and studied European languages, idealistically hoping for a job with the German Foreign Service.

In January 1933, Hitler was appointed *Reichskanzler;* in April, the Offenbach Fencing Club rescinded her membership, citing newly passed Nazi legislation that, while it excluded Jews from the civil service, did not extend its reach to private organizations. No outcry ensued, however. The Reichstag was burning. With a physician father who was Jewish and a Protestant mother, Mayer wouldn't be spared, not even in California, the even harsher laws soon ratified in Nuremberg.

The Olympics, Hitler had said, are "a ploy inspired by Judaism that cannot possibly be put on by a Reich ruled by National Socialists." But by late 1933, Propaganda Minister Joseph Goebbels induced a rare change of heart. The Berlin Olympics would be a means of introducing the new Reich to the world: At a cost of 20 million reichsmarks, and in the span of only three years, unprecedented stadia and infrastructure were built; for the duration of the Games, no anti-Semitic media were broadcast or published (though the indefatigable *Der Stürmer* managed one commemorative issue);

huge Nazi flags were hung from balconies (though Jewish households were only allowed, or compelled, to fly the Olympic rings banner); Leni Riefenstahl filmed the proceedings.

The Jewish Question of 1936 was whether Jewish athletes would be allowed to compete. In early 1933, the Nazi delegation assured the IOC that Jewish athletes would be permitted, at least, to qualify—a stipulation that could have camouflaged rigged results. (Ultimately, Nuremberg's ban of Jews from training facilities and shuttering of Jewish sports clubs made such meddling extraneous.) The Amateur Athletic Union, the governing body of the American team, proposed a boycott; the American Jewish community petitioned President Hoover to condemn "the Naziad." Fearing an international incident, Hitler and Goebbels relented. Two token "Jews"—athletes hastily determined to be *Mischlinge*, or mixed-blood—were invited to join the German team: Mayer and high jumper Gretel Bergmann. (Similarly, *Mischlinge* ice hockey player Rudi Ball competed in the Winter Games in Garmisch-Partenkirchen; 1936 was the last year that Summer and Winter Games were held in the same year and same country.)

Mayer, now residing in the Bay Area, maintained silence until she was formally invited, at which point she chose not to celebrate but to act—and not with a thrust or a parry, but with a "riposte," the conversion of a defensive maneuver into an offensive strike. Using the official letterhead of Mills College, where she was teaching German, Mayer wrote to inform the Nazi government that she'd join the German team only if her full rights as a German citizen were restored. But was this a daring ultimatum? Or merely the desperate lunging of a young woman separated from her family and fans? Neither the government nor the *Reichssportführer* responded: Inaction, which is dangerous on the piste, is frequently the cunningest diplomatic tactic. Eventually Mayer decided to accept and join her homeland anyway—perhaps reasoning that her performance could convince the authorities in a way her correspondence couldn't.

Over one hundred thousand *Israeliten* had fled Germany since Hitler assumed power, and here was one woman, wielding a toy sword, wanting in. She was naïve, opportunistic, ignorant, a selfish, frivolous girl. It often seemed as if Mayer was as excoriated by American Jews—the Yiddish press enjoyed calling her "calculating" and "cynical"—as she was in Germany. Or would have been, had the German public been allowed to know of her presence. Goebbels embargoed her: She was not reported on, unphotographed; "no comments," he decreed, "may be made regarding Helene Mayer's non-Aryan ancestry or her expectations for a gold medal." The Führer shook her hand as he greeted all the German athletes; apparently, not even he could identify her.

Mayer won silver in her main event, individual foil. Thirteen "Jews"—most of them uncomfortable with that distinction—medaled at the Nazi Olympics, many in fencing. Endre Kabos of Hungary won two golds in sabre; the female fencers who won gold and bronze in individual foil, Ilona Schacherer-Elek of Hungary and Ellen Preis of Austria, were also "Jewish," and they stood solemnly with Mayer atop the medal platform as Mayer upstaged them both in a dramatic white outfit, bedecked with a swastika. At the conclusion of the ceremony, she, with that long limb, gave the Nazi salute—memorable, public, captured on film. Returning to the States directly after, Mayer refused to explain her behavior; later, she'd claim it might have helped protect family still in Germany (her brothers, Eugen and Ludwig, survived the war in labor camps).

After Berlin, she was ranked number one in foil in America eight times between 1934 and 1946. But there were no Olympics until 1948, by which time Germany was decimated; Mayer's longtime relationship with an industrial designer, Joseph Sinel, had come to an end; and her health was failing. She'd quit Mills College, citing clinical depression, and was teaching at San Francisco City College when the diagnosis came: breast cancer. She immediately sought out an advantageous marriage. By the time she'd wed Baron Erwin Falkner von Sonnenburg—a former indifferent Nazi and flight engineer—and repatriated to Germany in 1952, the cancer had metastasized to her spine. She died in 1953, at the age of forty-two, and was buried in Munich.

It's a strange and inexplicable fact that more major Jewish fencers were murdered in Nazi camps than were accomplished athletes of any other sport. Otto Herschmann died in Izbica; János Garay and Oszkár Gerde in Mauthausen; Lion van Minden and Simon Okker, veterans of the 1908 London Games, in Auschwitz. Attila Petschauer was recognized as an Olympian in the Davidovka concentration camp by the commandant, Kálmán Cseh von Szent-Katolna, who'd competed for the Hungarians as an equestrian. But this was not Amsterdam 1928, it was Ukraine 1944, a milieu less renowned for fair play. Von Szent-Katolna's torture of Petschauer came to resemble, consciously or not, competition's darkest perversion: Guards forced the champion to climb trees naked while they hosed him with freezing water until he succumbed to hypothermia.

(Endre Kabos, the 1936 Berlin gold medalist, died when the lorry he was using to ferry ammunition for the resistance exploded on Budapest's Margit Bridge.)

The next time the Olympics were held in Germany, it was 1972 and the country was called West Germany. A Palestinian terror squad massacred eleven Israeli team members: two wrestlers, a wrestling coach and referee, three weightlifters and a weightlifting judge, a shooting coach, a track and field coach, and Andre Spitzer, the fencing coach, who'd co-founded Israel's fencing academy. He was shot in the head. To be a Jew after the Holocaust would mean, for better or worse, to sharpen one's blade.

SPEAK EASY:
ON BOHUMIL HRABAL

Once upon a time a friend of a friend was drinking at a pub in Prague—U Zlatého Tygra (At the Golden Tiger). That this friend of a friend was a Fellow American should tell you that this was post-'89—after the Velvet Revolution, when hordes of Czechs and Slovaks revolted against Sovietism, jingled their keys on Wenceslas Square, and elected a literocracy: a playwright-president (Václav Havel), who appointed fellow writers to portfolio positions: poet-ministers, novelist-ambassadors. This Fellow American had arrived in Prague to witness history, get drunk for cheap, and get laid (perhaps he was also writing a novel). Alienated but empowered by Reaganomics, eager to tour the ruins of the Cold War—his generation's only war—this latter-day Hemingway was to participate in the mass capitalization of the Eastern Bloc's capitals: Once the Baltics had rebelled, the Berlin Wall fell, the Warsaw Pact went, and with it went Moscow. Soon the U.S.S.R. had no satellites, save those used transmitting TV footage of it all.

Plzeňský Prazdroj (aka Pilsner Urquell, Bohemia's definitive pilsner), Krušovice (a more refined, smoother beer, stereotypically "for the ladies"), Staropramen ("the workers' choice")—this friend of a friend consumed them all and eventually had to urinate. An old man leaned in the doorway to the surely dim graffitied bathroom. He had his hand out and was demanding twenty crowns—in German since he didn't think our hero understood Czech: *Zwanzig koruny, bitte.* Did the friend of a friend find this strange? Maybe not: To this day the bathrooms of many postcommunist countries are superintended by older people—pensioners, most of them women—who subsist on the few koruny, złote, forints, or rubly required for a urinal or stall, loose squares of toilet paper, a palmful of pink powdered soap.

This friend of a friend, probably too drunk to realize that twenty crowns was too much, paid the man, went in, unzipped. While he's pissing, let's remember that Czech has creative genteelisms for male genitalia that measure up to any other language's: "Feather," "pen," "chimney," "bird and eggs" are all in routine usage. Upon emerging, our hero noticed the same man teetering at the farthest corner of the bar, surrounded by journalists and photographers. To be an American abroad is to be taken advantage of; all expats must expect some shaving off the top, a bartender's trimming. Back at his table he asked a waiter who the erstwhile attendant was, to which the waiter raised an actor's eyebrow: "Bohumil Hrabal," he replied. *"Nejlepší česk´y spisovatel"*—"the best Czech writer."

That story is essentially un-fact-checkable, which is appropriate for Hrabal, king of the drunken anecdote. Hrabal perfected the genre during all those nights spent at U Zlatého Tygra, where, as he told his wife, Eliška Hrabalová, he performed research by the liter, studying his stoolmates, who were, practically, his literary collaborators.

Before street addresses were introduced in Prague in the late eighteenth century—it proved easier to collect taxes from a numbered house—the city identified its establishments by heraldry lintelled over doorways. A golden tiger still prowls above the entrance to 17 Husova Street, formerly a brewery. The tiger is a violent animal, a symbol of strife, the sneaky counterpart to that nobler feline, the lion, official mascot of the Czechs, of Bohemia.[1] By the way, the bar where this anecdote came to me was U Rotundy (the Rotunda), or U Cěrného Vola (the Black Ox), or, I don't know—anyway, sometime in winter 2001.

But "anecdote," which word Hrabal's critics used to both praise and denigrate the informal form of his writings, is inaccurate. The term "anecdote"—cognates exist in every Slavic language—derives from the secret chronicles of Procopius of Caesarea, biographer of Justinian I, and last of the historians of Antiquity; *anecdota* means "unpublished writings." Officially unpublished for nearly a decade in Czechoslovakia, censored for almost his entire life, Hrabal suggested another term for his works: *pábení*, Englished by the writer Josef Škvorecký as "palavering," meaning "idle chatter" or "flattering babble," here intended to characterize looping, loopy conversation, as evinced by its Latin root, *parabola*, source also of that recursive form the parable. This is talk, or talky writing, that begins somewhere, goes elsewhere unrelated, only to return to its origins: its original subject and also, regardless of the intellectual flights taken, an earthy humor.

Pábení has a secondary definition: It's the word used for any conference conducted between parties with varying conceptions of civility, as in a parley between natives and foreigners. Hrabal's sense of the term encompasses both meanings, as his fallen narrators—born

1. Historically speaking, the word Čech, in Czech, possesses two meanings. It defines both a citizen of today's Czech Republic and a person from the lands of the former kingdom of Bohemia. The Czech Republic comprises the territories of two crowns: Bohemia and Moravia. A Moravian is a Czech insofar as he is a Czech citizen, but would take exception to being called a Bohemian.

bourgeois, reassigned to manual labor—meander between collegiate discussions of Goethe and the lowdown talk their factory colleagues employ, the ramblings of the un- or antiintellectual proletariat.

How Hrabal's palavering diverges from this second sense is that it's never dialogic: His books, most lacking quotationmarks, can be read as a single monologue, delivered by one man, half conquered and half conqueror—the *pábitel*, or "palaverer." "As a rule, a *pábitel* has read almost nothing," Hrabal once explained, "but on the other hand has seen and heard a great deal. And has forgotten almost nothing. He is captivated by his own inner monologue, with which he wanders the world, like a peacock with its beautiful plumage."

Nowhere is this palavering better developed than in Hrabal's autobiographical trilogy, translated only now in its entirety by Tony Liman, and in *Dancing Lessons for the Advanced in Age*, which, though it was Hrabal's first published novel, in 1964, is pretty much the last word in Hrabalovština. That term was invented as both a description and an embodiment of Hrabal's invented language: an amalgam of acrolect book Czech and Bohemian and Moravian slangs, infused with trade vernacular and ideological verbiage traduced from German and Russian. The trilogy—among the last texts Hrabal wrote and a fresh discovery for Anglo-American readers—is surely one of the supreme attempts at autoanalysis by a European writer under communism, while *Dancing Lessons*, translated by Michael Henry Heim (the title should really, if less mellifluously, be *Dancing Lessons for the Elderly and Advanced*), is a lighter, idiosyncratic affair: a nimble foxtrot through a sparsely punctuated hundred pages in which a period or question mark, an exclamation point or even a semicolon, would seem to interrupt the intoxicated flow of language like the pinch of the bladder that precurses the breaking of the seal:

> Bondy the poet once went to see my nephew, with his two babies in their baby buggy and because the pub closed after they'd drunk only three buckets of beer they took one home for the night and poured it into the washbasin and went on with their academic debate till they fell asleep, and my nephew woke up thinking a pipe had burst, but it was only poor Bondy pissing his two buckets onto the rug, after which he tumbled back into bed and didn't get up until morning when the babies began to bawl, and he looked around and shouted Eureka! out of the blue and started cheering and jumping up and down on the pisssoaked rug and shouting, Listen, everybody, not only people who aren't with us are with us, no, even people who are against us are with us, because you can't cut yourself off from your times, there you have it, ladies, now you see why poets love to drink and meditate, and just when things are looking grim the heavens open up and out comes a thought making its way to the light...

Turning foodstuffs to drink, brewing takes that which sustains and makes it debilitating. Turning water to wine is a comparatively meek transubstantiation. Wine is quaffed in Europe's sophisticated West; vodka—"little water"—in the cruder East; whereas bloating the Middle is beer. That beverage begins as grain; the land's bounty of wheat and oats and hops are gleaned (hops were introduced to brewing in the same century the Slavic tribes received an alphabet: the ninth) and fermented. Much in the same way, Hrabal harvested the floor talk from his day jobs—the iron and steel foundry at Kladno, the paper-compacting plant on Spálená Street in Prague—and pulled from that raw jawing, literature.

Born in 1914 in Brno, in Moravia, then part of the Austro-Hungarian Empire, Hrabal reached drinking age while living in Nymburk, in Bohemia, and working behind the walls of his stepfather's brewery, which, like all Czechoslovak businesses, was nationalized after WWII. Hrabal was a lusty adopter of Bohemia in every sense. Leaving Moravia's religiosity and folkways behind, he headed for more modern, Germanic precincts: the capital of a free Czechoslovakia between 1918 and 1939, and again after 1989, and of the Czech Republic after an independent Slovakia deaccessioned in 1993—Prague was his ultimate destination.

Innumerable poems, stories, and shoddy ad campaigns have fantasized that the river running through Prague, the Vltava—the Moldau in German—is a river of beer. On one bank is the city's administrative center; on the other, the nation's—the Castle, apostrophized by another son, Franz Kafka. Prague is a city of churches where no one goes to church, a city of synagogues without Jews. Literary Prague—aping the literary life of the empire's imperial cities, Budapest and Vienna—once enjoyed more of a café culture, conducted not in Czech but in German. Kafka and his future executor, Max Brod, along with Oskar Baum and Franz Werfel, were ersatz Viennese who aspired to the capital's caffeination, taking their beans with a dash of cream. Not for them the Slavic demimonde, the twilit taverns strewn with sawdust, their rusty tanks and taps—the Eastern accents of this Western metropolis were too gauche for the authors of *The Metamorphosis* and *The Song of Bernadette*.

Hrabal's literary predecessor was not Kafka but Jaroslav Hašek, author of *The Good Soldier Švejk* (often

Germanized as *Schweik*), whose hero is the prototypical inscrutable "fool." Švejk, cherished paragon of Czech consciousness, is either a moron or a crafty subversive, as he manages to evade action in WWI by being taken captive, in a stolen Russian uniform, by his own side's troops. Hašek, no shrunken consumptive, was bibulous and monumentally fat; his supranovelistic scribble wasn't a rarefied diary or excruciatingly psychological correspondence like Kafka's—Kafka and Hašek were exact contemporaries, born in 1883, twenty blocks apart—but rather whimsical items about murders and rapes for the local Czech press. Hrabal was the educated heir to the Germans, but he was more temperamentally suited to Hašek's company of syphilitic prostitutes and, as it were, syphilitics. German Kaffeekultur gave rise to expressionist and Symbolist texts, whereas Czech beer culture, *pivní kultura*, was defiantly narrative and lurid—as if coffee served as a cipher merely to center talk, and beer was talk's incitement.

Alcoholism would seem among the least concerns of communism. Already boasting one of the higest per-capita beer consumption rates in the world—surpassed in 1989 only by East Germany's—Czechoslovakia, like every Soviet protectorate, engaged in pro-forma propaganda discouraging drinking, especially in the workplace and during compulsory military service. The state couldn't actually afford for its citizens to go sober: With the breweries being state-owned, the more intoxicated the people, the richer, in every way, the party. It was ironic, then, that the perfect communist comrade was a dutiful teetotaler—not a man but a fictional character.

Homo socialist realismus—the literature would produce

its own readership, indistinguishable from its characters. Socialist Realist literature had to be about and for the proletariat; it had to depict the daily life of that population; that depiction had to be in a realist style, meaning it had to be accurate to the ideal of proletarian life and contain no experiments or formalisms; and, finally, it had to support but not independently further the objectives of the Communist Party (these being the diktats decided upon at the debut meeting of the Union of Soviet Writers in 1934). What resulted, in the Sputnik countries of the Warsaw Pact as in the Soviet Union, was a canon of childish unsubtlety—a fabling corpus in which nothing could be plotted without a moral, whether explicit or implied. The goal of this literature [sic] was not to entertain but to instruct, to make the perfect comrade by making a new type of writer—not a poet of inky individuality but rather, as that formidable poet Stalin put it, "an engineer of human souls."

A mad, maddening tautology: A Socialist Realist writer must write about reality in a realistic style while remaining partisan and at all times reinforcing the party line. When these two impulses came into conflict, the writer risked shading into the realm of irony or satire, and suddenly what had been didactic and simple became complex and revolutionary. This was the literature of those who wrote for oblivion or the drawer, for a dimly free future or for a cynically regarded, because illegal, posterity. Such writers, who remained (mostly) unpublished under communism, who, if they published, did so (mostly) in samizdat, represented the Eastern Bloc's only authentic international style, but only in retrospect. In its day its practitioners were scattered across too many countries and too many languages, with each responding both to a general Soviet politics and to the particular censorships of their home nations (it appears to have been easier to get away with writing subversively in Yugoslavia than in Russia, for example).

Socialist Realist fiction was too obviously occupied with schematic surface: A man is discharged from the Red Army a hero and returns to reorganize his hometown around a hyperprogressive cement factory (the novel *Cement* by Fyodor Gladkov). It was all exterior, a series of events or plot points demonstrating fate, synonymous in these books with political calling. By contrast, the corpora of censored or banned writers were usually more interested by the inner life—the mind, the one space from which no citizen can be exiled. Show a veteran working productively in a plant and you have created propaganda, but tell the thoughts of this man, tell us what he feels when he boozes at night and beats his children and wife, and you have an artwork—a dangerous artwork.

It was Hrabal's genius to redeem Socialist Realism by taking it literally, to its literal extreme, in the creation of verbatim documents of people trying to conform to societal norms, failing, and still wanting to succeed. Avoiding boring the bar with platitudes about the soul's oppression by totalitarianism, Hrabal preferred the objective approach of reproducing speech, from which any attentive patron might infer the appropriate conclusions.

In the autobiographies, Hrabal transcribes his own speech but has it pour out of the mouth of his wife, the narratrix Eliška, also called Miss Pipsi. Countess Tolstaya wrote a memoir of her husband that rivals even Gorky's classic reminiscence of Tolstoy; Anna Dostoyevskaya wrote similar memoirs; Hrabal tweaks that venerable tradition by ventriloquism. He has pre-empted posthumity by having his wife address the reader directly, when she's not reporting to Hrabal's mother, Marie Kiliánová, a failed actress. Hrabal exploits this uxorial distance to parody himself and gently rib his wife. While he has intense discussions about Action Painting and Allan Kaprow's Happenings with his painter friend, the "Explosionist" Vladimír Boudník, Eliška Hrabalová contents herself with nice needlepoints of Prague's spired skyline. The trilogy's first volume, *In-House Weddings*, narrates the couple's shy courtship; the second, *Vita Nuova*, has Hrabal beginning to write and publish; and the third, *Gaps*, fills in the rest with fame, Hrabal relaxing with his kittens at his dacha in Kersko, and traveling worldwide until, eventually—in a destiny perhaps fitting for someone so liquored—he's "liquidated," forbidden to publish.

Dancing Lessons is a wilder affair accomplished with a similar technique: Hrabal transcribed the ranting of his stepfather's brother, Uncle Pepin, veteran of "the most elegant army in the world," the Imperial Austrian army. In the novel, Pepin's "ludibrious" logorrhea (and wordplay) is given to an unnamed man whose metanarrative—he tells a story about how he used to tell stories to a bunch of "beauties," sunbathers in bikinis—touches on such subjects as Freud, the Czech nationalism of Karel Havlíček, and the transition from the monarchy to the First Czechoslovak Republic. Throughout, this narrator—"as sensitive as Mozart and an admirer of the European Renaissance"—relates and interprets his own dreams in a manner that combines Viennese psychoanalysis with Parisian Surrealism or Dadaism. Artists of every Mitteleuropean city put in time in Left Bank Paris, and the avant-gardities they encountered often found more potent, darker expressions back home: Hrabal's cutup techniques; the collages of Jindřich Štyrský and Vítězslav Nezval. All this geographic and cultural complication reminded Hrabal's readership that even as Soviet tanks rolled in to crush the 1968 Prague Spring uprising, the city's cinematic streets were filled with extras from Czech history: concentration-camp victims; school chums of T. G. Masaryk, the first Czechoslovak president; wannabe *poètes maudits;* old deposed gentry who'd flirted with Empress Maria Theresa.

It's this same panoramic, parabolic view that defines the perspective of the autobiographies: Hrabalová, as her husband has her explain, was Sudeten German by birth and Czech by accident, after her family was split up following WWII when the Beneš government expelled German nationals from western Bohemia. While her relatives lived prosperously in republican Vienna, Hrabalová moved into her husband's cramped peeling-plaster flat on Na Hrázi Street in the ramshackle Prague suburb of Libeň, where she was distrusted on account of her origins. The personal experience of history serves to refute notions of categorical good and evil, suggesting instead a pan-European complicity in postwar decline. The sheer convolution of alliances and birthrights justifies Hrabal's principle of historical passivity, which is just another term for a drunkard's politics.

If the state asserted that drinking was bad for work, Hrabal held that without drinking he wouldn't have been able to work at all, badly or well—either as laborer or novelist of labor. Hrabal's protagonists are all committed workers, and nobody writes about work with

292

more dignity than he who, like most Czech writers—save those approved by the regime—suffered the lowliest of manual jobbery for decades. The Pepinized palaverer of *Dancing Lessons* is a cobbler; in the autobiographies, Hrabalová calls her husband "doctor," and though Hrabal earned a doctorate in law from Charles University, he never practiced. He worked as a railway lineman and train dispatcher (experiences featured in *Closely Watched Trains*), insurance agent, traveling salesman, metalwork foreman, and sceneshifter in a provincial but influential theater. Hrabalová herself toiled as a waitress, providing her husband with insight for *I Served the King of England*, while Hrabal's stint as a baler and compactor informed *Too Loud a Solitude*, his most celebrated novel. (In the autobiographies, Hrabal has his wife note that among the many hundreds of books he saved from pulping were copies of his own early volumes—sent for destruction after his work incensed the censors after 1968.)

Only in a city where your garbageman was your greatest novelist, tasked with trashing his own output, could Václav Havel have coined the phrase "the power of the powerless," which served as the title of a provocative essay and as the commiserable epitaph for a generation of Eastern Bloc artists. Havel, for a time, had been frequenting Hrabal's local haunts to encourage him to add his signature to Charter 77, the Czech dissidence platform Havel coauthored, but Hrabal repeatedly refused, preferring not to further jeopardize the publication of *Too Loud a Solitude*—an action, or inaction, perhaps selfish or aloof but consistent with Hrabal's aim: to continue publishing, if only illegally. It was this very surrender that must have represented, to Hrabal, the essential power of the powerless: the power to opt out, to maintain daily normalcy while daily making vanguard art.

As major writers during the communist era, so minor cultures in the Europe of empire. The Czechs and Slovaks are still peoples at the crossroads, always at the mercy of neighboring nation-states. Mitteleuropa, which, according to Hrabal, terminated in the Russified East at the last Hapsburg train station—which would be in Lemberg, now Lviv, Ukraine—was never a toponym to be found on maps but rather a transnational entity founded on the skill of its underclass, the Slavs. Tour any railroad shed, church, palace, or decrepit municipal building in Germany, Austria, Hungary, or Poland and it was, most probably, built by Slav labor—the most mobile of a faction that, in the midst of Europe, was perpetually imperiled by its lesser numbers, lack of technology, and cloistral languages prickly about Germanic calquing. The power of the powerless, as Hrabal realized, was an inheritance much older than communism; *Dancing Lessons* proclaims this in its epigraph, from the Czech philosopher Ladislav Klima:

> Not only may one imagine that what is higher derives always and only from what is lower; one may imagine— given the polarity and, more important, the ludicrousness of the world—everything derives from its opposite: day from night, frailty from strength, deformity from beauty, fortune from misfortune. Victory is made up exclusively of beatings.

Prague's Charles Bridge hosts a famous miracle rub: a statue of John of Nepomuk, patron saint of the Czechs, who was dressed in a suit of armor and tossed off the bridge for not divulging the queen's confessions to her husband, King Wenceslas IV. Give the saint's bronze plaque a short pat or brush with a cuff and your wish will be granted, the superstition goes: St. John's pediment is shiny with use, its escutcheon's embellishments almost entirely worn away by centuries of pilgrims. A decade after publishing his memoirs, Hrabal was a walking, talking statue—a lucky living icon, faded from regular toasting.

The problem with being a notorious imbiber is that everyone wants to have a drink with you: even Bill Clinton made the trek to the Golden Tiger to shake the writer's shaky hand, a pickled relic. Some Czech critics after the fall of communism thought it their task to argue that Hrabal's drinking was about drinking; others chose to believe that the author's consumption was a protest, an attack against the state expressing itself as an attack against the self. It's this ambivalence that is at the heart, or cirrhotic liver, of Hrabal's compulsive venture. In this sense, debauchery perversely becomes a method of abstention: Regimes come and go, but alcohol is always legal. ("Reality is alcoholic," he once wrote.)

One winter afternoon in 1997, leaning out of his hospital-room window to feed the pigeons, Hrabal fell—from the fifth floor; the same floor he noted Kafka lived on and considered jumping from at the Oppelt House on Prague's Old Town Square; the same floor Rainer Maria Rilke, another Prague native, lived on in Paris and to which he consigned his doomed character Malte Laurids Brigge—not to mention Prague's enduring penchant for defenestrations. Hrabal, whose fall was rumored to have been a suicide—thanks to quintaphobic allusions to these fates sprinkled like birdseed throughout his later texts—never spotted a coincidence he did not advantage.

As the world watched the Berlin Wall come down on television, East Germans were heading to West

Germany to buy televisions. That type of consumerism supported literature for a few years—post-'89 editions of Hrabal's books sold out quickly—but what seemed at the time like the first drops of unprecedented promise seem now just the final dregs before eurozone homogenization. Books by Hrabal and Ivan Klima and Milan Kundera were bought for the same reasons televisions were: because they could be. Goods were goods, and the free market was good. Hrabal's manuscripts were always grammatically idiosyncratic because he wrote on a Perkeo Schreibmaschine, a popular model of German typewriter that the author had bartered from some Soviet soldiers during WWII. Being German, it lacked the acutes, haceks, and rings of Czech letters. Today we're free to interpret this materialist effect on a text as a mechanism of capitalism—the larger country exporting its typewriter to the smaller country, thereby affecting its future literature—just as in Hrabal's day the effacement of an autonomous culture was a communist concern. The power changes, the drinks remain the same.

FROM THE DIARIES

Museum Fact (Rijeka)

The shape of the anchor derives from the shape of the
arrow. An anchor is an arrow shot into the sea.

Critical Typo

"[...] if one considers for a moment the reverse perspective developed by Byzantine ant [...]"

HUNG LIKE AN OBELISK, HARD AS AN OLYMPIAN: AN ABECEDARIUM OF ENGLISH-LANGUAGE PUBLISHING IN PARIS

"A" IS FOR AVANT-GARDE

Before *l'avant-garde* came to characterize a movement in the arts, it was a military position: It referred to the front line of an advancing army, the soldiers sacrificed for the progress of the rest. It was in this way that the term was understood by the Napoleons. Over one thousand enemy cannon were captured in the Battle of Austerlitz, in which Napoleon I defeated the Russians and Austrians in winter 1805. The bronze from this artillery was melted down for an obelisk, erected in the Place Vendôme in Paris. Because of its proximity to the publisher's offices (16 Place Vendôme), this phallus of French glory became the imprimatur and namesake of the Obelisk Press, an English-language avant-garde and erotica publisher active throughout the 1930s, responsible for issuing works by the likes of James Joyce and Henry Miller. Obelisk's Napoleon was a Jew from Manchester, Jack Kahane. Following WWII, Kahane's eldest son, Maurice Girodias, founded the Olympia Press, redoubling Obelisk's crusade against Anglo-American censorship by publishing the likes of William S. Burroughs and Vladimir Nabokov. Olympia financed this vanguard by publishing explicit pornography—referred to in-house as "d.b.s," "dirty books"—that, like the artistic works of the house's marquee authors, challenged the obscenity laws of the countries of their linguistic audience: Britain and America. Olympia's porn also proved popular among American GIs stationed in Paris—men lonely for sex and the language of home.[1]

"B" IS FOR BATAILLE, GEORGES

Ignored in his own lifetime but posthumously lauded by Derrida, Foucault, Barthes, and Baudrillard, Georges Bataille (1897–1962) was a Catholic seminary dropout and a French writer of surrealistically sensualist fiction and poetry, and mystical philosophy. His best novel, *Histoire de l'oeil* (*Story of the Eye*), today a classic of obscure symbolism and underage sex, was published in 1928 and peremptorily banned. American Austryn Wainhouse's 1953 translation was called *A Tale of Satisfied Desire*, a title received from Girodias himself, who hoped to prevent the authorities from noticing any connection between the French and English editions. The English edition was published under the pseudonym Pierre Angélique, while Bataille's French pseudonym for the book had been Lord Auch, literally Lord to the Shittery, *auch* being a condensation of *aux chiottes*, slang used to reprove a person by telling them off "to the toilets."

"C" IS FOR CHESTER, ALFRED

Alfred Chester, born in 1927 in Jewish Brooklyn to Russian immigrant parents, can be regarded as a typical Olympia author: a *littérateur* who took fiction seriously, and financially supported that seriousness with the hack

1. Alternatively, and perhaps more convincingly, Obelisk's name and colophon are said to have been inspired by the ancient Egyptian Obelisk of Luxor. Dating from the reign of Ramses II, hieroglyphed from bottom to top, that monumental column had guarded the entrance to the Luxor Temple and was a gift of goodwill from Egypt to Louis-Philippe I, the last King of France. It was erected, in 1836, in Paris's Place de la Concorde, just a handful of blocks from the Vendôme column and the future site of the press's offices.

writing of a pornographic novel. Due to a rare childhood disease, the pasty, pudgy Chester went bald at a young age and took to wearing outlandish, ratty wigs. In 1953, Chester decamped New York for Paris, and in 1955 published his sole Olympia d.b., entitled *The Chariot of Flesh* (the *The* was dropped in future editions), under the name Malcolm Nesbit. In 1959, with money from the sale of a story to *The New Yorker*, Chester returned to New York, where he became one of the foremost critics of the '60s, writing witty, scabrous reviews for *The New York Review of Books*, *Partisan Review*, and *Commentary*. But sensing his true calling was in fiction—his novels are *Jamie Is My Heart's Desire* and *Exquisite Corpse*—Chester abandoned journalism and moved to Tangiers, where, with the help of pills and alcohol, he lost his mind and friends. He was deported from Morocco (which, in those tolerant days, was quite the achievement) and found his way to Israel, where he died a probable suicide in 1971. Chester self-defined as homosexual, though he gave Cynthia Ozick her first kiss, once offered to marry Susan Sontag, and seemed not to have difficulty producing heterosexual porn (Olympia's misogynistic sex world was almost exclusively hetero, plus lesbian). *Chariot of Flesh* is an excellent example of a rush-job d.b., though it is also notable for scenarios that speak to the author's personal proclivities:

It was difficult to believe that this tearful boy sucking my penis was the same as the one who had raped Carla. In any case, I flung him away. He returned, and I pushed him again, harder than I intended. Coming back, he deliberately provoked me into hitting him, and he continued to do so. We both became a little wild, and I pounded him with all my strength. It was a while before I realized how much he was enjoying it. He moaned and sighed; his penis was in an enormous state of erection. I'd gone so far, I couldn't stop, and I continued beating him, pinching him, tearing at him until he was bloody. With each wound I inflicted, his passion rose, and he rubbed against my body, giving it small wet kisses. He dropped into a heap at my feet, begging me to kick him, and I did, again and again, and each time he came back to stroke, lick, kiss my ankles, knees or thighs. Half-crazy I threw myself on him; his buttocks rose under me, and suddenly we were locked together. And while we rolled and swayed, I continued pounding him and pinching him as if this last horrible act must purge me of all the terrible degeneracy of the past two weeks. My member throbbed in and out of him, tearing at him, and finally I came.

"D" IS FOR DONLEAVY, J.P.

James Patrick Donleavy was born in 1926 to Irish immigrants in New York. Joining the U.S. Navy brought him to Europe. After WWII, Donleavy settled in Ireland and wrote. His first and best book, *The Ginger Man*, about the sexual exploits of Sebastian Dangerfield, was published by Olympia in 1955, but would bring down the press a decade later. Naïve Donleavy had expected his book to be published in the manner of Henry Miller's, which is to say respectfully, as literature. However, Girodias decided to publish it as Volume 7 in the Traveller's Companion series of raunchy sex books (Chester's *Chariot of Flesh* was Volume 12 of the series, whose other titles included *Rape*, *The Loins of Amon*, *The Libertine*, and *Tender Was My Flesh*). Piqued, Donleavy made the cuts necessary to avoid prosecution under Britain's obscenity laws and resold his book to a U.K. publisher in 1956, depriving Olympia of an audience for its edition. Adding to the lawsuits already proliferating, the expurgated version of *The Ginger Man* appeared in America in 1958. As the novel went on to sell tens of thousands of copies, Girodias felt that his press was due a portion of the royalties. There were problems, however, with Olympia's filing of copyright and with Girodias's always late reports of sales to the author, causing courts to rule in Donleavy's favor. Girodias and Donleavy would litigate against each other across two decades and two continents. In 1968, Olympia went bankrupt and was put on the block. Despite Girodias's attempts to keep the auction secret, Donleavy sent his then-wife, actress Mary Wilson Price (later, Mary Guinness), to Paris, where she bid against Girodias for ownership of his press. Price's deeper pockets won out and Olympia remained her property until her death. With the press that had sued him for rights to the royalties of his book now part of his own portfolio, Donleavy was essentially suing himself, and *The Ginger Man* killed the press that, a decade earlier, had given it life.

"E" IS FOR ÉDOUARD MANET

Olympia was named after *Olympia*, a painting by Édouard Manet (1832–83). Manet's entry into the 1863 Salon, the annual exhibition of the Académie des Beaux-Art, had been the rejected *Le déjeuner sur l'herbe*, which, in its subsequent showing in the Salon des Réfusés, scandalized with its depiction of a nude woman (modeled by fellow painter Victorine Meurent), whose nudity alludes to mythology, but who is enjoying a picnic with men in modern clothing. In 1865, Manet offered the Salon his roughshod, frank portrait of a lounging odalisque, or prostitute (also modeled by Meurent), being attended to by her African servant. Upon its inexplicable acceptance, *Olympia* caused a furor that Manet had to have expected. Still, he complained to Baudelaire: "Abuses rain upon me like hail. I have never before been in such a fix. ... I should have wished to have your sound opinion of my work, for all this outcry is disturbing and clearly somebody is wrong."

"F" IS FOR FRANCE
France is a French-speaking country located just across the English Channel from the most formidable English-language literary market outside the United States. Lost Generation conspirators as disparate as Fitzgerald, Hemingway, and Stein found the cheap, libertine Paris of the '20s conducive to reflection on American home. But their freewheeling, freespending spirit was crushed in 1929 with the onset of Depression. As American novelists, painters, and composers evacuated the Left Bank in droves, Kahane's Obelisk opened shop. The spirit of France's third and fourth republics, from the fall of Napoleon III, the last French emperor, to postwar reconstruction in the wake of Nazi devastation, is best embodied by Obelisk and Olympia's smutty paperback books, which liberated the world once clearing customs between Calais and prudish Dover.

"G" IS FOR GIRODIAS, MAURICE
Olympia's founder, "a second-generation Anglo-French pornographer," as he described himself, was born Maurice Kahane in Paris in 1919. The Nazi occupation compelled him to exchange his Jewish surname for his mother's Spanish sobriquet. As Girodias, he survived WWII by publishing a weekly film guide, *Paris-Programme*, and supplying paper to the Reich. Following the war, Girodias and his publishing ventures were

accused of committing every conceivable offense under the guise of free speech, including obscenity, indecency, defamation, and what would later come to be called hate speech and child pornography. With Anglo-American censorship disappearing by the late '60s, Gallic glamour fading under de Gaulle, and Olympia collapsing around him, the occasionally dishonest, always disorganized Girodias relocated to the United States, where his attempts to establish various American Olympia imprints were perennially frustrated. Girodias was forced to return to France and died in Paris in 1990. Though chiefly known for publishing prose, Girodias was also talented at writing it, as evinced by this excerpt from *The Frog Prince*, the first of his three autobiographies. Here the author loses his virginity to Didi, a Provençal waitress:

> For my part, I am so carried away in delight that I've completely forgotten my own desires. A need more subtle than mine has me captivated. I ask nothing more than to serve my beautiful Didi, for she and I are now bound by a common passion, which is for her body. The desire in my hands penetrates her flesh deeply. She loves that beautiful skin of hers as it glows with the pleasure of my caresses. My clumsy admiration arouses in her a narcissistic voluptuousness, for she takes my beginner's errors for subtle refinements; and she no longer knows what is happening, she's deliciously disoriented. I thank my stars, I treasure my luck, I even congratulate myself on my ignorance.

"H" IS FOR HARRIS, FRANK

James Thomas (Frank) Harris, born in Ireland in 1856, was a short, husky sex maniac who slept and talked and wrote his way around the world, paying his bills as a cowboy, lawyer, journalist, playwright, and "sandhog" (caisson excavator) on the Brooklyn Bridge. Kahane met Harris in 1912 in Manchester, where Harris was lecturing at the Midland Hotel in support of his book *The Man Shakespeare*, which opined that the playwright had encoded his personality in the soliloquies of his leading men and argued that Mary Fitton, maid of honor to Elizabeth I, was the Dark Lady of the sonnets. That book was unanimously derided, though it could not do as much damage as *My Life and Loves*, Harris's prolix memoirs in four volumes, which he self-published throughout the '20s, destroying himself financially. After Harris's death in Nice in 1931, however, Kahane put out a reprint, and *My Life and Loves*, rife with vain, preening coitus, would become an exceptional seller for both Obelisk and Olympia for decades. A fifth volume of lewd hagiography appeared in 1954, ghostwritten in grand impersonation of Harris's style by Alexander Trocchi, and is commonly regarded as the best of the set.

"I" IS FOR INSIDE SCIENTOLOGY

Inside Scientology: How I Joined Scientology and Became Superhuman was written by former Scientologist Robert Kaufman and published by Olympia U.S.A. in 1972 (Olympia U.S.A. was one of the press's American incarnations, founded after Girodias lost Olympia Paris and became, like his father, an expatriate). Kaufman's book was the first to publicly criticize the Church of Scientology and also to reveal its organizational secrets by reproducing founder L. Ron Hubbard's staff instructions and training techniques. The Church is said to have immediately responded: Allegedly, it mailed thousands of letters to Olympia's U.K. associates, informing them, on forged Olympia letterhead, that Olympia U.S.A. had gone out of business. One morning, a blond woman appeared at Girodias's office, claiming an interest in his legal affairs. According to Girodias, she drove him to New Jersey and abandoned him, under false pretense, at the Port of Newark, having planted marijuana on his person. Girodias was charged with trespass on property without legitimate purpose and possession of a controlled dangerous substance, but this being his first offense, he was only given probation. In 1974, however, a letter accusing Girodias of violating the terms of his U.S. visa was sent to Henry Kissinger at the State Department, on the occasion of Olympia U.S.A.'s publication of the horny dystopian novel *President Kissinger*. Girodias would be forced to leave the country unless he could find another way to maintain his status. The Church of Scientology, which Girodias suspected was behind the Kissinger letter, would then be responsible for Girodias's marriage to medical student Lilla Cabot Lyon, a union that briefly extended his American residence.

"J" IS FOR JOYCE, JAMES

Hoping for literary glory, Kahane wished to reproduce the success of Sylvia Beach's publication of James Joyce's *Ulysses* through her bookstore, Shakespeare & Company, in 1922. By 1929 all the great avant-garde English-language publishing houses of Paris had died—Shakespeare, Three Mountains Press, Contact Editions—and so, in search of an unattached name with which to launch his venture (which he was then calling the Fountain Press, operating in collaboration with printer Henry Babou), the dandyish Kahane pestered the spinsterly Beach into introducing him to that blind Irishman he called God. For 50,000 francs, Kahane purchased the rights to publish five thousand words entitled *Haveth Childers Everywhere*, the first excerpt of Joyce's last novel, *Finnegans Wake*. *H.C.E.* was published by Obelisk in 1930 in a deluxe edition of six hundred copies (one hundred printed on "mother-of-pearl Japanese vellum paper"). Two years later, Obelisk published Joyce's *Pomes Penyeach*, with illustrations by Lucia Joyce, the author's daughter. Kahane, in a letter praising the sketches, admitted he found her father's texts unreadable.

"K" IS FOR KAHANE, JACK

Jack Kahane, born in 1887, the Mancunian son of Romanian Jews, first made his name as a poet and dramatist, and as a polemicist who accused Hans Richter, famed German musician and principal conductor of Manchester's Hallé Orchestra, of too infrequently programming French repertoire. Richter quit the orchestra in the wake of Kahane's press campaign while the young arch-Francophile, newly understanding the value of publicity, went on to found the Swan Club, Manchester's leading literary salon, the denizens of which included playwrights Harold Brighouse and Stanley Houghton. Kahane served in WWI, was wounded, and convalesced in France, where he met and married Marcelle Girodias, the Spanish-born Catholic French daughter of an engineer who'd built railroads across Spain, Portugal, North Africa, and South America. During his recovery, which was also the couple's honeymoon, Kahane began writing fiction. His most popular novel was his first, a bubbly but prim concoction called *Laugh and Grow Rich*. Kahane's other books include six erotic novels written under the name Cecil Barr, after a favorite pub, the Cecil Bar, and his 1939 *Memoirs of a Booklegger*. Natalie Barney held Friday soirées; Gertrude Stein and

Alice B. Toklas had their klatsch on Saturdays; while Sylvia Beach's bookstore was open for business daily; but by 1929, as those great salons disappeared, and Americans left for home, Kahane began to envision two possibilities for his literary future. First, he could step in to publish the work of eminences like Joyce; second, he could support such idealism by making money off British tourists interested in buying English-language books, of all kinds, that were banned in their own country. Kahane was the only expatriate publisher in interwar Paris who wasn't independently wealthy and so found it necessary to profit from everything he chose to put between covers. Kahane's Obelisk published work by Joyce, Miller, D. H. Lawrence, Richard Aldington, and Cyril Connolly, alongside mild smut such as *To Beg I Am Ashamed* ("the autobiography of a London prostitute") and *Mad About Women*, by "the Marco Polo of sex," N. Reynolds Packard, Rome correspondent for the New York *Daily News*. Obelisk died when Kahane died, in September 1939, with the Nazis invading Poland, the Vichy regime a winter away.

"L" IS FOR NAKED LUNCH

Olympia originally rejected William S. Burroughs's seminal novel because, literally, its manuscript was soaked—it'd been steeped in alcohol, burned by cigarettes, and nibbled by rats. Always a footloose collation of pages, *Naked Lunch* would be resubmitted in a fresh copy, with organizational help from Allen Ginsberg and Gregory Corso and typing assistance from Jack Kerouac, who also suggested its title. Girodias accepted and published the manuscript in 1959. Purportedly, Girodias was convinced to acquire Burroughs's book not by any intrinsic quality of the writing, but thanks to the scandalous publication of excerpts in a magazine called *Big Table*, a name Kerouac had suggested as well. Barney Rosset at Grove Press purchased the American rights, but proceeded to warehouse ten thousand copies of the book, awaiting the resolution of Henry Miller's *Tropic of Cancer* obscenity trial to know whether works like Miller's and Burroughs's would be allowed American distribution (Obelisk had published Miller's book in Paris nearly three decades earlier). However, following the press interest in Burroughs's raucous appearance at the 1962 Edinburgh Festival, a landmark literary gathering that also featured Miller and Norman Mailer, Grove decided to release the novel, censors be damned. If not for this Scottish coup, *Naked Lunch* would have hungered much longer, as Miller's case was resolved only in 1964 and censorship in America was not itself censured until 1966 with the Supreme Court decision in the matter of *Memoirs v. Massachusetts*. Mary McCarthy lent her crucial support only three months after publication. A 1963 newspaper strike provided the opportunity for the launch of *The New York Review of Books*, the inaugural issue of which featured McCarthy's *Naked Lunch* assessment, which remains among the best: "The literalness of Burroughs is the opposite of 'literature.'"

"M" IS FOR MILLER, HENRY
Henry Miller dealt with both Obelisk and Olympia and so had working relationships, however strained, with both Kahane and Girodias. The relationships were consummated simultaneously when Obelisk first published Miller's *Tropic of Cancer* in 1934, two years after it had been submitted to the press. It took that long for Kahane to come to terms with its subject matter and to feel comfortable printing it after the relatively tame titles of

Sleeveless Errand and *The Well of Loneliness;* Joyceiana aside, Miller's was Obelisk's first important literary work. The cover image of a woman being abducted by a gigantic crab—Cancer—was the work of Maurice Girodias, then still Maurice Kahane, fifteen years old and not even allowed to read the work himself. After such a delay, Kahane had no more excuses for not publishing when money for the printers was loaned him by Miller's lover and fellow Obelisk erographer, Anaïs Nin, who'd borrowed the money herself from her mentor and occasional tryst, the psychoanalyst Otto Rank. Nin's own Obelisk book, *The Winter of Artifice*, was the last title published in Kahane's lifetime, released a week before the beginning of WWII, nine days before the publisher's death. That book was financed by another Obelisk author, Lawrence Durrell—Miller's friend and, again, a lover of Nin's. Henry Miller lived a long and productive life (1891–1980) in two cultures, so it's unsurprising that his books, lovers, and friends gave rise to so many connections. Frank Harris's tailor in New York was none other than Heinrich Miller, a German immigrant to Yorkville, Manhattan, and Henry Miller's father.

"N" IS FOR NABOKOV, VLADIMIR

In 1955, Parisian literary agent Denise Clarouin introduced Girodias to her colleague Doussia Ergaz, a muse to Russian émigré writers and, occasionally, their representation. At the drunken business lunch that followed, Ergaz sold Girodias a manuscript previously rejected by four American publishers: a licentious, cerebral book about a European scholar's obsession with an American suburban girl, *Lolita*, which Olympia published that same year. Its author, the Russian exile, lepidopterist, and chessmaster Vladimir Nabokov, was then teaching literature at Cornell University and, with an immigrant's fear of losing his livelihood, initially wanted his novel to appear under the *nom de plume* V. Sirin, which he'd used to publish in Germany amid the heyday of Russian Berlin. Eric Kahane, Girodias's younger brother, translated *Lolita*—Nabokov's third novel written in English—into French, though the novel would be banned in France until 1958 (in an odd reversal, *Lolita* was always legal in Britain). Putnam, the American publisher, claimed it was prepared to defend any challenge to the book in court, ready for what Nabokov would refer to in correspondence as "lolitigation," but the glory of Stateside prosecution was never to be. Instead, the deal Nabokov signed between Olympia and Putnam enriched all involved. The novel sold over one hundred thousand copies in the first three weeks, thanks to masterful publicity and hints of illicitness with no real illegality. Putnam editor Walter Minton, who first read the Olympia edition thanks to the influence of his showgirl girlfriend, Rosemary Ridgewell, became one of the most influential editors of the decade. Nabokov quit academia to live the rest of his life in Swiss hotels. Girodias, however, squandered his nymphet's fortune—which would have run his press for years—in the construction and operation of a two-floor pleasure palace. Initially wanting to call this establishment Chez Lolita, Girodias reconsidered after he was threatened with legal action; he named the place La Grande Séverine, after its address, 7 rue Saint-Séverine. The place featured an Oriental red room; a blue room called Le Salon Cagliostro, after its tarot-card theme; a Winter Garden replete with rococo birdcages; La Salle du Grand Siècle, a candlelit formal restaurant; La Batucada, a Brazilian-themed dance club; Club de Jazz (later Le Blues-Bar), which hosted the likes of Chet Baker, Memphis Slim, and Marpessa Dawn; La Salle Suèdoise, a late-night restaurant specializing in light Scandinavian fare; and Chez Vodka, a Russian cabaret with a balalaika orchestra.

"O" IS FOR HISTOIRE D'O

Histoire d'O, or *Story of O*, is the story of a woman named after the most open, accessible vowel in the alphabet. O, a fashion photographer, is taken to a château in Roissy, a Paris suburb, by her lover, René. There, she is sexually—and, shockingly to feminism, willingly—enslaved: She is whipped, raped, and kept manacled in dungeons while being repeatedly sodomized by a succession of ebonite dildos. She is branded on her buttocks; her labia are pierced with a ring connected to chains by which she is led around, crawling. *Story of O* was published simultaneously in French and English in 1954, under the pornonym Pauline Réage, with a preface signed by Jean Paulhan, a respected critic for the *Nouvelle Revue Française*, editor at Gallimard, and member of the Académie française. Thanks to Paulhan's imprimatur, the book was a *succès de scandale* and bestseller, the author's identity an avidly sought secret. The French press doubted that Réage was a woman and proposed as author André Malraux, Raymond Queneau, Jean Paulhan himself, and even the American writer George Plimpton. Forty years after publication, though, Réage was publicly outed by Olympia scholar John de St. Jorre (writing in *The New Yorker*) as Dominique Aury, a Gallimard employee, and a prominent English-French translator. Aury, who was privately suspected for decades of being O's author, maintained that her novel had been a love letter to Paulhan, who had guarded her identity after he captured her heart. As Paulhan was years older than

Aury and already married to an invalid who'd outlive him (Paulhan died in 1968), Aury's *O* had been intended as a complete gift of herself to the man she could not possess. However, Dominique Aury was also a pseudonym, used for the author's translation work, and ultimately de St. Jorre chose to protect the true identity of the novel's creatrix. The real writer of *O* is named only in the definitive bibliography of the Olympia Press, written by book smuggler and erotician Patrick Kearney and edited by Angus Carroll. There we are told that Réage/Aury is, or was, Anne Cécile Desclos (1907–98). But Desclos's is not the only pseudonymous conundrum involved with *O*'s publication: The translator of the book's 1965 American edition was Sabine d'Estrée, believed to be Richard Seaver, translator of Samuel Beckett's French work and husband to a woman whose middle name was Sabine. The first English version of *O* was execrable, with Olympia's translator translating the name "Madeleine" as "cake." Because brother Eric was busy, Girodias had entrusted the work to Baird Bryant, dilettante novelist. Bryant would abandon literature for cinematography; he was one of the cameramen who, at the 1969 Rolling Stones concert at Altamont, California, caught on tape the murder of gunman Meredith Hunter by Hell's Angel Alan Passaro, which can be seen in the documentary film *Gimme Shelter*.

"P" IS FOR PORNOGRAPHY

My breasts, if it is not too bold a figure to call so two hard,
firm, rising hillocks, that just began to shew themselves,
or signify anything to the touch, employ'd and amus'd her
hands a-while, till, slipping down lower, over a smooth
track, she could just feel the soft silky down that had
but a few months before put forth and garnish'd the

mount-pleasant of those parts, and promised to spread a grateful shelter over the seat of the most exquisite sensation, and which had been, till that instant, the seat of the most insensible innocence. Her fingers play'd and strove to twine in the young tendrils of that moss, which nature has contrived at once for use and ornament. / But, not contented with these outer posts, she now attempts the main spot, and began to twitch, to insinuate, and at length to force an introduction of a finger into the quick itself, in such a manner, that had she not proceeded by insensible gradations that inflamed me beyond the power of modesty to oppose its resistance to their progress, I should have jump'd out of bed and cried for help against such strange assaults. / Instead of which, her lascivious touches had lighted up a new fire that wanton'd through all my veins, but fix'd with violence in that center appointed them by nature, where the first strange hands were now busied in feeling, squeezing, compressing the lips, then opening them again, with a finger between, till an "Oh!" express'd her hurting me, where the narrowness of the unbroken passage refused it entrance to any depth.

From *Fanny Hill, or: Memoirs of a Woman of Pleasure*, first pornographic novel in English, by John Cleland, published in installments beginning in 1748, republished by Olympia in 1954, defined as protected under the First Amendment of the Constitution by the U.S. Supreme Court in the matter of *Memoirs v. Massachusetts*, 1966, which effectively ended literary censorship in America.

"Q" IS FOR QUENEAU, RAYMOND
Raymond Queneau (1903–76) was a French poet, novelist, literary theorist, Gallimard executive, and the co-founder of the Oulipo movement (an acronym for

ouvroir de littérature potentielle, or workshop for potential literature), dedicated to experimenting with writing under formal and stylistic constraints. Translation: His work is difficult to translate. Queneau's most artistically successful book is 1947's *Exercises de style,* in which the same story is told multiple times and in multiple ways, such as in retrograde and in rhyming slang. Queneau's most commercially successful book, however, was 1959's *Zazie dans le Métro,* whose English edition was published simultaneously by Olympia under the same French title in a translation by Eric Kahane and Akbar del Piobo, a pseudonym for American artist Norman Rubington. A film version by Louis Malle was made in 1960. *Zazie,* which concerns the adventures of the eponymous young girl placed in the care of a transvestite uncle to allow her mother time alone with a lover, explores the possibilities of punning in colloquial French. Its opening word is "Doukipudonktan," a phoneticized portmanteau of the correct *"D'où qu'il pue donc tant?"* ("How come he stinks so bad?") The now-standard English translation, by Barbara Wright, reads "Howcanaystinksotho," while "Holifart, watastink" was Olympia's original.

"R" IS FOR RIJEKA
Kahane was shelled and gassed at Ypres in 1916, his health forever ruined. After his hospital discharge, marriage, and honeymoon recuperation, Kahane resumed his duties, serving as a transport officer with the Fourth Army in Dunkirk and Italy. Stationed in the port of Fiume—today known as Rijeka, Croatia—Kahane's job was to ensure that the Italian railways ran on time to facilitate the return of Allied troops to Britain. Austro-Hungarian Fiume's population had been majority Italian, until the *novecento,* when the Hapsburgs began encouraging

Croatian emigration. The city had been administered by the Hungarian half of the empire from Budapest, but following the armistice it was under British control and Italy (especially the Italian Right) had begun claiming it, if only unofficially. Meanwhile, the city's port moored ships from the fleets of Britain, France, Austria, and Italy. When the Treaty of Versailles failed to award the Dalmatian territories to Italy, Italian nationalists felt insulted and sought to restore their dignity through the figure of Gabriele D'Annunzio, warrior-poet. A crazy blackshirted fascist—he popularized both the politics and the fashion—D'Annunzio had emerged from the war a hero, not only as an artist but also as a cavalry officer and fighter pilot. When it emerged that Fiume itself would not be awarded to Italy, D'Annunzio, with the support of Mussolini, who'd just founded the Fascist Party, marched on the city in September 1919. There he claimed Fiume for Italy against the will of the Italian government. The government condemned D'Annunzio; Mussolini's Fascists denounced the government; and D'Annunzio, calling himself Il Duce before Mussolini, ensconced himself in Fiume, which he declared an independent state called the Regency of Carnaro, where he instituted the laws of ancient Rome, including capital punishment. When the Treaty of Rapallo between Italy and Yugoslavia called for Fiume to be incorporated into Croatia in 1920 (under its Croatian name of Rijeka), D'Annunzio responded by declaring war on the country of his birth. But with the Italian fleet blockading the harbor and shelling his villa, the poet-provocateur retreated. By this time, Kahane was already in France, where he was asked to approach the Yugoslav delegation at the Paris Conference on behalf of Italy, covertly offering to purchase Fiume/Rijeka from Yugoslavia; further, the Italians offered to surrender Spalato and build a new port for that city. Kahane's remuneration would have been the concession for the port's construction, but the scheme came to nothing. Fiume/Rijeka was Kahane's first encounter with the fascism that his sons would experience more directly.

"S" IS FOR DE SADE, MARQUIS

La Grande Séverine, Girodias's nightspot, was located down the street from the fifteenth-century Saint-Séverin church. While excavating the building's cellars for an expansion, workers unearthed skeletons from the church's medieval burial grounds. Converting this (said to be cursed) basement into an underground theater, Girodias turned impresario, staging theatrical works for the public and friends. These included a revue entitled *Les Playgirls* as well as a stage adaptation of Norman Rubington's *Fuzz Against Junk* in a French translation by Eric Kahane. Girodias's brother was also responsible for a 1959 adaptation of Donatien Alphonse François de Sade's *La Philosophie dans le boudoir* (*The Bedroom Philosophers*), the dialogical original of which Olympia published in 1953. Olympia also released editions of the ithyphallic marquis's *Justine* (first published under the Obelisk imprint), *Juliette*, and *The 120 Days of Sodom*. While *La Philosophie dans le boudoir*'s opening night was a success, the Paris vice squad—increasingly intolerant in de Gaulle's France—arrived two nights later and closed the play down. Girodias, who unlike other porn publishers never much kept a low profile, defied the ban, mounting the stage the next night to read, as an opening act, the text of the decree that shuttered his show. The police did nothing, however, perhaps because that night the audience included de Gaulle's former minister of education; the writer Romain Gary and his wife, actress Jean Seberg; the filmmaker Roger Vadim; and actress Catherine Deneuve. The following night, though, the vice squad returned and the theater never reopened. La Grande Séverine soon exhausted its resources and credit, closing forever. Olympia Paris would not survive the club by much, and by 1965 Girodias had moved his operations to America.

"T" IS FOR TRILOGY

Alexander Trocchi, Scottish writer and pornographer, co-founded *Merlin* with his American wife, Jane Lougee, in 1952 as a journal for "innovation in creative writing." Their partners included Austryn Wainhouse, Richard Seaver, and British poet Christopher Logue. It was Seaver who discovered Samuel Beckett in French, helped translate him into English, and brought the Irish writer to the attention of *Merlin*, which published an excerpt from *Molloy*. Girodias, who'd befriended the *Merlinois*, as he called them, and who supported the journal by employing its editors in the writing of d.b.s, was introduced to Beckett (1906–89), and published *Watt*, the future Nobel laureate's first book in English, as part of a series called Collection Merlin in 1953. Another of the *Merlinois*, South African Patrick Bowles, translated *Molloy* into English in collaboration with its author, who translated *Malone Dies* and *The Unnamable* on his own. Despite the fact that Beckett considered the three titles individual entities, Girodias published them as a trilogy in 1959, fixing for posterity the format and order in which we read them today.

"U" IS FOR UNEXPURGATED

"Sleeveless errand" is superannuated slang for a fool's

errand, or fruitless endeavor. "Sleeveless" derives from "sleave," or "sleive," meaning raveled thread or the raw edge of silk, implying uselessness. An Old English verb, to "sleeve" meant to divide or separate. To sleeve silk meant to prepare it for weaving by passing it through the "slay" of a loom, sometimes called a "sled." The "sleeve" itself was the tangled, coarse end left over from the process. *Sleeveless Errand* is a novel by Norah C. James, written in 1928 and scheduled for publication by the British Scholartis Press in 1929. But in February of that year, on the eve of publication, London police raided every bookstore that had ordered copies and confiscated their stock. What followed was a sleeveless prosecution. The Crown found the book lascivious, while supporters praised its (illusory) literary merit. Offending passages included such verbiage as "bloody hell," "balls," "homos," "whores," "for Christ's sake," "like hell," and "bitch." Kahane read about the fracas in a newspaper across the Channel and managed to obtain a confiscated copy (most of the print run had been pulped). He didn't enjoy it as literature as much as entertain it as business opportunity. Believing that the book was attacked because a prominent politician had been maligned in its pages—though neither he nor James ever mentioned any names—Kahane conceived the idea for a prurient but entirely legal Parisian press, which profited from exploiting the definitional differences between British and French pruderies and libels. In March 1929, Kahane purchased English-language, French-publication rights to *Sleeveless Errand*, taking out advertisements in the London press announcing that "in the event of other books of literary merit being banned in England," he was "prepared to publish them in Paris within a month." *Sleeveless Errand* was Obelisk's first title.

319

James said that had she known that portions of her book would have offended, she would have removed them. Kahane, contrarily, relished the economics of transgression and emblazoned on a blue-green wrapper across his edition's cover the catchphrase: the complete /and unexpurgated text.

"V" IS FOR VALERIE SOLANAS

In 1967, while establishing Olympia U.S.A., Girodias lived in New York at the Chelsea Hotel. His neighbor was a writer named Valerie Solanas. A friendship began, and Girodias came to appreciate Solanas's antimale play *Up Your Ass*, as well as a manifesto entitled, and for, *S.C.U.M.*, the Society for Cutting Up Men. Girodias commissioned Solanas to write a novel, offering her an advance of $2,000, and Solanas—a friend and collaborator of Andy Warhol's—introduced Girodias to the pop artist at a screening of the rough cut of his film *I, a Man*. Solanas could not finish her novel, however, and offered Girodias her manifesto instead. In June 1968, Girodias abruptly evacuated New York for Montréal. The day after he left, Solanas entered Warhol's studio and shot the artist three times, damaging organs. That evening, with Warhol undergoing surgery, Solanas surrendered to police in Times Square. Warhol's shooting was front-page news until Sirhan Sirhan shot Robert F. Kennedy in Los Angeles two days later. Capitalizing on the Warhol shooting as best he could, Girodias immediately published *S.C.U.M.*, treating it as an exhibit in Solanas's public trial by quoting in a press release her statement to the police that her motives for shooting Warhol were "very involved but best understood if you read my manifesto." There was a rumor, possibly spread by Girodias himself, that the deranged Solanas, dissatisfied with

what had been Girodias's delay in publishing her manuscript, had actually been after him, that she had stopped
by Olympia U.S.A.'s Gramercy Park offices first, but,
finding Girodias gone, instead walked, gun in hand, to
Warhol's Factory at Union Square. Girodias was to said
to have known she was coming and thought it best to
depart for Canada.

"W" IS FOR WYNDHAM LEWIS

Marjorie Firminger, born in London in 1899, began her
artistic career as an actress, playing gadfly girl Penelope
Foxglove in Kenneth Barnes's play *The Letter of the Law*.
Despite good notices, this was Firminger's last stage success. When she met the author, painter, and raconteur
Wyndham Lewis (1882–1957), Firminger was eking out
a living writing about fashion for women's magazines.
Lewis occasionally stopped by Firminger's Chelsea
apartment and encouraged her to gossip, relying on the
younger writer for insight into Lewis's friends, who'd
become Firminger's too: Sidney Schiff, novelist, and
Richard Wyndham, painter, among others. At this time,
Firminger was writing a novel herself, a fact she kept
from the intimidating, domineering Lewis. That novel,
Jam To-day, was a messy satire, and a masochistic act of
social suicide. The title is borrowed from Lewis Carroll's
Through the Looking-Glass, in which the Queen tells
Alice: "The rule is, jam to-morrow and jam yesterday—
but never jam to-day." Though the Queen's quote might
derive from a Latin pun (*iam* in Latin means "soon,"
or "presently"), Carroll's phrase has come to signify
unfulfilled promise or delayed gratification. Firminger
herself greedily gobbles her preserves from the very first
page: Friend Sir Michael Bruce, author, is lampooned as
Lord Jerry Poon; the book's lesbian heroine, Bracken

Dilitor, was based on friend Heather Pilkington (whom Firminger had introduced to Lewis upon Lewis's request to meet a lesbian); and Pilkington's real-life lover, Wyn Henderson, friend to shipping heiress Nancy Cunard and collaborator with Cunard on the Hours Press in Paris, appears as Mrs. Wikk, "over six feet and colossally fat." Word about the book traveled, and even before publication Firminger's friends began to desert her. Firminger, though, remained convinced of her right to transmute life into art—a conviction influenced by Lewis's practice. *Jam To-day* was accepted for publication by Herbert Clarke, of the Paris-based Vendôme Press, and appeared in print in 1931, only to be promptly seized by British customs as obscene. Only a week later, Clarke died of a stroke and Vendôme's list was bought by Kahane, who rebranded Firminger's novel with the Obelisk phallus and offered to publish her future books, but none was forthcoming. *After Thirty*, *That Cad Jane*, and *Love at Last* were left unfinished. A married Lewis, returned from an extended trip to Berlin, where he would fall under Nazi influence, distanced himself even further from Firminger, who remained obsessed with him, refusing to abandon her pretense toward their relationship. In 1932, Lewis published *Snooty Baronet*, a novel that follows its writer-hero, the one-legged, Scottish minor noble Sir Michael Kell-Imrie, as he makes his way through a world of mediocrities, unworthies, incompetents, and poseurs. One of them is his infrequent lover, hack writer Valerie Ritter, whose works were "quite unprintable, except in de luxe editions privately printed in Paris or Milan." A "giggling fantoche" with halitosis, Val's face "has a swarthy massaged flush. (If you look too close, it is full of pits; under the make-up is a field of gaping pores—her nose is worst in this respect: some day it will disintegrate for all practical purposes)." Like Firminger, Val self-destructed, having alienated "all those bright nebulous monomaniacal patrons, of Gossip-column-class—on to the hem of whose garment she had clung like grim death—but who had shaken her off, of one accord, and by common consent, about a year since, when she had pooped in their faces." The author of *Jam To-day* married, divorced, and worked in a department store selling hats. Firminger's legacy was Lewis's slight; Lewis would withhold their correspondence from his own collection of letters. She died in 1976, humiliated still.

"X" IS FOR XXX

X's anonymity has stood in for the miscellaneously prurient, a shorthand for the scatological or otherwise forbidden. It stands for 10 in Roman numerals and has also served as both a symbol of negation ("no") and the traditional signature of illiterates. The origins of its myriad applications are obscure. Two Olympians incorporated this anonymizing, lurid letter into their pseudonyms. XXX was the pseudonym of Diane, or alternately Diana, Bataille, wife of Georges, also known as Princess Diane Kotchoubey de Beauharnais, and the author of *The Whip Angels*. Greta X was John Millington-Ward, who wrote exclusively about *le vice anglais*—flagellation. As Greta, this dignified, older Englishman—Olympia's most commercially successful d.b. writer throughout the 1950s—wrote *There's a Whip in My Valise* and *Whipsdom*. He also wrote under the names Angela Pearson (*Scream, My Darling, Scream; The Whipping Club; The Whipping Post; Whips Incorporated*), and Ruth Less or Lesse (*Lash*). Under his own name, Millington-Ward was a theorist of education and the author of such valuable textbooks as *New Intermediate English Grammar* and *Proficiency In The Use Of English: 10 Lessons of Guidance and Practice*.

"Y" IS FOR YOUNG ADAM

Young Adam is a book by Francis Lengel, aka Alexander Trocchi, who wrote both d.b.s and more-serious literature for Olympia under the gynonym Carmencita de las Lunas and the alias Oscar Mole. He used the name Lengel for pornography; de las Lunas was used to write *Thongs;* and Oscar Mole was appended to Trocchi's translations, which included an Englishing of Apollinaire's *Les Onze Mille Verges.* The indefatigable Trocchi was also Terry Southern's first collaborator on the latter's update of *Candide,* but Trocchi recused himself to meet d.b. deadlines, leaving Southern to work with Mason Hoffenberg on the subversive sex farce *Candy.* Subsequently, Trocchi turned literary agent, introducing Southern and Hoffenberg to Girodias, who published their coauthored novel to enduring success. Trocchi was a one-man, rush-hour Grub Street and was even prodigious, or profligate, against his will: When his update of *Fanny Hill,* entitled *Helen and Desire* (1954), was banned in France, Olympia reprinted it under the title *Desire and Helen* (1956). *Helen and Desire* was the first Lengel book, but *Young Adam*—also from 1954, about a bargeworker plying Glasgow to Edinburgh who discovers the corpse of a woman he knew, and is sexually stirred—was his most successful. In the late '50s, Trocchi left Paris, moved to the United States, and, life imitating art, worked on a garbage barge on the Hudson River. He returned to England a decade later, continued writing (in 1960 publishing his masterpiece, *Cain's Book,* also concerning a libidinous bargeworker), but

324

summated his posterity by injecting heroin on a live TV talk show. He died in 1984, having spent his last years operating a used-books stall in London. A *Young Adam* film appeared in 2003 starring Ewan McGregor. It was rated NC-17; Sony Pictures, the movie's American distributors, wanted to cut McGregor's full-frontal-nudity scene for Stateside release, but the actor protested and the scene was retained.

"Z" IS FOR ZAY, THEODORE

Theodore Zay, ostensible Hungarian nobleman, wrote only one book for Obelisk, never reprinted. That novel, *Love Counts Ten*, subtitled *A Sensational Story / of the Night Haunts of a Great City*, concerns young gigolo Ernest von Sternheim, who services both sexes in Weimar Berlin. Sternheim falls in love and seeks retirement at age twenty-seven, but the stock market crashes and our tender whore loses his fortune. After his lover dies of consumption, Sternheim blinds himself in a suicide attempt as inept as his author's prose style (I am relying on summaries, however; *Love* is among the most difficult of Obelisk titles to obtain). At novel's end, our hero, broke and unable to satisfy his clientele, is left preternaturally old, selling matches on a Paris street corner. Theodore Zay is certainly a pseudonym, given the location of Obelisk's offices just across the Seine from the Left Bank's Quai d'Orsay (and the Musée d'Orsay, where Manet's *Olympia* hangs). In bleak January 1939, the price of paper was already so prohibitive in France that *Love* was printed in Belgium. The true identity of "Theo d'Orsay" remains unknown.

Selected Bibliography

Campbell, James; *Paris Interzone: Richard Wright, Lolita, Boris Vian and Others on the Left Bank, 1946–1960*

de St. Jorre, John; *Venus Bound: The Erotic Voyage of the Olympia Press and its Writers*

Ford, Hugh; *Published in Paris: American and British Writers, Printers, and Publishers in Paris, 1920–1939*

Girodias, Maurice; *The Frog Prince*

Girodias, Maurice; *The Olympia Reader*

Kahane, Jack; *Memoirs of a Booklegger*

Kearney, Patrick (ed. Angus Carroll); *The Paris Olympia Press*

Pearson, Neil; *A History of Jack Kahane and the Obelisk Press*

FROM THE DIARIES

Sounds of Odessa

Clip-clop, clip-clop: Horse hooves on the cobbles?
Or the mating call of stilettos?

Sights of Odessa

Potemkin Villages are fake villages; the Potemkin
Stairs are real steep.

Odessa Fashion

Odessa fashion is extremely resourceful: A sailor's
stripes are the same as a convict's.

Odessa at Work

A man demands money just for owning a monkey.

Odessa Geography

Wherever an ashtray is, is the center of the table.

London Stumble

(Lateness accrues debt to be repaid in compliments.)
But he stumbled into the pub saying, "It's dark out and
you look great."

POND MEMORIES:
ON GEORGES PEREC

Once upon a time there was a pond, which was filled with small worms who fed on even smaller worms. To survive, the littlest of the worms had to hide in the slimy shallows and secrete themselves amid the weeds. But whatever the littlest worms lacked in practical resources, they made up for in imagination. Because as the littlest worms waited in the shallows—as the littlest worms lived—expecting at any moment to be devoured, they found themselves inventing legends, lore: a tradition. They called the pond they were in the Great Pond and named its four paradisiacal rivers: the one that brought gold and silver (the slime), the one that brought flowers (the weeds), the one that brought pearls (the frog-spawn), the one that brought coral (the fungi). Birds had once nested at the pond's banks until their nests had been scavenged and their eggs had been crushed and so bits of the crushed eggshells floated atop the water and gazing up from below the littlest worms called the bits "the stars." The littlest worms called a pumpkin—rotting at the shoreline, barely visible through the murk—"the sun." The littlest worms honored one another with titles like "Trout" and "Pike," "Whale" and "Leviathan," and even managed to assemble a code of little-worm-law, with hundreds of little-worm-commentaries, thousands of little-worm-rules and little-worm-regulations...

And then, one day, a herd of swine came crashing through the pond—their brute hooves breaking through the water's surface, which is the heaven of the worms—destroying everything...

"In the Pond" is a short tale by Isaac Leib Peretz, who was the Whale, the Leviathan, of Yiddish literature: among the largest and most slippery and so most inassimilable authors in the Yiddish canon.

He was also Georges Perec's great-great-uncle.

Perec, who had no Yiddish and so was familiar with his ancestor's work only in French translation, was nonetheless proud of his lineage, and mentioned it often: in conversation, in interviews, in books.

In his best book: *W, or The Memory of Childhood*, from 1975.

In Chapter Eight of that book, Perec speculates that his forebears fled the Inquisition and took their name, Peiresc, from their refuge in Provençe. The Peirescs, in Perec's account, then dispersed throughout the papal states, and from there to Mitteleuropa and vicinities east: Russian Poland, Romania, Bulgaria. Perec's parents were of the generation that made the return journey west: His father, Icek Judko Perec, informally André, and his mother, Cyrla Szulewicz, informally Cécile, separately left Warsaw for Paris just after WWI. Perec himself was born in Paris in spring 1936. In spring 1940, Perec's father, a volunteer soldier in the Twelfth Foreign Regiment of the French army, was wounded by German fire and died. In winter 1943, Perec's mother was interned at Drancy and then deported to the country of her birth—to Auschwitz.

All of which might explain the son's penchant for genealogy.

The orphaned son's mania for forms (evolved), structures (imposed), branches, clades, lines of descent.

In 1942, two years after his father's death, a year before her own, Perec's mother brought the future author to the Gare de Lyon, bought him a copy of *Charlie* (the tame kiddie predecessor of *Charlie Hebdo*), and sent him off to Villard-de-Lans, under the protection of relatives and the International Red Cross.

> The tiniest worms who weren't trampled died of fright and the tiniest worms who didn't die of fright succumbed to broken hearts.
>
> The rest committed suicide.
>
> Only one—the tiniest of the tiniest worms—survived, and when he declared to the bigger worms (who'd been fast asleep at the bottom of the pond) that the heaven above them now was a new heaven—when he declared to the bigger worms (who'd been fast asleep at the bottom of the pond) that the old heaven had been decimated by a pogrom of stampeding beasts, and so that the worm-heaven was not eternal—that only this universal-heaven presently above them might be eternal—then the bigger worms understood: this survivor-worm had lost his mind...
>
> They treated him with the utmost compassion and conveyed him to a subaqueous insane asylum...

In Peretz's tale—given in my own loose English above—a pondful of diminutive squirmers try to temporarily reshape and so transcend their imperilment through fiction: through the invention of stories.

To put it bluntly, worms writhing in muck countering that muck by creating a law, and a culture = Jews in the backwater shtetls of Russian Poland immersing themselves in Torah, Talmud, kabbalah, anecdotes, and jokes.

In Perec's *W, or The Memory of Childhood*, an adult man who is, or who says he is, Perec records and so relives his childhood, a time during which he was trying to temporarily reshape and so transcend his imperilment through fiction: through the invention of stories. Foremost of which is the story of the island of W, or the reconstructed story of the island of W, a grotesque childhood fantasy that Perec first put to paper (with fist-around-the-crayon illustrations), or claims that he first put to paper (with fist-around-the-crayon illustrations), around the bar-mitzvah age of thirteen, and that, he further claims, he'd never been able to escape, he'd never been able to completely forget, in all the intervening decades.

W—whose "shores offer no natural landing stage, but only shallows with treacherous, barely submerged reefs, or straight, steep, unfaulted basalt cliffs"—is located "far away, at the other end of the earth." Its government is a criminal or at least inhumane regime based entirely on a perversion of Classically Grecian physical culture. That is, based entirely on culling the winners from the losers: survival of the fittest.

To put it bluntly (as Perec himself does): W with its squalid barracks, training facilities, and tracks, where male athletes are starved, stripped to the skin, and forced to compete against one another in relentless contests of running, jumping, and mortal combat = the Nazi death camps.

Peretz, in his short Yiddish tale, is making a metaphor. Perec, in his much longer French tale, is admitting to a metaphor. The Yiddish writer trusts his readers to understand the correspondences and, despite the grim nature of the correspondences, to take pleasure from that understanding. The French writer offers no such solace. To him, symbolism has been degraded, and so feels degrading. Symbols are for fascists.

Perec's technique, then, is to put everything out in the

open—everything, including technique. This isn't precious avant-gardeism, but principle: To write prose after Auschwitz is barbaric, only if you can't admit that it's merely prose. Only if you can't admit that your metaphors, that all metaphors, are insufficiencies and, as such, failures.

Religious Jews in danger and seeking a reprieve will pray by reciting the verses of Psalms that begin with the letters of their names. Psalm 119 is often used for this purpose, as it's composed of twenty-two sets of eight verses, all the verses in each set beginning with the same Hebrew letter, with the sets arranged alphabetically—*alephbetically*. Alternately, Uncle Peretz and Nephew Perec might've opted to read out Psalm 144, which contains their surname: *Eyn peretz* is the verse in Hebrew, which means, essentially, "Let there be no break." The majority of Jewish liturgy not taken directly from Torah comprises devotions arranged by permutations of letters and interpolations of sums: For centuries, rabbis have written acrostic prayers that spell out their own names, and any visit to any synagogue on any day of the week at any of the three daily services will tell you that the number of times a text is repeated is just as crucial, theologically crucial, as what that text might mean.

Perec was the heir to this mystical—kabbalistic—practice, which he secularized and refined through his association with the Oulipo (an acronym for *ouvroir de littérature potentielle*, "the workshop for potential literature"), a French writing group founded in 1960 by Raymond Queneau and François Le Lionnais, whose ranks included Italo Calvino. The Oulipo turned research into the art itself, as members sought to identify sets of constraints by which novels and stories might be produced—calculations and formulas by which the clichés of freewriting might be avoided in favor of making something "new," of making something "original."

Oulipian constraints included, but were not limited to: use of anagram, use of palindrome, word-count limits, vowel-count limits, word replacements (in which every occurrence of a noun is replaced by another noun; for example, if noun = "massacre," then that last fragment should read "in which every occurrence of a massacre is replaced by another massacre"), vowel replacements (in which the word "noun" might be turned to "noon," the hour, or "naan," the flatbread, or "neon," the gas). Then there's the snowball, which is a text in which the words get progressively one letter longer, or the melting snowball, which is a text in which the words get progressively one letter shorter, and, of course, the lipogram, from the Greek *lipagrammatos* ("missing letters"), in which a text is written without the use of one or more letters. Literature's most famous lipogram is *La disparition (A Void)*, an antidetective novel published by Perec in 1969, whose three hundred or so pages omit the letter "e." The book's hero, Anton Vowl, must search for his vowel, just like the book's author must search for his family, his past—given the plethora of "e"s in "Georges Perec," the quest is, ultimately, for the self.

A futile quest for the self's completion.

W, or The Memory of Childhood focuses on a different letter: that dissonant consonant "W," which as Perec's English-language translator David Bellos has pointed out, should be pronounced, as it should be interpreted, in the French style: *double-vé.*

Throughout the book, this letter will stand for *une double-vie,* and Victory, and Vichy, and Rue Vilin, and

Various other things.

The book is dedicated, however, "for E."

V and E (no relation)? Or V.E. (as in the Day, May 8, 1945)? Neither. Both.

W, or The Memory of Childhood is not as convolutedly arranged as the vowel-voided masterpiece that preceded it and certainly plainer in plan than the masterpiece that followed: *La Vie mode d'emploi* (*Life, a User's Manual*, 1978). The basic tenet here is alternation. The "W" sections—the purported fictions of Perec the child, "made literary" by Perec the adult—are presented in italics in odd-numbered chapters. The autobiographical sections —the purported facts of Perec the child, "made correct" by Perec the adult—are presented in roman in even-numbered chapters. And that's it, ostensibly. Absent is all the author's most notorious trickery: the predetermined chapter lengths and character groupings (in every sense of the word "character"), the cycling of settings and even of activities (eating, sleeping, art-creation, *ménages à trois,* and more)—all that listmaking, author-as-martyr-to-data craziness for which Perec was venerated even before he died of cancer at age forty-five.

Forty-five words:

> Today, all survivors of atrocities are expected to "testify"
> or to "bear witness," as if after having been deprived of
> every other trapping of civilization the last token to be
> taken from them must be their imaginations—their privi-
> leges of self-reinvention, and even of self-doubt.

334

"Most of them are swallowed up by the sea in the first
three or four hours, but some kind of hope gives certain
survivors the strength to live on for days, weeks even. A
few years ago, one such was found more than five thousand miles away from where he had been shipwrecked,
lashed to a barrel, half eaten away by seasalt [...]"

Perec's books are among the greatest to have been written about the Holocaust, chiefly because the Holocaust
barely appears in them. Or barely appears in them as
anything but a system. A pitiless, constantly operating
system that converts humans into fictions. Into self-fic-
tionalizing fictions.

Perec/Peretz in Hebrew—פרץ —happens to be the root
of such words as "break," "breach," "gush," "spurt," "jet
of water."

AUTO-FLÂNEURISM:
ON TOM MCCARTHY

A novel character emerged from the mists of Second
Empire France and roamed the boulevards of Romantic
culture, seeking to connect their disparate objects and
events into the cohesive beauty that technologized urban
life was proposing as elusive. This man was Baudelaire's
flâneur, but not only—this master of accents and disguis-
es, this master of personas. In depressing St. Petersburg
he was the anonymous hero of Dostoyevsky's *Notes from
Underground*. In depressing Kristiania, he was the anonymous hero of Hamsun's *Hunger*. He was Malte Laurids
Brigge, lonely in Paris, in Rilke's *Notebooks*. He was
Antoine Ronquentin, lonely in Bouville, which is a city
so forlorn that it doesn't even exist, except in Sartre's
Nausea. It took Walter Benjamin—a Marxist German
Jew who'd spent WWI translating Baudelaire—to sense
this man's pale precarity and sadness, and to sense them
as being kindred to his own, and endemic to a type. He
decided that all these narrator-characters separately
wandering through cities as if their cities were already
books weren't quite aesthetically aimless, but desperate—for meaning, for money; they were casualties of
capitalism feverishly scavenging the marketplaces for
discarded old symbols to link together again and sell
back to the public as new.

WWII spared this type, but left the metropoleis
in rubble. Many of the best avatars went abroad—as
W. G. Sebald did, leaving Germany for England. All
of Sebald's books were narrated by solitary German
émigrés virtually indistinguishable in biography from
the author himself, who tramped through multilingual
archives, libraries, museums, and cemeteries, to collect

materials on the history of Germany's war crimes for use in essays that faded in and out of fiction; some of it original, some of it appropriated from earlier, which is to say guiltless, writers from the German margins, like Kafka (Jewish), Adalbert Stifter (an Austrian chronicler of the countryside), and Robert Walser (a Swiss writer who spent much of his life institutionalized), whose sentences Sebald adapted without acknowledgment. These silent borrowings were frequently accompanied—antiillustrated—by black-and-white photographs that the author or his surrogates collected on rambles and were unable, or unwilling, to caption.

Since Sebald's death in 2001 his influence has only grown, especially outside of Germany—rather, especially in countries that fought Germany, and remained fascinated by its madness. To be sure, it's Sebald's techniques that are thriving—his pondering of a set of facts *in situ*, as a means of interpreting himself—while his preoccupation with the Holocaust has been transposed to more-current crises. It helps, on a first reading of Sebald, to have already read your Benjamin, and Adorno, Wittgenstein, and Freud. But it doesn't help, on a first reading of Sebald's heirs—say Geoff Dyer, Teju Cole, and Ben Lerner—to have already read your Sebald. Their books come off as too weak to shoulder the comparison, as the writer-narrators—who share traits if not also names with their authors—practice backpacker-*flânerie* through the major capitals in the style not of exile but of tourism or study-abroad. Certainly Dyer's Jeff (in *Jeff in Venice, Death in Varanasi*), Cole's Julius (in *Open City*), and Lerner's Adam (in *Leaving the Atocha Station*) and Ben (in *10:04*) are still doing the most serious work of trying to patch a creative self out of the strangers they meet and the artworks they experience, and the way they go about it is often intelligent (Lerner), compassionate (Cole), and droll (Dyer). Still, all of those books of self-alienation through travel are suffused with the shaming suspicion that a ticket home will always be available—even if that's only because everywhere in the world can feel like "home," or much of it has been homogenized to resemble it, at least. But globalization isn't the novelist's fault, or not completely.

Further complicating this generational transition are computers, which make getting lost or losing touch nearly impossible and the occupation of symbol-scrounging more efficient: Online is the ultimate semiotic trash-heap, and, given its ubiquity, its corruption of the imagination appears absolute. There's just too much of everything to repackage for a writer to still be bothering to invent. This, finally, is the theme of *Satin Island*, a trenchant travesty of the Sebald genre by Tom McCarthy, the British avatar of the transnational writer-in-residence avant-garde.

Satin Island opens in Turin—rather, at its airport, Torino-Caselle. The narrator—the browser or curator of this tricksy text—is referred to only as U. This man with the second-person name is a British anthropologist employed by a consulting company called the Company to advise on branding issues, most recently for the undefined Koob-Sassen Project. (This has to be a reference—and online supports my hunch—to Hilary Koob-Sassen, a multimedia artist friend of McCarthy's and the son of Saskia Sassen, the Dutch sociologist who coined the academic/PR term "global city.") U. is stuck idle at the gate, without a plane to board; U.K.-bound airspace is closed due to an unidentified private jet flying rogue. He cracks his laptop and wastes his wait by searching—which means delivering a mini-disquisition on—the Shroud of Turin, with a vehemence that suggests his regret at not having visited the relic offscreen. He contemplates Jesus's crown of thorns and likens its shape to that of a hub airport. He searches "hub airport," and educates himself, and so the reader, on how the most convenient terminals are designed like wheels, whose spokes facilitate "communion between any two spots [...] despite no direct line connecting [them]." Further clicked links tell him and so tell us that the hub model is used "in fields ranging from freight to distributed computing." A childhood memory intervenes: U. recalls coasting his bicycle downhill and being unnerved by the property of backpedaling: "that you could move one way while rotating the crank in the opposite direction contravened my fledgling understanding not only of motion but also of time." He feels this way again now, despite being older and grounded: "the same awkward sense of things being out of sync, out of whack."

As the pages mount, no true plot unfolds, though the circular meme keeps expanding: Crowns/hubs/bicycle wheels morph into pools of oil, jellyfish, deployed parachutes, and the *tawaf* (or the circumambulations of Muslims around the Ka'aba), and though each symbolic correspondence is attached to its own incident in the news—an oil spill, and the case of a skydiver who died of a sabotaged chute—none involve U. as anything other than a witness to the cycle, a victim of the mechanization of the associative mind. Pursuing media patterns compels him to create "Present Tense Anthropology™," a discipline he has the patience to proprietize, but not to develop. And it keeps recommending, but also frustrating, topics for the "Great Report," which the Company has commissioned to be "The Document, the Book, the First and Last Word on our Age." Needless to say, U.

will never finish writing it. Or he will and this is it. Or, perhaps, all of *Satin Island* is just the result of a flaw in the file's transmission—in the way that its title reproduces how the words "Staten Island" appeared to U. in a dream. A roughly round spit of land whose vast garbage dump is now defunct: U. becomes obsessed with this most maligned of boroughs, but, while in New York to deliver a lecture, never makes time to hop the ferry for a visit.

FROM THE DIARIES

The Only Caravaggio in Russia

B keeps insisting that this painting at the Odessa
Museum is the only Caravaggio in Russia, though
Odessa isn't in Russia and the painting's not a
Caravaggio.

*My Friend's Estimation of his Grandfather, a Forgotten
Hungarian Painter*

"It was like he'd only seen, seen and misunderstood,
one Cubist painting in all of his life—one day, as if
by accident, in Paris—before returning directly to
Budapest and attempting to imitate it. Rather, before
returning directly to Budapest and attempting to
nationalize it. To make Cubism Hungarian. For him
that was enough."

THE DEATH OF CULTURE, AND OTHER HYPOCRISIES: ON MARIO VARGAS LLOSA

I call it the newspaper problem: About a decade ago I wrote an essay on contemporary poetry for a newspaper that will remain nameless and had the occasion to quote a line by "Eliot." The editor sent back many changes, the most minor but telling of which was that the quotation was now attributed to "the English poet T. S. Eliot." Vaguely piqued, I asked what the editor was trying to clarify: Was he afraid readers wouldn't realize the quotation came from a poem? Or was he afraid readers might confuse the Eliot who wrote it with, say, George Eliot, the pseudonymous author of *Middlemarch*? Anyway, I noted that the "English" qualifier was misleading: Though T. S. Eliot had taken British citizenship, he'd been born in America. The editor, then, sent on another suggestion: "the American-born English poet T. S. Eliot." I, having lost all the patience I had as a twenty-something-year-old, replied by modifying that tag to: "the American-born, British-citizen English-language poet, essayist, dramatist, teacher, publisher, and bank teller Thomas Stearns Eliot (1888–1965)," after which the editor finally got the point and canceled the assignment.

Of course, it's tempting, even now, to keep spinning that description out, into "cuckold, chain smoker, cat fancier, and anti-Semite"—not just to have my revenge, but also to demonstrate how culture works or doesn't. I can't help suspecting that if I were writing a decade or so in the future I would be expected—despite all information being findable online—to explain what a "bank teller" or "publisher" was, not to mention what it once meant to write criticism, as opposed to a consumer review.

Notes on the Death of Culture: Essays on Spectacle and Society is a nonfiction diatribe by Mario Vargas Llosa, or (should I say) by the Spanish-language Peruvian novelist, lapsed Catholic, last living public face of the Latin American "boom," and 2010 Nobel laureate in literature Mario Vargas Llosa, the author of over two dozen previous books. The subject of this one is "our" lack: of common culture, or common context, common sets of referents and allusions, and a common understanding of who or what that pronoun "our" might refer to anymore, now that even papers of record have capitulated to individually curated channels and algorithmicized feeds. *Notes* begins with a survey of the literature of cultural decline, focusing on Eliot's "Notes Toward the Definition of Culture," before degenerating into a series of squibs—on Islam, online, the preeminence of sex over eroticism, and the spread of "the yellow press"—most of which began as columns in the Spanish newspaper *El País*. All of which is to say that Vargas Llosa's cranky, hasty manifesto is made of the very stuff it criticizes: journalism.

Vargas Llosa's opening essay reduces its Eliotic ur text to its crassest points, but my own version here must be crasser: After all, I have six browser tabs open and my phone has been beeping all day. Eliot defines culture as existing in, and through, three different spheres: that of the individual, the group or class, and the entire rest of society. Individuals' sensibilities affiliate them with a group or class, which doesn't have to be the one they're born into. That group or class proceeds to exercise its idea of culture on society as a whole, with the elites—the educated and artists, in Eliot's ideal arrangement—leveraging their access to the media and academia to influence the tastes of the average citizen, and of the next generation too. As for what forms the individual, it's the family, and the family, in turn, is formed by the Church: "It is in Christianity that our arts have developed," Eliot writes; "it is in Christianity that the laws of Europe have—until recently—been rooted."

"Until recently" refers to the year of Eliot's essay's publication: 1943. Vargas Llosa departs from there, to examine the work of George Steiner, whose 1971 book *In Bluebeard's Castle* was a caustic reply to Eliot, from the perspective of the counterculture, which both Steiner and Vargas Llosa define as "postculture." In Steiner's account, which, again, I'll have to abridge, the post-Napoleonic supremacy of the European bourgeoisie caused culture to fall into tedium and decadence, becoming the outlet for the "transcendence" formerly promised by religion, only now transmuted into the form of "explosive, cataclysmic violence" (the quotes are Vargas Llosa's). "For Steiner," Vargas Llosa writes, "European culture did not simply anticipate but it also desired the prospect of a bloody and purging explosion that took shape in revolutions and in two world wars. Instead of stopping these blood baths, culture desired to provoke and celebrate them." In other words, God died as the last casualty of the Napoleonic Wars, and the wars of the century that followed laid waste to the human. What remains is the reign of what Vargas Llosa calls "the spectacle": techno-entertainment and capital.

So, a history that begins with Eliot's Anglo-American expatriate striving proceeds through refugee German-Jewish anxiety and ends with the communist, poststructuralist French: Guy Debord. Now we're

344

ready for what used to be called, with colonial scorn, the fringes, the frontier: South America. But instead of pointing out that the most interesting literary culture on the planet, post-1968, was being made by Cortázar (Argentina), Donoso (Chile), Fuentes (Mexico), García Márquez (Colombia), Puig (Argentina), and, hey, himself, Vargas Llosa instead mourns the lack of an audience, as if novels ever could, or should, make the same box office as a blockbuster.

It's here, in the essay "The Civilization of the Spectacle," that Vargas Llosa falls into contradiction—exhorting more people to read more, even while decrying the deleterious effects of "democratization":

> This is a phenomenon born of altruism: Culture could no longer be the patrimony of an elite; liberal and democratic society had a moral obligation to make culture accessible to all, through education and through promoting and supporting the arts, literature and other cultural expression. This commendable philosophy has had the undesired effect of trivializing and cheapening cultural life, justifying superficial form and content in works on the grounds of fulfilling a civic duty to reach the greatest number.

But Vargas Llosa doesn't stop at that. Later in this essay he notes: "It is not surprising therefore that the most representative literature of our times is 'light,' easy literature, which, without any sense of shame, sets out to be—as its primary and almost exclusive objective—entertaining." And if you need more to file under the Grumpy Old Novelists rubric: "Chefs and fashion designers now enjoy the prominence that before was given to scientists"; "The vacuum left by the disappearance of criticism has been filled, imperceptibly, by advertising"; "Today … people usually play sports at the expense of, and instead of, intellectual pursuits"; "Today, the mass consumption of marijuana, cocaine, ecstasy, crack, heroin, etc., is a response to a social environment that pushes men and women toward quick and easy pleasure."

Even if Vargas Llosa is correct, there's a difference between being correct and being stylish. The psychology's too obvious, applicable equally to a novelist as to a reader: To complain about the death of culture is to complain about dying yourself. It's a displacement of mortality. Vargas Llosa turned eighty in 2016. I take no joy in kicking an old man when he's down. I'd rather re-read his earlier books, and remember how his character Zavalita expressed rage—expressed Vargas Llosa's previously productive rage—in *Conversation in the Cathedral*: "He was like Peru, Zavalita was," Vargas Llosa wrote there, because Peru and Zavalita had both "fucked up somewhere along the line."

But where? When was the fuckup? Vargas Llosa's novels have never hesitated to traffic in the same high-low blend he now bemoans. It's impossible to think of the way the narration is split among cadets at a military school in *The Time of the Hero*, or the way the teeming jungle causes timelines to mix in *The Green House*, without thinking of film; it's impossible to recall Vargas Llosa's stint as a TV talk-show host without finding its fictionalization in *Aunt Julia and the Scriptwriter*, later adapted for the screen itself; *Who Killed Palomino Molero?* and *Death in the Andes* owe much of their plotting to noir. And then there's the lowest, the nadir: politics. Vargas Llosa, abjuring the inevitable socialism of his youth, ran unsuccessfully as a pro-American candidate for the Peruvian presidency in 1990; *The Feast of the Goat* and

The Dream of the Celt are rife with intellectuals who deign the compromises of diplomacy and dine out at the laden tables of neoliberalism.

In novels like *The War of the End of the World* and *The Storyteller*—the former set during the Canudos conflict, just as slavery came to an end in Brazil, the latter set among the Machiguenga of the Peruvian rain forest—Vargas Llosa had no trouble juxtaposing native cultures with the conquest's importations. He has always believed that one tradition can, and does, reinforce the other, but it seems that his belief gutters out when the indigenous becomes the popular. After all, to be an Amazonian chief is to be a legend to your tribe alone, but to be a famous Latin American novelist is to be paparazzied for your foibles. About a week before *Notes on the Death of Culture* was published, Vargas Llosa left his wife of fifty years for Isabel Preysler, a Filipino-born Spanish socialite, model, and former beauty queen known as the Pearl of Manila, and as the ex-wife of Julio Iglesias. *Hola!* magazine carried the "exclusive" story, rife with intimate photographs and quotations (the relationship "is going very well," according to the novelist). My favorite headline read:

ENRIQUE IGLESIAS' MOM JUST BROKE UP THE MARRIAGE OF NOBEL WINNER MARIO VARGAS LLOSA

Since the scandal, his numbers have been up, in English and in Spanish, on the only Amazon that people seem to care about. Culture is how we pass the time between hypocrisies.

ALL FOISON, ALL ABUNDANCE: ON FLORIO'S MONTAIGNE AND SHAKESPEARE'S FLORIO

John Florio—lexicographer, raconteur, and supposed model for Shakespeare's schoolmaster Holofernes in *Love's Labour's Lost*—was born in London in 1553 to an unidentified Englishwoman and an Italian Protestant who'd fled the Inquisition. Later that year Queen Mary I reinstated Catholicism, which sent the family packing for France, Germany, and Switzerland. Florio didn't return to London until the reign of Elizabeth I, and subsequently served as Italian tutor to Queen Anne of Denmark, wife of James I, who gave the Church of England a Bible and so gave English to God. Florio's posterity consists of twin ironies. The first is that despite compiling the first comprehensive Italian-English dictionary, Florio most likely never set foot in Italy. The second is that his most enduring translation happens to be from the French.

Florio's 1603 version of Montaigne's *Essayes* survives not because of its writing but because of a single reader—Shakespeare, whose initial encounter with the French philosopher was via Florio's "enflourishing" eloquence. Stephen Greenblatt and Peter Platt have annotated selections in *Shakespeare's Montaigne*, and the result is a crash course in Elizabethan lit, a multiculti study of the development of English, and, above all, a revisionist biography of a monumental dramatist who not only cribbed the classical education he lacked but also responded to his sources with a fierce and censorious intelligence.

Montaigne's presence behind the scenes was already remarked upon, and lampooned, in Shakespeare's lifetime. Ben Jonson's *Volpone* proposed a Florio-like Italian writer from whom "All our *English* writers... Will deigne to steale... Almost as much, as from MONTAGNIE." By the time the variora of the plays had been assembled, in the late eighteenth century, the influence was such a matter of record that an unscrupulous party forged the signature of "Willm Shakspere" on a copy of Florio's work and sold it to the British Museum. Emerson, who regarded the signature as genuine, noted that when the museum bought a second copy, for public use, the volume contained the—authentic—autograph of Jonson.

Approximately 750 words peculiar to Florio's style show up in Shakespeare's plays and sonnets after 1603 ("apostrophe," "bellyful," "consanguinity"), twenty of them used in the *Essayes* for the first time (or for the first time in English). In "Of the Cannibals," Florio's Montaigne writes that the just-discovered peoples of the New World:

> hath no kind of traffic, no knowledge of letters, no intelligence of numbers, no name of magistrate, nor of politic superiority; no use of service, of riches, or of poverty; no contracts, no successions, no dividences, no occupation, but idle; no respect of kindred, but common; no apparel, but natural; no manuring of lands, no use of wine, corn, or metal. The very words that import lying, falsehood, treason, dissimulations, covetousness, envy, detraction, and pardon, were never heard of amongst them.

Compare this with Gonzalo's fantasy after he's shipwrecked on the island of *The Tempest:*

> *I' th' commonwealth I would by contraries*
> *Execute all things; for no kind of traffic*
> *Would I admit; no name of magistrate;*
> *Letters should not be known; riches, poverty,*
> *And use of service, none; contract, succession,*
> *Bourn, bound of land, tilth, vineyard, none;*
> *No use of metal, corn, or wine, or oil;*
> *No occupation; all men idle, all;*
> *And women too, but innocent and pure;*
> *No sovereignty—*
>
> *...*
>
> *All things in common nature should produce*
> *Without sweat or endeavor: Treason, felony,*
> *Sword, pike, knife, gun, or need of any engine,*
> *Would I not have; but nature should bring forth,*
> *Of its own kind, all foison, all abundance,*
> *To feed my innocent people.*

Jonson's accusation of theft rings true, but only if the criterion is verbiage. The conceptual usages are crossed. Montaigne's unexplored utopia is meant in earnest; Shakespeare is poking fun at both his character and his source—at the leisurely, moneyed abstractions of gentleman metaphysics. Shakespeare takes the same approach to "Of the Affection of Fathers to Their Children," in which Montaigne directs the aged patriarch to entrust his fortunes to his offspring, who will provide for him, which is precisely what doesn't happen in *King Lear*. This is the basest element Shakespeare dug out from Florio's Montaigne: an innocence, or naïveté, to react to. Because Montaigne was an essayist, he had to state his ideas, which, if they came into contradiction, he had to either acknowledge or resolve. Shakespeare, writing for the stage, costumed each of his characters in the rhetoric of an essayist, and in their conflicts they dramatized ideas. The playwright, who altered histories, bent time, and insisted on locating landlocked Milan, Padua, and Verona on coasts, plagiarized not out of ineptitude but out of vengeance. Each of his quotations is a commentary.

FROM THE DIARIES

Sentence from an English Language Workbook Found in Sofia

"I go to work on Monday. I work on the second floor.
I turn my computer on. The roof is on the ceiling."

A Phrase that Must Be, but Is Not, Originally Yiddish

Lies are advice to God.

INNER SYNTAX:
ON EIMEAR MCBRIDE

God alone might've written the Bible, but the Irish provided the punctuation. While the Roman Empire collapsed into the vernacular across the European continent, monks immured inside the cold stone monasteries of that cold stone island hand-copied Latin and Greek versions of Scripture. Their "manuscripts" revived Antiquity's systems of notation, resurrecting spaces between words and pauses between thoughts, and turned the Flesh of body text into the Word of divine revelation through the sacrament of quotation. The first thing God says to the first man, Adam, is, "Don't pick the fruit from a certain tree." Next, God says, "Man must have a partner," and so He puts Adam to sleep and removes a rib He turns into a woman: a half-formed thing, a dependent.

A Girl Is a Half-Formed Thing is the first novel by Eimear McBride, the latest in that illustrious line of Irish typographical reformers (born *anno Domini* 1976). Her book forgoes quotationmarks and elides verbiage for sense, sound, and sheer appearance on the page. For emphasis it occasionally wreaks havoc on *capItalS* and reverses *lettre ordre*. It is, in all respects, a heresy—which is to say, Lord above, it's a future classic.

It helps, then, that its plot is among the oldest: childhood, or innocence and its loss. Genesis is narrated in an omniscient third person: Eve picks the fruit and is shamed. McBride opts for a first-person heroine-narrator who drinks, takes drugs, and enjoys, but is traumatized by, sex. She's a lapsed Catholic, and always a cowed but dutiful daughter. She tells us all this, obliquely, and never says her name.

But then, *A Girl* begins before the name. The narrator speaks from the womb, as she's about to be delivered to a kind but care worn mother and an absentee father: "Thinking I think of you and me. Our empty spaces where fathers should be. Whenabouts we might find them and what we'd do to fill them up." The "you" being addressed is not the reader, as it might appear, but the narrator's brother, two or three years older, and afflicted with a brain tumor. If it's initially daunting to sift this prose for its relationships and even identities, it's because McBride insists that familial intimacy inheres linguistically too; this is how we all speak to our own loved ones, and about them to ourselves.

Here is the narrator speaking to her brother of their mother:

> She was careful of you. Saying let's take it slow. Mind your head dear heart. And her guts said Thank God. For her gasp of air. For this grant of Nurse I will. Learning you Our Fathers art. And when you slept I lulled in joyful mysteries glorious until I kingdom come. Mucus stogging up my nose. Scream to rupture day. Fatty snorting like a creature. A vinegar world I smelled. There now a girleen isn't she great. Bawling. Oh Ho. Now you're safe. But I saw less with these flesh eyes.

After only a chapter or two, the style is justified, and the reader converted. In a fallen world of banshee winters, abuse, abandonment, and neurosurgery, it's almost a sin of pride to care about grammar. By the time the narrator's father dies, life itself can seem like a McBride sentence: a maddened rush to the terminal without comma.

Endings, finalities, periods, anything that impedes

the flow of experience into thought, and of thought into speech: English usage imposes restraints, but then so does the Catholic Church, and even Dublin's River Liffey has dams to contend with. Throughout *A Girl*, McBride opposes her narrator's unbridled fluency, which is her vitality, to the myriad forces—the family, nuns, priests and men, many men—that would arrest it into clauses, laws, rules, and diagnoses, and it's this opposition that provides the cohering drama. This is why in a book in which the narrator struggles with her brother's decline, and with her rape by an uncle, the tragedy that would ultimately enfold them all is the adoption of a conventional clarity: the unambiguous statement, or fact, is aligned with adulthood, and so with death.

Of course, to be fully formed—to grow up—means to be tainted by this mode of communicating, as the narrator is in a catechism with her mother about their departure for another town: "It's time to go about our business. What's that? Moving house. Why? Because he bought this and I don't want it anymore. But I don't want to move Mammy. Don't start. But we've always lived here. We're. Moving. House. Because. That. Is. What. I'd. Like. To. Do. And. If. You. Don't. Too. Bad. Because. I'm. The. Mother."

Later, the narrator will catechize herself, as she recovers an appetite for sex, or power:

Pimply faces white as never seen the light and crusty
lips and dirty hands... Just leave me alone. But he didn't
answer. That voice already burning in what they don't
know for all their talk. What am I? God. Is that right.
How would that be? But there's some bit feels savage. That
doesn't know the wrong from right and sees the way to
venge. I might. I am. I will.

The narrator, approaching her late teens, decides to leave alone for the city, and so becomes briefly legible, if only because she hasn't brought along her "you." On her visits home, she regains him, her brother in his failing health and pronoun, but the accounts she gives of her independence—of an independence he'll never have—are now notably internalized, unspoken: "I met a man. I met a man. I let him throw me round the bed. And smoked, me, spliffs and choked my neck until I said I was dead. I met a man who took me for walks. Long ones in the country. I offer up. I offer up in the hedge. I met a man I met with her. She and me and his friend to bars at night and drink champagne and bought me chips at every teatime."

McBride herself, at seventeen, moved to London to study acting at the Drama Centre, wrote this novel a decade later, and spent nearly another decade trying to publish it. Once she succeeded, *A Girl* succeeded, winning a bundle of prizes, and the inevitable comparisons to the Irish tradition—Beckett's monologues, Joyce's Molly Bloom soliloquy in *Ulysses*, and the ontogenetic prose of *A Portrait of the Artist as a Young Man*—and to the Irish/British female avants: Edna O'Brien, Virginia Woolf, Ann Quin, Christine Brooke-Rose. What all that praise had in common, besides that it was deserved, was the sad sense that the English-language novel had matured from modernism and that in maturing its spirit was lost: It was now gray, shaky, timid, compromised by publicity and money, the realisms of survival.

McBride's book was a shock to that sentiment, not least because it is about that sentiment. *A Girl* subjects the outer language the world expects of us to the inner syntaxes that are natural to our minds, and in doing so refuses to equate universal experience with universal expression—a false religion that has oppressed most contemporary literature and most contemporary souls.

INADVERTENCE:
ON ALAN TURING'S CENTENNIAL

Alan Turing, the British mathematician, morphogeneti-cist, breaker of the Nazi's Enigma codes, and inventor of programmable computing, chose to commit suicide by eating an apple soaked in cyanide. But only after he'd chosen to be chemically castrated by way of estrogen hormone injections in order to avoid prison on a charge of "gross indecency," a euphemism for the sex he'd had with a man who later burgled his home. Turing's report of the burglary was what led to the final reenactment of original sin. He was forty-one years old.

Summer 2012 was the centennial of Turing's birth and, to mark the occasion, a number of books and, fittingly, ebooks have appeared, granting belated honor to a man who did more to defeat the Axis than Montgomery, Marshall, Eisenhower, Zhukov, or Konev. Turing himself, though, wasn't satisfied with the deci-phering "bombe" he'd built at Bletchley Park, where the British cryptanalysts were based throughout the war, and much preferred the Automatic Computing Engine he designed for the National Physical Laboratory in London in 1945. The bombe was just a glorified, if medi-evally torturous, calculator, capable of a single function. Turing's ideal was a Renaissance machine—a computer that could do it all.

Andrew Hodges's magisterial *Alan Turing: The Enigma*, published in 1983 and made available for the anniversary in an expanded edition with a foreword by the cognitive scientist Douglas Hofstadter, is still the definitive text. Its six hundred pages don't presume to solve Turing's life so much as to respect the equation: colonial Indian conception; itinerant boarding school in the English countryside; King's College, Cambridge; his encounter with the German mathematician David Hilbert's *Entscheidungsproblem* ("decision problem"), which led Turing to a reformulation of Kurt Gödel's theory about the limits of what can and cannot be expressed. The *Entscheidungsproblem* asks whether any proposition can be considered universally valid, which is to say logically derived as either all True or False—the answers are as binary as 1s and 0s. Hilbert's interest was in whether all propositions could be so fundamentally defined. Whereas Gödel clung to arithmetic, Turing conceived of a more materialist, or mechanized, solution: His propositions would be represented as algorithms, to be sequenced into a machine that would test whether the sequence itself, or the machine's processing of it, could ever end. At least Gödel's problem was ended: The answer was neither Yes nor No, but "Undecidable."

After publishing his results in a 1936 paper, "On Computable Numbers," Turing decamped for Princeton. *Alan Turing's Systems of Logic: The Princeton Thesis* (ed. Andrew W. Appel) contains, after its sheaf of explanatory material, a facsimile of the document that earned him his doctorate. "Systems of Logic Based on Ordinals" addresses "incompleteness," a suggestive concept in Turing's sad life but one that, in a Gödelian context, deals with sequencing propositions that can be "intuitively," as opposed to only logically, derived. Turing hazarded an audacious hypothesis: Although intuition itself might never be computable, the appearance of intuition was. With this, Turing was able to imagine a humanoid computer, possessed of an "artificial intelligence." In his formulation—eventually codified as the Turing Test—this computer would become human if and only if another human recognized "him" as such. (It

359

would seem that, in Turing's milieu, gay men couldn't hope for a similar dignity.)

A last book, a last poignancy. *Alan M. Turing: Centenary Edition*, by Sara Turing, could only have been written by one type of human—a mother who'd outlived her son. First published in 1959 and since fallen out of print, this memoir of a genius who was also a champion marathon runner, cyclist, and rationalist eccentric (wearing a gas mask to protect against pollen) is now reissued with an essay by Turing's elder brother, John. Until Turing's arrest, John had never suspected his brother's homosexuality; Sara seemed, or attempted to seem, never to believe it, just as she never believed that his death was a suicide. Her recollection concludes:

> Many friends, either by reason of his temperament and recent good spirits, or because of his "unlimited flow of ideas and great enthusiasm for putting them into practice," have been led to believe that his death was caused by some unaccountable misadventure. Besides, his inadvertence alone had always involved the risk of an accident.

"Inadvertence": She is referring to Turing's fussing with cyanide. Yes? No? Or Undecidable?

HER OWN ASYLUM:
ON ANNA KAVAN

Anna Kavan, a British fiction writer of genius, first appeared as a character—the heroine of *Let Me Alone* (1930), the third novel by Helen Ferguson, later known as Helen Edmonds, earlier known as Helen Woods, born probably in Cannes, probably in 1901. By 1938, after publishing six novels, she'd internalized the discord between her Home Counties realism and her itinerant life, had a psychological break, been institutionalized, and dedicated herself to heroin addiction. She had also come to identify with her most autobiographical, but also most mystical, character, taking Kavan as a pseudonym and then as her official surname. This new life required neither quotationmarks nor husbands (both Edmonds and Ferguson had mistreated her); neither children (one died in WWII, another died in infancy, a third was adopted and given up) nor parents (her father died young, possibly a suicide; her mother was a vain socialite who may have sexually auditioned her daughter's lovers). But it did require a new prose style: stripped, brittle-boned, shorn.

In the mid-'40s, Kavan met Dr. Karl Theodor Bluth, a physician and writer who'd escaped from Nazi Germany. He became a close friend and business adviser (after the war, Kavan earned a living renovating homes in bomb-cratered Kensington) and helped administer her injections. Most of Kavan's other friends were gay, including the Welsh author Rhys Davies, who became her amateur editor. Thanks to the Rolleston Committee, tasked by the Ministry of Health in the '20s with relieving drug dependence throughout the U.K., Kavan's most reliable dealer was the government itself.

But when the vice laws changed in 1965, Kavan was forced into counseling. After Bluth died, she suffered the black market, and stockpiled all the opiates she could, dying in 1968, her head atop the Chinese lacquered box in which she kept her stash. The police, searching her home, claimed they'd recovered enough heroin "to kill the whole street."

Kavan's corpus has been made available again in new editions, appearing throughout the 2010s. The most notable rereleases are *Asylum Piece* (1940), a story collection retelling the author's first experience in a mental ward; *Sleep Has His House* (1948), an account of insomnia; *Ice* (1967), a post-nuclear-war novel; and *Julia and the Bazooka* (1970), a compilation of narcotized fantasies. But *I Am Lazarus*, first published in 1945, is the best introduction to Kavan. Its fifteen fictions show the fullness of her career, from febrile impersonations of Eliot and Hardy and the even graver absurdity of mimicking Kafka to her later efforts at making them cellmates. (Kavan on their mutual konsonant: "Why does the 'K' sound in a name symbolize the struggle of those who try to make themselves at home on a homeless borderland?")

Lazarus allows genuine characters—Dr. Pope, Thomas Bow—to enjoy the company of abstractions like "the adversary" and "the adviser," and establishes London as the capital of a private Mitteleuropa. Throughout, Kavan's motif, the imperiled woman, is as inescapable as her setting, the clinic or sanatorium—whitewashed, windowless, almost unfurnished, almost unfurnishable rooms where some days the patients are voluntaries and other days they're prisoners, even if they've committed themselves. Nature itself becomes an inmate, convalesces.

From "Palace of Sleep":

> The wind was blowing like mad in the hospital garden.
> It seemed to know that it was near a mental hospital, and
> was showing off some crazy tricks of its own, pouncing
> first one way and then another, and then apparently in all
> directions at once.

From "Who Has Desired the Sea":

> The late autumn sun came into the ward about two in
> the afternoon. There wasn't much strength in the sun
> which was slow in creeping round the edge of the blackout
> curtains so that it took a long time to reach the bed by the
> window.

"A Certain Experience" recounts the impossibility of
relating the experience of discharge, as the narrator cannot be certain that the asylum is not rather everything
that surrounds it, beyond "the courtyard with its high
spiked walls, where shuffling, indistinguishable gangs
swept the leaves which the guards always rescattered
to be swept again." "Now I Know Where My Place Is"
concerns a grand hotel the narrator either stayed at as
a girl or only remembers from a photograph—though it
might also be a dream or, as the previous fictions have
conditioned us to imagine, yet another institution. "The
Blackout" and "Glorious Boys" concern the Blitz—the
privations, the darkness. During peace, "asylum" is for
the insane. During war, it's for everyone else.

FROM THE DIARIES

American Woman Complimented by Greek Man

"You look like one million dollars. Because you are tall."

Bucharest Hostel

The paint has flaked from the wall in the shape of the country I will found for you, my love.

BIBLIOTHANATOS, OR
EPIGRAPHS FOR A LAST BOOK

Once, in the future, a man wanted to keep a secret safe from everyone. He wrote it down into a book.

Once, in the future, some child will have to look up what a book is on the computer. What a book was.

Once books go, can we still use the word "binding" or "bound"? What will bind us together now, what will be bound? Certainly nothing between covers.

In other words, what to make of "margin" or "marginal" in a postbook world?

I like the archaic English for book: "boke." As in Chaucer, at the end of *Canterbury Tales*, disavowing himself of "the boke of Troilus, the boke also of Fame, the boke of the five and twenty Ladies, the boke of the Duchesse, the boke of Seint Valentines day of the Parlement of briddes." It's like "book," but only in past tense.

Pages are more fraught than screens. With a page you're reading, you always know there's a page you're not reading just on the other side.

Bookmarks: (personal) envelopes, pencils and pens, an ermine's baculum (penis bone), my father's expired driver's license, a scrap of a dead neighbor's *ex libris* on which I wrote the word "bibliothanatos"; (historical) Mao had bookmarks made featuring his sayings, "Be serious, be active," bamboo bookmarks from Nepal, corn husks from Czechoslovakia, American bookmarks made as advertisements for Heinz in the warty shapes of pickles; it's believed that Queen Elizabeth I (1533–1603) first popularized bookmarks; the term now indicates a computer function that holds an online "page" detailing the life of Elizabeth (inaccurate).

Revelations is the last book of the Bible, at least of the New Testament. It seems too obvious that the Bible should end with Apocalypse. No good novelist would have allowed it.

W, a librarian friend, mentioned that he'd cataloged approximately thirty books called "The Last Book," or a variation on that title.

People enthuse about the smell of books, but it is only the smell of dust. This instructs in mortality: After the book is composed, it decomposes. That (and other reasons) is why there are multiple copies.

People enthuse over touching a book: texture, heft in hand. It should be noted for posterity that if you closed your eyes and ran your fingertips over a page, you could tell which parts of that page were blank and which held ink. Words were palpable, words felt palpable, until the advent of recycling, and digital printing, the 1990s.

The taste of books. Monks poisoned the page tips of forbidden books to punish their readers. Rabbis placed honey there to encourage their students to lick and go forward. Lick and proceed.

At least that was the story I heard from my uncle (not a monk, his name is also Cohen).

I asked, "But then when you finished the lesson and shut the book, wouldn't all the honeyed pages stick together?"

He said, "The problem with your generation is not just that you can't tell a story, it's that you can't listen to one neither."

III. DREAMLANDS

OPEN SESAME

A writer stands outside of a story yelling, "Open Sesame!" and then, what do you know, the story, as if it were a seed, opens. And treasure is found inside. That treasure, of course, is just another story, and it all begins again.

Or else, say the writer is no different from any other of his tribe—say he's actually a thief. And the story is no story, but really a mountain. "Open Sesame!" then (this writer continues), the mountain opens, and my meaning is revealed.

A version of this nonsense—this magician's stage business—occurs in the tale "Ali Baba and the Forty Thieves," popularly known from *The Thousand and One Nights*.

But Ali's tale is not to be found in the oldest manuscripts of that collection. Some believe it to be the invention of one Youhenna Diab, known as Hanna of Aleppo, an Arab Christian storyteller said to have communicated it to Antoine Galland, the first translator of the *Nights* into French; while other scholars argue for a purely Western source and believe that Ali is the incorrupt fiction of Galland himself (though Richard Burton, the first translator of an unexpurgated *Nights* into English, claimed that *Ali* was to be found in an Arabic original, a mythical manuscript often forged but never found).

Indeed, Galland (1646–1715) is the earliest source for this exclamation: "*Sésame,*" he has his Baba say, "*ouvre toi!*" while the ponderous Burton (1821–90) has given us not "sesame" but "Open, O Simsim!"

In the first two decades of the nineteenth century, the brothers Grimm collected what seems to be a German variant of the tale under the title *Simeliberg*. In their telling, a mountain somewhere in the Reich opens to disclose its myriad riches when addressed by the word *Semsi*: *"Berg Semsi, Berg Semsi, thu dich auf."* The Grimms, who were, we should remember, philologists by training and compilers of a dictionary, explain this *Semsi*—given in subsequent editions as *Simsi*, and *Semeli*—as an archaic German word, or name, for "mountain." Wilhelm Grimm, the younger of the brothers and the better writer, notes: "This name for a mountain is, according to a document in Pistorius, very ancient in Germany. A mountain in Grabfeld is called Similes and in a Swiss song a Simeliberg is again mentioned. This makes us think of the Swiss word '*Sinel*' for 'sinbel,' round."

Was Ali Baba Galland's creation, or only a character adapted from European folklore? Should we think that Galland, that forty-first thief, in an ostensible translation of Arabic into French, gave us, instead, an immemorial German children's story in Oriental guise? Thus far we have an errant Arab "original," a French *Sésame* from the seventeenth century, a German *Semsi* collected in the early nineteenth century, and an English "Simsim" from later that same century. Our understanding is complicated even further when we think that Burton, whose English is the latest of the revisions discussed here, has left us with the seemingly most authentic salutation: His "Simsim" is nothing but the Arabic word for "sesame"— *Sesamum orientale*.

Which came first, Simsim or *Semsi*? The *Sésame* or a more germinating seed? As this is the "Middle East," opinions and arguments support every agenda, obliterating synthesis. In favor of the primacy of sesame: That seed was prized by Babylon for its ability to ward off, or remove, evil curses. In favor, why not, of an Oriental heritage for *Semsi:* That word, whether or not it means or names a Teutonic mountain, might be a mondegreen of Arabic's greeting, the peaceful *Salaam.* Where does that leave us—wedged between the cave wall and the protecting boulder admitting no light? Searching still, as scholars have always searched, for an Arabic source for a German folktale/French art story that, in our Englished day, has become the quintessential narrative of Arabia?

The mountain opens for the voice, the voice rolls away the sepulchral stone—and treasures lie within, they lie behind, proverbial silver, metaphor's gold; the precious gem of language, made when all the facets of all the languages join as one. Words are borrowed in preparation for this call—words, sounds, translations, tralatitious mistranslations—but by whom, in what way?

Where did I first hear this cry? Not as a reader of Scheherazade's mortal, crepuscular entertainment, but as a fanatic of weekend TV. In cartoons come Sundays, when Bugs Bunny twitched his ears, ashed his cigarlike carrot, and gave out to a rock face in gumptious New York immigrant-speak, "Close, seza me!"

(I write this in the summer after the sixth anniversary of the American invasion of Iraq—civilization's cradle, birthplace of the *Nights.* In Iraq, Ali Baba served as U.S. military slang to characterize "the natives," much as Vietnam's Charlie was used to dehumanize the enemy of that previous lost war. But, in time, thanks to occupation, many Iraqis themselves began using the epithet Ali Baba to describe the American soldiers who regularly looted Iraqi museum property and homes; soldiers who need demonstrate no causality, nor do they need any magic formula to burst down doors—just force.)

ME, U, BAKU, QUBA

One thing about dictatorships, they're either very expensive or very cheap to fly to. There's no such thing as a midrange regime: Extremities charge extremities. I know a guy, it cost him $4,600 just to get to North Korea (Newark-Beijing-Dandong, and then across the DPRK border in a Jeep). I know another guy, it cost him $2,800 just to get to Laos (Newark-Tokyo-Bangkok-Vientiane). I flew nonstop from JFK to Baku, Azerbaijan, visa included, for all of $500. The plane was a brand-new Airbus A340; the pilots were military-grade, and the senior or just older pilot wore medals on his chest that resembled poker chips: two black, one yellow, which at Trump casinos, back when there were Trump casinos, would've been redeemable for $1,200. The flight attendants, uniformed in sky-gray and blood-red, were gorgeous: The men were creatic gym creatures bursting out of their polo shirts; the women were dripping with make-up and curvaceous, their skirts slit as high as it gets, at least in the world of Islamic female-flight-attendant fashion. The three exorbitant meals they served over the course of the ten-hour, thirty-minute, 5,812-mile/9,353-kilometer flight were culturally specific (mutton stews and breads) and hot (very hot). The in-flight-entertainment selection was operated by individual seat-back touchscreen and generous and included, alongside the standard Hollywood and Russian offerings, an impressive selection of Azeri content, all of it bearing the seal of the Ministry of Culture and Tourism of Azerbaijan. I tried to catch up on *Star Wars*, the prequel trilogy, in order to prepare for the upcoming release of the sequel trilogy, though by the middle of *Episode II—Attack of the Clones*, I'd had enough and switched to

374

an Azeri property, but it was only in Azeri—no subtitles, no dub—and so I wasn't able to ascertain whether the lawyer was the good guy, or the bad guy, or not a lawyer at all and instead a slick plastic surgeon on trial for corrupting his wife.

The plane was mostly empty, with no more than two dozen other passengers, about half of whom would terminate in Baku, with the other half Israeli—Russian-Israelis, *Parsim* (Persian Israeli), and *Teimanim* (Yemeni Israelis). Leave it to the Jews to find out that AZAL, the Azerbaijani government's official airline, or flag-carrier, had been subsidizing ticket prices from America, and so the cheapest way to get from New York to Tel Aviv was to go through Baku and wait. I'm not sure that this subsidy policy was created for the express purpose of saving Jews money, but then neither am I sure that it was created to encourage visits by American tourists and business travelers. Instead, dictator president Ilham Aliyev just cares about being able to boast domestically that his country now has biweekly direct flights from/ to New York. The airport, which Aliyev is constantly renovating, as if he were intent on expanding it in tandem with the expansion of the universe, is named for his father, Heydar Aliyev, the previous dictator president. At its center is a glitzy foreign-flights terminal that resembles the Galactic Senate from *Star Wars*. The landing was baby-gentle, the deplaning swift; the Israelis dispersed to window-shop duty-free caviar and Rolexes until their departure for Ben-Gurion.

I was processed through immigration and customs, asked no questions, but photographed twice. The first person in Azerbaijan to ask me any questions was my cabdriver: "What you doing here?" And, "What you pay?"

I answered the "what I doing here?" with, "I'm a tourist," because to say that I'd come to this majority-Muslim authoritarian country as a writer, let alone as a journalist, would be like saying I'd come to prey on your youth, or to masturbate into the Caspian. I answered the "what I pay?" with, "How about 20 manats?"—because that was the amount suggested by "Zaur J" on a messageboard on TripAdvisor.com. Other posts had suggested 14, 16, 25, 30, and taking the 116 shuttle bus to the 28 May train station for 40 qepik, which was roughly a quarter.

I settled on 20, because it wasn't my money. A bit over $12. The driver suggested 25. Which was a bit over $15. He still hadn't asked where we were going.

Azerbaijan is a nation bordered by threats and built atop lies. This makes it not too different from any other nation, except: To the south is Iran, to the north is Georgia and a hunk of Russian Dagestan (which doesn't do much to buffer the rumblings of Chechnya and Ossetia); to the west is a short border with Turkey and a long, troubled ton of border shared with hated Armenia, with which Azerbaijan has been engaged in an on-and-off war over the Nagorno-Karabakh exclave since 1988; while to the east is the largest enclosed inland body of water on earth, the oil-and-natural-gas-rich Caspian, whose greatest local landlord is SOCAR (State Oil Company of Azerbaijan Republic), which partners with and administers contracts for the AIOC (the Azerbaijan International Operating Company), a consortium of extractors headed by BP (U.K.), and including—in order of declining equity—Chevron (United States), INPEX (Japan), Statoil (Norway), ExxonMobil (United States), TPAO (Turkey), ITOCHU (Japan), and ONGC Videsh (India). To make it clearer, Azerbaijan is a seabound country with dwindling but still significant reserves of oil, outsized reserves of natural gas, the highest Shia population percentage in the world after Iran, an ongoing conflict with an Orthodox Christian neighbor, close-enough experience of the Georgian/Abkhazian and Chechen Wars, a sense of Russia as representing the highest of culture, yet a sense of Putin as the lowest of thugs, bent on recapturing a toxic mashup of Soviet/Tsarist glory, and so perpetually reconnoitering the Central Asian steppes for the next Donbass or Crimea. Dropping oil and natural-gas revenues have sparked a rising interest in the previously inimical—because Sunni—Salafism blowing north from Iranian Kurdistan and south from Ciscaucasia. As of 2016, over 1,500 Azerbaijani citizens were in Syria fighting for ISIS.

Baku, the capital, a city of approximately two million people, is a brash glam cesspit of new construction—newly stalled since the global banking crisis and, again, since oil and gas have plummeted—surrounded by ruined farmland. To pass from Baku to the countryside is to pass from the twenty-first century to the nineteenth, skipping the twentieth entirely, which was such a downer anyway, everyone pretends not to notice. Throughout the country there isn't a dominant culture, but an only-culture. Azerbaijani state power, though notionally secular, has the force of Islam and the same vertical structure: bow and scrape. The country's best criminals are treated like businessmen, and the country's best businessmen happen to be members of the ruling family. To get a good job, you have to have good connections. To get good connections you have to be born to a good family. To be born to a good family you have to be blessed by a good God. If you find yourself—like, say, the 7.4 million people in Azerbaijan who don't live in Baku—unlucky enough to be excluded from this system of patronage, or nepotistic oligarchy, you're fucked. All you can do, in your fuckedness, is put on a fake face and submit. Spend all your money on your car, or your clothes, so that you seem wealthier. Name your firstborn male child after the president or the president's father so that he seems more employable. Have more female children, because only women can marry up. Take pride in the new pedestrian promenade along the waterfront. In the skyscrapers you don't work in. The malls you can't afford to shop in. Embrace the falsehoods and lead a double life.

So, the truth of why I'd come here—if truth can be spoken, or even spoken of, in Azeri (whose word for truth, *haqq*, also means justice, and payment): I was in Baku only to get the hell out of Baku—to go to the edge of Azerbaijan and up into the Caucasus, the easternmost of the western mountains, or the westernmost of the eastern mountains, where, tectonically, Europe crashes into Asia. I was headed there to enact a submission of my own: to fall down at the Adidas-sneakered feet of the Mountain Jews—a sect of overwhelmingly short, hairy, dark-skinned Semites—who, as craggy cloud-bound slope-dwellers, seemed perfectly positioned to offer me the wisdom I was seeking, without any annoying lectures on Orientalism.

I wanted to ask these Jews—these fellow Jews—what to do: about how to handle, how personally to handle, the tragedy of capitalism as it withers into kleptocracy; about how to deal, how personally to deal, with Islamic fundamentalism and the compounding quandary that is Zionism; about how to survive as a writer—how to scheme and scam to get by as "a writer"—in a world that doesn't read.

While I didn't seriously suppose that the Mountain

Jews had all the answers, I did suspect, or hope, that they themselves would be the answers. After all, they— their community—might comprise the longest-running mafia in recorded history. Or semi-recorded—because the Mountain Jews have never written their own history, because writing is too fixed, too fixing, and surely too unremunerative. Instead, they abide in strangers' pages, shrouded in the oral.

Among their legends are the following, which I'll list in order from "OK, I'll Give You the Benefit of the Doubt," to "Definitely Didn't Happen":

Toward the end of the eighth century B.C.E., the Assyrians conquered the Northern Kingdom of Israel, Samaria, and deported between one and ten of its tribes— between one and ten of the so-called Lost Tribes—for resettlement in their capital, Nineveh, present-day Mosul. But the Assyrian king, Ashur, whom the Mountain Jews associate with Shalmaneser V, mentioned in II Kings, grew so enraged by the Israelites for refusing to forsake their God and for the success they had in commerce that he exiled them to the edge of the empire—to the Caucasus Mountains, where they flourished.

Toward the end of the eighth century B.C.E., Hoshea, last of the Israelite kings, attempted to gain his kingdom's independence from Assyria and, as recorded in II Kings, stopped paying the official tribute—10 talents of gold, 1,000 talents of silver—upon Shalmaneser V's ascension to the throne. Shalmaneser V moved to recoup his losses by imprisoning Hoshea, laying siege to Samaria, and seizing the property of between one and ten of its tribes— the property of between one and ten of the so-called Lost Tribes—whom he or his successor, Sargon II, exiled to the edge of the empire—to the Caucasus Mountains, where they flourished.

Toward the end of the eighth century B.C.E., under the reign of Hoshea, around twenty thousand Israelites fled the destruction of their kingdom—or left to seek unimperiled trade routes between east and west—or traveled en masse to Nineveh to post bail and free Hoshea from debtors' prison, but failed—or traveled en masse to press an alliance against the Assyrians with the Egyptian King So (either Tefnakht of Sais or Osorkon IV of Tanis) but went astray. They passed through Assyria, Babylonia, and Persia before settling atop the Caucasus Mountains, where they flourished.

The more scholarly proposals of Mountain Jewish origin, the few of them there are, prove just as fascinating/ unsatisfactory:

Jews came from the Israelite Kingdom to Persia ca. eighth century B.C.E.; Persian Jews came to Greater Caucasia— the area between the Black and Caspian Seas—ca. fifth century C.E. With the incursions of Goths and/or Huns from the Black Sea region, across the Pontic steppe, the Parthian and/or Sassanid Empires (third century B.C.E. to third century C.E., the former) (third century C.E. to seventh century C.E., the latter) required a border defense force. Considering the Jews to be exemplary warriors, the Parthian and/or Sassanid kings resettled them in the Caucasus.

In the fifth century C.E., Sassanid King Yazdegerd II forced all the peoples he conquered to convert to Zoroastrianism and embarked on violent persecutions of Assyrian and Armenian Christians and Persian and Armenian Jews, with the result that the latter two fled, either together or separately, to the Caucasus.

By the eighth century C.E., a nomadic Turkic people called the Khazars, or Kuzari, had relinquished their syncretic religion of Tengriism (worship of the Turkic sky god Tengri), Islam, Christianity, and Judaism and converted exclusively to Judaism. Formerly a trading partner between Byzantium and the Sassanids, and then between Byzantium and the Ummayads, the Khazars now became enemies of both, as well as of Kievn Rus, whose prince, Sviatoslav I, razed their de facto capital, Atil— located along the Volga—whose population sought shelter in the Caucasus.

In or around the ninth century C.E., one or more of the minor khanates around the Caspian attempted to break what it or they regarded as a Jewish monopoly on maritime and overland trade by expelling its or their Jews from the coastal plain to the Caucasus. Or one or more of the minor khanates sent its or their Jews up into the mountains to act as a frontier guard. Or sent its or their Jews up into the mountain passes to act as basically inspectors and toll collectors—enforcing tariffs, imposing duties. Or else the Jews, either compelled to quit or perhaps even quitting the coastal plain of their own accord, went rogue up in the Caucasus, and appointed themselves frontier guards, inspectors, and/or toll collectors—extorting tribute and/or protection payments from any and all passing through.

By the late 1600s, Jews of Persian descent, fleeing the persecutions of the Persian Safavids for the fraying borders of the Lak Gazikumukh Shamkhalate, had established themselves on the shores of the Caspian near Derbent—today the second largest city in Dagestan, and the southernmost city in Russia—in a settlement called Aba-Sava. The Shamkhalate, in a bid to prevent the Safavids from advantaging its weaknesses and annexing

381

its holdings, struck an alliance with Catherine the Great. The Jews, who traded with everyone—the Shamkhalate, the Russians, the Safavids—had alliances with none. Aba-Sava was destroyed in either the second, or third, Russo-Persian War, and its Jews were half slaughtered, half scattered, and found shelter only under the Russian-aligned reign of Fatali Khan, ruler of the Quba Khanate, and conqueror of Derbent, who dispersed them to remote mountain towns of his dominion.

Regardless of which interpretation you hold with, the situation seems to be this: Somehow, a loose group of Jews that spoke a dialect of Persian that contained elements of Hebrew—a dialect now called Judeo-Tat, or Juhuri, or Gorsky—found themselves virtually alone high up in the rebarbative Caucasus, where—for a period of two hundred years, or two thousand years, give or take a grain of salt—they seem to have controlled most of the mountain passes, and so most of the caravanning traffic, on that tangle of routes as gossamer as thread that the German geographer Ferdinand von Richthofen (1833–1905) immortalized as the Silk Road (*die Seidenstraße*).

Few goods could cross the Pontic steppe—between Persia, Arabia, India, China, etc., and Europe—without the Mountain Jews taking a cut. Few good merchants could avoid saddling and gapping their peaks—unless, just before the Bolshevik Revolution, they wanted to take the Transcaspian Railway from Tashkent, Samarqand, or Bukhara, to Turkmenbashi, and then a steamer across the Caspian Sea to Baku, then the Transcaucasian Railway to Batumi, and then a steamer across the Black Sea to Odessa—unless, just after the Bolshevik Revolution, they wanted to take an airplane.

But then, even since the invention of the airplane and

intermodal freight, the Mountain Jews haven't done too poorly.

Of the approximately two hundred thousand Judeo-Tats, or Juhuros, or Gorsky Jews in existence (*gora* means "mountain" in Russian), half live in Israel, and about twenty thousand in the States; many of the rest are in Russia, mostly in Moscow—and in Azerbaijan, mostly in Baku. Only a few still live in their ancestral *auls* (fortified, or once upon a time fortified, settlements), midway up the flanks of mountains along two of the Caucasus's three major ranges, many of which are inaccessible today because the lines they obey are of faults, not borders; and though the armies camped atop the crust can't stop the sediment, Azerbaijanis can and do stop Armenians from crossing, and Armenians can and do stop Azerbaijanis from crossing, and each stops the other from crossing into the de facto independent but unrecognized republic of Nagorno-Karabakh; Turks stop Armenians from crossing and Armenians stop Turks from crossing; Georgians stop Russians from crossing, and Russians stop Georgians from crossing (not only the Russian republics of Dagestan, Chechnya, Ingushetia, North Ossetia, Kabardino-Balkaria, and Karachay-Cherkessia, but also the partially recognized breakaway-from-Georgia state of South Ossetia; the partially recognized breakaway-from-Georgia state of Abkhazia; and the breakaway-from-Georgia autonomous republic of Adjara).

What unites all these lands, besides their tramontane routes, are their Jews, whose ancestors had known all these lands under earlier names and no names, and had traded with all of their peoples in their own languages. It was this ability to slip between states, endonyms, exonyms, and tongues that enabled the Mountain Jews' survival, their continuity like rock, and earned them the contempt of countless dynasties that predeceased them. It was also what caused the Nazis to recognize them as Jews, and to treat them accordingly—indeed, they were the most Eastern Jews the Nazis ever encountered and, after studying their customs, not excluding polygamy, it was decided that their Judaism was more "religious" than "racial," though that didn't prohibit the occasional massacre. The Soviets, however, in compiling their statistics on national minorities, formally indexed them not as Jews but as Iranians. With the Soviet collapse, Sunni extremists started kidnapping Mountain Jews for ransom in Dagestan and Chechnya (Mountain Jewish communities always pay ransom), so that today, Azerbaijan seems to be their safest haven in the Caucasus—the only country to have realized the benefits of touting its Mountain Jews as mascots of ethnic comity, while shrewdly using them as regional dragomans and trade intercessors with Russia.

Because if Azerbaijan has become the Mountain Jews' sanctuary, Russia is now their bazaar—its appetites have made their fortune. Mountain Jews of my own generation, who came of age under Yeltsin's two terms of larceny and greed, moved into Moscow, St. Petersburg, and the vast cities of Siberia that have less name recognition, but more manufacturing infrastructure and coal mines. There they went about privatizing. Here's what privatizing means: When a state that owns everything disintegrates, suddenly everything's up for grabs; if you want a shop, or a factory, or an entire industry, say, you just show up and claim it as yours; the cops can't kick you out, because there aren't any cops—the cops don't stay cops when they're not getting paid—and so you dig in, and, should other parties arrive to stake their claims, you just have to hope that you have more and bigger men, and more and bigger guns, than they do. To give two examples—not to formally accuse them of having done anything like this, but merely to admire them if they had—God Nisanov (b. 1972), and Zarah Iliev (b. 1966). Both moved to Moscow in the early '90s and immediately went underground, taking over kiosks throughout the drafty cavernous Metro, whose stations had been designed to serve as bomb shelters, but now were also becoming groceries and malls. Nisanov and Iliev began shipping produce to the capital, setting up construction firms, and investing in real estate. Today, they're the largest commercial real-estate developers in Moscow, with properties including the Evropeyskiy Shopping Center, the Radisson Royal Hotel, the Radisson Slavyanskaya Hotel, myriad office parks, and wholesale and retail commodity markets (food, appliances, electronics, etc.). As of 2015, Forbes estimated the net worth of each at $4.9 billion, which tied them for the title of twenty-fourth-richest person in Russia. In 2014, Nisanov was awarded the Order of Friendship by Putin and was elected to the executive committee of the World Jewish Congress.

Both Nisanov and Iliev were born in the most venerable of the Mountain Jewish *auls*, Quba. Pronounced "Guba." Actually, they're from a Jewish enclave located just outside Quba, which in Azeri is called Qırmızı Qəsəbə, and in Russian is called Yevreiskaya Sloboda (Jewish Town), though under the Soviet period its name was changed to Krasnaya Sloboda (Red Town). Now, it shouldn't seem particularly strange that a village of fewer than 3,800 people produced two friends who grew up to become billionaires together. But it should seem particularly strange that this village currently boasts four billionaires, and at least twelve (by one count) and eighteen (by another) worth in the hundreds of millions. They include, as already noted, major property developers and commodity importers, but also car importers, clothing importers, and the managers of the Azerbaijani government's oil and gas portfolios.

I'd been introduced to the existence of the Mountain Jews, and of Quba, by a man a friend of mine met at the banya—a Russian bathhouse, in Brooklyn. This man happened to know, or in the course of sweating conversation claimed to know, my friend's relative, a Brooklyn (non-Mountain) Jew who does something I'd prefer not to understand with slot machines and has spent time as a ward of the state. I was told that this man from Quba, whose phone number my friend obtained for me, imported apples to New York—to the Big Apple, which, last time I checked, grows plenty of its own...

In any event, I called the man's number, introduced myself, in English, as a novelist—not as a journalist. I figured, because my friend had told him to expect the call, that he already had my name and I was searchable online; I also figured the man lived in America, he knew what a novelist was—he knew that it meant "vicarious-thrill seeker," or "coward." He immediately tried frustrating my interest, but I continued to pester, and finally got him to set a meeting. Which he canceled. I got him to set another meeting, and he canceled again, but at least had pretensions to courtesy and gave me a local, Baku, number. I searched the number online, and it was the same one listed on the site for the Mountain Jewish community office, whose address was the same as that of the Mountain Jewish central synagogue. But by the time I realized all that, I'd already convinced an editor to commission me and signed a contract. A check for expenses had cleared my account. Not only that: I'd already flown halfway across the globe and was sitting on the bed of my hotel, the Intourist, laptop on my lap, phone suctioned to my cheek, being reminded—as the number I kept dialing kept ringing—why I'd always preferred writing fiction...

I went to the address listed on the site, ostensibly just a leisurely stroll from the Intourist, but either the address was wrong or the street sign was: Under the Aliyevs, many of the streets in Baku have been stripped of their Russian names and given appellations in Azeri. Some of the more conscientious businesses list both street names on their sites. Most, however, don't bother. Then there's the issue of Azeri orthography, which further complicates map usage. Formerly, Azeri had been written in Perso-Arabic; in the 1920s the Latinesque Common Turkic alphabet was adopted; in 1939, the Soviets forced the adoption of the Cyrillic alphabet; after Sovietism, Latinesque Common Turkic was reinstated, and it was only in 1992 that the schwa, or ə, so prevalent in the name of the street I was searching for—Şəmsi Bədəlbəyli—was called into service to replace the diaeresistic—umlauted—a. One map listed Şəmsi Bədəlbəyli as Shamsi Bedelbeyli, and another as Shämsi Bädälbäyli (apparently a formidable Azeri theater actor and director). Whatever its spelling, the boulevard I eventually stumbled upon was a double-boulevard, and wide, but composed of many tiny lanes thronged with many tiny cars; its northbound and southbound congeries were divided by an island of freshly planted parkland—the grass not yet sprouted over the sprinkler heads—beyond which, on the distant side, was the dormant worksite of a massive condo project: Beaux-Arts trimmings atop concrete bunkers separated by gravel lots like bulldozer caravanserais. Catercorner to the condos, I found it: the community office, the central synagogue—the Baku HQ of the Mountain Jews. It was an immense new building of austere Art Deco detailing that, given its sharp-cornered cleanliness and shine, seemed two-dimensional, like an architectural rendering, a placard of itself:

THIS WILL BE BUILT ON THIS SITE.

It was amazing to me that this structure had another dimension—it was amazing that I was able to step inside. Though only for a moment.

A man strode up and, in response to my asking in Hebrew, said he spoke Hebrew. He was tall, skinny like he had a parasite, and wore a flatcap and trenchcoat indoors. He was between thirty and forty, I'd guess, but had a sparse scraggly beard—like he'd five-fingered it off the face of a surly teenager. He wouldn't give his name—I mean his own name—or he couldn't. It turned out that he couldn't speak Hebrew, or what he spoke of it wasn't just jumbled, but jumbled with rigor: morning (*boker*) was evening (*erev*) and vice versa, six (*sheysh*) was seven (*sheva*) and vice versa, the ark (*aron*) was a prayerbook (*siddur*). After showing me around the synagogue proper, he took me into the facility's community-center portion and showed me a wall of portraits of Mountain Jewish heroes of Azerbaijan's wars, and another wall of portraits of Mountain Jewish leaders posing alongside Putin, Netanyahu, both the Aliyevs, George W. Bush, Sheldon Adelson, and assorted Azerbaijani mullahs from the government's Committee for Religious

388

Organizations. Then he hit me up for a donation—he didn't confuse the word for charity, *tzedakah*. I gave him 5 manats, and asked if he knew any Mountain Jews who'd be willing to take me to Quba. He shook his head—meaning he didn't know? or didn't understand?—shook my hand, and ushered me out the door.

From the six or so years I lived and worked as a journalist throughout Eastern Europe, I was used to this stripe of wariness. No one who grew up in an authoritarian regime likes to or, honestly, can answer a question directly. Everyone hesitates, dissembles, feels each other out. Feels out, that is, the type and degree of trouble that truthfulness, if they're even capable of truthfulness, might get them into. In most post-Soviet countries this Cold War ice can usually be broken or, at a minimum, thawed, by a bribe, or through the vigorous application of alcohol. But here, in this Muslim country whose signature intoxicant was tea, alcohol wasn't an option.

So I headed back to Brooklyn.

By which I mean: I went to find the Azerbaijan Chabad House.

Chabad Lubavitch is a Hasidic religious movement based in Brooklyn, which—like a yarmulke-wearing, spiritually focused version of a UN taskforce or NGO—dispatches its rabbis all over the world, to provide essential religious services in places where there aren't many Jews—in Asia, Africa, even Antarctica, though they're especially active in places where there haven't been many Jews for a while, thanks to the Soviets and/or Nazis. They're basically a missionary organization, except they don't convert so much as reclaim: They bring the unaffiliated back into the fold. Now, that's a laudable brief for an organization to have, but there's also a dark side, in that Chabad, at one extreme, is something of a messianic cult (some of the rabbis proclaim an uncomfortable fealty to their deceased leader, Menachem Mendel Schneerson, the Lubavitcher rebbe), and insists on imposing its parochial brand of Ashkenazi Judaism—Eastern European Hasidic Judaism—no matter the local tradition or preference.[1]

There's also this pesky issue that a few of their rabbinic emissaries have had with, OK, money-laundering.

What might've licensed that behavior is a quirk of history: European Jews, not just in the East but throughout the continent, had almost always been required by the governments of the countries they lived in to identify as Jewish. Even after forced registrations became census requests, Jews tended to continue the practice on their own: If they gave charity to or attended their synagogue, there was a fair chance their home city or province's community had their name and address on file, and it was these files, these community rolls, that made the Nazi genocide that much more efficient. After the fall of Sovietism, amid the aforementioned rash of privatization, nascent independent countries like Poland and Czechoslovakia found themselves steeped in unclaimed property, a lot of which had belonged to Jews, a lot of whom were dead. Meanwhile, young ambitious Jews of the postwar generations, many with limited Jewish education and even limited Jewish identification, were busy reorganizing their official communities into nonprofit

1. Just one example: In 2004, Rabbi Sholom Ber Krinsky, a native of Boston and a scion of Chabad assigned to Vilnius, proclaimed himself Chief Rabbi of Lithuania, a country whose Jews, called *Mitnagdim*, or "opponents," spent over two hundred years resisting what they regarded as the intellectual torpor and heretical mysticism of Hasidism, from the moment of that movement's founding in Poland/Ukraine, up until the depredations of the Holocaust.

religious entities. Having varying levels of access to their prewar rolls, they applied to state, provincial, and city governments, not just for the restitution of their rightful infrastructure—their synagogues and cemeteries—but also for the restitution of the properties of their exterminated members who'd left no next of kin. Not many of these Jewish communities had rabbis; Chabad had rabbis—trained in America and Israel. Chabad sent its rabbis to open Chabad Houses—from which they directed prayers, classes, food-and-clothing drives, and life-cycle ceremonies (mostly funerals)—and while the preponderance of the sect's emissaries stuck to mission principles and successfully renewed Jewish life, a few were tempted, or invited, to infiltrate the administrations of their governmentally sanctioned communities and took up posts as official chief or head rabbis—which gave them nominal power over the management of community real estate portfolios, some of which were extraordinarily lucrative. For instance: much of the downtown tourist districts of Krakow and Prague. Local influential Jews, inured to the inversions of Sovietism, in which the state was the criminal, and they were merely businessmen, would cut deals with the Chabad rabbis assigned to them, supporting the movement and smoothing its way in return for using this reclaimed infrastructure to clean their money—say, a Russian Jew from Odessa who in the 1990s amid the ludicrous inflation and loan defaults of independent Ukraine gets involved in the counterfeit luggage racket, and launders his profits through a storefront in a community-owned, because community-restituted, building that before it'd been nationalized by the Soviets and devastated by the Nazis had belonged to a Jewish family that'd been liquidated in the camp at Bogdanovka. I once, at a very tender, pious, and moronic age, tried to report on this phenomenon—a phenomenon that, in retrospect, I now find utterly rational and tolerable—and, in return for my sanctimony, in the course of a single day, one man threatened my life, and another man handed me an envelope crammed with cash that kept me housed and fed and working on a novel for nearly all of 2004. Suffice to say, I'm no Chabad booster. But still, if I could never completely bring myself to trust Hasidim, I could at least trust Hasidim to be Hasidim.

Chabad has its Azerbaijani House on Dilara Aliyeva Street, which used to be called Surakhanskaya, and under the Soviets was Pervomayskaya. I couldn't figure out whether Dilara Aliyeva was related to the dictator president Aliyevs, or just shared their surname (two people said yes, online said no), but I do know that she founded an antidomestic abuse organization and was a member of the opposition People's Front, who died in what Russian media described, not without bias, as a mysterious car accident on the Azerbaijani/Georgian border in 1991.

The head of Chabad in Baku, conforming to expectations, introduced himself as the Chief Rabbi of Azerbaijan; his business card read "Cheif Rabbi" [sic] of "The Jewish Community of European Jews." Whatever. I addressed him in Hebrew, just to be a schmuck, but also because it felt like the only language to use in Baku for a conversation with another guy from New Jersey. Rabbi Shneor Segal—robustly obese, copiously bristled, the suit I'd bet from Shemtov's on Empire Boulevard, the Borsalino I'd bet from Primo's on Kingston Avenue—asked me to put on tefillin and tallis to pray, and after I did, because prayer is the price of admission with Chabad, he asked me to explain my presence. I was a tourist, I said. From where? Brooklyn. Ah, he said, Brooklyn. Born there? Born in Atlantic City. Ah, he said, New Jersey.

It was English after that. I told him we had mutual acquaintances, and named the rabbis in Prague and Krakow. He knew them. I named their wives, their children. He softened, reclined, released his belly over his belt. We talked about his difficulties getting a lease on a space to open up a kosher restaurant—there were so many people to "pay," and so many people he might slight through a failure to "pay," and all of them would be his only customers. We talked about my difficulties getting in with the Mountain Jews, and I wondered if he was in touch with any—if he knew any who'd take me around.

His face lit, and then his phone lit, and he was scrolling through his contacts. He was giving me a number, but what he said was: "I'm giving you a *mitzvah*."

There was this Mountain Jewish kid, he said, who was an orphan. His father had absconded, way back when. His mother had just died. He was having problems earning a living, but at least he had a car.

Some SMS'ing, and emailing, later, everything was arranged. This Mountain Jew agreed to pick me up, next day, at the Intourist.

One thing about the Intourist, before I continue: The original Intourist—the hotel of choice, or of no-choice, for foreign visitors under Sovietism—had aged so shoddily that it had to be demolished. But after the demolition, some oil and gas execs, feeling so nostalgic for what'd surely been a heap of reeking plumbing and intermittent electricity, commissioned a replica built on a plot just a block away.

The Mountain Jew, who was late to pick me up, was a

companionable slab of stymied maleness, aimless in his middle twenties, in too tight blue jeans, too tight black T-shirt, swart face with lots of scruff, lots of Asian: epicanthic folds.

If I'd had to guess his ethnic or racial affiliation from his appearance alone, I definitely wouldn't have said Jew or Azerbaijani or any other of the undifferentiatable (to me) Caucasians, so much as Man Boy—a peaceful beaten international tribe whose members are usually unemployed and single.

No surprise, then, that he seemed happy to be of help to me. Though I didn't understand straightaway what that meant—to be hanging outside of his clan like this— to have to depend on the white-bread Jews, the Chabad crowd...

I'm going to have to make up his name, of course, because some of the things he explained could get him in trouble with other Mountain Jews, and some could get him in trouble with his government. Also: He requested. I couldn't deny that I was a writer; I couldn't have been anything else: As he drove his dirt-colored but punctiliously tidy Hyundai, I was writing down everything he was saying.

He spoke Judeo-Tat, or Juhuri, which he called Gorsky, and also Azeri and Russian—and spoke to me in bits of broken Hebrew and English.

Kinda sorta.

I'm going to call him U. Because that's as close as I can get to You—and that's whom I've been trying to talk to.

We'd agreed on two days, 40 manats a day. He'd be driving me to Mountain Jewish sites. In Baku and in Quba—beyond. But after we'd stopped at a SOCAR station and I'd paid to fill up the tank, he took me to a Zoroastrian fire temple.

There's so much gas—"natural gas," as the English phrase goes, to distinguish it from what Americans call "gasoline" and the rest of the world calls "petrol"—seeping out from under the earth here that in certain areas you can light a match and the air will burn, and will keep burning, until the gas deposit runs out. Zoroastrians erected their temples around such natural fires—around "vents"—though now this temple, the Baku Ateshgah, is lit artificially, its ancient flame having been snuffed by the substrate damage done by adjacent oil drilling. Because of the subterranean deposits, you can't really dig (for anything but oil or gas), and if you can't really dig (for anything but oil or gas), you can't really bury your dead. That explains Zoroastrian air burial. Zoroastrians will lay a corpse out on a rock. The vultures swarm. Put it all together: Flames springing up from the ether; a corpse up on a rock; vultures plucking out its liver: Prometheus.

U took me to mud volcanoes (which locals explain as "vents" from which only mud erupts, after the exhaustion of their flammable deposits); he took me to what he called the Olympic Stadium and the Olympic Village—driving me through their abandoned concourses, grinning at my incredulity. The issue here—though it only seemed to be an issue for me, not U—is that Baku never hosted an Olympics. Earlier in 2015, it hosted the European Games, which the government apparently insisted on referring to as the Olympics—the bona fide quadrennial gold-silver-bronze Olympics™—intellectual property laws be damned. In 2017, these facilities are slated to host the Islamic Solidarity Games, which U called the Islamic Olympics. I wondered, "Do women compete?" U said, "How can they compete?" Later I found out that not only were women excluded, but also that they didn't even have a bogus Olympics of their own anymore—not since the Women's Islamic Games was discontinued after Tehran 2005.

I took U to a dinner of kebabs, and he reciprocated by taking me to meet his friend, another Mountain Jew, he said, though the friend denied this, and it was only after I admitted my confusion that he said, "If you're not in the business, then it doesn't count" [which meant: Being an ethnic Mountain Jew was not quite the same as being a professional Mountain Jew: a mafioso]. U and I met him, let's call him Asshole, in a video-game parlor above a carwash, and played video Monopoly—alas, not the Atlantic City but the London version. We hunkered around the console and drank tea—always black, never green or red, nothing herbal—compulsively, Asshole and U smoked compulsively, and I went bankrupt— every game. U wouldn't play anything else in the arcade, because Asshole wouldn't—not Pac-Man, not Tetris, not the vintage-Soviet foosball table encased in a plastic bubble so pockmarked and cloudy that the guys who yanked at the bars could only guess at the ball—at its position—at its existence. Indeed, there were too many guys, doing too much bar-yanking. There weren't any women in the place. But then, there weren't any women in any place in the country—not without their husbands or brothers. I asked U how he went about meeting women, and Asshole replied—in a sense. He ashed his cigarette, right onto the console, and said that all women who smoked cigarettes were whores. All women who drove were also whores. He didn't mean "women who had sex for fun and free," but "women who had sex for money." I asked, What about women who smoked while driving? According to Asshole, they were "double whores," who'd cost me even more than landing my pixelated thimble on his Regent Street, which he'd outfitted to capacity with flashy red hotels. I went bankrupt again and put on my jacket, to signal that I was ready to head back to the Intourist. That's when Asshole asked, "Didn't [U] tell you not to wear red?" He hadn't—no one had—"Why?" Only gay men wore red, Asshole told me, as a signal to other gay men.

The next morning, it was unavoidable. Rainy, drear, unavoidable. From the moment that U picked me up at the Intourist, he was suggesting itinerary alternatives. Still, I held firm: We were driving up to Quba.

Which should've been an ascent of an hour and a half, but U took two hours, three, like he was dreading it.

I tried to suss out why—trying to seem guileless—by asking him about himself, and then about Asshole, before moving onto Quba, and then to its more notorious natives, but U just hunched at the wheel and turned every question around on me: He wanted to know how much my apartment cost (including electricity? but what about WiFi?), how much my phone cost (included with the plan? but what was the plan?), how much his car would cost in America (where cars are cheaper), how much it would cost to fill up his tank in America (where, ridiculously, fuel is cheaper too), and I had to admit that I didn't know anything about cars, and I didn't want to waste my phone's data, or its battery, on enlightening him.

"Women in America no care if you no have car?"

"No," I said. "At least not in New York."

"Why—because you must to have also plane, helicopter, yacht?"

We passed a roadside stand that sold sturgeon

wraps—hunks of BBQ'd sturgeon squirted with pome-granate sauce, sprinkled with saffron, wrapped in lavash—and U insisted: lunch. As we ate, U pointed across the highway toward a mountain, and said that up in that mountain was a cave, and that in that cave was a bevy of stone growths that resembled penises, and that Muslim women, just after they were betrothed, would visit said stone penises and kneel down to kiss them, to ensure the *prima nocte* potency of their husbands. Out of courtesy I finished all my slick greasy fish, which now wobbled perilously atop the summit of my stomach of yogurt and eggs and unwashed veg from the Intourist breakfast buffet. It was time to go, but U was unrelent-ing: tea.

But I was still meth-level caffeinated from the night before—between that and my jet lag, I hadn't even gone to sleep yet...

We drove up toward the mountains, passing apple orchards. Apparently Quba is famous for its apples. I mentioned the apple-importer guy from Brooklyn who'd introduced my friend, and so me, to Quba, and realized, from U's response, that the guy's occupation had been a joke or a put-down. If you're from Quba and a rube asks what you do for a living, you say, "I import apples." It's the gangster version of Ivy League pricks who when they're asked where they went to school say, "In New Haven." "In Boston."

Quba isn't a one-horse town. It's a half-horse town. The rear half. Smelly (from car emissions, outlying factories, sewage), hideous. Besides apples, Quba's also known for its carpets—known for its carpets whose woven wool must inevitably soak up all the smells—and while the few formal stores display their wares flayed in windows, the bazaars roll them up and tie them and

lean them against walls like they're about to be executed by firing squad: carpets like multicolored, arboreally
patterned bodies—carpets like multicolored, arboreally
patterned bodybags.

The town ends with a river, the Qudiyalçay. I asked U
what Qudiyalçay meant and he said, "Qudiyalçay." He
wasn't in the mood to talk, but then he sensed my disappointment and said, "The name is to do with water."

On the other side of the Qudiyalçay was the only
town in the world outside of Israel that still has a 100 percent Jewish population: Qırmızı Qəsəbə/Yevreiskaya
Sloboda/Krasnaya Sloboda. Jewish/Red Town.

We stopped at the cemeteries—the new first, the old
next. U went to say kaddish at his mother's grave. The
newest graves were set with stones engraved with classy/
cheesy full-body portraits: There were guys who'd died
in their twenties, dressed in suits straight out of *Scarface*.
"How did they die so young?" I asked, but U didn't answer. Instead, he pointed to a grave depicting an obese
Mountain Jew who'd died, U said, at age thirteen, from
diabetes. Another grave featured the portrait of a family
who'd died in a plane crash over Siberia. The plane itself
was etched into the stone above the family's group hug.
The pilots had been inexperienced or drunk, apparently. Or inexperienced *and* drunk. The oldest graves were
on another hill, crowding the pagoda tomb of Rabbi
Gershon ben Reueven, the Admor Gershon, the town's
founding rabbi, supposedly a miracle-working sage but
legendary among no other community.

At my prodding, U roused Yury Naftaliev, the
Azerbaijan state deputy for Quba, who kept the keys
to the synagogues, yeshiva, and mikveh. Physically,
he was as spare and thin as his rhetorical style, strictly facts: About two thousand Jews currently live in

Krasnaya Sloboda; the settlement has suffered a 75 percent loss of its population over the last decade, with most
going to Baku, Russia, and Israel; Krasnaya Sloboda's
last chief rabbi, Rabbi Davidov, left for Jerusalem; another rabbi, Rabbi Lazar, left for Moscow. I had to tug all
this out of him—through U, who turned my English into
Gorsky and Russian, and Yury Naftaliev's Gorsky and
Russian into English. How many synagogues are there
now? Two. How many before Sovietism? Thirteen.
The Gilaki synagogue, named after Gilan Province in
Iran, is the winter synagogue, because it's heated. The
Kuzari or Six Cupola synagogue, which has six cupolas,
is the summer synagogue, because it's unheated. But
wait—why name one synagogue after an Iranian province, and another after the Khazars? Does this mean
the Mountain Jews claim descent from Persia, or from
a tribe of shamanistic bartering Tatars who converted?
Yury Naftaliev shrugged—"Some do"—and hustled us
along. The perverse pleasure this fascistic beadle seemed
to be taking in prevailing upon U and me to remove our
shoes at every site seemed to have less to do with pre-
serving the preciousness of the rugs, and more to do
with power—with cutting an American down to size, on
holy ground in holey socks. My feet were cold, and then
the rest of me got cold and irritated, not least because the
questions I was asking were innocuous—100 percent his-
torico-theological—but still were being rebuffed. Do the
Mountain Jews follow the prayer order and pronuncia-
tions and Torah cantillations of the Ashkenazim, or the
Sephardim, or the Bukharans—or do they, or did they
ever, have their own? No comment. Do the Mountain
Jews accept the Talmud, like the Krymchaks, or reject it,
like the Karaites? No comment. I'd read that the primary
Mountain Jew holiday is Tisha B'Av—the ninth day of

the month of Av, which commemorates the destruction of both temples—why? Yury Naftaliev just held up his palms as if to say, "Why not?" I decided to pursue an easier, number-based and yes/no line of inquiry: I asked U to ask Yury Naftaliev how many Torahs the community had, but the totalitarian janitor just handed me a prayerbook, printed in 2014 in Israel on what felt like toilet paper. I asked U to ask Yury Naftaliev if he would unlock the ark, but Yury Naftaliev refused, until I dropped 5 manats—and then another 5 manats—into the donation box, and he, with a bitter twist to his mouth, opened the doors and there, inside, was a panoply of Torahs, the scrolls encased in olivewood filigreed with silver and gold and draped with silks. How old was the oldest? Over three hundred years. From where? Iran. Wouldn't this appear to substantiate the theory that the Mountain Jews came up from Persia under the Safavids? And, while we're at it, if your winter synagogue that, by the way, doesn't seem heated, contains an intact Persian Torah scroll over three hundred years old, which would make it one of the oldest intact Persian Torah scrolls in existence, why didn't you mention that earlier? But Yury Naftaliev was already shutting the ark, locking it, heading outside, and U was on bended knee doing up his laces.

Yury Naftaliev led us past a former synagogue, now a pharmacy. Yet another former synagogue would be converted into a Mountain Jew museum, he said, but only if they raised 200,000 manats. Restoration was expensive. Exhibits—with interactive computer terminals, because no Azerbaijani museum was complete without interactive computer terminals (which half the time didn't function)—were expensive. Suddenly, everything became about money, as Yury Naftaliev just continued

401

with the community-chest version of U's pricing habit: talking about how much it cost to run the mikveh, and how much it cost to run the yeshiva—to buy the desks and chairs and books, to pay for all the meals. About a dozen kids sat in a classroom in the yeshiva, studying the Hebrew alphabet—which was strange. In that it felt staged. Potemkin villagey. Walking into a yeshiva at some random hour on some random weekday at the end of October—two months after the Azerbaijani secular school term started, and a month after the Jewish New Year—and finding a dozen kids just starting to puzzle out the first few letters of the *alephbet* is like happening to drop by Citi Field on a whim, only to find out it's Opening Day and there's a home game v. the Phillies.

On the wall of the yeshiva was a calendar illustrated with images of Mountain Jewish synagogues, one for each month (it's amazing they had enough for the year)— the synagogue in Derbent (the photograph taken either before or after it was repaired from its firebombing by Chechen Muslims in 2012), in Makhachkala (the photograph taken either before or after it was repaired from its vandalizing in 2007), in Nalchik (the photograph taken either before or after it was repaired from its vandalizing in 2000; a Chechen Muslim plot to blow up the synagogue was foiled by the Russian FSB in 2002), in Buynaksk (now closed), and in Oğuz (open sporadically). The synagogue of this month, October, was the newest, dedicated in 2013, a glistening white Oriental pile in Grozny. The calendar was published by STMEGI, a Russian acronym for the International Mountain Jewish Charity Fund, a serious philanthropic but also seriously tax-exempt organization, founded by German Zakharyayev, a Quban (b. 1971), now resident in Moscow, who, beyond being another billionaire developer (the Sezar Group), has the singular distinction of having contributed a new Jewish holiday to the calendar, through his successful petitioning of the Israeli government to establish the twenty-sixth of Iyar—which corresponded to May 9, 1945, or Russia's WWII V-Day—as "The Rescue Day of European Jewry." I flipped back to spring, and sure enough, the holiday was there. I asked U to ask Yury Naftaliev if I could have the calendar. "No." I asked U to ask Yury Naftaliev if I could buy the calendar. "No." How can I buy my own copy, then? "You cannot to." You're telling me this is the only copy? "Yes."

None of this miserliness was making any sense. Because, as I couldn't help but notice—as Yury Naftaliev couldn't help but ignore—cropping up among the old Jewish sites he'd been bringing U and me to, overshadowing all of their carved wood and stained glass and even the six cupolas with their six-pointed stars, was some of the most lavish, most ugly-lavish, new real estate I'd ever been around. I'll clarify: On the Quba side of the Qudiyalçay were chickens, cows, tractors, and hovels—grimness. But on this side, here in Krasnaya Sloboda, were Lamborghinis, Ferraris, and villas that intermarried craven faux-Euro fin-de-frippery with the crassest of Stateside suburban McMansionism. If every Baroque has its Rococo, every Vegas has its Dubai, but this architecture was so outlandish, it verged on the extraterrestrial—there was nowhere to go beyond it. Some of the villas had five floors, some had six, most had turrets, many had elevators. Fountains in the yards, gargoyles, putti. Guardtowers, spiked fences, CCTV cameras. One had a helipad on its roof. Another had a rooftop pool. I asked to be taken to Zakharyayev's— to ask him if he had another of his calendars lying around—but U hesitated to transmit the request, as if he'd forgotten how to speak Gorsky, or Russian, while, at the same time, Yury Naftaliev frowned, as if he were gradually remembering that he understood English after all. I persisted, and asked where God Nisanov's house was, where Zarah Iliev's house was, and snap, just like that, my audience with the officious offseason caretaker of the summer homes—at least of the summer-vacation destination—of some of Russia's most wealthy and most powerful men was over. Yury Naftaliev, that dignified creep with a hedgehog for a mustache, bum-rushed us into the car, and stalked back to the yeshiva—gone.

Leaving, U was gritting his teeth. I was silent but angry, so U jacked his phone into the stereo and cranked the volume on some Israeli Mizrahi snake-charmerish club music, before switching to a Chabad chorus nasal-singing *niggunim*, Sabbath songs: *ayayayayay*. We were headed back to Baku, chased by rain. But then U drove off the highway, and, putting cheer in his voice, or just yelling, declared that we were stopping—again. He explained that there was this seaside joint he'd just suddenly recalled, but then—a half hour later, as we were parking in its empty lot—he was getting misty relating how ever since he was a child, "It was always really the most very special [to him]." It was a restaurant, whose theme might've been that it was too forlorn to even remember its theme, comprised of clusters of dacha-like dining cabins scattered out on the beach, and as unoccupied as the beach, which backed onto a cement apron with a rusted kiddie carousel and a crumbled dysfunctional zoo, all of whose animals appeared to have escaped except a pair of chimpanzees—a species that was supposed to be intelligent. The two flailed around their cage, howled as if the cold had driven them insane, and quieted only after U slipped them cigarettes. Not to smoke, of course, but to eat. This, according to U, was all the chimps here ever ate: cigarettes. U's brand was Marlboro Red (ersatz, made in China). A giant waiter stomped up, barely acknowledging us, and we higher primates fell in behind him and were conducted to the cabin farthest from the central pavilion containing the kitchen—a gesture that, like every other Azerbaijani host/guest gesture, seemed simultaneously respectful, insulting, and arbitrary. The cabin was a log affair, with gaps between the logs that let the wind in, and a wall-wide acrylic window to the Caspian. The surf was mean and thrashing. I was shivering, and in response to my asking whether the radiator was working, and whether it was adjustable, U just assured me that it was nicer here in summer. He'd come here, he said, this past summer, with this girl from Baku he was in love with, who worked as a supply liaison for a business that contracted with the U.S. military, which had a presence—a base? refueling rights? U waved off my questions—in Azerbaijan. Every discussion, about every person in U's life, began and ended with the same two (redundant) facts: what kind of job they had, and what kind of money they made. Either they had a bad job or a good job, either they made bad money or good money—there was nothing between, nothing decent.

Anyway, this girl. Who worked as a supply liaison for some business that did something with, or for, the U.S. military—whatever that was, it was a good job, which made good money. She was beautiful and loved him too. He wanted to marry her, but he couldn't. "Because she isn't Jewish?" Yes, he said, but not just that. "What,

405

then?" He couldn't marry her because he had a bad job, he said, and made bad money. Actually, he corrected himself: Officially, he had no job, and made no money. And "no" was worse than "bad." He'd brought the girl here for their final date—they both knew it had to be final. She was about to marry another man, who had the same good job and made the same good money with that same vague business—this other man who was also a *supply liaison*, which U kept repeating as if I was supposed to know what that was, because he so obviously didn't. I just nodded, as U—recovering from awkwardness—went on to praise this rival, who wasn't a rival; U was making a martyr of himself, as a way of consoling himself, swearing how happy he was for the groom. For the bride too. But especially for the groom. The waiter returned and just stood there, chair-sized hands on the chair at the head of our table, his concern for us—for anything—as absent as a menu. U ordered dumplings—qatabs. Stuffed dough fried on a convex griddle called a saj. Negotiations ensued, and the varieties that were compromised on were translated to me as Beef, Grass, and Camel. The Beef was beef, the Grass meant greens that might've been grass, and the Camel must've been diseased and/or geriatric. We finished eating and smoked, and the tea came. The ineluctable tea. If you drink what you're poured, you have to piss constantly. If you have to piss and your cabin isn't bathroom-equipped, you have to go outside. I opened the door, which spooked a stray dog that was harassing the chimps. The dog roamed toward me and foamed. I pissed hurriedly on the sand, on the cabin's steps, my own shoes, and dashed inside.

10/26
Shalom chaver, what's up? I'm just letting you

know I'm back in New York, exhausted. How are you? That animal they were selling at the bazaar and you said you were always finding everywhere for free, I just remembered I was wrong, the English name for it isn't "porcupine," but "hedgehog." Different animals. I'm going crusading for a girl for you, don't worry. Though your chances/ the crop certainly will be better in Tel Aviv. When are you going to be there? And Yury Naftaliev, is Naftaliev the patronymic (father's name) or the surname? And if it's the patronymic, what's the surname (lastname)? Also what's his official title, just Head of the Quba Jewish Community?

Todah me'rosh, Josh

10/30
Yo yo, kak dela? What's going on? I hope you got my last email—did you? Even if you're busy or depressed or both just type me a line or two? Just so I know to roll doubles for you or else sell Whitehall or Fleet Street or the Water Works or the Electric Company to get you out of jail and passing Go again. Just so I know that all is kosher. I have a few other questions if you wouldn't mind answering. Nothing too difficult.

OK ok kol tov, j

11/4
Habibi, kak dela? What's the news? Is everything all right between us? Did you get my two

last emails? Doesn't make sense to me that you wouldn't, because we were in touch without a hitch in Baku. I'm nervous. So even if you're hassled as fuck running around a tourgroup of Russian blondes to Fire Temple #9, just take a moment and send up a flare, a smoke signal, whatever. Are you there? Are you angry with me? Are my emails being blocked? Do you/can you use encryption?

11/14

Writing you from a different address, after you haven't responded to any of the emails I sent from Gmail, so maybe my Columbia email will work. Can you Skype? Encryption? Is this Aliyev reading this now? Hey, Dicktator Prez, you reading my friend's email? You better not have fucked with him.

I'm a slightly important American writer, according to several glossy magazines, and *The New York Times*.

Nothing. I never got a single response—not a word.

I wrote the Chabad rabbi in Baku, and told him to tell... U to be in touch. I'm not sure whether the Chabadnik passed on the message, but at least I'm sure of this: I did nothing to offend U. I mean, I was just doing my good bad job for good bad money—I didn't do anything on purpose...

I just slammed the cabin door behind me, and sat, panting. U grinned and refilled my tea, and then I let him light me a cigarette and as its sour formaldehyde fur taste came on, he picked up the thread of the girl:

How beautiful she was, how much they loved each other. How much he wasn't able to regret anything.

And then he mentioned his mother dying, and his father—who'd crashed like a wave over his childhood and then retreated.

How shaming that was—shaming of everyone, and even of the community.

It was just after his mother was diagnosed with cancer that he was given the chance to restore his honor and name.

U was telling me something, but I wasn't sure what—something about his life, about this girl's life, and about family—what all of that can mean to a Jew not jetting through, a Jew not from America but from the mountains.

What it was like to be a son, a fatherless son, who had to deal with the patriarchs of Quba.

He was explaining, not least, our reception there.

So: There was this man from the community. He was older, like of U's mother's generation—a Mountain Jew who might've known U's father, but who never mentioned knowing U's father, who owned a large commercial bakery at the foot of the Urals in Siberia. It made cakes, it made breads, to ship to groceries—supermarkets—hypermarkets throughout Russia. Don't think of kerchiefed babas dusted in flour kneading and rolling and waiting for their loaves to rise. Think bulk, preservatives, plastic packaging. Still, this large commercial bakery was one of the smaller things this man owned. He also owned malls and linen and clothing stores and linen and clothing factories, not only in Siberia. But all that U would have to concern himself with was the bakery. This man needed a guy he could trust, one of his own guys, to serve as manager. And despite the hardness that some of his ventures required, this man's emotions were such that he still wanted to do a young struggling Mountain Jew a favor. If U, who'd had some harsh breaks, hadn't been calloused by them, why should his benefactor be? Why not share the success? But the way the successful wholesale bread baker and retail linen and clothing manufacturer would explain it to U was that this wasn't a favor but a *mitzvah*. Which meant that U had to agree. U was flown to Siberia—to the city of Perm—to manage the bakery. It was a good job, which paid good money. He was given an apartment; the apartment had a flatscreen TV. It had a washer/dryer. It was centrally located and spacious. U spent all his days at the bakery, supervising baking. Keeping the bakers in line. Ordering the baking ingredients. Equipment maintenance. Quality control. But more often than not, he did nothing. The breads and cakes baked themselves. Everyone behaved. At night he went back to the apartment and sat. He sat and did nothing. He had no friends in Perm. No family, of course. The bakery owner was never around. He was flying constantly among all his other properties. U would go weeks without talking to anyone. Without talking personally, he meant, in person. The bakery personnel feared him. He himself was afraid of fraternizing, and of being taken as soft, pliable, doughy. He ached he was so lonely. Phone calls with his mother just exacerbated. Her loneliness increased his, and her cancer was advancing. Russians on the street, taking him for a Chechen, a Muslim, would taunt and threaten him. They'd try to beat him. But more often than not, he'd escape. He considered suicide.

Then one day, he left. He gave notice. He didn't give notice. He forgot. He bought a ticket with what money he'd saved, what money he hadn't sent back to his mother, and went back to his mother. Baku. The man who owned Siberia was furious, which meant the man's business partners who were also his family were furious, and the man had an extended—an overextended—family. No one was going to do U a kindness again. He'd blown his chance and was out. He was on the outside, permanently. He was no one's *mitzvah*. Which limited his prospects for marriage within the community. And being broke and Jewish limited his prospects for marriage outside the community—with the girl he loved, the girl who loved him, this beautiful Muslim *supply liaison*. He'd only taken the job, he said, to earn enough to win the favor of her family. And a Jew has to earn a lot, he said, to win the favor of the family of a beautiful Muslim *supply liaison*. The rain picked up. The waiter cast stones toward the rabid dog off and brought the bill. U said he was paying and not to argue. He was considering moving to Israel.

FROM THE DIARIES

Adoration of New Magi

Yea they wandered from the east bearing black plastic
idols, in search of signal from across the desert. They
followed the pulse, the perk: one bar, two bars, three—
a horizon. Over yonder lay their reception, their promised service. They summoned their hosannas with
buttons, pressing mystical combinatorials of numbers
that represented letters, and the symbols pound (#)
and star (*). The static cleared as they approached
the presence: the one and only truly imageless god,
a carrier that, now that they'd crossed into the zone
of its coverage, would never drop them.

Le Pont Mirabeau

In poetry, the river is a symbol of the unceasing flow
of time, resistance to which is futile. Like trying to
isolate the exact moment at which a "leap" becomes a
"fall." The precise instant at which the will gives way
to gravity. Many minor poets have died attempting to
perform this calculation, only to have it be declared
that they "committed suicide." The best poets, however,
tend to die under more desperate circumstances. They
jump to find the word for the opposite of "bridge."

ON THE TRANSIT OF TOLEDO

In the world above our world there lives a race of perfect beings—beings who are perfect because they are unities, because they are wholes—who are always being called down to this world by half-wits and fools, and who only occasionally, in rare foolish moments of their own, heed that call and decide to descend. They come down to us, they come down to us slowly, but then inadvisably they speed up their descent as our summons of them becomes more and more impatient and insistent, and, in passing through the nearly imperceptible white sheet that separates their world from our world, they are mutilated, they are maimed. In their passage, their perfect forms become imperfect: deformed.

These deformed forms then proceed to drag themselves around our world, around our highly flawed and polluted planet that we call earth, complaining for years, for decades, even in some extreme cases for over a century, about how good it used to be, about how good they used to have it, and how utterly repugnant and defective they are now—whining about how Up There was so much better than Down Here, and about how they were lured Down Here by false representations, *by misrepresentations*—they were victimized, defrauded, cozened by lies—and they go on like this, these deformed forms, moaning and groaning and just generally making an intolerable fuss for as long as it takes them to fully embody their grievance, for as long as it takes them to become nothing but their rage, in doing so once again attaining a state of total purity, at which point they are allowed to ascend: they are allowed to travel back through that flimsy atmospheric sheet to the world from which they came, and in the process of that

413

return, they mysteriously reacquire their original perfections.

I have the fantasy that were this legend I've just related to you to be translated into the terms of some dead language, like Ancient Greek or even Latin—were this legend to be translated in that impossible direction, the past—that some wayward ancestor of mine might recognize my description of what's now known as Neo-Platonism. My admittedly completely imperfect description of what's now known as Neo-Platonism.

If Platonism is the belief in perfect forms dwelling in some higher world or alternate dimension, then Neo-Platonism is the conversion of that belief to Judeo-Christianity: a revision in which these perfect forms enter our world through a fall—they enter through a fall from grace.

Our earth becomes their exile, and their bodies—which they acquire in their plummet, and which have to piss and shit and age and become flabby and weak and cancered and stuck in traffic—become their exile too.

These forms are us, of course. Or they become us. They are our souls, and they can't wait to get out of here, and be rid of all this dumb flesh and unread email.

There are certain ridiculous bureaucratic situations I've gotten into while traveling, or while on a quest for employment, in which I've been asked my nationality, and even my gender and my religion—questions which have always irked me and which I always answer as follows: "I am a divine soul trapped in a loathsome body, from which I seek release."

414

In response, the bureaucrats who are interviewing me just give their nod, the nod of officialdom, which indicates neither understanding nor non-understanding. They shuffle their "forms" and possibly check the box labeled "Crazy."

Sometimes I am searched, and my bags are searched. Sometimes I am hired and pitied.

But I am not crazy.

I am just a Neo-Platonist, or a practicing Neo-Neo-Platonist, as I suspect all writers are (though they might not be aware of it).

I hazard this assumption, outing my colleagues as co-religionists, because this doctrine that derives from Plato and was subsequently Judeo-Christianized—the Jews bringing to it the pessimism of the fall, the Christians bringing to it the optimism of the rising-again—strikes me as the ultimate religion of writing and, especially, of translation.

Let me rephrase.

I know what I want to say, but I don't know the words in which to say it. And this, I want to say, is the problem—a theological problem.

Let me rephrase.

As a writer, I go about my dull daily life with a book in my head. And, despite that dull daily life, let's call my head a type of heaven.

Up in the heaven of my head, this book is perfect. It's complete. It's complete and finished. From the first word to the last, though I don't know what those words might be, though I might not even know anything about it: not the characters, the situations, the settings. All I know, all I have to know, is that it's brilliant, this book of mine, and that it's above me, like a star floating high, and that without even the slightest effort on my part, it's shining brightly Up There—I know it's shining even during daylight.

But then I get ahead of myself, and I can sense that anyone who's been following me so far is now getting ahead of me too: you know where this is going—you know because you've experienced this yourself. You become a bit haughty, a bit conceited. Maybe you get somewhat drunk or high or lusty one night and in that flush of excitement you find yourself calling this book down—you call this book down to the page or screen.

You call this book down to its wording.

As surely you know, this is where the work begins.

Because it can take forever, or it can feel like it takes forever, to do the coaxing. You say, "Please come down, book, you're so very beautiful." And you get no reply. Which makes you feel the same as when any fellow human being you're enamored with doesn't reply to your entreaties—it only makes you more enamored, more possessive. You flirt with the book—with *your book*—you continue to flatter it—to flatter *her*, *him*—and maybe you get a sentence, or even a paragraph, for your troubles. This, in turn, inflames you, and you move on to cajoling, inveigling, wheedling, making use of every suasion in the synonymicon, making promises you can never fulfill. *Making*—here is that word again, that Platonic word—*representations*.

You have to be insane to be doing this.

That's what everyone tells you. That's what you tell yourself. You must be insane and conceited and absolutely in love.

And you must also be in love with disappointment.

Because the book that descends is not the same book

that was hovering so peacefully in the empyrean. The book that descends is never that same book. It's rather like a parody or satire of that book, but it's not funny. Or it's not funny to you.

The book that you now have in front of you, worded onto the page, or onscreen, is just a beaten ugly incarnation of its original perfect being, and it's your fault. You have only yourself to blame. Because you couldn't control yourself. Because you just couldn't have left it twinkling in the ether. You had to call it down, you were so afraid, so jealous, that someone else might possess it. But now it's yours, it's all yours, a justly perverse reward for your needy greed and hubris. Now, instead of perfection, you possess a monster.

Which brings us to translation.

Translators are much like writers: they tend to be sedentary and yet have tumultuous romantic relationships. But they differ from writers in one crucial respect: they never believe the books they are working on to be perfect, or *to have been perfect*—they never believe the books to which they have dedicated their lives to have originated in some uncorrupted primordial form, some prelapsarian and unspoiled sublimity.

This is because they know a book's problems. They know all of its problems, as well as if not better than does the book's so-called writer.

And yet still they love these monsters. Or they try to love these monsters.

They do so by putting these repellent gawky mutant creatures into another language.

The idea is that the language of a book's initial wording is like an ungainly body, which cannot contain the soul that it has captured.

It is the task of the translator to remove that language and to replace it with another—it is the task of all translators to remove all the languages that have come before them and to replace them with their own, flensing the body of a book time and again until the ideal linguistic body for the book has been found and the soul of the book, the eternal and immortal soul of the book, has been most suitably accommodated.

Of course, in doing so, they are setting themselves up for failure. Because: no book that is a book of words can ever be returned to the realm of the celestial.

But at least a translated book makes explicit the desire for that return—a translated book makes the sincerest attempt of which I'm aware at achieving that desire.

This is what translation has done for my own books, the books for which I must take responsibility and apologize—in many languages apologize.

Ana asif. Ani mitztaer. ¡Lo siento!

Of the books that are called mine that I especially loathe, and am especially ashamed of, I can always say: "But they might still become perfect again in Swahili!" "They might yet achieve their apotheosis in Icelandic!"

Because who's to say that the language of perfection is not Swahili or Icelandic?

The answer is: writers in Swahili and Icelandic.

Samahani. Fyrirgefðu.

For them, the language of perfection might be Arabic or Hebrew or Spanish.

I'd like now to mention two verbs in English that aren't strictly English: from Greek, English has "to catasterize," while from Latin, English has "to stellify." The words are synonyms, the former a self-consciously antiquarian adaptation by the "rationalist" 1600s, the latter an earlier adoption by Middle English. Both are translations of a type. They mean "to turn something into a star," or "to be turned into a star." They mean this literally, astrally: to be "translated" from corporeality into a constellation. In Classical mythology, this is the reward of great heroes like the hunter Orion, and, in my mythology, this is the reward that translators bestow on unheroic writers: they catasterize us, they stellify our books.

Or they recatasterize, they restellify, to constellate our culture.

It was as unheroic heroes that, in the spring of 1085, the armies of Alfonso VI of Castile rode into the city that we call Toledo, deposed the Umayyad Dynasty, and brought to a close nearly three centuries of Moorish Muslim rule, in a campaign that the Castilian Spanish language, but not the Arabic language, refers to as *Reconquista*. The new Christian reconquerors found that this city called Toledo (which was also a kingdom, and, in Arabic, a *taifa* of al-Andalus) possessed a mixed population, which spoke, read, and wrote a mongrelity of tongues: Arabic, Hebrew, Latin, and *lingua Tholetana*, the local Romance vernacular. Concomitantly, the city's Muslim religious institutions possessed large libraries with a polyglot of books that had, perhaps, only a single commonality: they were largely incomprehensible to their new owners.

In order for the Spaniards to take fuller possession of what they'd fought for, a movement came about to translate these works and make them legible. This movement, which in the imagination of history has acquired the moniker the Toledo School—as if its impulse immediately sterilized itself with campuses and deans—succeeded in bringing an unprecedented amount of the scientific and mathematical and philosophical thought of the Arab world, and of the scientific and mathematical and philosophical thought that the Arab world had itself translated from the Greek, into "modern" Castilian Spanish and so into "modern" Europe. Because it is a fact that while the Romans copied Greek statuary and painting—Greek surfaces—it was only the Arabs, and, to a degree, the Persians, who took it upon themselves to preserve the less superficial appurtenances: Greek thought and literary culture.

Here, at least, is the iconic image that history has passed down to us—that translators have translated for us: an image not of an ecclesiastical library but of a balmy gardened *patio* (which means something much different in Spanish than it does in English), which is also the traditional depiction of the Muslim Paradise. In the middle of this *patio* is a babbling fountain, and surrounding this babbling fountain are overstuffed pillows on which lounge overstuffed Muslims and Christians and Jews, who, having put aside their dogmatic squabbles, discuss the divisions of the quadrivium and trivium, the differences between *the spirit* and *the soul*, and which words in which languages might be used to render each.

Of course, this depiction is sheer surface too: it's false, a fantasy as shallow as the pool into which the fountain's nonsense spouts.

And yet the books associated with this School are real. For example, what appears to be the School's first notable translation, John of Seville's version of Qusta ibn Luqa's *On the Difference Between the Soul and the Spirit*, which sought to elucidate distinctions between those two ghosts that haunt us: the Judeo-Christian perduring *soul*, which animates the body, and the passing *spirit* of Arabic medicine, which influences the body's health.

It was through the syncretic diligence of this enigmatic enterprise of the city called Toledo that we, today, can make platitudinal reference to the works of Plato, and of the Neo-Platonists—to the works of Aristotle, Euclid, Theodosius, Menelaus, Archimedes, Hippocrates, Galen, and Ptolemy, whose wisdom was widely ignored if not proscribed by the Christian Middle Ages, but intently and respectfully amended by the likes of Al-Kindi, Al-Razi, and others: Ibn Sina known as Avicenna, Ibn Rushd known as Averroes, and Al-Khwarizmi known as Algoritmi, the author of algebra the concept and *Algebra* the book. The Toledo School produced versions of Aristotle's *Physics*, *On the Heavens*, *On Generation and Corruption*, and *Meteorology*, the lattermost of which fixed the four elements of Creation: fire, air, water, and earth. Ptolemy's *Almagest*—whose Arabic copy drew the School's most industrious translator, Gerard of Cremona, to the city called Toledo—informed us that the heavens were a sphere, and that the equally spherical earth squatted motionless at its center, with the equally fixed stars clustered into constellations and orbiting as a single unified mechanism around it, and it even lists those stars: all 1,022 of them... I could go on and on, listing these works like the stars they are themselves—after all, it's simpler to do so than to divine the true nature of the organization that set them spinning...

It's telling that, having perused numerous chronicles of this cipherous School, I have yet to find one that seems definitive, or even convincing.

What appears to be the case is that the Toledo School was actually two schools, diverse in era and errand. The first was founded by Raymond, archbishop of the city called Toledo between 1126 and 1151, which years Muslims call 519 and 545, while the second—the resurrection—was picked up a century later under the reign of Alfonso X. The first was a church institution, operating out of the Toledo Cathedral, with a team that included Jews, Mozarabians (Arab Christians who hewed to the liturgy of the Visigothic Church), and monks from the Order of Cluny, translating—together, separately, successively, however—from Arabic into Latin, or from Arabic into Castilian into Latin, which meant that their works were intended for clergy and educated audiences abroad, because the local laity couldn't read Latin. The second incarnation, however, was a government institution, in which the king himself served an editorial role: Alfonso X insisted, apparently, on jettisoning the church's Latin for the people's Castilian, which meant that the works being translated were now intended to be readable by all people who sought education, the "general public."

The history of the Toledo School or schools can be read in the *microcosmos* of its major nonliterary achievement: namely, the compilation of the Toledan Tables—astronomical charts, lastingly referred to as "Ephemerides," that were used to predict the movements of the sun, moon, and planets, or the five planets that had been identified at the time and deified as Mercury, Venus, Mars, Jupiter, and Saturn. The bounty of the Toledan Tables was assembled by Al-Zarqali, called

Arzachel, a Muslim astronomer of the city called Toledo, whose work was translated by Gerard of Cremona around the year 1140, and then revised—with the help of the Jewish astronomers Yehudah ben Moshe and Yitzhak ibn Sid—and redubbed the Alfonsine Tables, around the year 1270.

It was these Tables that set the standard for Renaissance astronomy, and though their compilers had accepted the Ptolemaic model that set our earth as the fixed center of all Creation, the Tables' data were so comprehensive and accurate that Copernicus, at the dawn of the sixteenth century, used them to disprove that geocentric misnomer and assert the systemic fixity of our sun and the universal fact of heliocentrism.

A millennium later, the Toledo School remains mostly mythic: a dream of an almost logical comity. So much is unclear, and never will be clear—such as, given all of the School's literary and, if you'll excuse me, STEM-related industry, why was no university ever established at the city called Toledo? And, were those among the School's translators who, as it's said, "had" Arabic willing collaborators with their European counterparts, or were they impressed into service, forced to translate their culture's books for their foreign masters in the interests of mere survival? I confess to being attracted to the cruel romance of this hypothesis: I imagine an inky office employing only editor-slaves and a publisher-king.

To be sure, translators have never had it easy, and it might even constitute an insult to contemporary practitioners of the discipline that those who are trying to kill them now are not royalty but plebs—we writers who kill our translators by our thanklessness, as much as by our thankfulness, which is to say by our obtuseness: such is the tribute that our renderers receive for giving our imperfect work a progressively less imperfect future.

Of all the legends of the city called Toledo, there is only one about which I am certain—rather, there is only one that I am certain cannot be disproven.

It states: The world is a place but has no places. It tells us: The things of this world can have no name that isn't constantly in the process of changing.

It was never the Creator's intention that our cities should be fixed to the ground. It was never the Creator's intention that our cities should be immovable.

The Creator decreed that what we now call locations—our present-day cities, towns, villages—inhere not in the earth but in the heavens.

At the moment of Creation, then, the constellation that Ptolemy called, and that we call, Centaurus emerged low in the sky directly over the spot where the city that we call Toledo now stands. This means that wherever Centaurus was the week after Creation was Toledo, and wherever Centaurus was the month after creation was Toledo, and so on, the city—or the perfect form of the city, which is the only form that we can recognize—remaining in constant galloping motion over the earth, remaining in constant trotting transit around us, while we, the earth's sad and evil people, persisted in ignoring this cyclical cartographical imperative.

We ignored it, and then, at some darkly aged point, we forgot it.

We lost all knowledge of where exactly the stars were in relation to the earth at the moment of Creation, and so, to this very day, we have no way of knowing the names

—the true precise precessional and changing names—of where we dwell.

Tonight, because it is night already somewhere, Toledo might be anywhere. It might even be here, above us, now.

Let us be greedy and call to it, then, in all of our languages.

Let us call it down.

IN PARTIAL DISGRACE:
ON CHARLES NEWMAN

¶ Partialness

In Partial Disgrace is the book's title, though the emphasis should be on that intermediary word—that unstable, pieceworkish, double-definitioned "partial." Charles Hamilton Newman—among the best, and best-neglected, of American authors—had intended to write a novel-cycle of three volumes, each volume containing three novels, for a total of nine. But when he died, in 2006 at age sixty-eight, all that had been completed was an overture—or just the blueprints for a theater, the scaffold for a proscenium.

¶ Arcadia

Charles Newman was born in 1938 in St. Louis, city of the Mississippi, of Harold Brodkey, William S. Burroughs, T. S. Eliot—three eminences who'd left. Newman never had that privilege. His father made the decision for him, moving the family—which stretched back two centuries in St. Louis, to when the town was just "a little village of French and Spanish inhabitants"—to a suburban housing tract north of Chicago, adjacent to a horseradish bottling plant. The prairie, the imagination, lay just beyond. A talented athlete, Newman led North Shore Country Day School to championships in football, basketball, baseball. Yale followed, where he won a prize for the most outstanding senior thesis in American history. He befriended Leslie Epstein, novelist, and Porter Goss, future director of the CIA under Bush II (more on "intelligence" later). Study at Balliol College, Oxford, led to a stint as assistant to Congressman Sidney R. Yates (D, Ninth District, Chicago), which lasted until Newman was drafted into the Air Force Reserve, which he served as paramedic. Korea was avoided.

In 1964, Newman returned to Chicago: "I have been forced by pecuniary circumstances to deal with other men's errors and nature's abortions, to become... an educationist!" He became a professor in the English department at Northwestern, where he turned the campus rag, *TriQuarterly*, into the foremost American lit journal of the second half of the century—weighty words for weighty writers like Jorge Luis Borges, Gabriel García Márquez, Czesław Miłosz, E. M. Cioran, Frederic Jameson, Susan Sontag, Robert Coover, John Barth. *TriQuarterly* was the journal that notified the city—New York, publishing's capital—of the progress in the provinces. Academia would resurrect American letters, at least relicate it in library stacks amid the slaughterhouses, the grain and missile silos. The counterculture usurping the culture, standards in decline, artistic degradation—the complaints of Newman's essays, *A Child's History of America* (1973), and *The Postmodern Aura* (1985), could also be used to rationalize his behavior: the dalliances with coeds, the boozing, the pills. With his job in jeopardy, his journal too, in 1975 Newman moved to Baltimore, where he directed the Johns Hopkins Writing Seminars.

This is where the account, or just Newman, gets hazy. He quit Hopkins, or was fired again, or quit before he was fired, or was fired before he could quit, went off to raise hunting dogs in the Shenandoah Valley (more on the dogs too, in a bit). The failure of that venture, or a feud with a neighbor that left him wounded in a shovel attack—either that or a brief bout of sobriety, or its attendant hypochondria that required better health insurance—led him back, by a commodius rictus of recirculation, to St. Louis, city of Brodkey (a stylistic peer), Burroughs (with whom he shared a tolerance for self-abuse), Eliot (whose adoption of a foreign identity prefigured Newman's own interest in Hungary—about which, again, stay tuned). After Chicago, this was his second homecoming, third chance. Fortune smiled gap-toothed. Newman was already the author of *New Axis* (1966, a novel following three generations of a Midwestern family from Depression striving, through middle-class success, to a striven-for, successful-because-failed, Aquarian rebellion), *The Promisekeeper: A Tephramancy* (1971, a novel that risks, as its subtitle suggests, a divination of the ashes of the American Dream, forecasting a country unable to communicate except in media references, satire, parody), and *There Must Be More to Love Than Death* (1976, a collection of three texts, of a series of twelve that would remain unfinished, each in a different vein: A junkie veteran suffers naturalism, an operatic baritone frets over farce, a photographic-memory prodigy is worried by the very concept of non-fiction). *White Jazz*—Newman's best completed novel, in which an overconsuming computer programmer finds satisfaction in his function as a mere line of code in the program of this country—had just been published. The year was 1985. Reagan had just been whistled for an encore.

For this act—Newman's last—let's green the stage, let loose a rolling hilly verdancy to billow as backdrop, caster the trees into position, dolly hedges to their marks, creating a clearing, a nymph's grove of sorts, surrounding a ruin—a folly—risen from the floor's trapdoor. Literature students wandered into this grove and declothed, quaffed grape, toked a strange lotosine

428

weed. The demigods who organized, or disorganized, these pagan proceedings were called by the names William H. Gass, Stanley Elkin, Howard Nemerov. This secret Arcadia hid under the ineffable epithet Washington University. But Eden is not to be returned to. Paradise, especially if one's birthplace, can never be regained. (At Newman's memorial service, Gass suspected the deceased "would find faults in paradise, because they sprayed their trees.")

It wasn't just that Newman loathed Wash U, or the suburban complacency that had taken hold outside the ivy tower—rather, it's that he felt most alive when bitching or blurbing the uncontainability of his own genius. Or resuming his cryptodipso routine, insulting fellow teachers and deans, setting himself on fire in class (an accident? or to prove what point?). Newman broke friendships, collapsed marriages, wore himself out in the constant commute between classes and his writing studio/apartment in cramped, indispensable-to-his-vanity-but-insulting-of-his-vanity Manhattan, and in the perpetual writing of this book, the perpetual rewriting of the books that would become this book as if it would sober him finally, which it didn't—fiction never does.

The dramatization — the self-dramatization — of Newman's finale should be accompanied by flute and harp, out of synch, out of tune in a disconcerting mode. An exit dance might be hazarded, but the steps should stagger, the bows should be falls, passing out. Let's clear the set—reel in the prop foliage, crank to the rafters those *deae ex machinis* of ever-fresher, ever-younger student lovers. All that should be left onstage is that ruin, that folly—the size of a respectable state university, the size of a respectable state, but abandoned in

429

midbloom—this masterpiece in pieces, this partial.

❡ Ruritania

For Newman—the peripatetic New Man—the imagined place was always a proxy, or preparatory study, for a reimagination of the self. The move to Chicago turned his family from prosperously rooted burghers to panting arrivistes; his sojourn in Virginia turned a genuine wildman into a playacting gentleman farmer, and it was his first trip to Hungary, in 1968, that turned an intellectual citizen of an unintellectual republic into an adventurer, or apprentice dissident—a champion of everyone's free speech because a champion of his own.

Hungary, the Midwest of the Continent: the Magyar state, Pannonia to Antiquity and Cannonia to Newman, is located at the very middle of Mitteleuropa, an East/West crossroads of Teutons and Slavs. The second crownland of the Austro-Hungarian Empire, it was carved into thirds and landlocked—losing its only port, called Fiume by the Hungarians, Rijeka by Yugoslavia—after WWI. The brief communist coup of 1919 gave way, in 1920, to a parliamentary government subservient to a sham regent whose most notable previous credential was his inept admiralty in Austro-Hungary's sinking joke of a navy. Miklós Horthy allied his nation with Hitler, who returned the compliment by invading in 1944. Nearly half a million Hungarians perished in WWII—nearly a million if Jews can be counted, or counted themselves, Hungarian. Soviet occupation, backing the puppet regime of Mátyás Rákosi, was challenged in 1956 by the election of Imre Nagy—a marionette who snipped his own strings. A multiparty system was, temporarily, restored; Hungary withdrew, for a breath, from the Warsaw Pact; revolution simmered in the streets. Moscow responded with tanks. Twenty thousand people died in the fighting. After crushing the resistance, the Kremlin installed János Kádár in a dictatorship that lasted until 1989, to the fall of the original "Wall"—not the concrete slabs of Berlin, toppled in the fall of that year, but the dismantling of the barbed-wire fence along the Hungarian/Austrian border, earlier, in spring.

The country Newman arrived in had just dragged itself out from under the treads, dusted off, and limped back to the factories. 1968 was the year of Kádár's New Economic Mechanism, an appeasement measure introducing certain free-market principles—giving nationalized businesses a modicum of control over what products they produced, in what quantities, even over what prices the products would be sold at—to an economy whose central planning was increasingly outsourced to Budapest. This was the period of "Goulash Communism"; Hungary was "the happiest barrack in the socialist camp" (whether these descriptions originated in Hungary or Moscow, or even in the West, and whether they were intended seriously or in jest, are still matters of musty debate). Hungarians could choose to buy either domestic crap or foreign pap in a selection unprecedented since the kaisers; they could even travel widely—from Moscow to Yalta, Kamchatka to Havana. The Hungarian press was less strict than that of any other Soviet satellite. All of which would account for how Newman got into the country. None of which would account for what he was doing there.

He was, crazily, editing a literary journal out of Budapest. Newman's *New Hungarian Quarterly* published samizdat literature but not in samizdat—in public. It disseminated English-language versions of poems,

431

stories, and essays whose Hungarian (and Czech and Slovak and Polish, etc.) originals were banned. Though Newman never became fluent in Hungarian, he did become expert at editing, for free, translations, also offered for free, more accurate and artistic than anything being produced at the time by the Western capitalist publishers and the university faculties that slaved for them—institutions that though they (mostly) lacked contacts with their Hungarian counterparts, anyway (mostly) followed the example of their Hungarian counterparts and chose the works they rendered based as much on politics as on aesthetics (not to mention the criteria of "marketability"—an American term translating to "censorship"). How Newman got away with it all, I don't know. Neither do I know how he managed to make repeated trips to Hungary throughout the '70s and '80s, nor how he managed to smuggle into the States a brace of the Hungarian dogs he'd breed—Uplanders, also called wirehaired vizslas—and two of his three Hungarian wives (Newman met his third Hungarian wife in the States; another wife was Jewish; yet another longtime companion, Greek).

I can only wink, drop the name "Porter Goss," and refer to a scrap of paper stuck in a crack of Newman's *Nachlass:* "An intelligence officer's most obsessive thought, *and I ought to know,* is whether his time behind the lines, in deep cover, is going to be counted toward his annuity" (italics mine). If Newman wasn't in the CIA, he was certainly interrogated by it. If Newman wasn't an agent, or even an agent-manqué, he would certainly have enjoyed pretending to be one, or the other, or both—shadowing in and out of character for his Hungarian hosts and for the KGB stooges who tailed them (after 1956, Hungary was the only communist country not to have its own secret police).

Ultimately it doesn't matter whether Newman's fascination with Hungary originated on-assignment, or merely as an inexplicable *esprit de parti*. The truth is that Newman always pursued estrangements and alienations, not just as opportunities to reinvent, but also as psychological defenses—as refuges, as amnesties.

In the Eastern Bloc, literature could define one's life, civically. A Hungarian's criticism of the regime could be a one-way ticket if not to gulag, then at least to penury and oblivion, whereas a famous, and famously self-aware, American abroad had to be on guard against incarceration as much as against romanticism, the fatuous touristic thrills. Newman's passport redeemed him, even while it mortified. He didn't like his face or his name, except when they were praised, and he didn't like his nationality, except when it could be condemned in prose that was praised. Whenever he lost faith in the struggle to keep life and literature as separate as Buda and Pest, he clung to the belief that they were interlayered, or overlaid, in the same way that Budapest is built atop the rubble of Aquincum, and Magyar identity merely the false construct of a racial purity atop the tribal burial mounds of Celts, Mongols, Turks.

It followed that Hungarian literature wasn't just the literature Newman helped to translate from the Hungarian; it was also all literature, in every language— about Austro-Hungary, Ottoman Hungary, Antiquity's Hungary, caravanning back to the clunky coining of the Hunnic runes. Newman's tradition would provide sanctuary for the liturgies of seceded churches, the decrees of rival courts, as much as for the slick escapism of interbellum pulp fiction—written in a fantastic dialect called Ruritanian: the world's only vernacular intended more for the page than for the tongue, the jargon preferred by creaky empires for diplomatic cabling with breakaway nation-states, and the unofficial argot of international dreamers.

Ruritania has become the generic name for a hypothetical or fictional kingdom located at the center not necessarily of geographic Europe, but of European psychogeography and literature—though British author Anthony Hope (a pseudonym of Sir Anthony Hope Hawkins, 1863–1933) initially founded it somewhere, or nowhere, between Saxony and Bohemia, in his trilogy of novels (*The Prisoner of Zenda*, *The Heart of Princess Osra*, and *Rupert of Hentzau*) characterizing it as a German-speaking, Roman Catholic absolute monarchy. Despite this classic setting being perpetually in the midst of dissolution, that dissolution would mean only, paradoxically, more ground. Even as class, ethnic, and religious tensions threatened conflict, territory was taken at every cardinality. War could not destroy it, peace could not bore it—every dark passage, be it to throne room or dungeon, met intrigue along the way. Ruritania's annexations would acquire it more names, as if noble honorifics: George Barr McCutcheon's *Graustark* hexalogy expanded it southeast to the Carpathians and called it Graustark; in Edgar Rice Burroughs's *The Mad King*, it's located east toward the Baltics, as Lutha; in John Buchan's *The House of the Four Winds*, it's a Scandinavian/Italian/Balkan mélange called Evallonia; Dashiell Hammett, in one of only two stories he ever set outside the States, had his nameless detective, the Continental Op, meddle in the royal succession of Muravia; Frances Hodgson Burnett further clarified the compass by positioning her Samavia "north of Beltrazo and east of Jiardasia," names that should be familiar to every good

434

mercenary as demarcating the borders of "Carnolitz." Newman called his Ruritania "Cannonia"—a toponym echoing the martial ring of "cannon," with the authority of "canon."

¶ Cannonia
Still, to map Cannonia 1:1 onto Pannonian Hungary might be to misunderstand how Newman regarded place: To him, books could be just as physical as cities. The trashed palace of pages he left behind recalls another unfinished project: Musil's *The Man Without Qualities*, set in an impostor Austro-Hungary called Kakanien. Though *Kaka* is German juvie slang for "shit," derived from the Greek prefix meaning "shitty"—if "calligraphy" is beautiful, "cacography" is ugly—Kakanien is also a pun on *K und K*, the empire's abbreviation for itself: *kaiserlich und königlich*, "Imperial and Royal," indicating Austro-Hungary's dual crowns. Musil's remains the prototypical modernist confusion—a book so coterminous with life that it could end only outside its covers, with the death of its author, or the Death of the Author (Musil was stopped by a stroke at age sixty-one, having completed only two of the projected three volumes).

Newman had always known his only option was what he called "postmodernism"—a knowledge that assuaged his yearning for "modernism," which was itself a balm for earlier aches. Though he'd always idealized the man in full, he was fated, was aware he was fated, to montage, sumlessness, pastiche. Ruritania will forever be trapped in the clockwork gears of the turn of the century, but by the time another century was about to turn, the drive to synecdochize all of Europe in Vienna, or in a Swiss sanatorium (as in Thomas Mann's *The Magic Mountain*), or even in the sci-fi province of Castalia (in

435

Hermann Hesse's *The Glass Bead Game*), had forsaken history for dystopia. If utopia was "no-place," dystopia—cacotopia—was Anglo-America: *Brave New World, 1984, Fahrenheit 451, Lord of the Flies, A Clockwork Orange.* Kurt Vonnegut, Philip K. Dick, J. G. Ballard. By the 1980s—when Newman was first surveying Cannonia—the genre goons were at publishing's gates, and they proceeded to divide and conquer: "Literary novelists" would take care of the *totum pro parte*—"the whole for the parts"—in an effort to maintain the ideal of an artwork that could still mirror all of reality; while the pop hacks who hadn't yet traded the page for TV and film would concern themselves with the *pars pro toto*—"the parts for the whole"—in an attempt to acknowledge that reality had sprawled beyond any consensus, exceeding the capabilities of any single novelist and the capacities of any single reader. (Throughout the Cold War, espionage and thriller novelists made effective use of this limitation: In presenting Western spycraft as important to, though inconsistent with, Western democracy, they revealed even their right to publish fiction as the privilege of a fiction—a delusion.)

Newman's ambition was to write this change itself. He would show and tell the evolution of literature, would narrate the revolutions of the wheel. His cycle would begin with a volume of three books in Musil/ Mann/Hesse mode—landmarks, monuments, all set in Cannonia, from around 1900 to 1924—follow with three books surrendering Cannonia's metonymy to Russian hegemony, 1925 through 1938 (comprising a second volume Newman claimed to have begun, since lost), and conclude with three books triangulating with realpolitik—with Cannonia, Russia, and America negotiating between 1939 and 1989 (comprising a third volume

436

Newman never began but described in correspondence—though he never mentioned whether the novel's '89 would've marked the end of communism).

In Partial Disgrace is the one-volume version of the first volume—the one-book version of the first three books that Newman worked on for the last three decades of his life. Its initial hero was, and still is, Felix Aufidius Pzalmanazar, "Hauptzuchtwart Supreme," which is to say a dogbreeder, trainer, and vet nonpareil, whose clients include Freud—himself an analysand in the first volume—and Pavlov—the presumed bellwether of the second. His son, Coriolan Iulus Pzalmanazar, "Ambassador without portfolio for Cannonia, and inadvertently the last casualty of the last war of the twentieth century, and the first great writer of the twenty-first," would become a "triple agent"— Cannonian, Russian, American. Their stories, along with tales of the Professor (Freud), and the Academician (Pavlov), were all to be told as the memoirs of Iulus, "translated, with alterations, additions, and occasional corrections by Frank Rufus Hewitt, Adjutant General, U.S. Army (Ret.)," who remains a presence in this composite—indeed, he's the parachutist who lands on the very first page, in 1945—and who was to emerge as the hero of the final volume, where he'd betray Iulus, or be betrayed by him, or—it's anyone's guess, anyone's but Newman's. The overarching theme of the cycle was to be the rebalancing of power, the shift from military brinksmanship to informational détente: If every side has the same intel, and so much of the same, it's only the purpose or the intention of the disclosure that matters. It's how nations reacted to these disclosures that interested Newman, and his cycle was to stage a *kampf* between those two great schools of behavior explanation: the Freudian

437

(transference) and the Pavlovian (conditioning).

Cannonia is a breeding ground, literally—not just for ideologies, but for canines. The eugenic pursuit of the perfection of diverse breeds of *Canis lupus familiaris* takes on a far more sinister, defamiliarizing set of associations when applied to *Homo sapiens*. The Nazis compelled the Reich's blondes and blues to mate their ways to an Aryan superrace, whereas the Soviets preferred to inculcate exemplary comradeship through "art"—a literature that would engineer its own public. Newman's consideration of speciation is of a piece with his investigation into the properties of metaphor: The question of whether it's irresponsible to try to perfect a breed is also the question of whether it's irresponsible to try and perfect a novel: What happens to breeds that don't please their masters? Are misbehaving novels, or novelists, to meet the same fate as untrainable mutts? Nature v. nurture is the case, which Newman insists is as much a referendum on the master as on the mastered: Is culture innate or cultivated or both? Finally, if a new breed can only be the combination of old breeds, just as a new literature must come from a miscegenation of the old—what are we humans to make of our prejudices?

To Newman, Freud's psychology compartmentalizes our being—as if life were just a train of alternating appetites and suppressions—whereas Pavlov's physiology coheres us as singularities, but as beasts. Newman alternately accepts and rejects these two conceptions, even while slyly offering a third: Men are no better than dogs, and no better than locomotive engines—though they can become the worst of both, especially in the company of women. (Felix's "three golden rules": "1. Ride women high. 2. Never take the first parachute offered. 3. Never go out, even to church, without a passport,

1,500 Florins, and a knife." Elsewhere he gives his son another trinity of "advice": "1. Neither marry nor wander, you are not strong enough for either. 2. Do not believe any confession, voluntary or otherwise. And most importantly, 3. *Maxime constat ut suus canes cuique optimus*"—which Newman glosses as "Everyone has a cleverer dog than their neighbor.")

In Partial Disgrace stalks its elusive prey through landscapes that resemble the Great Plains (that is, if they'd been treated to their own Treaty of Trianon), stopping for refreshment from lessons in obedience theory ("The animal, like society, must be taken into liberality without quite knowing it," Felix avers), from lectures on theater, dance, music, art, and the ethnology of the nomadic Astingi, Cannonia's sole surviving indigenous tribe ("They thought the Cossacks wimps, the gypsies too sedentary, the Jews passive-aggressive, the gentry unmannered, the peasants too rich by half, the aristocracy too democratic, and the Bolsheviks and Nazis too pluralistic"), and from high-minded entr'acte harangues ("Cannonia and America had a special and preferential historical relationship, [Iulus] insisted, beyond their shared distaste for oracles and pundits, as the only two nations in History of whom it could be truly said that all their wounds were self-inflicted. And what could Cannonia offer America?—the wincing knowledge that there are historical periods in which you have to live without hope").

"History" appearing thrice in one sentence—and once even capitalized, Germanically? But what of that other word, "disgrace"? Grace is for the religious; disgrace is for the damned. Humans once hunted for sustenance; now they hunt for sport. To go through the motions of what once ensured survival, now purely for entertainment, is ignominious, but vital—the ignominy is vital. Even if the rituals have become as hollow as rotted logs, or as unpredictable in their ultimate attainments as the rivers Mze—Newman's double Danubes, whose currents switch from east to west to east—the very fact that we remember any ritual at all is enough to remind us too of a more essential way of being. Our various historical, racial, and ethnic selves are cast in a masquerade, which makes a game of integration. Yesterday's work is play today, as contemporary life converts all needing to wanting. That's why when the hound points and we squeeze the trigger, when we slit the knife across the quarry's throat, we experience disgrace—a fallen estate, an embodiment of Felix's Semper Vero, his ancestral holdings lost to laziness and debt. Agriculture has become a hobby for us millennials. Along with reading and writing. But "once upon a time," everything was sacred. The traditions haven't changed, only our justifications of them have, and so though when we're faced with tradition we're disgraced, our disgrace is only partial. The holiness remains.

¶ Partiality
But, again, to be partial is to be polysemous, and another meaning is "to favor," "to incline"—as a hill becomes a mountain, where a settlement is raised, around an empty temple. Newman's disgrace brings solace, as the storms of spring bring flowers. Newman's disgrace is secular grace. "Not even a curtain of iron can separate Israel from its Heavenly Father," Rabbi Joshua ben Levi said in third-century Palestine. "An iron curtain has descended across the Continent," Winston Churchill said in 1946 at a college in Missouri. The *eiserne Vorhang*—the iron curtain, or firewall, an innovation of Austro-Hungary—is

a sheet of civic armor dropped from a theater's proscenium to prevent a conflagration that starts onstage from spreading to the audience. Newman lifts this barrier and invites his readers to ascend and bask in the flames.

FROM THE DIARIES

A Certain Angle

"Remember," the receptionist said, after loaning me a pen, "it won't write unless held at a certain angle."

The Mind Too

"[The pen] dries up if you don't keep it flowing."

A

... difficult letter to form while writing on moving tr...ins... buses.

Posterity

Posterity might think I had terrible handwriting. Truth is, I wrote everything on planes.

REORIENTALISM:
ON MATHIAS ÉNARD

Edward Said, May Peace Be Upon Him, regarded Orientalism as an Occidentalist illusion, and the Orient itself as "a theatrical stage affixed to Europe" upon which Westerners from Napoleon to Flaubert projected their lavish fantasies of violent *djinns* and nymphomaniacal *houris*, which were ultimately more revelatory of the psychic yearnings of European culture than of the daily lives of diverse Easterners: Turks, Egyptians, Iranians, and Syrians.

Today, nearly forty years after the publication of *Orientalism*, Said's thesis has been elevated to the status of dogma in Western academe, and among Western writers who—having lost the public imagination and so fighting increasingly internecine intellectual skirmishes—have taken to issuing soft *fatwas* against one another for the sin of writing from the "perspective" or "experience" of a person (a fictional person) of another ethnicity or race. Meanwhile, Arabic and Persian writers—the Others themselves—keep being jailed, tortured, and having their heads cut off.

Compass, Mathias Énard's masterly novel that attempts to redeem the specter of the Orient (it won the Prix Goncourt in 2015), refers to Said prophet-style, as "the Great Name." After acknowledging that the Palestinian-Manhattanite polymath "had asked a burning but pertinent question: the relationship between knowledge and power in the Orient," the narrator goes on to say, "I had no opinion, and I still don't, I think; Edward Said was an excellent pianist."

Which is all that matters—if not to Énard himself, then to the narrator, an insomniac musicologist named

Franz Ritter, who lies bedridden in Vienna, the "*Porta Orientalis*," fervid with his memories and an unspecified but assuredly fatal illness. There's no room in Franz's sickroom for debate about what it means "to appropriate," or "to be appropriate"; his only concern is for beauty, because beauty—especially nonverbal beauty, musical beauty—is a foretaste, or forehearing, of paradise, where we'll all finally speak the same language again, akin to the twittering of birds.

Énard—the French author of *Street of Thieves* (2012), a novel set during the Arab Spring, and of the widely lauded *Zone* (2008), a novel about Mediterranean Europe, Nazism, and the Yugoslav wars presented all in the course of a single train journey, and a single five-hundred-page sentence—here posits aestheticism not as a political substitute, but as a political "compass": If you take pleasure from music, if you're good at performing or, above all, composing good music, then in his cosmology you're innocent, even if you happen to be what the Saidists would call a "colonizer."

In *Compass*, Orientalism is offered up as a third way or "alterity"—the Orient not a place, even an imaginary place, but a passage, a circumvention of the East-West dialectic. The novel's characters—modulated from major to minor to major again—live in literal pipe dreams, which they access through opium, sex, the delirium of infirmity (syphilis or tuberculosis being the historical choice), and an almost fundamentalist submission to the religion of art. The narrator Ritter has written scholarship about how "revolution in music in the nineteenth and twentieth centuries owed everything to the Orient"; how Mozart, Beethoven, Schubert, Schoenberg, et al., used "the Other to modify the Self, to bastardize it, for genius wants bastardy." He sits up through the night like a donnish Scheherazade, lecturing the darkness on the discredited discipline of Orientalism, through a survey of the careers of the Orientalists he's known: disreputable loners all; emeritus drifters at home nowhere, or only in museums, library archives, and more ancient forms of ruins. There's the Prussian archaeologist and "madman," Bilger; the Aryanologist and "specialist in Arabic coitus," Faugier; and Ritter's inamorata, his *Unsterbliche Geliebte* (Immortal Beloved), Sarah, a Jewish Parisienne who has captured his heart (her research interests include legends of medieval European cardiophagy, or heart-eating). As Ritter counts down the clock to morning—to the sun, which rises in the cardinality of his obsession—he turns to recounting times past, excavating the precipitous collapse of his profession in the last days "before Google" and ISIS, when he and his colleagues still traveled through the region, and lived it up on fieldwork grants in Tehran (until the Islamic Revolution), and Damascus, Aleppo, and Palmyra (until the civil war).

Ritter inflects his fictional peregrinations with nonfictional prose-flights concerning musical Orientalism, which read like Thomas Bernhard editing Wikipedia, or a Levantine-themed edition of *Grove's Dictionary of Music*. Famous names and motifs—Mozart's *Rondo Alla Turca*, Beethoven's *Marcia Alla Turca*—entwine with excuruses on obscurer maestros: A brief account of Gaetano Donizetti, a composer of bel canto, leads to a biographical sketch of his brother, Giuseppe, who "introduced European music to the Ottoman ruling classes." Occasionally, Ritter's virtuoso solo will take in literature too, but even then his predilections tend to veer from the canon, with ruminations on Robert Musil followed by a portrait of his second cousin Alois Musil, an Austro-Hungarian priest who'd "set off, on camel-back, in the company of a few Ottoman gendarmes 'loaned' by the *kaimmakam* of Akaba, into the desert to find the famous pleasure castle of Qasr Tuba, which no one had heard of for centuries, except the Bedouins."

This is where Ritter's Orientalism dovetails with Said's: Both are alternative histories of the West, the stifled chronicles of its cravings for emancipation (from liberalism), or escape (from *la vie bourgeoise*). But while Said meant his thesis in a corrective spirit, Ritter means his as a tragedy—not least because he's expressing himself in prose, which is a fallen medium. Words, the medium of poetry but also of criticism, have to be translated to be made comprehensible, while music is universally coherent, the expression of pre- or post-verbal emotions in time.

"All art constantly aspires toward the condition of music": Walter Pater's fusty dictum is a neo-Romantic *cri de coeur* for Énard. All of his books share the hope of transposing prose into the empyrean of pure sound, where words can never correspond to stable meanings, but can merely indicate the energies underlying an attempt at stabilizing meanings and the bitterness that ensues when those attempts inevitably fail (even in Charlotte Mandell's resoundingly successful translation). Ritter's record of this pursuit is the record of his pursuit of love—but of a distant love, a doomed love—a love that won't be returned: not by Sarah, not by the "foreign" cultures he dwells among, and, most grievously, not by music itself. He becomes the bard of a world growing smaller even as its rifts become larger. He's the composer of a discomposing age, lamenting that "these days only Khomeini talks about love."

THE LITERATURE OF TWO EASTS

> The essence of wisdom is silence. If a word is worth a *sela*,
> silence is worth two. When I speak I regret, and if I do not
> speak I am not regretful. Until I have spoken I am ruler
> and master over my speech, but after I have spoken, the
> words master me.

The above transgression of silence was not blacked
onto a scroll by a Buddhist scribe or delivered to an
acolyte by a Zen monk from atop a Himalaya. It is, instead, the eighty-sixth section of the *Sefer Hasidim* (*The
Book of the Pious*), attributed to Judah ben Samuel the
Pious of Regensburg, founder of Ashkenazi or Western
Hasidism in the late twelfth–early thirteenth centuries.
That collection of folk wisdom is also responsible for instructing its readers not to write notes in the margins
of books—a proscription that covers, one would think,
the margins of the *Sefer Hasidim*—and for forbidding the
killing of lice at table.

Not just style and subject, however. Zen Buddhist and
Hasidic Jewish stories also share a handful of forms: a
Q&A format in which a student approaches an illustrious Master—in Zen a sensei, in Hasidism a rabbi, known
in Yiddish as a rebbe, or a tzaddik (a sage), or a maggid (
a preacher)—in order to pose a question whose only answer is a slap, a laugh, or a seemingly nonsensical retort
intended to reorient the senses (the highest expression of
this might be the Zen koan); a type of anecdote relating
the piety, and/or meekness, and/or miraculous powers
of the Master, often related after the Master's death by
a student or relative-disciple; and, most literarily, the
miniature wonder-tale that communicates both at face
value and as parable or allegory.

A monk asked, "Why is it that an outsider is not allowed to take over?" Master Zhaozhou [778–897, China] said, "Who are you?" The monk said, "Enan." Master Zhaozhou said, "What is your question?" Enan asked, "Why is it that an outsider is not allowed to take over?" Master Zhaozhou patted his head.

The people of a certain city begged the Baal Shem Tov [Israel ben Eliezer, 1698–1760, Poland] to force his disciple Yehiel Mikhal to accept the position of rabbi, which they had offered him. The Baal Shem Tov ordered him to accept, but he persisted in his refusal. "If you don't obey me," said the Master, "you will lose this world and the next world too." "Even if I lose both worlds," his disciple answered, "I won't accept what does not befit me." "Then take my blessing instead," the Master said, "because you have resisted temptation."

The prime attribute uniting these literatures might be called a fascination with "authority." Secular literature gains authority from the lives of its authors and from the outlets of its publication, but in the realm of oralia, especially in the realm of religious oralia, authority derives directly from the Master himself, that barefoot bearded embodiment of righteousness who is rarely if ever his own transcriber. The text is what the text is because the Master said it was, and it's the disciple's task to transmit that text accurately, and only then to interpret its meaning. The disciple becomes the Master at the very point at which his interpretations have themselves achieved the authority of primary texts, by having been transmitted accurately and interpreted by subsequent disciples, and so on, and that is the way a tradition works—a tradition, which is continual, as opposed to a culture, which is reactionary. In the anecdotes above, Master Zhaozhou's lesson seems to be that Enan's very acknowledgment of a hierarchy, in which he is a disciple and Zhaozhou a Master, will prevent Enan from ever becoming a Master himself. This paradox acquires an explicitly moral dimension with the Baal Shem Tov (the name itself is moralizing: Baal Shem Tov means "Master of the Good Name"), who ends his exchange not with emptiness but with an injunction against sin or evil.

A disciple told: Whenever we rode to our teacher, the maggid [Dov Baer, the Maggid of Mezeritch, 1710–72, Poland]—the moment we were within the limits of the town—all our desires were fulfilled. And if anyone happened to have a wish left, this was satisfied as soon as he entered the house of the maggid. But if there was one among us whose soul was still churned up with wanting—he was at peace when he looked into the face of the maggid.

The Master [Ryōkan Daigu, 1758–1831, Japan] never displayed excessive joy or anger. One never heard him speaking in a hurried manner, and in all his daily activities, in the way he would eat and drink, rise and retire, his movements were slow and easy, as if he were an idiot.

The two literatures have similar origins: They both began as the tralatitious lore of the peasantry, of the poor and uneducated village and town, as opposed to the city (the Baal Shem, founder of Eastern Hasidism, was an indifferent Talmudist who worshipped mostly in forests; Huineng, Zen's Sixth and last Patriarch, was an illiterate woodcutter when he went to study under the Fifth Patriarch, Hungjen); they both grew out of a revolt against religious intellectualism, Zen as a meditative response to the increasingly hermetic tenets of Chinese Mahayana Buddhism, Hasidism as an ecstatic rejoinder to the rote primacy of Lithuanian Jewish scriptural interpretation; they both became famous to the world as the aloud musings of charismatic leaders forced into itinerancy, moving constantly among monasteries and rabbinic courts in order to attract adherents and charity, and too to evade persecution.

A monk asked, "What is the depth of the deep?" Master Zhaozhou said, "What depth of the deep should I talk about, the seven of seven or the eight of eight?"

The Baal Shem said: "What does it mean when people say that Truth goes all over the world? It means that Truth is driven out of one place after another, and must wander on and on."

About their codifications.

The Blue Cliff Record and *The Book of Equanimity* (aka *The Book of Serenity*) were collated in twelfth-century China, while *The Gateless Gate* was compiled a century later toward the decline of the empire's hyperliterate Song Dynasty, at the time of the fragments of Kalonymus ben Isaac the Elder, Samuel the Pious, his son Judah the Pious, and the latter's apostle Eleazar ben Judah of Worms, whose Western Hasidism—half a millennium before the Hasidism of the Polish and Russian Pale—developed as a theological reckoning with the carnage of the Crusades and the escalation of the oppressive conduct, commercial, and sumptuary laws that followed.

Hasidism's canonical stories were assembled from their diverse sects for translation only at the turn of the twentieth century, however, a time when assimilated

Jews in Germany and the Austro-Hungarian Empire felt themselves alienated from their ancestral ceremonies and languages and were negotiating their returns to the wilds of Yiddish and a Hebrew revivified through Zionism. Not coincidentally, this Jewish dream of a comprehensible patrimony emerged just at the apex of Europe's interest in the Orient—in the folkways, literature, and esoteric philosophies of Asia.

European penchant for the *Orientalistik* grew out of the design style known as *chinoiserie*, whose motifs were brought to the continent by emissaries of the Dutch East India Company in the seventeenth and eighteenth centuries. Its manifestations included the decoration of porcelain with ostensibly Chinese and Japanese tableaux, and the erection on noble estates of pagodas of a theoretically Buddhist architecture. In literature, this vogue culminated with Hermann Hesse's *Siddhartha*, the *Bildungsroman* of a boy pursuing enlightenment in the India of the Gautama Buddha, though its elements are apparent in all of the arts, from the background patterning in paintings by van Gogh and Klimt to the use of the gong in the First Symphony of Mahler.

At the same time, Jews of the great European cities who'd be come changed by what they considered to be the more authentic lives lived by their Pale coreligionists included not only Martin Buber, amassing his landmark *Die Erzählungen der Chassidim* (*Tales of the Hasidim*, from which the selections here are adapted), but also Benjamin and Scholem, who immersed themselves in the contradictory doctrines of messianic redemption (which early Hasidism was fascinated with) and Jewish statehood in Palestine (with which later Hasidism has maintained a skeptical relationship).

Foremost among those artistically converted by

experience with Judaism's East was Kafka, who befriended Yitzchak Löwy, an actor of the traveling Yiddish theater, and the writer and dilettante Hasid Jiří Langer, a Jew who was born secular but became an errant disciple of the third and fourth rebbeim of the dynasty of Belz. Kafka recounted in his diaries numerous tales told to him by both Löwy and Langer, Talmudic episodes, and miscellaneous midrashim—and he managed to get many wrong or confused—but aphorized in a letter to Max Brod: "Langer tries to find or thinks he finds a deeper meaning in all this; I think that the deeper meaning is that there is none and in my opinion this is quite enough." (Kafka also admixed the Oriental: *The Great Wall of China* is a kabbalistic fable in Asian garb; its unabating wall could just as well be Jerusalem's Kotel.)

By the time of the Holocaust, Western Jewry's appropriation of Eastern Jewry was so complete and influential that it itself had become a kind of original: not an authentic thing to be sanctified, but a hybridity to be emulated. Writers, after all, are readers too, and though they might be cut off from an oral tradition, they do have recourse to regretting that estate by transforming the oral in books. After Kafka, there derives a host of Jewish and distinctly Israeli writers occupied with the free excavation of the overtly antiquarian in the hopes of finding whatever style next—style, the artist's religion.

FROM THE DIARIES

Traveling

While traveling and sitting perfectly still, he could feel the many objects in his many pockets all pressing in on him. He felt his wallet press against his right leg, while his left leg bore the weight of an American passport, $40 American in tens, and an oversize key to a seventh-floor apartment in Yalta. Train tickets, clipped together, pressed against his left buttock. Three cigarettes left in a pack pressed up against his left breast from the pocket above his heart. Their combined weight pressured him, pushed through his pockets and into him, until he himself was pocketed—until all that was left of him was an essential point, which had to bear these weights, still beating.

ISRAEL DIARY

7/31/2015

The plan was, if my brother and sister-in-law had a girl, to fly just after the birth. If they had a boy, I'd fly the next week, just after the bris. They had a boy. The boy had a bris. Between the birth and the bris I bought a ticket (expensive). At the bris, my brother announced he was naming his son after his, and so my, paternal grandfather, Benjamin (nickname: Benjy? Benji? Not Bibi).

I ate, I drank, I stopped by my apartment for my bag and got to Newark still tipsyish about three hours before my flight. Check-in and security sobered me up. About an hour before the scheduled departure, the screens reddened: delayed.

Nearing midnight, the flight was canceled and rescheduled for the morning.

Flights to Israel are the worst flights to cancel—the worst for airline employees, that is. One woman, just one, a woman so short that even standing on a box she could barely clear her desk, now had to deal with over one hundred Long Island Jews, and the enraged coordinators of a massive bar mitzvah party from Teaneck.

I stayed over at the airport, camped out on the floor. A guy in a knitted kippah—a fellow stranded traveler—stretched out too close to me on the tiles.

"What do you do?" is how he introduces himself.

I say, "I'm an uncle."

Avi's from Woodmere, Long Island—"I'm an uncle too. What are the chances?" He has a sister and nieces in Jerusalem. Then, suddenly, he's talking about the Holocaust. He's trying to explain how and why his parents came to be in the States and not Israel—he thinks that requires an explanation. Then he's trying to explain why he didn't make aliyah, like his sister did—he thinks that also requires an explanation. He says he thinks he knows a friend of mine, from yeshiva.

8/2

Tel Aviv. Staying in too-cool-for-school Florentin, south Tel Aviv, on a street called Hazanovich, in what'd been described to me by the friend of a friend, whose family owns it, as a courtyard apartment. Turns out the courtyard is a parkinglot, and the apartment is a room. Not air-conditioned, hot—living here's like living in the crook of a knee, or inside a scrotum between two chubby legs rubbing up against each other, chafing. The chubby legs in this analogy being two busy thoroughfares: Sderot Har Tsiyon and Derekh Shalma.

The friend of a friend's grandparents used to live here, their first apartment after coming to Israel from Yemen in or around 1950. The friend of a friend had been listing the apartment on Airbnb, until he was forced off the site for having garnered too many complaints and one-star reviews. At least I'm staying here for free. I keep reminding myself, I'm staying here for free.

8/4

I'm here to write a novel about Israel. Which is not what I told the woman who checked my passport at Ben Gurion. I told her I was here to visit cousins.

So many dangers in writing about Israel. So many failures. Especially for Israeli novelists.

To my mind, Israel is the only contemporary Jewish subject, or the last contemporary Jewish subject not kitsch. Reading a popular novel about Israel (there aren't more than a few) is like reading a Holocaust novel (of which there are many), but backward: the last page (death or escape from death) coming first, the first page (bourgeois respectability, bourgeois self-loathing) coming last.

Right to left: Popular Israeli novels are just novels about the Holocaust read right to left.

8/7

"The politics of the novel": The meaning of this phrase has changed in my lifetime. Or maybe just my interpretation of it has.

Once upon a time, preonline, the phrase used to mean: "the politics espoused in a novel, by its characters and author." But now, it seems, I take the phrase to mean: "the politics implied by the very act of writing or even reading a novel in the year 2015, with everything beautiful gone to blazing hell, and so much else to do, especially so much else to do that's easier and more comforting."

To exercise literacy has become a political act in and of itself.

The politics of the novel are now just the novel.

About cousins (not mine): In line to pay at Hummus Beit Lechem, unable or unwilling to ignore the discussion in front of me, I'm reminded that Mizrahi Jews (Jews from Arab countries) have strange ways of talking about their cousins. They will refer to a male cousin in the feminine, which sounds to me and to most Ashkenazi Jews (Jews from Europe) like a grammatical mistake. But it's not a mistake so much as a sign of how intensely invested Mizrahi Jews are in filiation, which itself is just a sign of the importance of blood to Judaism. To refer to your male cousin but in the feminine (*ben dodah*, literally "son of aunt") signifies that your relation to him comes through his mother—it defines his mother as the sister of one of your parents. Similarly, to refer to your female cousin but in the masculine (*bat dod*, literally "daughter of uncle") signifies that your relation to her comes through her father—it defines her father as the brother of one of your parents. The genealogy of this grammatical quirk seems Arabic, which has eight different terms for cousin, each describing a different kinship type: son of paternal uncle, son of paternal aunt, son of maternal uncle, son of maternal aunt, daughter of paternal uncle, daughter of paternal aunt, daughter of maternal uncle, daughter of maternal aunt. In Arab countries, as among Arab Jews, everything, apparently, is about your blood. For me, however, everything is about your language, which is the conduit, and the only consanguinity you can choose.

8/10

Florentin: The neighborhood reminds me of Williamsburg ca. 2000, which is not a compliment. Of course, by "Williamsburg" I mean "north of the Williamsburg Bridge." Because south of the bridge are the Hasidim—more Hasidim than in all of Tel Aviv. I miss them something terrible.

My daily routine, now that I'm finally over the jet lag: wake up at 6:00 a.m., write for four hours, get to Hummus Beit Lechem just when it opens. Order a hummus with egg, which is served with pita, pickled veg, and half a raw onion. Eat while reading *Haaretz*. Buy cigarettes and smoke my way back to writing by noon. I can choose between two routes; rather, between two sides of Herzl Street, neither of which gives any shade from the sun. One side has a store that sells birdcages. The other side has a store that sells birds. Both are run by

457

Ethiopians and both are called "Song of Sheba."

I quit by 7:00 p.m., and head out again for a shwarma or a falafel or a sabich, then wind down the day at a bar, reading the books I bought at Ha'Nasich Ha'Katan and Robinson, and drinking beer and arak until I'm sleepy (by 11:00 p.m.). The books, in Hebrew: *Dolly City* (*Dolly City*) by Orly Castel-Bloom, *Hitganvut Yechidim* (*Infiltration*) by Yehoshua Kenaz, and last but not least, *Ha'Yored Lemala* (*The Acrophile*) by Yoram Kaniuk, a great writer who was once very generous and kind to me, and whom I can't avoid, or can't avoid missing, not just because Tel Aviv was very much "his city," but also because it's been two summers now since he died.

In English, translated from the Arabic: *The Secret Life of Saeed: The Pessoptimist* by Emile Habiby.

8/12

I'm not going to Jerusalem. That's my decision, and I'm enjoying its perversity.

It's insane to visit Israel but skip Jerusalem—to resist its gates, to refuse its walls—to fail in my duties to God, family, and the Israel Ministry of Tourism.

I remember how back when I dated H, I took her to Katz's Deli and she ordered a salad. Another time when I took her, she ordered nothing.

Denying herself and/or provoking me was the thrill.

I wonder whom I'm denying and/or provoking now.

A guy at a café who talks about his life exclusively in terms of "terror": Instead of saying, "I was born," he says, "I was kidnapped." Instead of saying, "My parents took me for a year to Ann Arbor, Michigan," he says, "My parents took me hostage."

8/13

A conversation about Israelis who don't serve in the IDF, and so: a conversation about the religious and the mentally and physically disabled.

My interlocutor, a fancy journalist, says, "Religious and disabled—there's a difference?"

I would've laughed at that in New York.

Not here.

8/14

Whenever army service comes up in café conversations, or just in café conversations with me, everyone says, "I was the worst soldier in my unit."

A mysterious line by Avot Yeshurun (Ukrainian-born Israeli poet, 1904–92): Should it be translated, "The isolationist life of a roof"? "The separatist life of a roof"? "The secessionist life of a roof"?

No, no, the translation by the great Harold Schimmel (Israeli poet, born in Paterson, N.J., 1935) is still the best: "The dissident life of a roof."

8/15

Didn't even try to go to the beach. (Or Gaza.)

8/18

I go about breaking, or half-breaking, my vow as I ride in the crowded nosepicker's sherut to Jerusalem.

But all I do in Jerusalem is get a cab—still, because I'm going east, to the West Bank, it takes me a while. No one's keen to drive me.

Y, a Palestinian, drives me out to a checkpoint, where I'm asked what I do and why I'm here. Intimidated by the uniform, intimidated by the gun, I mumble something in English about tourism, and it's only after I put the barrier wall behind me and get out of the cab, it's only after I get out of the next Kia Picanto converted into a cab—after the settlements, after the ruined fields, after the blockaded roads, and all the plastic and aluminum garbage glowing in the sun along the only open road to Jericho—that I come up with a more honest answer: I'm an uncle.

LINES OF OCCUPATION:
ON YITZHAK LAOR

How great is the God Who allows a poet to be born at the same moment as his nation! Let us praise Him! Let us praise Him with flute and timbrel! Let us praise Him by criticizing Israel!

Yitzhak Laor—Israel's most celebrated dissident, and perhaps its greatest living poet—was born in 1948 a month before the founding of the Jewish state. The town he grew up in, Pardes Hannah—Hannah's Orchard, named not after the biblical Hannah, mother to the Prophet Samuel, but after Hannah Rothschild, scion of the orchard's funding family—is today a scruffy backwater redeemed only by its bright groves of citrus trees. Forsaken halfway between Tel Aviv and Haifa, Pardes Hannah in 1948 was a Jewish oasis surrounded by Arab villages soon to be destroyed. By the time Laor could have been conscious of his neighbors, they'd vanished, through intimidation and by force. Gone were *their orchards*. Gone were *their citrus trees*.

Laor was first recognized for his resistance—the most modern of mediums. As students at Tel Aviv University in 1972, Laor and fellow reservist Yossi Kotten became the first two Israel Defense Forces soldiers to invoke "selective refusal" (in Hebrew, *sarvanut selektivit*) with regard to their compulsory military service. The line they drew in the sand was the Green Line, the border that separated Israel from the lands it took during the Six-Day War: Laor and Kotten refused to serve in any mission perpetrated in what are now called "the Occupied Territories." This act of becoming a "Refusenik"[1]—retrospectively marking a generational shift from the happy heroes of 1948, 1967, and 1973 to the grunts mired in Lebanon in 1982—proved a national sensation, prompting popular condemnation and earning Laor a short term in a military prison. But it also proved his seriousness as a political voice and gained readers for his poetry—politician-readers, soldier-readers, even lay readers.

For more than three decades, Laor has ignited controversy, and the success of his verse, novels, stories, and the play *Ephraim Goes Back to the Army* has given rise at times to outright paradox: When he won the 1990 Prime Minister's Prize for Poetry, Israel's highest such award, Yitzhak Shamir, then prime minister, refused to sign the official declaration. Laor should not be read as the bane of officialdom, however, but rather as the stern comfort of the Israeli soldier who can no longer pretend to be the courageous warrior; his poetry is both the balm of those who serve only the orders of their own conscience and the prophetic exhortation of those he describes in his poem "Balance":

> The gunner who wiped out a hospital the pilot
> who torched a refugee camp the journalist
> who courted hearts & minds for murder the actor
> who played it as just another war the teacher
> who sanctioned the bloodshed in class the rabbi
> who sanctified the killing the government minister
> who sweatily voted the paratrooper
> who shot the three-time refugee the poet
> who lauded the finest hour of the nation

1. Refusenik" is the sardonic invention of radical journalism. The original Refuseniks were Soviet Jews refused the opportunity of *aliyah,* or moving to Israel. In Hebrew, "conscientious objectors" are *sarvanim,* from the root *serev,* "to refuse" or "to decline."

who scented blood and blessed the MiG. The moderates
who said let's wait & see the party hack
who fell over himself in praising the army the sales clerk
who sniffed out traitors the policeman
who beat an Arab in the anxious street the lecturer
who tapped on the officer's back with envy of the officer
who was afraid of refusing the prime minister
who eagerly drank down the blood. They
shall not be cleansed.

The translation is mine, because no English translations of Laor's poetry have yet appeared in a book of his own, and where they have appeared, online and in left-leaning poetry anthologies, they have been poor if not incorrect. The decision of who gets translated into English is often less a matter of quality than of politics—the lack of a market for translated literature requiring its subsidy by a writer's home state—and one can imagine Israel's unwillingness to promote a writer like Laor abroad.

It comes as both a disappointment and an inevitability, then, that Laor's first book to make it into our language is nonfiction. *The Myths of Liberal Zionism* is a work of political critique as literary criticism, a treatment of statecraft as an adjunct to poetic craft, and it is also an attack on the famous writers of Laor's generation, whom he reads as providing humanitarian cover for Israeli abuses. Amos Oz, A. B. Yehoshua, even David Grossman, who lost a son in the 2006 Lebanon war—Laor accuses these and others of sanctioning, through impotent dissent and empty rhetoric, the tragic status quo. Novelists who pen pietistic eulogies but have never resisted their governance; public intellectuals who absolve liberal guilt but have never directly opposed the moral compasses of their readership—"They shall not be cleansed."

According to Laor, the singular Myth of Liberal Zionism is Liberal Zionism itself. Like the beasts Behemoth and Leviathan, a *Zionis liberalis* is inconceivable to Laor, because whereas his Liberal believes in openness and the policies of empathy, his Zionist—more than a century after Theodor Herzl recalled Palestine as the *Judenstaat*—believes that millions can be denied their patrimony, dispossessed, abused, and even murdered in the name of Jewish statehood.

As Laor writes in the preface to his essay collection, composed in Hebrew, then translated into French (published by La Fabrique éditions as *Le nouveau philosémitisme européen et le "camp de la paix" en Israël*), then from French into the following, with the rage intact:

> History is always written by the mighty, by the victors. Even if we do not talk openly of bloodshed, of the price of our blood compared to "theirs" in the ongoing equation between sufferings, every discussion about Israel must bear in mind that over ten million people live in this nation-state and the territories occupied by it. Half of them are Arabs, but almost four million of them live under military occupation, with virtually no law protecting them. Fifty percent of all the prisoners in Israeli prisons and detention centers—in other words, ten thousand people—are "security prisoners," as Israel calls them, in other words Arabs from the occupied territories who are sitting in prison after being convicted by military courts, or detained without any trial at all. Close to four million people are currently living under the longest military occupation in modern times, stripped of the right to vote on the laws that have governed their lives for more than four decades.

Laor's version of history is to be incensed that history should even have versions. His disdain for the very concept of myriad concepts is informed by a vicious integrity—by his credentials not only as a conscientious objector but also as the son of refugees from the Shoah—and reinforced by his poetic practice. For him, the essential truth underlying historical ambiguity can be found only in and through common language, and one wonders, reading him, whether the ultimate synoptic history of Israel and Palestine would not be a poet's history, a linguistic history—a version that can be all versions, once the vocabulary has been agreed upon: vocabulary having to do with, for example, the sanctity of "life," or *chayyim*, a word that in Hebrew is uniquely plural, and so, as Laor reminds us, cannot be lived by one person, or one nation, alone. Any philological account of this conflict must begin with the name of the younger aggrieved party: "Palestinian" is the word for a people created by the fall of the Ottomans, an empire destroyed in WWI along with two other vaunted houses of the nineteenth century—the Habsburg and the Romanov. Ottoman decline left the Muslim and Christian Arabs living in Palestine to seek for themselves nationhood and a cultural identity distinct from Turkish suzerainty. Meanwhile, the rise of pogroms in Russia, and pervasive anti-Semitism within a host of newly nationalistic countries liberated from the multiethnic inclusivity of empire, turned disparate Jewish populations—from Hasidim in rural Poland and Ukraine to worldly businessmen in Berlin and Paris—into "the Jewish People," dedicated to reestablishing a country that no Jew had ruled in more than two millennia.

Palestine was then a British "mandate"—that term denoting an indefinite interregnum between colonial rule and colonized self-governance. In 1917, with the war entering its gory senescence, the Balfour Declaration—an open letter from British Foreign Minister Lord Arthur Balfour to Lord Walter Rothschild, Hannah's grandnephew and the premier Jewish philanthropist of his day—took pains to assert that the newly proposed Jewish homeland shall not "prejudice the civil and religious rights of existing non-Jewish communities in Palestine," and so defined the rightful Palestinian inhabitants of Palestine apophatically, or by negation, as what they were not.

That declaration and the subsequent White Papers of 1922 and 1939 were effectively nullified in the wake of the Shoah (much of the Arab world was aligned with the Axis), and by Jewish paramilitaries such as Lehi, Haganah, and the Irgun, which led raids on Arab settlements and British military depots. Israel's founding, coming six months after the United Nations passed Resolution 181, which advocated Palestine's partition into Jewish and Arab states, immediately triggered a war when the provisions of that resolution were violated, by Arab aggression and by Israel's very existence. Israelis call this the War of Independence; Palestinians refer to it as the *Nakba*, or "Catastrophe." Here is another Catastrophe: At the time of this writing, that term, *Nakba*, previously allowed in Arabic schools and textbooks, has been removed from all curricula in the State of Israel by order of the Education Ministry.

The manipulation of language is no metaphor for political manipulation; *it is political manipulation*, and every government that has ever sought to convert its citizenry has turned to words—the medium of the media that is also the domain of the poet, who is a veritable president of words. (In Israel the presidency is a powerless office, yet possessed of symbolic significance.) According to Victor Klemperer, by 1933 the German language had swollen with an array of new compounds involving the word *Volk*: *Volksfest* ("a festival of the people," later the führer's birthday), *Volksgenosse* ("comrade of the people"), *Volksgemeinschaft* ("community of the people"), *volksnah* ("one of the people"), *volksfremd* ("alien to the people"), *volksentstammt* ("descended from the people"). Klemperer, a Jew and leading lexicologist of the Reich, along with Karl Kraus, of decayed, feuilletonistic Vienna, are perhaps Laor's foremost political precursors—*Nestbeschmutzern*, or "people who dirty their own nests" (leave it to German to have a word for this)—and the best popular theorists of how a change in public language can manifest a change in public consciousness.

Indeed, this reification of language is a tenet of all Abrahamic faiths. Allah, through the angel Gabriel, dictated the Koran to Mohammed; in the Torah the world itself is made by Word: "Let there be light," and there was, and we're told "it was good," and so it is good still. Vitriolic critic of a country that proudly defines its citizenry in the terms of a *Volk—Das Jüdische Volk—*Laor makes the following tally. Since Israel's inception, more than four hundred Arab settlements have been dismantled, and not a few have had their ancient toponyms Hebraicized—Rami to Ramat Naftali, Majd al-Krum to Beit Ha-Kerem, Ja'una to Rosh Pina. This first summer of the Netanyahu government, just as *Nakba* was deleted from the schoolbooks, the Transportation Ministry proposed to redo Israeli street signs so that even the names written in Arabic would be Hebrew transliterations (e.g., the city of Jaffa would be written as the Hebrew

467

Yafo on Arabic signs, not as the Arabic *Yaffa*).

These official measures, Laor insists, just legislate the bias with which the conflict is reported in Israel and in those countries, like the United States, influenced by Israeli *hasbara*, or "explanation"—the Hebrew term for wartime lobbying. According to the Nakdi Report, a set of guidelines drafted by the Israeli Broadcasting Authority, the epithet "East Jerusalem" is strictly verboten. During the First Intifada, Israel fought, according to the American press, not an organization like the PLO but "the Palestinians." Israeli soldiers are regularly "kidnapped," whereas Hamas "fighters" can only be "arrested." A Palestinian action is normally "terrorism"; an Israeli action is routinely a "response." To be fair, the official Palestinian Authority newspaper did, at millennium's end, call "the Jew" "the disease of the century," but Laor insists on criticizing only his own.

It isn't every day that poetry sheds a metaphor, but that is exactly what happened on May 14, 1948, the date of Israel's founding. By the time of David Ben-Gurion's proclamation, "Zion" ceased to be a proleptic ideal or symbol and began to be an archaeological site with borders to defend. The imagery of the daily prayerbook, and of Diaspora poets like Judah Ha-Levi ("O Zion, won't you ask after your captives—the exiles who seek your welfare, the remnants of your flocks?"), would be reread as versified prophecy, while new writers— "Sabras," native Israelis nicknamed after the indigenous prickly cactus—would need to find new metaphors to exploit in a revivified language. Previously a historical tongue wherein each letter controlled a bodily organ and represented an attribute of the Godhead, Hebrew

468

was now put to more-mundane uses: finding verbiage for landed things; for flowers, trees, and animals; for politics; for warfare.

Laor's book begins with a simultaneous study and condemnation of this matured, normalized literature—a corpus of Hebrew letters that didn't lament an absent patriarchal God or the travails of Exile but, instead, rejoiced in workaday existence. Yet this purported normalcy would degenerate into a type of propaganda in which the Israeli patriot was always in the right, a golden boy-man liberating Judea and Samaria from the Arab hordes in ecstatic self-realization. Canon-building became an initiative of nation-building, as nascent public and government alike clamored for a *shira meguyeset*—a "mobilized poetry," able to defend the homeland at a stanza's notice. Zealous revisionism wasn't confined to Israeli bookery but also informed such American films as *Exodus*, starring Paul Newman as a miraculously brawny, virile Jew—half biblical Israelite, half Aryan redivivus. Laor notes, however, that "this trend was somewhat obstructed with the advance of Israeli cinema, perhaps because it was hard to find enough blue-eyed blond actors to fill all the parts."

If the decades following 1948 found Israelis aspiring to Aryanhood, then the roots of that loathing grew from decades previous, from the Nazi desire to cast European Jewry as entirely Oriental—the infamous *Der Stürmer* cartoons of the fattish Jew with the hooked nose and tasseled fez, the cigar and ruby rings. Laor argues that the Nazi genocide represented a purgation of this stereotype, and that the Jew emerged from the war intensely Westernized, as if Auschwitz's fires had burned away all traces of Otherness and now the Jew was fit to be not just a citizen like all Western citizens but the very paragon of a *polis*, the Western citizen par excellence. In Laor's interpretation, if the Holocausted Jew is today regarded as the special guardian of Humanism, then the new Oriental Other or Easterner can be said to be the Arab, and especially the rock-throwing, half-literate Palestinian. Laor accuses the brandnames of Israeli letters of continuing to play up these roles, posing as diligent humanists internationally while turning a blind eye to, or even encouraging, the bloodshed at home.

Laor's polemic engages divergences of East and West in two ways. He accuses his peers of advocating a vague peace in translation, in such forums as *Le Monde* and *Die Zeit*, then vociferously supporting recent incursions domestically, in Hebrew. He further accuses them of discriminating between putatively Eastern and Western influences within Israeli Jewry itself. Although Ashkenazim, or European Jewry, constitute a minority of Israelis, their traditions have always been privileged. Despite the presence of the Sephardim—Jews ingathered from Arab lands, for whom Arabic was a primary language—culture for Israel still means *Kultur*, the cult of *Bildung*: Beethoven, Rembrandt, Goethe, with maybe a Russian or two, or Marx, included for good measure. This primacy, in turn, is evinced as the subject of most exported Israeli fiction—how European "we" are, how well educated, how polished. Israeli writers like to mention that Tel Aviv boasts the highest concentration of Bauhaus architecture in the world.

According to Laor, it is precisely this identification with the West that allows Oz and Yehoshua to be perceived as "liberals," perhaps even *to be* "liberals," yet to distort the facts mercilessly: Oz claiming in the foreign press that the Camp David accords failed because Yasir

Arafat insisted on being granted the Right of Return (the right of Palestinians to return to confiscated lands, which critics rightly fear would overrun the country and outpopulate the Jews), whereas Laor (and subsequent intelligence) claims it was because Israel refused to negotiate shared custodianship of Jerusalem; Yehoshua insisting on a binational *Pax Semitica*, even while recommending an embargo on Gaza and justifying sanctions against the West Bank, agitating in *Haaretz* in 2004 for "not a desired war, but definitely a purifying one. A war that will make it clear to the Palestinians that they are sovereign," and threatening "all the rules of war will be different... we will make use of force against an entire population."

By contrast with the Ashkenazi, Israel's Sephardi or Mizrahi ("Eastern") majority are largely absent from Israeli fiction, even from that of writers born to Mizrahi families, like Yehoshua, whose mother was born in Morocco and whose father's people have lived in Jerusalem for five generations. Laor takes Yehoshua to task for disavowing his heritage, and he censures Oz, born Amos Klausner, son of a renowned Russian family of Judaic scholars, for writing novels that praise Jewish Europe, or Jewish Europeans in Israel, while ignoring a sizable swath of his country's demographic.

Laor—whose own father, a Galician immigrant to Germany, changed his surname from Laufer upon emigration to Palestine—is particularly perplexed by Oz, a writer who denies his origins in life yet cleaves to them on the page, eulogizing in his memoir, *A Tale of Love and Darkness*, those Jewish "Europhiles, who could speak so many of Europe's languages, recite its poetry, who believed in its moral superiority." Oz does this, Laor maintains, to make a statement about the qualifications of the victims of Nazism, despite the fact that most of the Jews the Nazis exterminated were far from being urban poetasters or linguists. Just as wherever Jewish literary history is discussed the Yiddish of Sholem Aleichem and I. L. Peretz is emphasized over the Arabic of Jewish writers like Anwar Shaul and Murad Michael, in popular iconography the image of the Lubavitcher rabbi appears intimately bound to that of Einstein, or Freud. To Laor, these reductions and lacunae imply a schizophrenia, a desperate reinforcement of older, weaker Jewishness as a stereotype of both what to venerate and never to be, commingled with a racist fear of Arabness that resolves itself in the institution of a synthetic Israeli identity.

Israel is the only country in the world whose politics were initially a poetics. Anytime a ground operation or air raid is launched, the orders implement the dictates of national verse. When Jews first ruled Jerusalem, there was no call for poetry. Then, with the Roman destruction of the Temple in 70 C.E., Jewry was thrust into history, or Exile, with a return to Jerusalem representing the end of history, as if the Messiah were not a person but the reunification of a People with its Land. In Exile, Mosaic law gave way to textual interpretation, which gave way to secular letters. Religion turned to a *religio poetae* —a faith in poetry, or aesthetics, with wordmakers serving as surrogate priests. Their liturgies were odes to a Zion past, and their panegyrics will live forever even if Zionism won't. The tragedy of Zionism is that history will outlive it, and that governments can never accomplish what should be the province of metaphor, or the divine.

That tragedy is best embodied in translation. Here is "A Citizen of the World," the only poem of his that Laor quotes in this collection of prose that comments on prose:

> We didn't grow up where our fathers grew.
> They didn't grow up where
> their fathers grew. We learned not to
> feel nostalgic (we can feel nostalgic for any tombstone
> decided upon) we don't belong
> anywhere (we shall belong with ease to anything
> when demanded) we move across
> countries, we sleep in fancy
> hotels, we sleep in cold
> barns, we love only to be
> loved, we rape only
> to be remembered, we enjoy
> only to register ownership, destroying
> mainly villages, declaring ownership
> then leaving, hating peasants, mainly
> peasants (if necessary, we'll also cultivate
> the land)

It's unfortunate that Laor's word choices in the last lines remain silent in English: "we'll also cultivate/the land." The solution to this problem is the solution to the entire Middle East. The last word in the Hebrew is *Adamah*, "land" in the sense of earth, ground, soil. An agricultural word, a common dirt-under-your-fingernails word, whose root, *Adam*, relates it to the name of the first man, made of mud, made of clay dug from Eden. The other way of saying "land" is *Eretz*, though it's more like saying "Land" (the patriotic phrase is *Eretz Yisroel*, the "Land of Israel," never *Adamah Yisroel*). Lacking capital letters, just as it lacks superlatives, Hebrew suggests differences of importance by near-synonyms, or by compounds. *Eretz*—used earlier in the poem, here translated as "countries"—is grasping, metaphysical, scriptural: Moses tried to enter the *Eretz* but failed; Joshua conquered the *Eretz* in the book that bears his name. The Land of *Eretz* is a biblical grant, an ethereal encryption of a heart's ideal, whereas the land of *Adamah* is a profane place to feed your flesh and water your blood—emphasizing its corporeality, the word for "blood," *dam*, is contained in *Adamah*—the impermanent ground beneath our feet; a temporal tract, or plot, which we could cultivate, "if necessary." Hebrew poetry since the time of Titus called for an *Eretz*, modern realpolitik realized an *Adamah*, and the poets of Laor's generation found that their grand subject could only be their loss of grand subject—the decapitalization of the Land/land their fathers had labored so hard to capitalize.

If the land of Laor's poem is *Adamah*, the poem's "we" cannot be taken to mean Jews, who live for an *Eretz* while maintaining residence in Brooklyn and citizenship worldwide. Instead, this "we," it must be assumed, are Israelis who "didn't grow up where [our] fathers grew," and so Laor means to speak only for, and to, Israelis of his own age and circumstances. It often seems that the Israeli-Palestinian conflict is just this, a textual problem. If so, then the muddle of meaning that must be analyzed lies in parsing not Palestinian from Israeli but "Israeli" from "Jew." Only once those epithets have been dissevered can some sort of dialogue begin, between two political entities and not between two (or three) religions, or Peoples. Until then, "Israel" will continue to be vilified as a word that means something other than what it should, while all critics of Israel will be accused of anti-Semitism.

Some poets have tried to write the future; others have tried to rewrite the past, or erase it. Although a good poem does not necessarily have to be a moral poem, a good state is necessarily a moral state. So anarchical as to be apocalyptic, so sensitized to the lamentations of others as to negate his own birthright, Laor in his essays asks not another Jewish Question but rather a universal question: Can a Zionist act morally if morality dictates Zionism's erasure?

FROM THE DIARIES

To Think

"To think there's weather, even here."

Traveling Without You

Traveling without you: traveling without clothes, without a body.

LITERARY ANIMALS

Today, the political metamorphosis of the novel ranges in every extreme: as some novelists debate gender and racial parity, while others let businesses sponsor their plots, to the point at which all their characters drive Mercedes (Mercedi?).

It frequently seems as if only one wrong remains to be righted, because it's not regarded as wrong: the use, or abuse, of the literary animal.

This, of course, is a matter as hoary and spavined as Rucio, Sancho Panza's donkey, and Rocinante, Quixote's horse—a matter as old as the Bible, immediately older than misogyny and racism. After all, it was a serpent that was responsible for the fall of Eve, and so for the fall of humanity, in Genesis. Rather, it wasn't just any garden-variety snake, but a snake that walked and talked and tempted our appetites, until we rewarded it for its surrogacy by mutilation: We forked its tongue and severed its legs and so forced it to hiss and crawl through the dust and blamed our massacre on God, Whom we kept shapeless and nameless and unaccountable.

Ten generations later, Creationdom was destroyed in a Flood, yet all the animals were rescued. Even the serpents. Even the worms, the parasitic worms, crept into the ark as individuals and out of it as prototypes. That vessel must've been a floating laboratory (but a laboratory of inbreeding or of hybridity?), as the two of each kind tamed each other (or mated with others?), until the waters receded to let their spawn be domesticated. Then Ham uncovered the nakedness—the feral nakedness—of his father, Noah, and was punished by having the skin of *his spawn* forever blackened. Ham's descendants became the animals to men and the men to animals, a middle caste of chattel to till the fields. Their salvation was just another punishment: enslavement.

Consider Fable #150 by that slave named Aesop: The lion spares the mouse's life and the mouse returns the favor and springs the lion by gnawing at the hunter's net. Now, consider that same scenario but with the animals' roles assumed by men: The behavior might be more, not less, of a shock. Allegories and parables are the political statements of censorious cultures and with democracy devolve into mere art. Bears and whales not to mention dogs and cats have been rendered endangered if not extinct—imaginatively, that is. We've so humanized them—we've so burdened them with consciousness, and even with conscience—that they've been exhausted, especially as symbols. In perpetrating this, we've proven ourselves to be the cruelest of creatures, because we are cruel to every creature. It is we who belong in the bestiaries. We've imposed our languages on animals (Ovid, Orwell), whose every utterance condemns us. We've usurped their bodies (Apuleius, Kafka), but treat that violation as collateral. We've even made our gods turn into bulls before raping women, and then to silence the women we've turned them into trees.

I know of no species worse than our own—worse than *my own*. Writing is the act of acknowledging my wildness.

478

TOP TEN BOOKS ABOUT ONLINE

¶⫿ *The Catalogue of Nibru* (Various, CA. Twenty-First to Twentieth Centuries B.C.E)

> I, the king, was a hero already in the womb
> I am a king treated with respect
> Not only did the lord make the world appear in its correct
>   form
> Lady of all the divine powers

These lines, inscribed in clay in Sumerian during the Third Dynasty of Ur, were initially confusing to the American archaeologists who around 1900 uncovered them from the ruins of the city of Nibru, or Nippur, in contemporary Iraq. They appeared to be poems, or the Sumerian equivalent of poems, but none cohered, or cohered as completely as the forty thousand or so other texts excavated from the area. And so the sixty-two lines of this incomprehensible tablet—of this intact yet stylistically fragmented tablet—were set aside, as the more formally explicable texts were decoded. In the course of that decoding, however, the same lines kept cropping up—as first lines: "I, the king, was a hero already in the womb" was the first line of a poem in praise of Shulgi; "I am a king treated with respect" was the first line of a poem in praise of Lipit-Ishtar; "Not only did the lord make the world appear in its correct form" was a song for hoeing; "Lady of all the divine powers" was a hymn to the love goddess Inana. This led scholars to conclude that this mysterious cuneiform slab was no avant-garde Gilgamesh (whose earliest version was also unearthed at Nibru), but a bibliography or curriculum—an index of the Sumerian canon intended for reference, or instruction. Literature began with the list: Online just made the links palpable.

¶‖ *Talmud* (Various, CA. 200 C.E. To Present)
A commentary on commentaries: a book divided into books, or tractates, whose every page is divided among debates about Jewish law (*Mishnah*, 200 C.E.), debates about the debates (*Gemarah*, 500 C.E.), the glosses of the twelfth-century French rabbi Rashi (in a strip down one margin), and over six centuries of *tosafot*, which are glosses on Rashi's glosses (in a strip down the opposite margin). Interspersed textblocks can feature extracts from legal codices by Maimonides (twelfth-century Egypt), Nachmanides (thirteenth-century Spain), Joseph Caro (sixteenth-century Palestine), and Elijah ben Solomon Zalman, the Vilna Gaon (eighteenth-century Polish Lithuania). To speak of the Talmud is to speak of a multiplicity seeking syncreticity, a jurisprudential pullulation: a work that intermixes Aramaic and Hebrew and exists in two forms (the earlier Jerusalem Talmud, the later Babylonian Talmud), each of which has appeared in disparate editions, with dissentaneous annotations and addenda. The Talmud's ultimate interpretive difficulty, however, inheres in the fact that for over a millennium its primary "text" had been overwhelmingly oral—commandments communicated face-to-face before being transcribed.

¶‖ *The Compendious Book on Calculation by Completion and Balancing*, Muhammad Ibn Musa Al-Khwarizmi (CA. 820 C.E.)
A book from Baghdad, written by a Persian astronomer

and mathematician credited with the introduction of what we now call Arabic numerals to Europe. Al-Khwarizmi's Arabic treatise, which is known to us solely through its twelfth-century Latin translation by Robert of Chester, delineates two ways of solving quadratic equations: the first by means of *completion*, or the movement of negative terms from one side of an equation to the other; the second by means of *balancing*, or the cancelation of equal terms on both sides of an equation. "The balancing" was *al-muqabala;* "the completion" was *al-gabr*, whose transliteration into "algebra" was relatively logical when compared with the Latinate corruption of its creator's name: from Al-Khwarizmi to Algoritmi—source of the modern "algorithm." By proposing the abstraction or transposition of all quantities into a representative language, Al-Khwarizmi founded a method by which all extant mathematical disciplines could communicate. His immediate concerns, though, were more mundane, as his treatise concludes by turning theory to practice and, like the search engines that continue its work today, becomes preoccupied with mercantile transactions: "A man is hired to work in a vineyard for thirty days for 10 dinars. He works six days. How much of the agreed price should he receive?"

◀▥ *Summa Theologica*, Thomas Aquinas (1265–74)
"It seems that those who see the essence of God see all things in God. For Gregory says: 'What do they not see, who see Him Who sees all things?' But God sees all things. Therefore those who see God see all things.... Further, whoever sees a mirror, sees what is reflected in the mirror. But all actual or possible things shine forth in God as in a mirror; for He knows all things in

Himself. Therefore whoever sees God, sees all actual things in Him, and also all possible things. [...] Further, whoever understands the greater, can understand the least, as Aristotle says. But all that God does, or can do, are less than His essence. Therefore whoever understands God, can understand all that God does, or can do. [...] Further, the rational creature naturally desires to know all things. Therefore if in seeing God it does not know all things, its natural desire will not rest satisfied; thus, in seeing God it will not be fully happy, which is incongruous. Therefore he who sees God knows all things." Use the Ctrl key to find and replace "God" with "Google," "Apple," or the "Five Eyes" (the United States, U.K., Canada, Australia, New Zealand: the five nations that share signals intelligence), throughout.

¶ *Index Librorum Prohibitorum*
(First Edition 1559, Final Edition 1948)
A book necessitated by books: Gutenberg's invention stilled the copyist's hand, and ensured that texts were no longer the exclusive possessions of the aristocracy and Church. The democratization, along with the secularization, of "content," suggested the establishment of institutional controls—if governments and ecclesiastical bodies had ceased to be the primary sources of reading material, they could at least license the printers who were, and regulate the materials they published. The first edition of the Vatican's *Index Librorum Prohibitorum—Index of Prohibited Books*—was superintended by Pope Paul IV, and blacklisted over five hundred works for reasons not just of heresy or blasphemy, but also of anticlericalism, and obscenity; further, it set rules regarding book distribution that curtailed the influx of

illicit texts from outside the Holy See's dominion. The *Index*'s second edition, authorized by the Council of Trent and so referred to as the *Tridentine Index*, relaxed the standards of its predecessor, in that it distinguished between books to ban, and books merely to censor, and was more forgiving toward scientific works, except for those by Protestants. Taken in all its editions, the *Index* was both a guide to the evil opinions of heliocentrists (Kepler and Newton), pantheists (Bruno and Spinoza), Romantics (Balzac and Zola), and fascists (Alfred Rosenberg and Gabriele D'Annunzio), as well as a registry of the occulted holdings of the Vatican Library, which was required to obtain a copy of every book it proscribed. Paul VI abolished the *Index* in 1966—and in doing so appended it to another *Index:* that of Church books the Church has repudiated. Still, the list lives on, and has now been made searchable, at beaconforfreedom.org.

¶ *Epistolae Ho-Elianae*, James Howell (1645–55)
An all-over-the-map, four-volume autobiography—which, because it's semifictionalized, and because it's written as correspondence, qualifies it for the distinction of the first epistolary novel in English—*Epistolae Ho-Elianae* is more regularly referred to by its more regular title, *Familiar Letters*. Its Anglo-Welsh author, Howell, was arguably the first English-language author to earn his living solely from writing. He was the quintessential freelance, producing histories, political tracts, polyglot dictionaries, and wisdom miscellanies (*English Proverbs*, 1659, noted: "All work and no play makes Jack a dull boy."). The variety of Howell's interests—and the variety of his prefreelance-writing employment: as a

tutor of and secretary to the nobility, and as the traveling representative of a glass manufacturer—accounts for the varied settings of his *Letters* (Germany, Italy, Poland, prison), and the varied nature of *Letters'* addressees (family, friends, ambassadors of the British Crown, fellow belletristic hacks, and sea captains encountered along the way). The only aggregating premise to this P.O. box of prose is Howell's naïve but endearing conviction that life and writing were synonymous and that everything that ever happened to him deserved to be written down. Beyond that: that everything that ever happened to him deserved to be communicated (published).

¶ *Gulliver's Travels*, Jonathan Swift (1726)
A "projector," to Johnson's Dictionary, is "one who forms schemes," and, in its second definition, "one who forms wild impracticable schemes." In Lagado, capital of Balnibarbi, Lemuel Gulliver is given a tour of the Academy of Projectors, an organization dedicated to "putting all Arts, Sciences, Languages, and Mechanics upon a new Foot." Which is to say, dedicated to putting them onto, or through, a computer, with which "the most ignorant Person at a reasonable Charge, and with a little bodily Labour, may write books in Philosophy, Poetry, Politicks, Law, Mathematicks, and Theology, without the least Assistance from Genius or Study." Gulliver relates: "It was twenty Foot Square, placed in the middle of the Room. The Superficies was composed of several bits of Wood, about the bigness of a Die, but some larger than others. They were all linked together by slender Wires. These bits of Wood were covered on every Square with Paper pasted on them, and on these Papers were written all the Words of their Language, in their several Moods,

Tenses, and Declensions, but without any Order. The Professor then desired me to observe, for he was going to set his Engine at Work. The Pupils at his Command took each of them hold of an Iron Handle, whereof there were forty fixed round the Edges of the Frame, and giving them a sudden turn, the whole Disposition of the Words was entirely changed. He then commanded six and thirty of the Lads to read the several Lines softly as they appeared upon the Frame; and where they found three or four Words together that might make part of a Sentence, they dictated to the four remaining Boys who were Scribes. This Work was repeated three or four times, and at every turn the Engine was so contrived, that the Words shifted into new places, as the square bits of Wood moved upside down."

¶ The Telephone Directory, Connecticut District Telephone Company (1878)

In 1877, an inventor from New Haven named George Coy witnessed a telephone demonstration by Alexander Graham Bell and immediately went about founding the Connecticut District Telephone Company—the world's first commercial telephone exchange. In 1878, the company published its first directory—neither a white pages nor a yellow pages, just a single sheet of stiff cardboard. The company's fifty subscribers were listed only by name. Numbers weren't required or even useful: An operator connected, and was privy to, all calls. The second edition of the directory, published a year later, was a bound affair, listing nearly four hundred names, alongside directions for telephone operation, guidelines for telephone etiquette, an advertisement for Watkin's Automatic Signal Telegraph (a business that took telegrams via telephone dictation), and informative essays on "Progress in Electric Lighting" and "The Microphone."

¶ "Statistical Mechanics and Irreversibility,"
Émile Borel (1913)
Not the first version of Swift's scenario (which has also been imagined by Leibniz, Pascal, Cicero, and Aristotle), but the first to involve *singes dactylographes*—"typing monkeys." Borel, the French probabilist, cracks his knuckles: "Let us imagine that a million monkeys have been trained to strike the keys of a typewriter at random, and that [...] these typist monkeys work eagerly ten hours a day on a million typewriters of various kinds. [...] And at the end of a year, these volumes turn out to contain the exact texts of the books of every sort and every language found in the world's richest libraries." The implication being that, given enough monkeys, typewriters, paper, and time, even Borel's sentences are destined to be written again, as is this sentence, and so on.

¶ *The Foundation Pit*, Andrei Platonov (1930)
"To change the world": Half a century before this became the sanctimonious mantra of Silicon Valley, it was the violent imperative of Soviet Russia. Platonov's darkling novel concerns a pit being dug to accommodate the foundations of a vast residential tower that will ultimately shelter the entire population of an anonymous city in the USSR. Once the tower is finished, all the people's former dwellings will be destroyed. "And after ten or twenty years, another engineer would construct

a tower in the middle of the world, and the laborers of the entire terrestrial globe would be settled there for a happy eternity. With regard to both art and expediency, Prushevsky could already foresee what kind of composition of static mechanics would be required in the center of the world, but he could not foresense the psychic structure of the people who would settle the shared home amid this plan—and still less could he imagine the inhabitants of the future tower amid the universal earth. What kind of body would youth have then? What agitating force would set the heart beating and the mind thinking?"

FROM THE DIARIES

What's in the Bag?

The man stood barefoot at the security checkpoint and said, "Cancer."

Overnight Flight WC

"That toilet's sure going to feel it in the morning."

Shooting

When they go to shoot something set in the city, but in the past, they tend to use certain neighborhoods as "locations." There are "locations" for every century, for every decade, for every year. This is what my cousin tells me. My cousin who earns her living renting out her apartment for shoots and so who lives on permanent vacation. Her apartment, she says, is very December 26, 1986, which was the date her husband left.

IMPROMPTU FANTASIAS:
ON BENJAMIN DE CASSERES

> I have thought of writing the lives of some great artist—
> Shelley, Manet, Beethoven, Shakespeare, Chopin, Keats,
> Sappho, Emerson, Nietzsche, Redon, for instance—
> directly from a complete inhalation of and meditation on
> their work without any regard to the facts. Wherever the
> known facts conflict with my mythus, I shall reject them
> or flatly deny them. It would be a fascinating under-
> taking—the lives of Shakespeare, Chopin, Verlaine,
> for instance, as I conceive them to have been from
> their faces and work alone.

Such an endeavor would take considerable egotism, and
that Benjamin De Casseres was possessed of that quality is no "mythus" but verifiable fact. In this essay, we
will try to be more responsible, though the sources are
obscure. Given that De Casseres wrote regularly for
newspapers and magazines in the most public city in the
world, New York, during the heyday of the most public
century before ours, the twentieth, it's troubling that so
little is known, and so little is the desire to know. There
is hardly any scholarship about him (besides footnote
mentions in a handful of doctoral dissertations regarding interwar New York literary society); none of his
books are in print; and the manuscript of his thousand-
page diary, *Fantasia Impromptu* (which is the source of
my epigraphical paragraph), reposes in the basement of
the New York Public Library, where I might have been
the first person to read through its pages since they were
interred there by De Casseres's widow, Adele "Bio"
Terrill, following her husband's death in 1945.

Benjamin De Casseres was born April 3, 1873, in

Philadelphia, to a Jewish family of Sephardic descent. And so, an outsider: This man so vocal about his Manhattan credentials was born out of town, in the sixth borough. Not Ashkenazi like the majority of American Jewry, he was a nonimmigrant from comparatively exotic stock, taking on an Anglo-Saxon and Puritan literary establishment "with a genius that is profoundly Latin to my latter atom." The family name derives from Cáceres, the ancestral capital of the same-named Spanish province, and De Casseres himself liked to speculate that he was related to a hero of his, Spinoza: One Samuel De Casseres married Spinoza's youngest sister, Miriam, became a rabbi and scribe, and offered the funeral eulogy for his teacher, and Spinoza's excommunicator, Rabbi Saul Levi Mortera of Amsterdam.

De Casseres moved to New York by the turn of the century, began losing his hair, smoking cigars, drinking. Physically, De Casseres writes of himself: "I am strong meat; false teeth and babies, lay off! Fat and Jewish; bedroom eyes; voluptuous flesh." Surviving photographs by Arnold Genthe show a paragon of sly dissolution, tempered by self-seriousness, in precariously situated pince-nez, dark worsted suit, and patterned, probably colorful, tie. (Genthe's nitrate negatives date from 1925.)

However, the most telling autobiographical detail might be that of the outsized ambition De Casseres did his narcissistic best to conceal. If the man was, as he weekly reminded himself in print, the equal if not better of any writer who ever lived, then he was so unwittingly, as if against his will. He was, he said, like Rip Van Winkle of the Catskills, in that he "grew famous while [he] slept. I slept all day and worked on a New York newspaper all night (1900 to 1920), and almost precisely at the end of twenty years I was astounded to

490

find out that I was famous not only in my own country but that I was being translated into French by no less a person than Remy de Gourmont, who was writing about me in the *Mercure de France* and *La France*."

From his back rooms at 11 West 39th Street, a building that no longer exists, De Casseres mass-produced articles for dozens of publications: to begin with, *The American Spectator, The Bookman, The Boston American, Chicago Examiner, Fra Magazine, Gay Book Magazine, The Greenwich Village Quill, Haldeman-Julius Monthly, Los Angeles Examiner, Metropolitan Magazine, New York Evening Post, The New York Herald, New York Journal-American, The New York Times, New York World, People's Favorite Magazine, The Philadelphia Inquirer, The Philistine, Reedy's Mirror, The Revolutionary Almanac, The San Francisco Examiner, The Smart Set, The Sun, The Washington Herald;* he wrote for Alfred Stieglitz at *Camera Work;* at the *American Mercury* he was edited by H. L. Mencken. On a typical day, De Casseres might write a column on literature to be syndicated by the Hearst Service, ad copy for a cheesecake manufacturer, and the script of a radio commercial for "health syrup": "I am a one-call salesman. If I don't succeed at first, I never try again."

De Casseres also amassed reams of drama and fiction: "And some days I love to write lines for poems I'll never write." His books and booklets include: *The Adventures of an Exile; Anathema!: Litanies of Negation; Black Suns; The Book of Vengeance; Broken Images; The Chameleon; The Comedy of Hamlet; The Communist-Parasite State; The Complete American; Don Marquis; The Eighth Heaven; The Elect and the Damned; Enter Walt Whitman; The Eternal Return; Finis; Forty Immortals; I Dance with Nietzsche; The Individual Against Moloch; James Gibbons Huneker; The Last Supper; The Love Letters of a Living Poet; Mars and the Man;*

Mencken and Shaw; Mirrors of New York; The Muse of Lies; My New York Nights; The Overlord; Robinson Jeffers, Tragic Terror; The Second Advent; The Shadow-Eater; Sir Galahad: Knight of the Lidless Eye; Spinoza: Liberator of God and Man; The Superman in America; When Huck Finn Went Highbrow; Words, Words, Words. One of his most personal preoccupations was editing *The Sublime Boy*, a volume comprising poems by his younger brother Walter, a depressed homosexual who committed suicide at the age of nineteen by hurling himself into the Delaware River. (Poet Edwin Markham, in a letter to De Casseres: "I am touched by your brother's failure to fit himself to this tragic existence, touched also by the pathos of his fate"; other of the surviving De Casseres correspondents: British sexologist Havelock Ellis, French writer Maurice Maeterlinck, science-fiction writer Clark Ashton Smith, paranormal investigator Charles Fort, Hollywood screenwriter Ben Hecht, poet Edgar Lee Masters, novelist Damon Runyon, and "Nietzschean" Oscar Levy.)

But De Casseres's posterity mainly rests on a single poem, "Moth-Terror," first collected in the *Second Book of Modern Verse* in 1919, edited by journalist colleague Jessie Rittenhouse. The poem was subsequently recycled into numerous reprints and subanthologies that proliferated in schools, colleges, and book clubs even after WWII (nothing ensures a future like the lassitude of anthologists):

> *I have killed the moth flying around my night-light; wingless and*
> *dead it lies upon the floor.*
> *(O who will kill the great Time-Moth that eats holes in my soul*
> *and that burrows in and through my secretest veils!)*
> *My will against its will, and no more will it fly at my night-light*
> *or be hidden behind the curtains that swing in the winds.*

(But O who will shatter the Change-Moth that leaves me in
rags—tattered old tapestries that swing in the winds
that blow out of Chaos!)
Night-Moth, Change-Moth, Time-Moth, eaters of dreams
and of me!

All these elements of a life—the journalism, the interminable pamphleteering of poesy, the feverish letterwriting to more celebrated contemporaries—can be bound between two covers that don't exist: De Casseres's *Fantasia Impromptu*, subtitled ridiculously "The Adventures of an Intellectual Faun." Unlike the precious polished texts of the chapbooks and broadsides De Casseres self-published, sent around to friends for free and offered for sale to the general public for 50 cents apiece, this daybook—and, often, late-night book—could never be collected into finished form. Excerpts last appeared in an unedited 1976 Gordon Press Selected Works reprint of a privately subvented 1935 Blackstone edition (Blackstone seems to have been De Casseres's own venture). "I can see the standpoint of the American publishers: an American thinker must be a fakir of some sort because fake is a national trait. They simply will not believe in the possibility of my existence—as an American. They can, and do, conceive me as a Spaniard or a Frenchman, but as a Philadelphia-born original—*Jamais!*"

Begun in 1925, soon extending to multiple volumes, De Casseres's diary was dedicated "to the thinkers, poets, satirists, individualists, dare-devils, egoists, Satanists and godolepts of posterity"; the introducing author continues, on the manuscript's frontispiece: "This book will be continued to the end of my life—a new volume about every two years. Please read carefully and to the end to get full flavor of book. It is all spontaneously set

493

down, and all literally my self." De Casseres kept making random undated entries into older, weaker age; *le prosateur* was going on seventy when he noted that the world had never appeared so threatening: "This *jealousy of likeness*, that is at the bottom of the German persecution of Jews today," and, "Adolf Hitler is as personal, private, and peculiar to the German people as my morning bowel movement is to me." Toward diary's end, just before his death, the physical evinces and affects as much as the written: Not only is De Casseres writing letters to God, he's also writing letters *as God*, to himself; the paper gets cheaper, thinner; typewriting gives way to handwriting, a tremored scrawl.

Interleaved with the metaphysical whimsy, racism, and misogyny ("God couldn't possibly be a female, for He keeps so well and so long the profoundest secrets of life"), along with a loathing regard for his own Judaism, is to be found a trove of the most startling epigrams our country has ever known—the work of an American La Rochefoucauld or Lichtenberg, a Karl Kraus or George Bernard Shaw. Indeed, these stacks of incomprehensible, often insipid pages could be edited down to a hundred-page book of surpassing aphorism; but because I haven't yet received that commission, and not everyone has the time for a library visit to pile through the archives, I offer the following—a De Casseres *Chrestomathy*, as Mencken styled his own collection of a career's worth of the miscellaneous but brilliant:

A practical man should have knuckles in his eyes; a poet should have them in his images.

To almost any American "thinker": the feet of your thoughts are always asleep.

All summits are cemeteries.

Art can only influence artists.

If you have no ideas, beware of your tenses and your grammar.

An emotion has more reality than a nail.

Hope is the promise of a crucifixion.

Whatever we do is a remedy.

Beauty is distance.

Only the ugly are modest.

Identity is partisanship.

The difference between Science and Theology is that Science is evolving ignorance and Theology is static ignorance.

We used to say, "It is raining." Now (1930) it would be more appropriate to say: "The bladders of the atoms have opened and torrents of electronic urine lave the asphalt."

Symbol.—I live behind a statue of myself.

Esoteric.—If you swallow your jewels you will have to recover them in your excrement.

Things that intoxicate me.—Gardens; the sea; mountain solitudes; great poetry and great prose; abstract ideas; profound sleeps; twilight; music; God, the sense of Wonder and Mystery; Satan; amorous sports; Bio's love; the peace of death; wine; fastflying automobiles when I am in one; the voice of little children; the word Shelley; the word Baudelaire; the words Victor Hugo; imaged coitions with ideal women of an impossible beauty; well-buttered lima-beans; spaghetti; the flash of a metaphor through my brain; praise from superior minds; the stars; checks, checks, checks.

Keep the masses happy. Unhappiness should be the privilege of the few.

To have written a book that no one has ever read is like having a face that no one has ever looked at.

Pleasure has no eyes.
All life aspires to mirrors.

PARAGRAPH FOR LIU XIAOBO

There is no need to magnetize honey just like there is *no call* for imprisoning writers of conscience (they're already imprisoned by conscience). To apostrophize the regime is to take away an apostrophe from the end of your name. You are ended. You own nothing. To seek to dismantle Chinese quote unquote communism with literature is to try to shatter a mountain just by singing at it. Soon enough you forget the mountain and focus on the song. Xiaobo—I have read you in translation and admire you greatly. I have signed a petition protesting your arrest. I am an unimportant American of Jewish extraction. Half my body is corn syrup, the other half is whole. We will probably only meet when we're dead.

FROM THE DIARIES

There Should be Words for the Following in German

... resentment-of-another's-culture, resentment-
of-the-authenticity-of-another's-culture,
resentment-of-the-perceived-authenticity-of-
another's-culture, resentment-of-one's-own-
perception-of-another's-culture-as-authentic,
the-darker-shadow-formed-by-the-overlapping-
of-two-or-more-shadows-on-the-dance-floor...

Germany to Jersey for the Holidays

Mom: a cathedral restored. Dad: a casino demolished.

THOUGHTS ON THE ROTHS
AND THEIR KADDISH

If you're a writer, you translate yourself. There's an idea in your head, or an image, and it must find its way to words. There has always been a tension, a tension or an opposition, between writing that seeks to record life as experience, in the private language of experience, and writing that seeks to refine or winnow life into final statements, into fixities, with more-public vocabulary, syntax, grammar. On one hand, think of William Faulkner, who sends personal and so imperfect memories stumbling stuporously across Yoknapatawpha. Then, on the other hand, think of the safer, saner Saul Bellow, who tells us intellectually what Chicago means, clearly, even conclusively. This push/pull between inhabiting the self and experience, and making the self and experience intelligible to others, is especially pronounced among writers who write in second languages, and, to a lesser degree, among writers who write about a culture that is not the culture they are writing for or toward. Someone like Bellow, born to immigrants, born to Yiddish, beginning to write in post-WWII America under the sign of bestsellerdom, must have felt compelled to explain more, to explain his intentions, in a fancy Hyde Park version of the way my own relatives, when they spoke English, often spoke. very. slowly. and repeated themselves and repeatedly YELLED! to make themselves understood.

The question all second-language, second-culture writers must ask themselves is simply formulated: "How much does one translate?" Which is to say, "How accurately?" Do we translate the names of foods (cholent), or of family members (machatunim), or the texts of our blessings? Do we stet them in their original languages, but then set them in italics? Do we explain what they mean—what they mean to us, or does their foreignness alone speak to that significance (*halevai*)?

Here is what I'm talking about: Henry Roth was born in the shtetl of Tyshmenitz (in Yiddish), or Tyśmienica (in Polish), in Galicia, in 1906, but came to America a year later. Yiddish was his first language, his *mamalashon*. In his exemplary *Call it Sleep*, published during the Depression (1934) with low expectations from the marketplace, but with the highest of expectations from art, the protagonist David Schearl (that is, David Scissors) is referred to by his father as his father's "Kaddish." No explanation is given of this. There is no expository clause or note that tells the reader this is a Yiddish euphemism for the firstborn son who will say the Kaddish prayer in memory of the father when the father is deceased. Two generations later, Philip Roth (no relation) would find it necessary to convey to his readers that his own Kaddishes (not *Kaddishim*) were recitations of the Jewish prayer of mourning (though the prayer's text itself actually never mentions death and merely praises God). What happened between Roth's Kaddish and Roth's Kaddish?

Speaking within the context of a single language—say, within the historical context of this language, the language of Anglo-America—the tension between private language and translation as explanation is often thought of as the tension between what is called "literary fiction" and the popular. Though I prefer to think of this divide as that between being, just being, and odious "identity," which is the corpse of a culture that must be buried deep.

In my generation, let us say, Amen.

DREAM TRANSLATIONS FROM
THE EARLY HASIDIC

Nachman of Breslov, born in Medzhybizh, present-day Ukraine, in 1772, was the founder of Breslov Hasidism and despite his death, in Uman in 1810, remains the movement's leader. This is why Breslovers have been called, have called themselves, "The Dead Hasidim." Fittingly, their essential principle is what the Rebbe referred to as *hitbodedut*: "self-seclusion," "auto-isolation"—a lone contemplative state to be sought not in a sanctuary but in nature, for the purposes of inspiring spontaneous personal prayer, not necessarily in Hebrew, but in one's most fluent tongue. Breslov, then, can be considered a sect only inasmuch as it's considered a sect of individuals, each of whom pursues a direct and utterly private dialogue with God. The Rebbe's chosen setting for *hitbodedut* was in the woods or fields; his chosen time was in the middle of the night—the time of dreaming. Psychoanalysis defined "dream" as wish fulfillment and so allied it with prayer. If it follows that a collective prayer can express a collective dream, then the Breslovers' rejection of community worship might express an unfulfilled wish for extinction: their own, or their people's, the world's.

In 2014, due to a variety of factors too traumatic and banal to recount, I found myself suffering from insomnia and immobilized by depression and sought psychiatric treatment. I would go to school and deliver my lectures in the mornings, then have two hours to kill—to thought-murder—before my afternoon appointments. I had no appetite for lunch, home was too far. I considered joining a minyan, I considered suicide. Instead, I wound up sitting on a bench in Bryant Park in Manhattan and reading and translating Hasidic texts, which led to my reading and translating texts from elsewhere and earlier in the Jewish tradition (the languages were Hebrew and Yiddish). The following selections are from two of the spiralbounds I was spiraling through at the time—call them wishful dream-journals, unfulfilled prayerbooks: succor for sleepless yearning.

Once, in 1802, in the woods outside Breslov, a young Hasid was troubled—about an upcoming marriage? or his sister's infirmity?—and wandered among the trees mumbling a prayer. Another young Hasid was also troubled—perhaps he too had a marriage? or sister?—and, at the same time, was doing the same, wandering and mumbling. Though they were unable to see each other, due to the density of greenery, it is said that they were able to hear each other and, indeed, not only were their practices the same, their prayers were the same as well. Their individual spontaneous prayers were identical, verbatim.

Chayey Moharan, the book's title, means "Life of the Rebbe." "Moharan" is an acronym: "Morenu, HaRav Nachman," "Our Teacher, Rebbe Nachman." It was written, or compiled, by a disciple called Reb Noson, and contains, amid homiletics and practical advice, numerous accounts of the Rebbe's dreaming. The Rebbe himself features in many of his dreams, and in not a few he importunes another dream-character, to demand an explanation—to demand an interpretation.

Rabbinic opinion differs as to how to interpret the interpretation of a dream that's presented in a dream, but it's significant that even the Rebbe's oneiric interlocutors seem to doubt the endeavor—to doubt the Rebbe's capacities or intentions. After a particularly wild dream (#83), about twin palaces and swords with multiple blades (one that brings death, one that brings penury, one that brings physical afflictions, etc.), and disciples who swallow sparks that seed strange creatures in their guts, the Rebbe begs "an old man" for his thoughts, and the old man grabs his beard and says, "My beard is the explanation."

> Another time, in 1868, a goy merchant from Kiev (or Lvov) was in Lvov (or Kiev) and strolling past a bank, from which an ornament, or the scaffold for the workers installing an ornament, fell—it fell on his head—and knocked him into a coma. The goy merchant was kept in hospital, where he babbled in a language suspiciously Hebraic. Brought to interpret was Reb Nachman Chazzen, or, in other tellings, one or both of the Lubarsky brothers (Reb Moshe and/or Reb Zanvil). The merchant, despite never being a Jew, was pronouncing a perfect rendition of Ma Tovu, a common Jewish prayer that, when he emerged from his coma, he was unable to remember or even recognize.

Another of the Rebbe's dreams seems too explicitly didactic (#85). In it, a man is flying one moment, and home the next—he's in a valley, and home again—he's atop a mountain, and home—he's picking golden vessels from a golden tree, home. Is this possible? How is this possible? These are the questions the Rebbe's somnic-surrogate—"the host"—asks a man who turns out to be an angel—"the guest." The angel's answer is—like the dream itself—too long and too intricate with references and puns, but basically he says: "You've been reading."

The Rebbe had a dream: I was sitting in my room [he said]. No one was around. I got up, went to the other room. No one was around. I went into the house of study, went into the shul, but no one was anywhere. I went outside. People stood around whispering. One laughed at me, another provoked me. Arrogant stares all around. Even my own followers had turned against me. Insolent stares. Whispers around.

I called to one of my followers: "What's going on?" He replied: "How could you have done such a thing?"

I had no idea what he meant and asked him to explain, but he left me. So I traveled to another country, but when I got there, people stood around whispering. Even there, my sin was known. Everyone knew my sin but me. So I went to live with the trees. They became my followers.

We lived together and whenever I required food or water or a book, one of my trees would uproot itself and go scampering into the city to fetch it. When the tree would return, I'd ask: "Has the commotion died down?" to which the tree would reply: "No, the rumor is stronger than ever."

— *Chayey Moharan*,
Reb Noson, aka Nathan,
Sternhartz (1780–1844)

Once there was a turkey that dwelled beneath a table, pecking at flecks and bones. The king quit, the doctors and nurses quit, the Rebbe was called for, came. The Rebbe took off his robes, sat under the table, pecked at flecks and bones. The turkey asked: "What are you doing here?" The Rebbe asked: "What are *you* doing here?" The turkey replied: "I'm a turkey," the Rebbe replied: "So I'm a turkey too."

They sat together through many meals, the king

feasting his queens, orgies of doctors and nurses. Then
the Rebbe gave the signal for his shirt, which was tossed
to him. He said to the turkey: "What—a turkey can't
wear a shirt?" So another shirt was tossed, and both
their breasts were covered. Many meals, orgies, and
so on. Then the Rebbe gave the signal for his pants. He
said to the turkey: "What—a turkey can't wear pants?"
And so on, until both were dressed from top to bottom
and human foodstuffs—delicacies not yet partaken of
above—were hurled.

> "One can eat what humans eat and still be a turkey, I
> assure you," said the Rebbe, "and what's more—one can
> rise to sit as humans sit, not under the table, but at the
> table, in the laps of the feet around us, more commonly
> referred to as chairs."
>
> And so they rose, and so they chaired. (The turkey
> once again became a prince.)
>
> — *Kochavey Or,*
> Reb Abraham Chazzen
> (1849–1917)

A king once told his vizier: "The stars tell me that he who
will eat from this year's grain harvest will go insane—what
is to be done?"

The vizier said: "We must set aside a stock of foreign
grain, for ourselves, so as to not become tainted."

But the king objected: "We do not have enough foreign
grain for everyone in the kingdom, and if we set aside a
foreign stock for just us two, we will be the only ones in
the kingdom with intact minds. Everyone else will be
insane and yet will come to regard *us* as insane."

"It is better, then, for us two to eat from this year's
grain harvest, but we will each put a cut on our foreheads,

so I will look at your forehead, and you will look at my forehead, and when we see the cuts, at least we will be reminded of our insanities."

— *Sipurim Neflaim*, Reb Shmuel Horowitz (1903–73)

One Sabbath a man came to the Rebbe and said, "I am lonely," and the Rebbe gave him counsel: "Take a wife."

The man did as instructed, but returned the next Sabbath and said, "Even with a wife I am lonely." The Rebbe said, "Have children."

The man did as instructed, but months—even years—later, his complaint remained: "Even with children I am lonely."

The Rebbe said, "Sleep."

What does this mean?

It means that one is never lonely in a dream.

— *Maamarim Yekarim*,
attributed to Reb Yisroel Dov
Ber Odesser (ca. 1888–1994)

This world compares to the next world as sleeping does to wakefulness. In a dream you are never ashamed. For if you were ashamed, you would never dream of sleeping with a woman—sex would never occur to you. You would never commit acts in your dreams that you would be ashamed of committing awake. The reason for this is that dreams at night stem from the daytime's imaginings.

Once, a certain Hasid—who commanded his son not to enjoy this world any more than was necessary, and not to let more than thirty days ever pass without a fast—died. But then it transpired that rivals had his corpse disinterred and flogged, which grieved all his adepts deeply. He appeared to one of his adepts in a dream and said, "This befell me because I used to live among tattered books

506

with their leaves all shredded and I took no initiative to reassemble and protect them."

    —— *Sefer Hasidim*

ATTENTION!

A (SHORT) HISTORY

To write something in which every sentence is a first sentence. To write something in which every sentence is as good as the first sentence.

READ THE SMALL FONT FIRST.

"To live as if every day were your first,"
"to live as if every day were your last"—conditionally.

READ THE LARGE FONT LAST.

To begin with sex.

DO NOT BE DISTRACTED.

To begin with loss.

DO NOT BE DIVERTED.

To begin with death.

THERE IS NOTHING TO READ HERE.

To begin with the end.

YOU ARE STILL WASTING YOUR TIME.

GUIDE

At the advent of photography, exposures could last longer than it will take you to read the first chapter of this essay. Such long exposures are responsible for many of our ancestors appearing stiff and expressionless. A single movement, no more than a sudden smile or frown, could blur the image, rendering it useless. For that reason, parents concealed themselves behind drapery and furniture in an effort to keep their children still. This essay is dedicated to my parents.

INATTENTION

"Every one knows what attention is" is a good first line. It arrests your attention, then lets it loose. It was written by William James and published in 1890 in *The Principles of Psychology*. But it is not the first line of that book, nor even the first line of its lecture/essay on "Attention."

To write a book in which every sentence is a first sentence, to write a book in which every sentence is as good as the first sentence. "To live as if every day were your first," "to live as if every day were your last"—conditionally. To begin with sex. To begin with loss. To begin with death. To begin with the end.

Every one knows what attention is, James asserts, but he doesn't let that stop him:

> It is the taking possession of the mind, in clear and vivid form, of one out of what seem several simultaneously possible objects or trains of thought. Focalization, concentration, of consciousness are of its essence. It implies withdrawal from some things in order to deal effectively with others and is a condition which has a real opposite in the confused, dazed, scatterbrained state which in French is called *distraction*, and *Zerstreutheit* in German.

The most distinctive aspect of this passage is James's insistence that the word "distraction"—I'll resist the italics—is French.

James's linguistic scrupulousness was shared by his brother, Henry:

> There was a new infusion in his consciousness—an element in his life which altered the relations of things. He was not easy till he had found the right name for it—a

name the more satisfactory that it was simple, comprehensive and plausible. A new "distraction," in the French
sense, was what he flattered himself he had discovered;
he could recognize that as freely as possible without being
obliged to classify the agreeable resource as a new entanglement. He was neither too much nor too little diverted;
he had all his usual attention to give to his work: he had
only an employment for his odd hours, which, without
being imperative, had over various others the advantage
of a certain continuity.

That passage is from a fiction called *The Tragic Muse*,
also published in 1890. It is neither its beginning, nor
end, rather, a passage from the middle of a middle chapter. *The Tragic Muse* is obsessed with the theater, as was
James. We're often the most obsessed with disciplines
for which we possess the least talent.

All that you should be able to recall—now, tomorrow,
next week, or month—is that a certain type of British
theatrical character written by a celibate homosexual
expatriate American might still have considered distraction French, in or around 1890, despite the word having
been Englished by Shakespeare's day, ca. 1600: "He did
me kindness, sir, drew on my side, / But in conclusion
put strange speech upon me. / I know not what 'twas, but
distraction" (*Twelfth Night*).

Loudness compels attention. You learn this before you
learn that crying is not music. Size and contrasting
colors do the same. You're taught this before you're
taught that smearing the house with a diaper's soil is no
way to sculpt or paint.

For some reason, you're here. Maybe it was a

co-worker's recommendation that did the trick, or else maybe you read a synopsis or an excerpt you accidentally clicked—in some way, regardless of the way, you got ahold of this book, and if you've gotten this far into reading it, your attention has been *apprehended*. You've paid money for this book in order to *pay attention*. You are skeptical, which is to say, unforgiving. You have enough money to afford this book or you have family or friends who do and who don't mind your borrowing, or you have the type of family or friends who gift books like this on auspicious, and even for no, occasions, in which case perhaps you're only being attentive because you're interested in just what type of person this gifter thinks you are—whether they think you're too attentive, to them, to yourself, or too inattentive, to either or to both.

But let's agree for a moment—the present—that you're interested in what attention is (despite your already knowing what it is). You think that attention is important, though maybe not important in and of itself as much as it's important to everything else that is important, like carbon or chlorophyll is, though you're not 100 percent sure what those are. You believe that we live in a time of "perpetual mediation," but you hate that phrase. You believe that we must practice some degree of "aesthetic ecology," but that phrasing too is odious; you're not sure how you've come to regard attention as both a "spiritual principle" *and* "a commodity." You believe our sensoria to have become an "unregulated marketplace"—in which advertisers compete to distract us the consumers from essential appetites, and the culture industry vies to muddle distinctions between art and product that have served us faithfully since the Enlightenment—through a redefinition of experience as "interactivity." You believe that this "commodification"—or "commoditization"—has led to a state of existence that "increasingly"—or "exponentially"—resembles a "battle for consciousness," a "resource war," the most important war of our time, perhaps, though also the most unimportant given that genuine wars still rage and campaign for our contemplation alongside what we still have to call *culture*, which is a word that must be used in italics ever since that innovation was introduced by the Renaissance—slanting text in cursive, as if the language were fleeing its sense. You're bewildered by the new drugs that are regularly synthesized "to engage" "attention," but to or for what you aren't sure; you aren't even sure of what exactly is being "engaged." You're bothered by new films and television shows premiering with fresh promises of an encapsulation of "a contemporary condition," by new websites launched to provide constant commentary on our inability, or unwillingness, to "disconnect," to seek "a primary text," and by new books published, texts secondary (academic), tertiary (popular), and quaternary (academic commentaries on the popular), always claiming to tell us precisely "what matters now," or "the meaning of the present," and yet in doing so are willing to pervert even the matter and meaning of the quotationmark, which has been used to denote true speech, that of God, or Christ, or a government, since Medievalism, but has, in our time, been used to denote speech that can never be "true." You don't know which to believe, whether your experience—which tells you that attention is something abstract, a state or condition—or your schooling or online—which tells you that attention is something concrete, a measurable neurological response to stimulus—or both. You want to know what happens when we "attend," and whether it's something of which only humans are capable.

You consider all this and find yourself spiraling into that comfortable yet disconsolate postmodern or post-postmodern or amodern, perhaps, contemplation of contemplation, a recursive consciousness wherein you find yourself in both every place and no place at once, wondering about the differences, if any, between a helix and spiral; between reminiscence and memory; wondering about the relationship, if any, between/among reminiscence and/or memory and attention; about the relationship, if any, between attention and the type of dreaming you do when you're asleep and the type of dreaming you do when you're awake; whether you're only rehearsing your attention while you're dreaming and, if so, if everything you find yourself attending to, whether consciously or unconsciously, is merely a result of a routine or script. You suspect there's a difference between conscious attention and unconscious attention but you're not sure whether the subconscious exists or plays a role in either or in both. You suspect that considering the perception of time might be a waste of time; that it might in fact be easier to be an animal who, whether they can attend or not, is far better than a human at attracting/seducing attention, especially for sex, by emitting extreme colors and sounds and smells without embarrassment, or perhaps with an embarrassment that eludes human perception. You suspect that you should be having more sex. You've already noted that William James's focus on the visual aspect of attention—"clear and vivid"—is ironic, given that his essay was originally written and presented as a lecture (aural); you wonder whether he himself noted this irony. You note too that Henry James's observation that his character—whose name and circumstances you perhaps are familiar with, or perhaps aren't—"could recognize [his distraction] as freely as possible without being obliged to classify the agreeable resource as a new entanglement" is both entirely paradoxical and crazy but also entirely logical and sane; you wonder whether James himself was aware of this or intended that his character be regarded as being aware of it. You muse as to whether reading makes you more attentive, while partaking in other media makes you less attentive. You consider experimenting with psychostimulants. You consider that all the new amphetamines being peddled everywhere might help you attend better and longer but, because they reduce bloodflow too, will certainly hamper your hopes for better sex. You wonder how it is that these drugs exist and are routinely prescribed when the disorder they're intended to treat—Attention Deficit Hyperactivity Disorder, ADHD—remains a mere description of symptoms, which is to say no, or little, or little to no neurological evidence exists that all these diagnostic acronyms that have invaded our language are in fact anything more than further psychological aberrancies, delusions, or pharmaceutical scams, and that those scams themselves, whose brandnames I'd prefer to be paid to mention in a book, are in fact just legal iterations or achiral reproductions of substances that have been classified as illegal perhaps because the deficiencies or circumstances these illegal substances treat cannot be so rigidly perceived as being physical or mental or even psychological so much as political or economic. You are enraged that everything becomes corrupted, but you are also inspired by that corruption. You know that change is bad but good and also a fact. You are aware that "attention" comes from the Latin *attentio*, which itself is a calque, through *ad tenso*, of the Greek *pro soché/prosoché*, which itself means "to grip," "to grasp," "to take with the hands or hold/mold with the fingers." You are aware that the word "buttonhole," i.e., to detain someone in conversation, is merely a corruption of "buttonhold," the loop of thread that cinches a button into place, which reminds you that men's shirts have buttons on the right but women's on the left because women, or certain women, used to be dressed by attendants for whom those left-side buttons were on the right side and most people are right-handed; which reminds you that we shake hands with the right hand only to show that we're not carrying weapons and that Britain and so most of its former colonies drive on the left side of the road because knights would ride their horses with their lances tucked under their right arms and if you met a stranger on the road you passed him on the left to keep your lance between yourself and him; which reminds you that the rest of the world not British followed the practice of the distracted French, led by Napoleon who was left-handed and so ordered his armies to march on the right so he could keep his sword between him and any oncoming traffic (left-handed infantry, because of scabbard placement, had to mount their horses from the right, while horses themselves are subject to laterality: Horses that take longer strides with the right foreleg, which means they tend toward the left, are more successful at racing, as most tracks are run counterclockwise); which reminds you that the earliest French trains were built in the original century of distraction by the British and so kept to the left and that what further distinguishes French railroads are the postings at their crossings that read: *un train peut en cacher un autre*, which means "one train may hide another," though it's always been a mystery to you as to whether that implies that one train might closely follow another or, the more impractical and depressing interpretation, that even as one train passes east, another passes west, and never again will they meet (even further distraction: It just so happens that the father of British rail transport was named William James, while another Henry James was a pioneer of map production, and the father of the contemporary cartographic scale, 1:2,500, in which one centimeter on a page is equal to twenty-five meters of earth); which reminds you that all boats and airplanes are supposed to pass on the right; which reminds you that when you cross by car between China and Hong Kong you have to switch from right-sided driving to left-sided; which reminds you that I have still not explained anything directly or tied together, left shoelace over right, all my Jameses, or whether we humans possess the same laterality that we have in our hands in our feet and so you go to the computer to search it up, searching "human foot laterality" or "right-footed left-footed humans," or you check your email instead and by the time you're finished checking you've forgotten what your original purpose in going to the computer had been; or you don't even go to your computer but stay seated or lying and reading, let's hope, though you're tired; which reminds you, ultimately, that a long sentence in the second person— rather my addressing you as you, rather my addressing all my readers as you and you as all my readers, but also as me (my truest readership), at relentless length—is just another weary technique to compel/exhaust your continued... mindfulness.

2. DIRECTIONALITY, SUMER, BABEL AND THE FLOOD, EDEN

(if you're averse to religion/myth, skip directly to chapter 4)

The world's oldest languages were chiseled into stone. As most people are right-handed,[1] the right hand held the mallet, the left hand the chisel. This is why Semitic languages are written right to left, as the dominant R hand does the powerful work, as the submissive L hand returns across the body, reaching, at the end of each line, its rest. Arabian dialects in use a full millennium before Christ advantaged this return and were written in *boustrophedon*, or "cow-path writing," in which lines alternate their directions, R to L and L to R. A tablet would start

---

1. Most people (approx. 70 to 95 percent) are R-handed; the remainder is L, save a smattering of the cross-dominant (ambidextrous). But the determining factors of handedness remain elusive. Geneticists cling to genetics, of course, though while some studies have shown dominance to be hereditary, others have demonstrated only a limited relationship (a 2006 study of twins set L heritability at approx. 24 percent). Sociologists point out that handedness can be influenced by culture, obviously, by intolerant adults who might consider leftyism a social liability (modern incarnations of the religious fanatics who believed the sinister left—from Latin's *sinistra*, meaning both "left" and "unlucky"—to be the idle hand of Satan). Some neurologists claim handedness is based on where the language and fine-motor-skills controls are based in the brain: For most of the population, they're in the L hemisphere, which controls the R half of the body. Other neurologists cite research that indicates that many people who have those controls in the opposite, or R, hemisphere, aren't in fact lefties, while many lefties have those controls in the L. Still other researchers have found evidence of what they call "pathological leftness," related to brain trauma during birth, while still others again seek a prenatal intrauterine developmental/hormonal imbalance as cause.

from R to L, the L-hand chisel would be returned to its rest; the next line would be written in reverse, L to R, extending the L hand to the other side of the body, only to start all over again in a wandering trail reminiscent, to Semites at least, of the way a cow plows a field.

Enter that most popular myth of handwriting instruction, which makes a virtue of clarity by asserting that all directionality is directly and exclusively conditioned by the materials used. As stone and clay gave way to papyrus and paper, as mallet and chisel gave way to implement and ink, Western writing had to deal with the threat of smudging, smearing, blots. Because writing R-handed from R to L would mean that the hand would pass over the text, smutting the ink that might still be wet, the West chose to write from L to R, constantly dragging the R hand across the body for each successive line.

History aside, the ultimate reproof to this explanation might be nothing more than a repositioning of cultural horizons (a realignment of horizontalisms): namely, a recognition of Asia, whose cultures invented paper and ink, and whose languages have been written unidirectionally and with impeccable clarity since time immemorial—in vertical columns proceeding always top-down, never bottom-up.

Regardless of the true course of Western development, writing was, is, and will continue to be an unnatural act—as curious as a *zyzzyva* (an American weevil, which is death to crops, but also the concluding entry in many dictionaries and encyclopedias, and among the most difficult of words to type on the QWERTY keyboard, in terms of "finger privileging," "row skips," "lateral shifts," and "repetitions").

"Attention" is the pretext—attention, no quotes, the text itself. The earliest unit of attention in literature—its first metric, or standardization of meter—was called, but only later and in Latin, the *incipit* (literally "it begins"). Today we're familiar with the incipit through the indices to poetry anthologies, which list the poems by their opening lines, though this tradition dates back to the clay-tablet catalogs that listed the introductory verses or stanzas of Sumerian compositions, which the archaeologists and linguists who uncovered them misidentified, quite understandably, as poems unto themselves:

When in ancient days heaven was separated from earth
The pelican emerged from the reedbeds
To overturn the appointed times
In the beginning

(My own verse—comprised entirely of incipit from the catalog of Nibru.)

The oldest text that can be associated with an author contains one of the oldest incipit: "In those days, in those far remote days"—a formula that prefaces countless histories and prayers. But while most anonymous Sumerian literature concerns the gods (An, Enlil, Enki, Inanna), this earliest non-anonymous work—this incipit of authorship, *The Instructions of Shuruppak*, a haranguing hunk of wisdom lit from ca. 2600 B.C.E.—concerns man:

In those days, those far remote days, in those nights, those far remote nights, in those years, those faraway years, at that time the wise one who knew how to speak in difficult words lived in the land, Shuruppak the wise one who knew how to speak in difficult words lived in the land.

525

> Shuruppak gave instructions to his son, Shuruppak
> the son of Ubara-Tutu gave instructions to his son Zi-ud-
> sura: My son, I will give you instructions: you have to
> pay attention! Zi-ud-sura, let me speak a word to you: you
> must pay attention! Don't ignore my instructions! Don't
> transgress my words! The instructions of an old man are
> priceless; do what I say!

No trespassing! Beware! Shuruppak's advice continues, and continues to present attention in its most elemental form—not just as caution, or warning, but as cuneiform, from Latin's *cuneus*, meaning "wedge"—the imperative as a wedge between wrong and right: "You must not buy an ass that brays"; "you must not locate a field on a road"; "never vouch for someone/never let someone vouch for you"; "if an argument starts, leave"; "don't rob homes, steal from people, or cut yourself with an axe"; "don't have sex with a woman not your wife"; "don't buy an onager"; "don't have sex with a slave girl"; "don't curse or lie or travel at night or eastward alone." Masculine advice, from an age when women and pack animals were considered similarly useful, though if you choose to ignore it maybe the ending—not the *excipit* but, more correctly, the *explicit*—will command your attention: "These are the instructions given by Shuruppak, son of Ubara-Tutu! Praise be to the lady who finished these great tablets, the maiden Nisaba, to whom Shuruppak, the son of Ubara-Tutu, gave his instructions!"

Everyone knows the myths of Genesis. Everyone knows Babel. The hubris. The confusion of tongues. At the time—one interpretation might divagate—humanity had been nomadic, tribal, hunter-gatherers following the seasonal animal migrations. But by erecting this tower to propitiate, or meet, the gods, they rooted themselves, became civilized, agriculturalists requiring new words for all the new seisms—the stuff—around them: "tower," "civilization."

Previously everyone had understood everyone, and everything, but then specialization evolved—divisions. Sin-Nasir the son of Shamash-Nasir was the mudbrick constructor, and spawned a dynasty of mud-brick constructors. His own son-in-law, Ishme-Ea, the irrigationist. Royalty, the city's class iteration of itinerant clan rule, collaborated with religion in the organization of labor to ensure crop and so community survival. The builders of Babel were the second chance of humanity, the first generation since the Flood. The fate of humanity, and the authority of God, will later become the fate of the Decalogue, and the authority of Moses, who breaks the first set of the commandments—because of an idol cow that wouldn't plow—and so has to ascend Sinai again to obtain a second set, a disgraced probationary copy.

This is the favored interpretation of utopianists, dystopianists, mystics, dreamers. Sennacherib felled the presumed model for the biblical tower—the anonymously constructed Etemenanki—in the conquering of Babylon, seventh century B.C.E. Nabopolassar restored the city, while his son, Nebuchadnezzar II, restored the tower—or ziggurat (and hung the gardens to please his wife).

Myth is based on history, is based on myth—they're baked in the desert sun, dried into one, softened with blood only to harden again. Just as the Tower of Babel is prefigured in the epic of Emmerkar ("Let the people of Aratta bring down for me the stones from their mountain, erect the great shrine for me, erect the great abode for me, make the great abode, the abode of the gods, famous for me"), the Flood of Genesis has its own genesis in the epic of Gilgamesh, but even there its existence is subsidiary. Gilgamesh wanders in search of Utanapishtim, aka the Faraway, the only survivor of a great deluge, hoping to get from him the secret of eternal life. The waters, then, have already risen—all accounts are after the fact:

> Utanapishtim spoke to Gilgamesh, saying: You want my hidden knowledge? It's yours!
> It begins in Shuruppak, a familiar city, located on the bank of the Euphrates. A familiar yet very ancient city, a dwelling of the gods—who had decided to impose a flood.
> Father Anu had sworn an oath to this flood, and so did his adviser, the hero Enlil, their servant, the god Ninurta, and their guard, the god Ennugi.
> The heir Ea swore with them as well, repeating their words to a reed fence: O reed fence, O brick wall, hear and take heed! O man of Shuruppak, son of Ubara-Tutu, demolish your house and build a boat! Abandon wealth and cling to life! Forsake possessions and survive! Build a boat and take on board the seed of all living!

Not only is this passage a memory—the deluge had long been drained, the earth long survived, by the time of Gilgamesh's pilgrimage—*but it also contains a memory:* the heir, Ea, "repeating" the words of the gods.

The Genesis version, while clearly related to the Sumerian, accounts for its existence entirely differently. Its nesting is as radical as that of the dove—the bird that told Noah land had emerged, that builds its nests both in trees and on the ground.

528

Here, amid the destruction of the world, a creation still—the creation of attention:

> And God saw that the wickedness of man was great in the earth, and that every imagination of the thoughts of his heart was only evil continually. And it repented the LORD that he had made man on the earth, and it grieved him at his heart. And the LORD said, I will destroy man whom I have created from the face of the earth; both man, and beast, and the creeping thing, and the fowls of the air; for it repenteth me that I have made them. But Noah found grace in the eyes of the LORD. These are the generations of Noah: Noah was a just man and perfect in his generations, and Noah walked with God. And Noah begat three sons, Shem, Ham, and Japheth. The earth also was corrupt before God, and the earth was filled with violence. And God looked upon the earth, and, behold, it was corrupt; for all flesh had corrupted his way upon the earth. And God said unto Noah, The end of all flesh is come before me; for the earth is filled with violence through them; and, behold, I will destroy them with the earth.

It's beyond dispute that reiteration, beyond being a feature of Hebrew—of all Semitic languages: "in those days, in those far remote days"—is a result of the Flood narrative as we know it being either the composite of multiple sources, or the compiled layers of a single source. The most notable of these versions or supplements are known as the Jahwist (regarded as a populist account, which calls the deity JHWH, which the King James translates as LORD, ca. seventh–sixth century B.C.E) and the Priestly (regarded as the account of an editorial elite, which calls the deity Elohim, which the King James translates as God, though the Hebrew is plural, ca. fifth century B.C.E.).

Taken alone, each version provides a reading of attentive capacities both human and divine—the Jahwist people's Bible presenting an anthropomorphized deity concerned with His creation's relationship to the earth; the Priestly testament of caste attempting to assert or analogize the unremitting nature of power.

If Genesis is a matter of strata, its attention is revealed as a layering too—the alteration, becoming the synthesis, of humanity's and God's. Here is that King James passage again, with the exclusively Jahwist verses *in italics,* the exclusively Priestly underlined:

> *And God saw that the wickedness of man was great in the earth, and that every imagination of the thoughts of his heart was only evil continually. And it repented the LORD that he had made man on the earth, and it grieved him at his heart. And the LORD said, I will destroy man whom I have created from the face of the earth; both man, and beast, and the creeping thing, and the fowls of the air; for it repenteth me that I have made them.* But Noah found grace in the eyes of the LORD. These are the generations of Noah: Noah was a just man and perfect in his generations, and Noah walked with God. And Noah begat three sons, Shem, Ham, and Japheth. The earth also was corrupt before God, and the earth was filled with violence. <u>And God looked upon the earth, and, behold, it was corrupt; for all flesh had corrupted his way upon the earth. And God said unto Noah, The end of all flesh is come before me; for the earth is filled with violence through them; and, behold, I will destroy them with the earth.</u>

The earlier account, if taken alone, has God *seeing*—amassing the evidence—and *grieving*—delineating the burden of considered judgment—as if in justification of His decision to destroy. The later account, which cannot be taken alone, moderates God's vision and denies His regret, as if humanity had already been prejudged as corrupted and the only issue that remained was its sentencing—no justifications offered, no appeals accepted.

In the first, God announces His intentions to all humanity. In the synoptic second, to a single representative.

The powerless and the powerful: Each entity sees God in its own image, and so is seen by Him, accordingly.

Put secularly: The same process is at work with attention.

Fleeing in reverse, to Eden. God is only the second entity the Bible allows to attend to the mind. The first is Cain, who slaughtered Abel, his brother, and showed no remorse. Both God and Cain are psychopaths, sociopaths, mad. God sought to justify His irrational violence. Cain lied—he lied to an omniscience—and denied ending his brother's life. By contrast, the martyr Abel is purely a symbol. If his parents' fate represents the perils of knowledge (one's own), Abel's represents the perils of knowledge (another's).

Cain was the planted cultivator of crops, Abel the mobile shepherd. Adam and Eve were neither. It takes an Eden to deny a paradise—Adam and Eve had no choice between a life lived in motion or stasis, amid the rural or urban (marked Cain went on to found the world's first city, which he called after his son, Enoch), in monogamy or polygamy, or singlehood. Instead, they dwelled in a dreamworld, were free to wander a garden whose plants grew on their own, whose animals bred and raised themselves and offered themselves as sacrifices to temporal hunger before spiritual hunger ever compelled an offering of sacrifices to God—this couple, matched from a rib, had only to lounge around unsheltered and nude, naming the animals and plants. In Eden, they were gods governed only by God, Who was their consciousness, repressed, or suppressed, whichever—Vienna had not yet been settled. But then Eve plucked an apple from the one tree forbidden her, the one thing, in a psychoanalytic reading, she had forbidden herself through her imagination of a supreme authority, and so, having transgressed and so been forced into a dialogue with her consciousness, was punished—or punished herself and her mate—with a Fall: a lifetime of tilling and weeding, naked shame, excruciating childbirth, property issues, and petty chores—the penultimate of which is to develop a psychological approach to each, the ultimate of which is to die. (The true serpent in this narrative is the tangle of the mind, its coils forcing humanity to yearn for a sustenance it can never have, let alone define.)

Our damnation, though, is granted a reprieve, every Sabbath: the weekly anniversary of the seventh day of creation, when even the numinous rests. Further, the Bible decrees every seventh year a Sabbatical Year—the fields must lay fallow, the people must live from gleaning alone, in an intimation or fantasy of Eden—and every seventh Sabbatical a Jubilee Year, during which all debts are forgiven, and all slaves manumitted, in yet another return to the garden. These septenary mandated vacations are all attempts to circulate time, as blood circulates in the body, to turn time's relentless progress into a regulatory cycle—a human model both of the seasons, and of the rotations and revolutions of the heavenly bodies. The purpose: to give humanity a hint of eternity on earth, and to keep it from a continuous contemplation of death.

The search for an origin point for these cycles might be fruitless. "In the beginning God created the heavens and the earth": The Bible begins with an acknowledgment that God's authorship was so supreme that it must have, by implication alone, created God Himself. The Bible, of course, is the ur metafiction, a book that describes its own giving, and it's for that reason—as well as due to the mundane fact that it's best to begin a fiction with its most irrational element, as a neutralizing principle—that most readers pass over this formulation without pausing to interrogate its strangeness.

But the Hebrew is even stranger: *B'rayshit bara Elohim.* While *B'rayshit* means "in the beginning," the word contains the root of the next word, *bara*, or "created."

This is obvious even to people who read no Hebrew, just by scanning the letters (skimming over the face of the deep):

ארב תיש ארב

This containment might imply that creation was within the beginning, or that the beginning of creation was merely God's acknowledgment of the circumstances of creation—of the instinct to make. What is definite, however, is that the two words share the same first letter, the *bet* or *vet*, the second letter of the Hebrew alphabet after the unvoiced, ineffable *aleph*.

It's notable that the Bible begins with the alphabet's second letter, and the first that can be pronounced. It's as if the *aleph* were the creationary instinct itself, the un-understandable cause.

The two forms of this second letter serve different functions.

Without a dot in its center—the dot called a *dagesh*—it's just another letter, a mundane component, a *vet:*

ב

With a dot, though, it becomes a *bet*, with the honor of also serving as preposition, meaning "in," "at," "with," "within":

בּ

It is this version that begins the Bible. It is this letter that begins both words that might, ultimately, share meaning.

In both versions this letter is closed on three sides but open on one—opening outward, like a home should, like a mind should.

It's been said that this very shape is intended to encourage humanity to question everything that happened after creation, but nothing of what happened before it. Further, the dot, the *dagesh*, has been said to represent either, at the incipit of the world, the world itself, floating in the incommensurable center of the primordial void, or the presence of humanity within it, a mark of punctuation suspended not at the end but at the start of God's pronouncement.

The *dagesh*, both mystically and comprehendingly, has always been an element of attention. It's been said that even those who cannot read Hebrew, especially those who cannot read Hebrew, must concentrate on it, for it provides, in time, at the initiation of time, a locus. Deconstruct the three walls of its house, one by one. Once they've fallen away, the last approach toward total unity with creation is to meditate on the very sound of the *dagesh*, which, on its own, like an *aleph*, like a punctus, is unpronounceable, or just a pause, a breath.

C. EGYPT, CADMUS/KADMOS, MEMORY, ORPHEUS TURNING

In the Greek-Egyptian port city of Naucratis dwelled an ancient god called Theuth, creator of mathematics, astrology/astronomy, gambling, and the alphabet, all of which he shipped down the Nile, following the current, to Thebes, capital of Egypt, to its King Thamus who, in godly form, was worshipped as Ammon.

At Thebes—imagine a palace—they discussed these creations, some receiving Thamus's approval, some his disapproval, but none was resisted more than the alphabet. Though its letters resembled papyrus reeds broken by a storm, none symbolized "papyrus," or "reeds," or "brokenness," or "storms"—unlike glyphs, Theuth's inventions did not individually depict or represent but rather aggregated, piling on their singular sounds in a process not unlike the building of pyramids, into words that served as conceptual tombs.

The language in which Theuth defended his art is not recorded, nor has it ever been explained why a deity would require a language.

He said (in my translation of a dozen translations): *I do not understand your resistance, your divine majesty—these characters of mine will make the people more wise and improve their memories, broaden their culture, widen their trade, and enrich your treasury.*

Thamus replied (smiling): *With all respect due to my fellow immortal—inventors are not the best judges of their inventions. Your characters will not inculcate memory, rather forgetfulness. The people will come to entrust their minds to writing, their thoughts and knowledge will become enslaved to the tablet and scroll, remembrance will be drained to depthless recall, truth will be usurped by forgeries, things heard and said will engender no change, the truest experience of the soul will be draped, as in a funeral rite, with a false appearance of omniscience, and all the world will become a kingdom of pure surface.*

I have never been able to read this myth without recalling its genesis—in a speech by Socrates, who never wrote, transcribed by Plato, who did.

The alphabet was introduced to humanity by Theuth, or by hermeneutical Hermes (according to Diodorus), by Palamedes (according to Euripides), by Prometheus (according to Aeschylus), by Cadmus/Kadmos (according to Herodotus). Cadmus was a Phoenician prince from Tyre, his father, King Agenor, one of twins born to an Egyptian princess named Libya and the sea-god Poseidon. Agenor ruled Phoenicia; his brother Belus ruled Egypt. Cadmus's mother, Telephassa, was the daughter of the Nile and a cloud.

When Zeus changes into a bull and abducts Cadmus's sister, Europa, her brother sets out to rescue her. (Bullish Zeus, it might be mentioned, was Cadmus and Europa's great-grandfather.)

It was on the Greek island of Samothrace that Cadmus reenacts the privilege of Zeus, by abducting a woman of his own—Harmonia, daughter of Ares, god of war, and of Aphrodite, goddess of love. Cadmus takes her to Delphi, where the oracle counsels him to forsake his quest and follow a certain ox with a crescent moon on its flank. Wherever that ox lies down, Cadmus is to found the citadel of Cadmeia, the palace of Thebes you'd imagined, future seat of the kingdom of Thamus. Many adventures, many misadventures, follow, incidents whose color might have required the Phoenician alphabet their hero accidentally packed along to

536

Greece—the slaying of a water dragon, the sowing of the dragon's teeth to grow soldiers, accursed jewelry— though for a full accounting I'd direct you to the Delphi of online and recommend a search by author, with the keywords "Hyginus" and "Pseudo-Apollodorus."[1]

Cadmus's marriage to Harmonia has been taken as an allegorical wedding of Eastern, or Phoenician, wisdom, to the Western, or Greek, cult of beauty. If the wisdom that Cadmus brought to the Greeks has been recorded, in writing, as writing itself—Phoenician, the world's first nonglyphic alphabet—then perhaps Harmonia's beauty can be read as being of a proportion between the capacities of language and its use. This distinction is evinced immediately after what the archaeological record proposes as the date of the introduction of the Phoenician characters to Greek—between the ninth and eighth centuries B.C.E., a century or so before "Homer."

It's through the codification of the Homeric canon that the culture of the oral/aural became the culture of the visual/manual, fixing the odysseys of the roving bards as hexametric. Interpretation went from being a matter of individually altering a primal myth in performance—to collectively establishing a textbound version

1. The Cadmeian messenger/linguist figure might not be the only composite at work: The ox Cadmus is instructed to follow was likely related to his great-grandmother, a nymph named Io, called Isis by the Egyptians, whose mythology regards her as another candidate for alphabetical innovator. In the myth's most basic telling, insatiable Zeus has a dalliance with Io and, so as not to be caught by his wife, Hera, turns Io into a cow. Hera, though, uncovers the indiscretion and condemns Io to a life of grazing under the watch of the many-eyed, insomniac Argus Panoptes. Zeus, in turn, sends Hermes to distract the giant, to slay him, and set Io free. Io wanders across the Bosporus (lit. ox passage), to Egypt, where she births Libya, Cadmus's grandmother.

as primary. Letters lined consecutively into words, lined consecutively onto a scrap of reed or parchment, became sentences: punctuated—ca. fifth century B.C.E. This textuality engendered a quest for accuracy among the stanzas—or so goes the origin myth of literary criticism. Inconsistencies were pointed out and disseminated by scholiasts such as Zoilus of Amphipolis as early as the fourth century B.C.E.: In Book V of *The Iliad*, Menelaus and Antilochus slay Pylaemenes, king of the Paphlagonians. In Book XIII, however, he's still alive to witness his son, Harpalion, be pierced by Meriones's arrow.

An ultimate sharpness: A Greek *stilus* marked and was a mark, which word became Latin's *stimulus*, a "prick" or "goad." What Greek understood as an instrument for marking, or the mark itself, Latin understood as meriting attention.

(for a further consideration of writing technologies, skip directly to chapters e and 10)

Among the myriad complexities, or complications, of the concepts being written about came the need for more words, and even the need for more letters— conceptual revelations that signaled a notable reversal in the history of language development, in which new vocabulary had always been syllabically exhumed from the old. Simonides of Ceos (ca. 556–468 B.C.E.) is credited with the invention of η, ξ, ψ, ω, though he is better remembered as the father of memory—in a sense, a son of Mnemosyne, who had only daughters, nine of them, Muses.

Simonides was one of Greece's finest poets—it's unfortunate that only scattered verses of his have survived. He might also have been the first poet to write for pay. Cicero relates that a wealthy Thessalonian noble named Scopas held a banquet and commissioned an ode in his own honor. But when Simonides delivered his text, which insulted Scopas by including, instead of praise, a stretch of remplissage referring to Castor and Pollux, the patron responded by withholding half of Simonides's fee. The wining and dining continued, until a message arrived that Simonides had two young male visitors waiting at the door. The moment Simonides left, the banquet hall collapsed; the roof fell in and crushed Scopas, his family and guests so completely that when their surviving friends went to bury them—friends probably previously resentful that they hadn't been invited to the feast, probably pleased now that they hadn't been—they weren't able to recognize the corpses.

Cicero, who has no time for superstition, glosses over the purpose of the young men's visit (anyway, it would've been clear to Cicero's contemporaries that the visitors were supposed to be Castor and Pollux themselves, reincarnated from their constellation in gratitude for Simonides's interest). Instead, the great Latin poet prefers to describe the great Greek poet's descriptive postmortem:

> It is told that Simonides was able by his recollection of the place in which each had been sitting to identify them for individual interment, and that this experience suggested to him that the best aid to a clarity of memory consisted in orderly arrangement.
>
> He inferred that persons hoping to train this faculty must select localities, form mental images of the facts they wish to remember, and store those images in those localities, with the result that the arrangement of localities

> will preserve the order of facts, and the images of facts
> will designate the facts themselves, and we shall employ
> the localities and images as if wax tablets and the letters
> written on them, respectively.

It's ironic that Simonides, a man who worked in language and its sounding (the oral/aural), found his truest talent and posterity in pictures (the visual/manual): seating arrangements becoming mental arrangements, pillowy loci, reclines of the mind. His associative method itself was just a pictorial translation of literary technique. Lessons crucial for survival—this banquet is reminiscent of that banquet, the relation of this roof to a chance of collapse recalls the relation of that roof to its certain collapse—relied on the mimeses of poetry, in which a toppled glass might be a wasted opportunity; a fork missing a tine, a piteous loss; a knife missing a handle, a raging danger; a full amphora, a glutton. In Simonides's system, analogies, metaphors, similes, and puns were returned from the domain of literature, to life—to their source as granaries or storehouses of memory.

But the decisive triumph of the look/see over the hear/listen occurred in the first century B.C.E., not in written language but, again ironically, in oratory—the spoken. Cicero developed Simonides's loci into a host of mnemonic or rebus techniques to aid in remembering his vast speeches to the senate. Each of his addresses was quite literally an address—a labeled chamber—and each object in that chamber visually or ideationally rhymed with a rhetorical portion: Say, a vacant comfy chair was the Exordium (whose purpose, according to Quintilian, was "to prepare the audience to lend a ready ear to the rest"); drying togas the stiff data of the Narratio; a broken jug of wine the disputation of the Partitio; and so on, through the Confirmatio, the Reprehensio, and the conclusive—door shutting—Peroratio.

Memory, having been externalized to books, had to be reinternalized—not again by the communal sharing of legend and lore, but by the lonely scholar, zealously guarding his precious manuscripts and tablets. If the present was still a repository of the past, it wasn't from any civilized consensus, but from elective affinity. The gods had ceased to be anything but representations of human foibles; the convocation prayer of Classical religion was art; the temples, already museums.

But before the turn from Antiquity, which turned from the throat, there is one final—one original—figure to meet: Orpheus, whose voice could charm the birds and beasts and fish, compel even the trees and boulders to dance, and divert the courses of rivers—at least according to Simonides, whose own powers of transference were perhaps getting ahead of him. Whereas Cicero claimed philosophy as the sole arbiter of his expression, Orpheus took his marching orders only from music, the strophes. Orpheus, whose name is related to *orbus*, meaning "self-contained," "solitary," was another "Homer," but while Homeric editing aspired to the authority of history, the Orphic hierophants made art whose authority not even a god could aspire to.

The myth of Orpheus is one of an artist falling in love with a woman, a dryad or arboreal nymph, Agriope in some accounts, Eurydice in others, who dies accidentally and young and so is ferried across the river Styx that flows into the domain of Hades. It is there that Orpheus ventures, intent on winning her back, to life and to himself. *Katabasis* is to go down, *anabasis* to come back up, and that's what all the Greek versions have Orpheus doing—prevailing—returning from darkness into light with his love on one arm, his lyre in the other.

Cicero was a student of Plato—not yet a reader of Plato, but an inheritor of his tradition through the academies—and so might have been familiar with the philosopher's interpretation of the Orpheus myth as a dramatization of the soul's conflict between appearances and the actual. According to Plato, Eurydice is merely a shade, an apparition, the clouded reflection of Orpheus's mortal—insufficient—love. Because Orpheus is unwilling to commit suicide for this love, preferring instead to resurrect it, or her, to his own estate, he can be no hero. Such is his ignominy that Aristotle said—in words preserved in Cicero's quotation—"Orpheus never existed" (though the philosopher meant physically—really—not in terms of integrity or honor).

But let's give audience to a retelling by a later Roman, a later master of Latin, Virgil—from the fourth book of his *Georgics*.

The background is this: Pluto, or Hades, god of the underworld, was lonely and so did as they do in the over-world, on Olympus, and abducted a wife—Proserpine, or Persephone, confining her to hell. In Virgil's version, Eurydice's wandering through the woods one noon when she's ambushed and pursued by a satyr (lust). Trying to escape, she's bitten by a snake and dies, descends. Orpheus follows, as in the earlier Greek versions, but here Virgil has him transact with the queen of death Prosperine, who might be resentful—the poet seems to imply—that nobody has come to *save her*.

Because Orpheus's voice has so dazzled the dead she wants him out and doesn't want anyone to follow, so she orders him to silence, and to return to life. Only Eurydice will follow, but so as not to attract others, Orpheus must not turn around:

> And now Orpheus reversed his steps, avoided missteps,
> as Eurydice, reclaimed, regained the upper air,
> following behind him (as Proserpine decreed),
> when a sudden frenzy seized his caution
> (a pardonable offense, if hell is capable of pardon):
> he stopped, and, forgetful at the lip of light,
> was ruined, by looking back at his Eurydice.
> His efforts were shattered like water, his pact
> with the mean queen, broken, as three storm peals
> were heard by the Avernus pools. "Orpheus," Eurydice
>   cried,
> "what craze has destroyed my wretchedness? And yours?
> See, the base Fates recall me, sleep lids my swimming eyes,
> goodbye: I am taken, enwrapped by night,
> stretching out to you hands no longer yours."

Virgil's rewrite of the Greek is both a sober, literarily sophisticated commentary on how humanity can never quite countenance the monitions—the advice and signs—all around (none apply, individually), and also a sardonic fable or parable of the cult that Orpheus's fate gave rise to, debauched Orphism. Regardless of its interpretation, Virgil's version is an indictment of an entire society that imitated every aspect of Orpheus but his talent—a Rome too emotionally weak and carousing, too orgiastic and invested in mysticism. His implication seems to be that raving devotion devolves, with the intercession of business or commerce (the deal with Prosperine), into frenzy, craziness, *dementia*, and *furor*—a descent, or dissent, from the verities, the virtues. The whole Roman Empire follows Orpheus in doubting Eurydice's love, which is nature's love, and, at the moment of turning, surrenders its honor. The mythic martyrs, the grand sacrificial sufferers, were all cold in the ground, shadows underground, by Virgil's time, and new heroes hadn't stepped forward yet to claim the laurels. Not for nothing is Eurydice described as an oak nymph.[2]

> She spoke and then she fled, abruptly, from his vision,
> like smoke emptying in air, never to be seen,
> though he grasped vainly at shadows and craved
> further speech. Nor did the ferryman of Orcus
> allow him to cross the marsh again.

The Latin for "grasped vainly at shadows," *prensantem nequiquam umbras*, and discernible in that verb (*prenso*, *prehenso*) is the tenebrously mental nature of the action: "prehension," "apprehension." That prefix, *pre*, is especially disturbing, to the contemporary mind indicating that even a variety of "presentiment," in the sense of "premonition," might attend this grasping. It's as if Orpheus has already foretold his failures, but vainly.

2. Ovid, only a generation younger, might have sensed this lapse and attempted to compensate. His account in the *Metamorphoses* includes four variations not found in Virgil's: 1.) Eurydice is not pursued by a satyr, but is innocently dancing through the woods with the naiads, celebrating her nuptials, when she's bitten by the snake; 2.) Orpheus, upon his descent, pitifully proposes to remain in the underworld—to live in hell—in order to be with his betrothed, though this offer is ignored, to the reader's—and maybe even to Orpheus's own—relief; 3.) after losing Eurydice— after her second death—Orpheus has sex exclusively with young boys, and 4.) ends metamorphosed into a Eurydicean estate—by being turned into a tree.

He reaches out hoping for Eurydice, aware that his hope has the consistency of fume.

It's here that Orpheus sheds everything Grecian and becomes completely Roman: lost, confused, howling cacophonously and without meter but with grief. In some traditions, Orpheus even loses the ability to sing. In others, he doesn't lose the ability but spurns it. He tours the oracles. He can't find himself, so he casts around, this once-great model, for models. Artists consult oracles only when they cease to be oracles themselves. A question is asked, the oracle answers, the Greek ones with orders, the Roman ones with riddles, or metaphysical jokes. The riddle itself, its winding way, becomes the life that must be led in search of a solution; though Orpheus, of all mortals, must've been aware, having been there, that the only true solution is damned.

He worships Apollo, trying to get a grip on his sanity, but while on a visit to a shrine to Apollo's adversary, the insane Bacchus (or Dionysus), at Thrace, he's torn apart by Maenads, who are enraged that he has propitiated a deity more calm or resigned, and too that out of his uncontrollable passion for Eurydice—or, per Ovid, boys—he's spurned their desperate advances. The Maenads scatter his limbs; his lyre ascends to heaven, becoming catasterized by the Muses who'd tutored him in its art into a congeries of stars most evident in summer, between spring's birth and the death of fall. Orpheus's head floats down the Hebrus to the Aegean, where it washes up like an unpronounceable rock on the shore of Lesbos, island of Sappho, who counsels: "We must accept that in a world like ours/our chief desires will be denied us."

The head is buried in Lesbos, where it becomes an oracle again, consulting on the Greek invasion of Troy,

involving Orpheus's tongue with the fate of another
female ideal—Helen.

No record exists of his reunion with Eurydice amid
the sulfur.

4. TENSION, ASCETICISM, AUGUSTINE, AUGUSTINE *IDIPSUM*

"Attention"—if you have it, you'll remember—derives from the Latin *attentio,* which itself is a development of *ad tentio,* "to reach out," the opposite of *in tentio,* "to reach in." The Latin calques the Greek, *prosoché/pro soché.* Both *attentio* and *prosoché* are nouns, but while the Latin verb *attendo* emerged coevally with the noun form, the Greek verb *prosochô* is considerably older and—like the hand favored over the mind—more actively, or just more noticeably, used.

It is a term indicating grasping, gripping, steering a ship, enlisting the wind to get to port even if the wind is against you. The nouning of verbs, the stilling of their motion—their ultimate definition—is a function of the written word, the page.

A noun is a passive thing, content with its content. Oral/aural culture urges its audience to take physical hold of ropes and wheels, while visual/manual culture is more given to holding the idea of ropes and wheels "in mind." To a character in a book, no less than to its reader and writer, all elements of a boat—the hull, the deck, the masts and sails—are merely mental, readerly. The tiller has my attention. The rudder is just *an extension* ("reaching from").

This holding, though, derives originally from archery. Not from the arrow, which on its own is useless, no matter whether dipped in cupidite saliva or Hydra poison, as were the arrows of Hercules the oracle of Orpheus recommended for the siege of Troy. Rather, put one hand to the bow, while the other draws, stretches back, *tendo,* "to tension." The bowstring, like the strings of the lyre, is made from sinew, the tendon, which, poor

Achilles, also serves as target. Late Latin, especially that of the early Church, describes itself in its straining of the transitive *tendere*—to "stretch," or "tighten." Classicism becomes a *distentio*—a "distension," or "distention"—a thing tautened too far, because spread too widely, to snapping, slackness, so that whatever strands remain are as effective as raveled thread.

In contradistinction to their adjectival uses in this language, the original Cynics had no irony, and the founding Stoics didn't have stiff upper lips, but snarls. Stoicism advocated for the primacy of the individual, free love, redistribution of resources, and an equality of the sexes so total that men and women, according to Zeno of Citium, should even dress identically. That such proposals were not only politically unfeasible, but also, perhaps, oppressive, effected a change in the philosophy. As the early Stoa of Zeno, Cleanthes of Athos, and Chrysippus of Soli gave way to the late Romanized Stoa of Epictetus and Seneca, Stoicism became less of a revolutionary fight for life as it could be and more of an applied philosophy for surviving life as it was.

"A masculine diligence/vigilance"—the phrase of Chrysippus, the first writer to use the noun, the virtue, *prosoché*, third century B.C.E.—became a domesticated "mental concentration"—*attentio animi*—a phrase of Cicero's, the first writer to use the noun, the virtue, *attentio*, in the first century B.C.E., just at the time of Antiquity's last philosophical rebellion. This happened again in the streets, but in the streets of Roman Judea, among the disenfranchised and impoverished. The imperium was degraded; its altars were abandoned. The old sacrificial rituals of the Jerusalem Temple profaned by priestly extortion, whether Pharisee or Sadducee, Jewish worship became cultic, a practice conducted in the synagogues that were innovations of Babylonian exile, but rebuilt in an occupied homeland. Religion retreated inward, or out to the rim of the Dead Sea. The most extremist were the most ascetic, Israelites who abstained from sex and alcohol, who fasted or ate no flesh, and lived, tentless, in deserts. The Essenes quit Jerusalem in the first century B.C.E.; the Therapeutae, whom Philo identified, disavowed property; the Ebionites and Elkesites premiated cleanliness to such an extreme that each of their bathings became a baptism. This is not to mention the elaborate Nazirite rituals of the Torah—no shaving—and the excess of scarcity in the Talmud—culminating in the career of Shimon bar Yochai, the rabbi who after criticizing Rome fled to a cave, shed his clothes, buried himself in sand, and studied day and night for thirteen years, eating only carob and drinking only water.

The century previous—just prior to the event that would reconfigure time, by establishing the millennia of heaven—apostles had congregated in the Galilee to hang on one man's every good word (gospel). That event, that man's hanging death, provided an unexcelled example of attention—a life lived not for this world but the next. Attention, or its lack, became, by the time of the first monks, who'd become the first saints, an issue to flagellate themselves over. The attentiveness that Christ demanded must be practiced—"Verily, verily, I say unto you, he that heareth my word, and believeth on Him that sent me, hath everlasting life, and shall not come into condemnation; but is passed from death unto life"—even at the threat of persecution, especially if you are pondering that threat and so not dwelling in the spirit. You must take hold of yourself and choke, in search of a state of absolute preparedness—against sin and for redemption.

Christian attention can be understood as a synthesis of the Jewish "thou shalts/thou shalt nots," and the Classical "know thyself." The result was a strange neither/both, in which curiosity was encouraged not for its own sake, rather, for its fatal satisfaction in belief. Jesus had encouraged his followers to hearken, look, and see, as if revelation were more conspicuous than a Herodian wall. But what was most evident to the apostolic generation was oppression, and if they still saw the goodness around them, they were also looking over their shoulders. This was a palpable bind: If you kept the faith you might die, but if you didn't, when you died, you wouldn't be resurrected. If the Word was not attended to, the Christian homiletic went, you wouldn't just lose your fortune and flocks, as in Sumer, or your mate, as in Greece and Rome, you would also lose your self—immortally.

But Jesus was not the only Christ. Manichaeism teaches that the world is divisible into spiritual light and material darkness, making it fairly evident which to reject. The religion's Persian founder, Mani, third century C.E., triunized his empire's religions, Zoroastrianism, Christianity, and Buddhism, which tendency to adapt local norms reified in a concern for ecology: "and you must protect earth and water and fire and trees and plants and wild and domestic animals and you must not hurt them." The seclused wisdom that Manichaeism contributed to its neighboring faiths corresponded with a marginality of lifestyle: moderate in consumption,

550

casual in worship, theologically tractable. Neo-Platonism was a sibling instantiation of the mutable and arcane. Its doctrine holds that the individual soul is a perfect reproduction of a single universal soul, but through that derivation has been exiled from its pristine state and so, to achieve wisdom, must effect its return. The Neo-Platonist Plotinus, also third century, counseled that to become the conscious steward of your soul, you must stop extending yourself and start intending, seeing inward. Nature teaches humanity only to be proprioceptive (aware of its bodies), exteroceptive (aware of its surroundings), and interoceptive (aware of pleasure and pain, hunger and thirst); you must learn to become introspective on your own, to mentally look within so as to "keep the soul's power of apprehension pure and ready to hear the voices from above."

To be sure, Plotinus, student of the founder of Neo-Platonism, Ammonius Saccas, meant the metaphysical soul, not the ethical or moral soul that could be remediated through the behavior-modification therapies preached by the rabbi from Nazareth, but still, it's evident that the withdrawal from society Plotinus called for was an admission that there could be no outer peace without an inner reckoning. Porphyry, Plotinus's disciple and author of *Against the Christians*, a tractate better read as being for his own brand of Christianity, leaves the reader with this image of his teacher: a man who, before he wrote, thought out everything he had to say and, only once it was all thought out, did he sit down to write, "as if he were copying from a book."

The imperium's adoption of Christianity marks the page—380 C.E.—the world had been firmly shut inside a book. Copies of the works of Clement and Origen had been in circulation for a century already, texts whose sole topic and warrant was the existence of a pre-ponderant, perfected text—Scripture, which was the truest Church. Clement and Origen's insight followed the Jewish practice: If you read the gospels, you'll believe, no other suasion required. Meanwhile, if you don't believe, it doesn't necessarily mean you're damned, only that you haven't read enough or correctly.

Augustine of Hippo (354–430), native of Numidia, taught at Carthage and Rome before arriving in Milan to teach literature and rhetoric. In Milan he met the city's bishop, Ambrose, an older man whose piety impressed him, and whose amiable fervor served as a catalyst for a spiritual crisis. Born Christian, Augustine had become involved in Manichaeism (whose holism indulged his instincts), and Neo-Platonism (whose mysticism stimulated his intellect). It's notable that in preparing to return to Christianity under Ambrose's tutelage, Augustine continued to practice both: Manichaeanally confronting the duality of his temperament; Neo-Platonically setting himself to returning his soul to its source. This process involved intense sessions of prayer, and of reading indistinguishable from prayer, both of which were constantly interrupted: "My spirit was wholly intent on study," he writes in his *Confessions*, the account of his conversion, "and restless to dispute."

Here we have Christianity's first acknowledgment that "intention"—Augustine's *ad quaerendum intentus*—might have held very different meanings for the religious and literate than for the religious and illiterate (had it been explained to them). Contrary to the assertions of Clement and Origen, the more attentively Augustine read, the more he doubted, or had to quit the page to cogitate. Though what seemed to him like disruptions were anything but—they were thoughts, this was thinking—

the fact remained that his mind was disturbed, or that he was disturbed by his mind (though any differencing of self and brain would have seemed a fiction to "Augustine").

The young seeker was hesitant to impose his distress on anyone else, however: Not only was Ambrose a cipher—Augustine was not prepared to understand his celibacy—he was also busy giving counsel to "multitudes [...] whose weaknesses he served." Ambrose ate little, slept little, and the rest of his mortality, he read:

> But when Ambrose was reading, his eye glided over the pages; his heart searched out the sense; though his voice and tongue remained unmoving. Often, when we had come (no man was forbidden from entering, nor did he require anyone to be announced), we'd watch him reading to himself in this manner, never in any other; and having long sat silent ourselves (for who would intrude on one so intent? [*intento*]), we'd be obliged to depart, assuming that in the short time he had to recruit his mind, free from the noise of others, he'd be reluctant to be distracted; perhaps he lived in dread that if he read aloud an author might deliver a statement so hermetic that a perplexed eavesdropper might ask him to explain it, or to expound on its argument; and though because of this method he was unable to complete as many volumes as he would have liked to, the preserving of his voice, which didn't take much speech to weaken, was perhaps the truer rationale.

Augustine ends the account with a sentence that reads like a couplet, begging to be enjambed and read aloud:

> quolibet tamen animo id ageret,
> bono utique ille vir agebat.[3]

Augustine's fourth-century account is by no means the first mention of reading silently—recall Plutarch's reports of Alexander the Great's skimming: "When he had broken the seal of a confidential letter from his mother and was reading it silently, Hephaestion quietly put his head beside Alexander's and read the letter too; Alexander didn't stop him, but rather removed his ring and pressed the seal to Hephaestion's lips" (emphasizing confidentiality); or of Julius Caesar's scanning: "When Caesar was engaged in a great struggle with Cato that occupied the senate, a brief note was couriered to Caesar. Cato tried to direct suspicion toward the matter, by alleging that the note concerned the conspiracy [Catiline's attempted coup], and dared Caesar to read it aloud. Instead, Caesar read the note silently and handed it to Cato. When Cato read the note, he found it was a lewd message from his own sister Servilia, who was in passionate, guilty love with Caesar, and he hurled it back in Caesar's face, saying, 'All yours—you drunk,' and then resumed his speech"—but it is the most notable, because of its concern. Ambrose was gleaning not for information or romance, but for spiritual guidance. Reading silently, you are protected from scrutiny, and become the lone judge of your comprehension—its deficiency. Reading silently, then, you become dangerous—even if the language itself, in Augustine's milieu, had become more innocuous. (A panoply of Semitic religions regarded and still regard their shibboleths as inherently magical, talismanic—it's difficult

3. No matter what was in his head, such a man cannot be misread.

to imagine Latin or Greek pronouncements capable of such Hebrew and Aramaic feats as animating and deanimating life, effecting levitation, and healing lepers.)

It's inevitable that Augustine's ultimate conversion would occur at the very moment that he himself attempted this new practice—of sealing the world into his crowded bony cenacle. Augustine had been reading—aloud—in his garden, in the company of his friend, Alypius, when, surmounted by doubt, he abruptly flung the book aside and fled under a fig tree to cry. From a neighboring house came the voice of a child, indeterminate in gender, reciting a rhyme whose refrain was *tolle, lege,* "take up and read." Taking this as command, a voice in the wilderness, Augustine hurried back to Alypius and returned to the Epistles of Paul: "I took hold of the book and opened it, and in silence read the first section on which my eyes fell," a selection from Romans 13, counseling him to "make not provision for the flesh," rather to don, as if replacing a hairshirt with chainmail, "the Lord Jesus Christ." This passage's sartorial metonymy—"Put ye on"—reads like nothing but a momentaneous costuming in the Neo-Platonic soul, though instead of Augustine being confirmed in the knowledge that all of life was to be but a constant tailoring of Oneness, a continuous measuring and cutting and sewing and wrenching apart, the Oneness, suddenly, enwrapped, enfolded him—seamlessly—one size fits all.

Appositely, the language of both the Bible and Augustine's own revelation is Manichean, with Romans exhorting, "Let us therefore cast off the works of darkness, and let us put on the armor of light," and Augustine himself concluding, "I wouldn't read any further, nor did I have to, because at the very end of the verse a serene light infused my heart, dispersing all the darkness." Instead it was Alypius who read further. Alarmed by Augustine's rapture, he inquired as to its cause. Augustine responded by passing the book to his friend who, without knowing where Augustine had stopped, continued—aloud—just where the proselyte had left off, with the first verse of the next chapter: "Him that is weak in the faith receive ye."

Augustine would go on to become one of the Church's preeminent Fathers and Doctors, a godly preacher who worshipped mutely but used quill and ink to frame the concepts of original sin (which he defined as carnal), just war (violence only in defense), ecclesiology (which asserted the duality of the Church, as both earthly institution and heavenly kingdom), and illuminationism (God as the ideal that allows one human mind to understand another: "If we both see what you say is true, and we both see what I say is true, then where can the truth be seen? Not I in you, nor you in me, but both of us in that unalterable truth above us"). Alypius became a believer too and, finally, the fig tree of Augustine's weeping was grafted to another planted earlier by Ambrose, who once counseled that a convert must always be supported: "Give abundantly of your attention [*attentio*], so you may, like the productive fig tree, strengthen your own virtue as a result of the presence and distinction of that other uncultivated sapling."

A book converted Augustine—an experience with a codex, the reading/writing technology that became the medium of choice for Christianity and so the world. Books, unlike scrolls, were durable; unlike tablets, foldable; and unlike both scrolls and tablets, they traveled well and were concealable, which was useful in an age of heresies that would burn the books along with their scribes. But Ambrose and Augustine's experience was not common. In their time, most books had to be shared, and were shared through reading aloud. Silence, then as now, was a luxury, as was and is time, or the ability to stop and consider a passage. No religion has ever commended its lectors for pausing their chants to ponder a text—no congregation likes to be kept waiting.

Still, don't pass over that word, don't treat it with its own meaning: *ducebantur*, third-person plural imperfect passive indicative of *duco*—so more accurately: "they were glided," "floated," "guided," "led"—"they" being Ambrose's eyeballs. His reading, then, must've been mostly passive and imperfect: rounding, surrounding, "scrolling" the page—Ambrose's gaze mimicking the rolling motion of the volumen, then "cinching"—fixing on topics of interest, or just on a snippet already familiar, or memorized. Both Ambrose and Augustine must've memorized much, turning their reading into reminding, or comfort. Despite Augustine's claim that silence slowed Ambrose, preventing him from reading his fill, it's difficult to credit the implication that there were enough new books around to make every reading experience novel (or deserving of attention). (Unfortunately, Augustine's *Confessions* leaves no word as to whether either he or Ambrose moved their lips, or used their fingers as pointers.)

While reading silently—letting throat and tongue rest, with even the lips stilled, the finger kept from pointing—the mind can mind itself. Freed of the body, it can skip and jump, rush ahead and fall behind, both in the text it's reading (earlier pages remembered, later pages expected), and in the text that is itself (memories

and expectations). There could be no difference, however, between Augustine's reading of a consecutive/
unidirectional book and of his own nonconsecutive
/omnidirectional intelligence. For him, time and space
were nonexistent, unless the space was here and the
time was now: presence, the present—*idipsum* or *id ipsum*,
favorite terms of his that mean, the both of them, "the
selfsame."[4]

The present is Augustine's object, subject, and surety.
As an older man he asked (an older man's question) how
the future seems to decrease, when it did not exist *yet*?
and how the past seems to increase, when it did not exist
still? He settled on a trinity as explanation: "It is because
the mind expects [*expecto*], attends [*attendo*], and remembers [*memoro*], so that what it expects becomes what it
remembers by way of what it attends to."

Attention, for Augustine, is the fundamental medium: It "has a continuity, through which what is present
becomes absent.

"Therefore, the future, which does not exist *yet*, is not
long; rather, a long future is only *a long expectation of the
future*. Nor is the past, which does not exist *still*, long;
rather, a long past is only *a long memory of the past*" (italics
mine).

It should be evident that Augustine, in this passage
describing what attention is and is useful for, embodies

4. Augustine encountered the term in Psalm 4: *In pace in id ipsum
   dormiam et requiescam*. "In peace in the selfsame I will sleep and
   rest." When Augustine read this psalm, presumably silently,
   and came to *id ipsum*, he "cried"—he read it aloud. Augustine's
   primary Bible was the Vetus Latina, based on the Greek
   Septuagint. (At the time, Jerome hadn't even embarked on his
   Vulgate.) The King James, which was translated directly from
   Hebrew, renders the phrase: "I will both lay me down in peace,
   and sleep."

his own process: expecting what he's about to say, attending to saying it, and in the next sentence remembering, by reflecting on what he's said.

> I am about to repeat a psalm with which I'm very familiar. Before I begin, my attention encompasses the whole, but once I've begun, all that becomes past as I speak it, and so is retained again in my memory. My activity is divided between my memory, which contains what I've repeated, and my expectation, which contains what I'm about to repeat. Yet my attention is continually present, and through it what was future becomes past. The more this is repeated, the more the memory is greatened—and the expectation, lessened—until even expectation passes into memory. This, in turn, ends the action, which passes into memory as well. Further, what takes place in the entire psalm also takes place in each individual portion of it, even in each of its syllables. This holds too for the even longer action of which this psalm is only a portion. The same also holds for the whole life of man, of which all the actions of men are only parts. The same also holds for the whole age of *the sons of men* [italics mine], of which all the lives of men are only parts.

This passage not only embodies what came before but also engages a phrase from the psalms, "the sons of men," both to demonstrate that memory can be recontextualized and to reveal which psalm he was repeating, which he has, at least partially, repeated. (The phrase recurs in over twenty psalms, including Psalm 4.)

Finally, though, it's the vocabulary of the *Confessions* that renders Augustine untranslatable. Like all Latin writers of his era, he makes no distinction between "soul" and "mind," using *anima* and *animus* interchangeably.

This could be because he, or his age, believed they were selfsame. Or else it could be because the only way to insist on a distinction is *to make a distinction*—to prioritize the mental—and, in the dim depths of autocognition, he sensed this and fled from the light. Perhaps he also sensed that the penitent cannot make such, or any, decisions, but rather must live in a perpetual attention to miracle, a religious life being a vigilant life—one in which attention is sustained, and sustaining, not parsed. To become aware of revelation is to lose revelation; to become conscious of the present is to gain only past.

E. DISARTICULATION AND ARTICULATION, PAPER AND INK AND IMPLEMENTS, COPYING, COPYING (*WRITING 1*)

The first translation of the Torah into Greek, the Septuagint, was undertaken by a committee of seventy-two rabbis who knew Hebrew or just one another so well that, despite being forced to work independently in seventy-two sealed chambers—party to a gambit intended to expose disagreement and so falsehood in the law—all their versions emerged utterly the same, down to the last word, the last letter, and so the law was revealed as incontrovertible truth and even the evil commissioner, Ptolemy II, was appeased (or so goes the Talmud's legend).

Jerome was the first single translator to attempt to put what had become known as the Old Testament into Latin, though, perhaps because his Hebrew was rudimentary, he made reference to the Vetus Latina (an earlier Latin compilation of disparate renderings), and the Septuagint, in the production of his Vulgate. Jerome died in Judea, was buried in Bethlehem, re-buried, partially, in Rome, though some say that his head was entombed just north at the Cattedrale di Santa Maria Assunta in Nepi, while others say that it's interred at the royal Escorial, just north of Madrid, where it's administered by monks of the Augustine Order. Augustine himself is relicated all over Italy, especially in Pavia, though during the Napoleonic Wars the prime reliquary was sheltered in Milan, where Ambrose lies intact. Decapitation, disarticulation: What was punishment for Orpheus was honor to the Church.

These men were taken apart like texts, recast, redacted, moved around—spreading as the Church spread, west across Europe, each new fragment a new connection to the source—spreading too as their books spread, as literacy animated *animae* and *animi*, but silently. By the eighth century, scriptural punctuation was standardized, and sentences began to begin with capital letters. In the vernaculars, orthography—how to *spillon, spellon*—spell—was reformed.

Monks copied by consulting copies, or originals, or by taking dictation—reading aloud becoming a specialized function. An anonymous scribe of the eighth century: "You can't believe how demanding the work is. Three fingers write, two eyes see. One tongue speaks, all the body labors."

The ninth century finds so many copyists, copying so many texts (subspecialization), that to banish confusion a mandate is passed: Monks must remain silent in the scriptorium. Communication among the scribes becomes sign language. Earlier, Judaism had innovated the use of chironomy, or finger signals, used by a secondary silent reader—a mute copy editor or proofer—to indicate to the primary audible reader the various cadences of scriptural cantillation, a practice later adapted for recitations of the Koran and Gregorian chant. Monks who needed a new book to copy raised their hands and pretended to leaf through nonexistent pages. If a psalter were needed, they'd crown their heads with their hands in a reference to the psalmist King David. A lectionary was called for by cleaning imaginary wax dripped by imaginary candles, a missal by crossing the chest. A secular work—of philosophy, medicine, law—if it wasn't banned, was requested by scratching the body, as if the itch of free thought were an infestation of fleas. Heresies

562

accumulated with knowledge. The Second Coming had come and gone, and Jesus was a woman. God was three, or one, or the one martyred on the Cross. The soul and the flesh were one, or two, or the soul was the Word while the flesh could be transubstantiated through bread and wine, or was only substantially represented by them, though regardless of whether communion was symbolic or not, it could only be administered by clergy (the mind, meanwhile, was of the soul, or of the flesh, or separate and mediating between). Christ was entirely mortal. Or entirely divine. Original sin never happened, Augustine be damned. The Spirit alone illuminated and the testaments were but fabrications. Only the pope could interpret the Bible, or everyone could, and salvation had a price, in silver or gold. Theses were nailed not stigmatiferously through wrists and feet but to doors. In 1085, Alfonso VI, king of Castile and Leon, conquered Moorish Toledo and sought to impose the Roman rite—substituting the Latin liturgy for that of Mozarabia (the Visigothic Church). A Latin prayerbook and a Mozarabian prayerbook were hurled into a fire. By the time the Latin was totally consumed, the Mozarabian had been only slightly damaged, though the king decided to ignore the intervention and enforce the Roman rite nonetheless.

Books out of vellum, or parchment, were more likely to be proven innocent at trials by fire. Books out of paper—cheaper and so more popular; the material more suggestive, more open to imprinting—were adjudged guilty, even before the kindling was sparked. Paper of bark, bits of fishnets, cloth rags, and hemp was invented by the Chinese around the first century B.C.E., was in popular use by the second century C.E.—Han Dynasty—and unfurled west through Arabia. The Song Dynasty, 960–1279 C.E., had produced the first paper money by the time the Muslims introduced the technology, for writing and not for trade, to Iberia. Water mills allowed its mass production (1282, Aragon), and watermarks allowed each surface to be identified with its maker, or user (1300, Fabriano). Recycling, or deinking a page to be pulped back to fibers and remade—repaginated—was invented by a jurist named Justus Claproth (1774, Göttingen).

The ink, the communicative medium either liquid, paste, or powder. A trinitarian colorant/pigment, a binder, additive/carriers. Ink itself is the unisonous binder. Chinese inks of plant dyes and blood, ca. twenty centuries before Christ (the God). Chinese inks of soot and glue, ca. three centuries before Christ (the man). At the time, India's ink was not yet India ink, but *masi*, concocted of burnt bones, tar, and pitch. Indigo was distilled from the leaves of legume plants, the *Indigofereae*. Jews favored snail ink, a purple that, when exposed to air, lightened bluer—from royalty's hue to a plebe colorant for garments. The Greek term for the cuttlefish genus is *Sepia*, which squirted their ink. Rome favored recipes using iron salts, such as ferrous sulfate ("vitriol"), mixed with tannins ("gall"). Europe opted for soaking hawthorn branches in water, boiling the water, then brewing again with iron salts and wine. Black inks based on carbon, made with soot bound with glue or gum arabic, common until the twelfth century, tended not to corrode paper as efficiently as did black inks based on iron. Neither Greek and Roman carbon inks, nor the ferric inks of the Church, were feasible for printing. Both blurred when applied to metal plates, when the plates were applied to paper. The solution was, literally, ink based on turpentine and oil.

The implement. White chalk, black charcoal, on cave walls and slate. Bone styli, sharpened into clay and wax. Chinese brushes of rabbit and deer hair. Bamboo sticks. Crayons, sticks of lead and grease. Egyptian reeds of *Juncus maritimus*, or sea rush, a relation to the papyrus they marked (the papyrus exported from, and giving its name to, the port of Byblos, entrepôt of all bibliography and the world's oldest continuously inhabited city).

The reed was replaced by the quill when papyrus was replaced by parchment (animal skin), or vellum (strictly calfskin), ca. fifth–third centuries B.C.E. Skin, being smoother, allowed for finer writing, tighter-spaced. The Phoenician letters required, or benefited from, it. These quills, from bird feathers preferably molted, not plucked, were denominated in declining order from their attachment to wing, the best being the pinion, the first. The left-wing feathers were for R-handed scribes, as those feathers curved away from the sight line and over the hand. Scribes opted to change nib angles—cut with a *penknife*—rather than the angles at which they held their pens, and so contorting their hands and depleting them. Nibs were cut square for glyphic alphabets, in nonglyphic alphabets only for R-handed scribes, while oblique cuts, at 25 to 30 degrees to the left, were for L-handed scribes, or for R-handed scribes in R-to-L languages like Arabic and Hebrew.

The quill's notched point, like an arrow's, the quill itself an arrow of all fletch. The feather—Latin's *penna*—that became the pen. Copper nibs, which appeared by the first century C.E., had to be dipped in ink between each character. The reservoir pen—an implement centered around a capillary that held ink sufficient for a line, or a complete document, which was inspired by the calamus, or hollow shaft, of the feather—debuted in the tenth century, the conception of al-Mu'izz li-Din Allah, Caliph of Egypt.

The unrefreshable pencil—Latin's *penicillus*, "small tail." When a gigantic deposit of graphite was found at the turn of the sixteenth century in Cumbria, England, the element was identified as "lead," and so the pencil's black core is misidentified still. Snapping, breaking. A casing, of juniper, debuted in Italy by 1560.

Patent of steel nib, 1803. Mass production of steel pens, 1822. The fountain pen, the popularization of the Caliph's invention, Petrache Poenaru, France, 1827. 1858, Hymen Lipman of Philadelphia received U.S. Patent 19,783: "I make a lead-pencil in the usual manner, reserving about one-fourth the length, in which I make a groove of suitable size, and insert in this groove a piece of prepared india-rubber (or other erasive substance), secured to said pencil by being glued at one edge. The pencil is then finished in the usual manner, so that on cutting one end thereof you have the lead, and on cutting it at the other end you expose a small piece of india-rubber, ready for use, and particularly valuable for removing or erasing lines, figures, etc., and not subject to be soiled or mislaid on the table or desk."[5]

5. In 1862, Lipman sold his patent to one Joseph Reckendorfer, who sued pencil manufacturer Faber-Castell for infringement. In 1875, the U.S. Supreme Court ruled against Reckendorfer, and claimed the patent invalid: "It is evident that this manner of making or applying the instrument gives no aid to the patent. [...] A handle in common, a joint handle, does not create a new or combined operation. The handle for the pencil does not create or aid the handle for the eraser. The handle for the eraser does not create or aid the handle for the pencil. Each has and each requires a handle the same as it had required, without reference

The point, the nib, the felt tip, the rolling ball—all are fixations. They fix the hand, even while marking the line between its functions: clarity to all, and recognition of self.

Prior to Gutenberg's typography, chirography—handwriting—had been a quest for ecumenical perfection. Medieval monks, practicing manuscripture, worked toward the perfection of a hand in which the authority of the collective was privileged over that of the personal achievement. This sublimation is evident in every scribal hand: from the earliest *scriptura continua*, inwhichthetextwasn'tseparated, to uncial, a totally Majuscule hand, named after the half inch that each line had to occupy, through the Carolingian hands, called after Charlemagne, who reigned like a Majuscule, though his reforms included the use of minuscules and commas, and the later Gothic hands (literally "barbarous," "vandalistic," to the Italians), which solemnized commas into cathedral struts, finials, and minims, enough to render them carceral, as if the characters were bars, imprisoning monks in cells of lonely literacy.

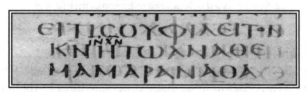

... to what is at the other end of the instrument, and the operation of the handle of and for each is precisely the same, whether the new article is or is not at the other end of it. [...] The law requires more than a change of form, or juxtaposition of parts, or of the external arrangement of things, or of the order in which they are used, to give patentability."

The ink of antique writing serves to mire words in vagary and doubt, giving rise to multiple print interpretations that in turn have acquired their own truths, and a species of religious disputation. Reproduced above is a fragment of the Codex Sinaiticus, the oldest complete Christian Bible, in the collection of Egypt's Saint Catherine's monastery, at the foot of the putative Mount Sinai.

Maranatha, one of a few Aramaic words in the entire New Testament, appears only once, at the conclusion of 1 Corinthians. Due to its obscurity, the word has always been transliterated, not translated, into Greek, Latin, and the English of the King James. A custom of confusion attends the matter of the whether *maranatha* is intended to read *marana tha*—"Come, O Lord"—or *maran atha*—"Our Lord Has Come." Had the Testament originally been typeset for the printing press, or on a computer and that space unicoded in its proper place, humanity would be able to tell whether that phrase was a call for Christ's Second Coming, or merely a creedal decree. God would be satisfied, though the reader's experience of the text would be poorer. The Codex Sinaiticus, the work of an unknown scribe or scribes, has been digitized in its entirety. Both variants of *maranatha* are available as translations online.

Handwriting must be legible enough to be read by all, yet it will always bear the mark of the individual. The modern recognition of distinct personalities in the formation of consonants and animation of vowels dates to the Renaissance. Paradoxically, the new writing hand that developed in Italy in the fourteenth century—a hand more fluid and so more suited to individual expression—became, with the advent of the press, the first font. What started as an *italicism*—or, alternately, as "cursive," from the Latin for "running"—ended as the standard setting for Renaissance publishers, especially for their translations of Latin and Greek that turned classical texts into Classics. Antonio Sinibaldi, scribe to the Medicis, had an elegant, gracile hand. He was put out of work by Gutenberg's press in 1480, but found a sinecure as a writing instructor and calligrapher. The usurpation of Sinibaldi—the first major scribe pensioned by machine—personalizes, with a valedictory flourish, the rift between humanity and technology.

Just as today a fervid minority denounces the digitization of literary experience, fifteenth-century literati responded to their own depredations. In 1492, Johannes Trithemius, Abbot of Sponheim, wrote *De Laude Scriptorum*, "In Praise of Scribes," a polemic addressed to Gerlach, Abbot of Deutz. Trithemius's intention was to uphold scribal preeminence while denouncing the temptations of the emerging press: "The printed book is made of paper and, like paper, will rapidly disappear. But the scribe working with parchment ensures lasting remembrance for himself and his text."

Trithemius asserted that movable type was no substitute for solitary transcription, as the discipline of copying was a better guarantor of religious sensibility than the mundane acts of printing and reading. As evidence he offers the account of a Benedictine copyist, famed for his pious perspicuity, who had died, was buried by his brethren, then subsequently, though inexplicably, exhumed. According to Trithemius, the copyist's corpus had decomposed but for three fingers of his composing hand: his right thumb, forefinger, and middle finger—relics, like manuscripture itself, of literary diligence.

6. SCHISMS, DIVISIONS, MONADS, SPECIES

Leave the monks to scribble their darkness, their scriptoria welters of fibers and bond weights, shades and delible densities. Return to the empire, Byzantine in every sense.

In 285, Diocletian split the imperium into eastern and western halves; the west was Rome, the east was established by Constantine I in 330, as Constantinople; Rome claimed that as the father and son were consubstantial, the spirit proceeded from them both; Constantinople claimed that as the son was of two natures, both human and divine, the spirit proceeded from the father alone; the *filioque* ("and from the son") clause of the Nicene Creed became the theological investiture of political strife; compromise was not achieved and in 1054 the Pope of Rome excommunicated the Patriarch of Constantinople, who, in turn, excommunicated the pope; in 1274, the Second Council of Lyons was convened to bridge the schism and reunite the churches; among the invited was Thomas Aquinas, who was to present his opuscule in defense of Rome, *Contra errores graecorum* ("Against the Errors of the Greeks"), but en route to the council, on donkeyback along the Appian Way, he smacked his head on a tree branch, and died.

The Nicene Creed began as a statement of principles in 325, and ended as a prayer with its incorporation into the Catholic mass in 1014; institutional discipline was assured by its spiration as personal duty. Aquinas's *Summa Theologica* (1265–74) maintains that prayer has three effects: The first is "merit," the second, "impetration," or to obtain a grace by entreaty, and the third, "spiritual refreshment of mind" (for which Latin

571

had developed a term since Augustine's time: *mentis*). Attention, *attentio*, is not required for the first two; intention, *intentio*—or the inchoative impulse to pray, "which God considers above all else"—is enough. Intent, though, is not enough for the third and last. To be repristinated one must be in attendance. Later in the *Summa*, Aquinas divides attention into three categories of its own: One must attend to the pronouncing of the words, to the sense of the words, and to God—though he allows that true attention to God would obliterate the two preceding types, and that such a relationship is the triumph of intention, of visceral inwrought resolve.

The textual, the lexical, was the Catholic fixation, while the Byzantines were always externally focused, and tended to conceive of prayer in terms of its material surroundings: precious metals and jewels, coruscant altarpieces, icons, mosaics, melodies swirling like censer smoke. Books were for knowledge, or rather Trinitarian recondities; by contrast, the Eastern Orthodox cathedral was an immortal monument to "wisdom" (*Sophia*, in Greek), and so the terrestrial seat of the spirit. (That spirit would not be as effective as the papal armies in the fight against the Ottoman Turks, however, and so in 1439 at the Council of Florence, Byzantium reluctantly adopted the *filioque*. Laity and synods repudiated the concession; Constantinople fell in 1453.)

The empire's ecclesiastical rift was doctrinal, dogmatic; its western linguistic fragmenting, vernacular. The troubadours and trouvères of the *langues d'oc* and *langues d'oïl*—Occitan/Provençal, Old Norman—sought not God but consistent patronage and sex, and were called after the vulgarized Latin *tropare*, "to find"; the Romance tongues were duly consummated. Latinate sapience became *saber*, gut "sense," acquired not from canonical copywork but devotion to experience. Old French dealt with this change in *conscius—con*, "common," *scius*, "knowledge"—by rendering its state into a faculty with "conscience," a defiantly secular judgment; the Old German *giwar*, not yet modern "awareness," hunted the inner self with prudence.

Curiously, it was English usage that retained at least a faint halo of religiosity. 1340, Richard Rolle of Hampole: "Thay may noghte flye to lufe and contemplacyone of God." 1337, William Langland: "Lerne logyk and lawe and eke contemplacioun." "Attention," meanwhile, was represented by Chaucer in 1374 in a decidedly utile, apprehensive, or arresting sense: "After at she hadde gadred [...] myn attencioun she seide us." Which treatment continued through Shakespeare, sixteenth century: "The tongues of dying men/Inforce attention," and Milton, seventeenth: "Attention held them mute." Tellingly, the first overt definition in English, 1526, William Bonde, conflated the religious and secular:

Attencion or intencion for our purpose here
is onely the attendaunce
study & diligence that man or woman gyveth to their dede
as prayer
word or worke
whiche they be in doyng or about to do.
And after saynt Aquinas this attencion may be iii maner
of ways
actuall
habituall or virtuall.

The 1600s, the seventeenth century, the Age of Rationalism, the Era of Empiricism: The very notion that a period might have a character is what characterizes the period. It was Christoph Keller, called Cellarius (1638–1707), who created the division of history into Ancient, Medieval, and Modern rubrics. Further epochs ensued, both in future and in retrospect. Throughout this time, whatever its label, arguments evolved as to whether organization depended on identification, or identification on organization, or whether a codependence obtained. Only once you defined what something was would you be able to tell how it was different from something else, in language as in science; only once you differentiated among things would you be able to define a thing, in science as in language. Both approaches were attempts to attend.

"Many things we confirm and deny, only because the nature of words allows us to do so, though the nature of things does not": concepts, minerals, plants, animals, human minds and bodies along with their functions and processes, had to be separated mathematically, as if numbers were a logical proxy for the illogic of letters. The author of that quotation might not have cared if you called him Blaise Pascal, René Descartes, or Baruch Spinoza—as long as you agreed with him.

Of the three, Pascal (1623–62) was the most profoundly religious; but though he'd been converted to Jansenism (a French version of Augustinism) by an appeal to the spirit, he sought to sway others to credence by reason alone: the famous wager of his *Pensées*, stating that there was more to be gained from believing in the existence of God than there was from not believing in it (atheism), and that it was precisely this potential for gain that rationalized religion. Likewise, when Pascal rhetoricized, "Philosophers who have mastered their passions—what matter would be capable of that?" the

574

implication was that the key to such mastery was ratiocination, of which humanity was the only matter capable. To resist ratiocination was to resist divine grace and to lapse if not into perdition—Jansenists subscribed to predestination—then guilt.

Descartes (1596–1650), who was an acquaintance of Pascal's, did not share his desire for faith, and applied logic not to prove the merit of a religious life, but rather to prove that the behaviors inculcated by religion could just as well be managed without it. His intention, in his *Passions of the Soul*, is "regulation": "There is no soul so weak that better management would not allow it to acquire mastery over its passions." To Descartes, the mind and body are separate, the body a type of technology whose metaphysical pulleys and levers are operated by "the passions"—note the innate "passivity"—which are not interiorly generated emotions, but rather the soul's experience of exterior phenomena. Unlike burns or wounds, however, the passions cannot be localized, because the soul cannot be localized, though according to Descartes the source of its stimulation could be "the miniature gland in the middle of the brain"—the pineal.

Spinoza (1632–77), who'd been excommunicated by Amsterdam's Jews, sought, instead, to define emotional experiences, which he called "affections," as mere manifestations of a universalizing Substance, "that which exists in, and is conceived through, itself: in other words, that of which a concept can be formed independently of any other concept." Spinoza's *Ethics* proposes the existence of this Substance, an illimitable power possessed of "attributes"—"that which the intellect regards as constituting the essence of Substance"—which express themselves through "modes"—which are "the modifications of Substance, or that which exists in, and is conceived through, something other than it-self." Spinoza's organization is hierarchical; Descartes's dual, though his *mens* and *corpus* are still haunted by the ghost of a soul. Neither philosopher fully addresses the ramifications of a distinction between existence and a consciousness-of-existence.

Instead it took the mid-seventeenth century to en-gineer this—in language, in a further contortion of "conscious": While Thomas Hobbes hewed to the com-munal definition—"where two or more men know of one and the same fact, they are said to be Conscious of it one to another"—John Locke pursued a more individual definition: "the perception of what passes in a man's own mind." It's as if a homonym were responsible for revo-lutionizing the political thinking of the Enlightenment to follow.

Before freedoms of speech and religion would be granted, every freedom—every feeling and act and thing—had to be categorized, classified, related, interre-lated. The world was discovered and discovered round in the fifteenth century; the sixteenth century found nation-states expanding into empires and staking their claims in New Worlds unseen by most but imagined by all. The next and only frontier was smaller, equal-ly unseen, but more unimaginable—the microscopic. Perception through language was radically changed when the constituent parts of an organism were made visible through glass.

Descartes was an optics theorist. Spinoza earned his living, and his death from silicosis, by tediously grind-ing and polishing lenses. Antonie van Leeuwenhoek (1632–1723) founded the science of microbiology by sighting, through 500x magnifying microscopes of his own invention, the microorganisms he called "animalcules." In 1674, he explored infusoria, or protists; in 1676, he set eyes on bacteria, selenomonads from the human mouth; and in 1677 he planted his flag in the fertile head of a spermatozoon (that flagellating squiggly initially suspected to be a worm, hence its name, "semen animal"). Larger organisms became seen as merely the sum of smaller organisms (the concealed the justificatory essence of the conspicuous), and so life itself was viewed not as an independent entity, but as an interdependent cycle (a mechanism, a machine).

Of all the exemplars of the seventeenth century's taxonomical drive, Gottfried Wilhelm Leibniz (1646–1716) is perhaps the most distinctive, and distinguished. His interest in what's now called semiotics—the study of signs: the relationship between signifier (word) and signified (thing)—resulted in a new *lingua franca*: a categorical language, which would classify every other language. Some of Leibniz's contemporaries sought to identify an Adamic, or Edenic, tongue; others experimented with artificial arrangements of prefixes, suffixes, and grapheme/phoneme (read/pronounced) roots, while Leibniz's own ideal was to utilize characters only. His was a pasigraphic or alingual attempt at a *characteristica universalis*, a universal characterization, or alphabet, of all human knowledge:

Though studious men have immemorially conceived of some type of language or universal characteristic by which all concepts and things might be arranged in harmonious order, and with the help of which disparate peoples might communicate their wisdom and each read in his own language what another has written in his, no

one has yet succeeded with a language or characteristic
that also includes both the arts of designation and operation, that is, one whose signs and characters serve the
same purpose that arithmetical signs serve for numbers,
and algebraic signs for abstract quantities.
(*On the General Characteristic*, 1679)

Leibniz's wouldn't just be a thinker's language, but a
thinking language, whose elements would be derived
directly from the things it described in the very way
those things were derived from their constituents—by
the principle of recombinant units:

All derivative concepts arise from a combination of
primitive ones, and those that are composite in a higher
degree arise from a combination of composite concepts.
(*On Universal Synthesis and Analysis*, 1679)

To Leibniz, all concepts were either primal or deriv-
able, and while primitives could serve as their own
symbols, derivatives had to be accorded designations
more descriptive, or just more relatable, than any mere
reduction or sum. It was this realization that inspired
Leibniz's development of binary notation—a system that
could represent the infinitude of the universe with only
two elements, or with one element, given that zero was
a nullity.

The ciphering accomplished by these 1s ("unities")
and 0s ("nothing")—in their alteration, or, in Leibniz's
phrase, *ars combinatoria*—was akin to God's "creation of
all things out of nothing," as Leibniz wrote to his patron, the Duke of Brunswick, in 1697: "Because instead
of there appearing no particular order or pattern, as in
the common representation of numerals, here appears a

beautiful order and harmony that cannot be improved upon."[6]

And so if 0 is 0, and 1 is 1, 2 will be 10, 3 will be 11; and 4, 100; 5, 101; 6, 110; 7, 111; 8, 1,000... This system, applied to the representation of ideas, allowed each to be symbolized by a character set that assimilated its full complement of relationships and referents. With this, any two concepts, and every stage of their compositing, might be evaluated, or equated, through logical operation.

In its most fundamental sense, Leibniz's binary is a model of existence itself, with expanses of void, or 0s, intervening between solid masses, or 1s—elementary particles that Leibniz called "monads": "nothing but a simple substance, which enters into compounds" (*Monadology*, 1714). Leibniz's monad was among the most influential revivals of Antiquity's atomism—the theory that the whole of life was but a coalescing of small parts. Though unlike other atomist units of the time— Descartes's "vortices," Pierre Gassendi and Robert Boyle's "corpuscules"—Leibniz's monad wasn't solely physical or metaphysical, but mental as well, having been founded on the insight that both things and ideas tended to assume the properties of the mind that was perceiving them: the thing or idea in itself constituting

6. Leibniz had served the ducal libraries at Hanover and Wolfenbüttel, where he'd engineered a new type of indexing— a bibliography that communicated a library's holdings both conceptually and materially. His schema called for books to be alphabetized firstly by author, and secondly by author within subject, producing a mental plan of the libraries' holdings, to be cross-referenced with the shelf list, which mapped the libraries' physical plan, where sections A–E covered Theology, F was concerned with Law, while Q–Z were left open to accommodate any fields not yet determined.

its primitive essence, variously derived by observation.

Leibniz's *Monadology*, like Spinoza's *Ethics*, describes and prescribes simultaneously. Both tractates are written in the styles by which their respective authors sought to rewrite all of existence—disciplined (Spinoza wrote in Latin), direct (Leibniz, in French), with terminology that when it didn't repeat, spawned relations in hypostatized genealogies. Though the tracts share common spirit, their methods are opposed: Spinoza, working *from* intuition *to* perception, divided Substance into *a posteriori* expressions; Leibniz, working *to* intuition *from* perception, added and multiplied *a priori* substances toward an expression of the "highest degree."

To Spinoza, everything about the sensory can only be derived; to Leibniz, however, anything that can be sensed is, in its essence, primal, though human engagement is not. Leibniz's monadism is fundamentally a notation of that engagement—the way the brain arrays disparate sights and sounds and smells and tastes and touches into integrated experiences. In Leibniz's formulation, all external phenomena exist as *petites perceptions*, "small perceptions" transmitted through the sensorium but registered, internally, only in combination—in their exceeding a certain threshold of combination—and so entering into what he calls "apperception," or "conscious awareness." Elemental phenomena cohere only through and as this compounding, at a threshold that changes with context: You—being familiar with this language—don't have to read every letter to read this "word," nor do you have to review etymology or grammar to comprehend this "sentence."

For Leibniz, the sole facilitator of apperception is memory, which aggregates perceptions across time and space:

All attention requires memory, and often when we're
not scolded and told to take notice of our present perceptions, welet them pass without reflection, and even
without observation, yet if someone directs our attention
to something immediately after, and, for instance, bids us
to recall a sound supposedly just made, we find not only
that we can but also that we had some notion of the sound
at the time.

(*New Essays*, 1704)

But ultimately memory isn't just continuance—rather,
it's a vehicle by which to decode creation:

It may even be said that in consequence of these *petites
perceptions*, the present is big with the future and weighted
with the past, that there is a conspiration of all things, and
that even in the least of substances eyes as penetrating as
those of God might read the total succession of all things
in the universe.

(*New Essays*, 1704)

In the same way that you can't look at the name of
God without reading it, God can't look at you without
being aware—given the deity's superior memory—of
everything you've ever been, or will be: biologically,
chemically, philosophically, religiously.

Despite Animals, Vegetables, and Minerals not differ-
ing from one another—or even from others of their own
Kingdoms—by stringent transpositions, such symbolic
logic became the model for speciation. In systematiz-
ing the basic distinctions among earth's organisms,
humanity categorized even itself—if only by placing

itself at the pinnacle: from Animalia, through Chordata, Vertebrata, Mammalia, Primates, Hominidæ, to *Homo sapiens*. Carl Linnaeus (1707–78), not the first *Homo sapiens* but the first to recognize himself as such, introduced binomial classification, or the *nomina trivialia*, for plants in his *Species Plantarum* (1753) and for animals in the tenth edition of his *Systema Naturae* (1758–59).[7] "It is not the character that makes the *genus*, but the *genus* that makes the character": It was the practice of Linnaeus and of earlier taxonomists like Andrea Cesalpino, Gaspard Bauhin, John Ray, Augustus Quirinus Rivinus, and Joseph Pitton de Tournefort to dispose their specimens through wishful intuition as much as by dissection or observation in the field. Their artificial taxonomies would later be replaced by clades, based on more rigorously quantifiable data, but it's this antique search for a qualifying "character" (Linnaeus), or "affinity" (Bauhin), that ramifies throughout the Enlightenment.

Jean-Jacques Rousseau (1712–78), memoirist and novelist, was also a political philosopher, composer, perambulist, and horticulturist, the author of a popular handbook, *Letters on the Elements of Botany*, written under the influence of Linnaeus. This concern in particular kept pace with Rousseau's old age, attaining its formidable dehiscence in *Reveries of a Solitary Walker*, a notably impractical guide written between 1776 and 1778 and left unfinished. It is the record of a man desystematizing himself—a man quitting the city's polluting throng

7. Linnaeus regarded Genus, species as innate, or God-given, whereas the preceding levels—Kingdom, Class, Order—he admitted were constructs and was content to treat them as mere foundations for refinement (the ranks of Phylum and Family were still-later partitions).

for the blameless clean solitude of the countryside, and in doing so realizing that even if all the world around him would be parsed and tagged, pinned if not stilled in amber, any and all conceivable taxa whether revealed or engineered would still be secondary to lived experience:

> Trees, hedges, and plants are the attire and clothing of the earth. Nothing is as sad as the sight of a plain and bare countryside, which displays to the eyes only boulders, clay, and sand. But enlivened by nature and arrayed in its wedding dress amidst the brooks and birdsong, the Earth, in the harmony of its three kingdoms [Linnaeus's Animal, Vegetable, and Mineral], offers man a spectacle filled with life, interest, and charm—the only spectacle in the world of which his eyes and heart never weary.
> (*Reveries of a Solitary Walker*, 1782)

For Rousseau, with his artist's soul, to attend is to appreciate, have to be utile, only diverting; he would be free to ignore Venus or Mars, the sum of an insect's limbs or of a fruit's seeds, a flower's petal structure, or the dimensions and twitches of the flyblown head of a dray horse, insofar as he sensitized that education to reveries, idylls, spells of dreaming.especially alone and especially amid nature. His observations didn't have to be utile, only diverting; he would be free to ignore Venus or Mars, the sum of an insect's limbs or of a fruit's seeds, a flower's petal structure, or the dimensions and twitches of the flyblown head of a dray horse, insofar as he sensitized that education to reveries, idylls, spells of dreaming.

Weather, landscape, would be translated inward; passions, translated outward; the inspiration of breezes, the influence of streamlets; pathetic fallacies would abound. The only season in which everything blooms is the

poetic occasion—that rarefied spring in which the study
of nature becomes a study of self:

> This occurred to me [he writes in his "Seventh Walk"],
> when my mind, oppressed by sorrow, recalled and con-
> centrated all its power to preserve the remains of a passion
> almost extinguished by the heaviness into which I'd
> slipped. I wandered the woods and highlands, not daring
> to think, for fear of reviving my afflictions. My imagina-
> tion, refusing to countenance the cause of my suffering,
> instead engaged my senses to register the fleet, charming
> impressions of my surroundings. My eyes roved from one
> to another, and, though it would appear inconceivable, in
> a variety so great something or other was bound to attract
> them the most, and transfix them the longest.
>
> I became fond of this recreation of the sight, which, in
> an unfortunate man, reposes, amuses, diverts the mind,
> and suspends the sense of his miseries. The nature of
> the surroundings profoundly assists the diversion, and
> renders it more seductive. Fragrant smells, lively colors,
> the most elegant lines, appear to vie with emulation for
> the right to our attention. Nothing but a love of pleasure
> is required to be in thrall to sensations so soft, and, if
> this effect is not produced in all people, it's due to a lack
> of inborn sensibility, and, moreover, to the fact that
> their minds, otherwise occupied, devote themselves to
> the sources of their stimulation only between times, or
> clandestinely.
>
> (*Reveries of a Solitary Walker*, 1782)

G. MALEBRANCHE, VITALITY, AUTOMATA, CONDILLAC

With Leibniz matter had been split; the matter that remained was motion. Nicolas Malebranche (1638–1715) was a philosopher in motion. He went forward and claimed that humanity could experience verities like truth and falsity only as relative notions, as sensations. But he also went backward by claiming that everything existed only wholly in God, and so human access could only be partial.

Like Pascal, Malebranche was Catholic and catholic (French); he dedicated his life to reconciling the philosophies of Descartes—things are ideas—and Augustine—ideas are divine. Like Spinoza, Malebranche sought to render everything as the effect of an initial cause, though while Spinoza settled on a pantheism that sundered God into a passive existence (*natura naturata*, "nature natured," or nature already created), descended from an active expression (*natura naturans*, "naturing nature," or nature that creates), Malebranche insisted on the role of human will, and spanned the vacuum.

To Malebranche and his fellow Occasionalists—Géraud de Cordemoy, Arnold Geulincx, and Louis de La Forge—the body cannot control the mind, the mind cannot control the body; rather, the two are linked in the soul, which in turn is linked with the Spirit (the divine). Malebranche's shared soul owes its divisions to Aquinas. For Malebranche, the human portion of the soul is what it intends, but the aspect that is God's is attentional. Intention is desire, attention—according to Malebranche's *The Search After Truth* (1674–75)—"a natural prayer" of the soul, for success at attaining its desiderata.

More-active interpretations of Occasionalism certainly resembled formal worship, with humanity submitting its will to the deity for approval or denial, turning experiences even as mundane as waking or reading or sleeping into sanctimonious events. More-passive interpretations regarded that cooperation as automatic and innate. Both versions, however, insisted on the perfection of all things within God, and the imperfection of how humans experienced them. By insisting that the flaw is always with the human half of the soul—with humanity's intentions and with its bodily and mental reception of what is sent—Malebranche became the first philosopher to systemize attention as transmission: mutual at best, at worst transactional.

But every transmission requires a medium. The human, without access to God or any other animating force, is just a golem, dusty matter without motion. A mechanism. A machine.

If the mechanical had quondam imitated the mortal—if cams and pistons had always been mere iterations of organs and glands—in the eighteenth century the mortal imitated the mechanical. Descartes regarded animals as machines and humans as no better than animals. Leibniz announced his capability in a letter to French theologian/mathematician Antoine Arnauld: "God has given a soul to every machine capable of having one."

Malebranche identified two types of machines, artificial, which are finite, which rust, and natural, which can infinitely reproduce, like species of flora and fauna. According to Malebranche, not only is humanity a natural machine but it is one that exists preassembled, or preformed, infinitely reproducing itself in mature just miniaturized form in utero, or, to be true to gender norms of the time, in sperm: as *homunculi*, or "little men," of small but proportional skeletons who upon birth, in one interpretation, or upon conception, in another, become attached to an entheastic soul and so are engaged, empowered.

What is telling is not that for most of the rationalists the power source of the human mechanism was God, but that for many of them God was the user, or operator, too, Whose eternal input was wisdom and Whose output included feces and urine.

In Classicism, animation was a matter of breath, life imparted by pneuma. Aether was established as a geographic heaven before becoming a conduit for esoteric communiqués. Aristotelian dynamics, which explained how and why things moved teleologically, in a type of physics of the soul, were powered through Medievalism by God, Who instilled in His flock *conatus*, or the will to exist, while His flock reacted with *impetus*, or the will to continue existing. But by the time Rationalism had developed its magnetic attraction to opposites, its perpetually pushing and pulling "desires"—between appetition (unconscious corporeal desire) and volition (conscious or willed desire)—science had animated itself. Physical motion was force applied to a thing to counteract its inertia; mental motion was force applied to language's inertia. Concentrations and distillations served both philosophical discourse and alchemy, in experiments that sought the essential energy of life: *virtus seminalis*, "seminal power."

Vitalism, dating from around 1600, classed matter based on its reaction to heat: When heated in a crucible, one type of matter changed form, though that form could be recovered (inorganic), whereas another type could not be recovered in form, due to the loss of a universal lifeforce (organic). Animals had this lifeforce in abundance; humans too, whose "mesmerism"—Franz Anton Mesmer (1734–1815)—was popularly regarded as animalistic. In 1781, Luigi Galvani's assistant touched a metal scalpel, charged with static electricity, to the exposed sciatic nerve of a frog. The amphibian sparked, twitched; Galvani deduced that the croaker itself was the source of the current. In 1800, Galvani's rival, Alessandro Volta, proved that animal electricity, or "galvanism," as he called it, was a myth, by obtaining the same effect without a specimen, just with alternating bars of copper and zinc separated by strips of cloth soaked in brine (to increase their conductivity): the "voltaic pile," or battery.

Rationalism was the theory, automation, the practice; the logic that replaced divine law dictated that the divinely given innards of any organism were technologically replaceable.

Automata: It's significant that the Enlightenment's first and best models of total attention also lacked free will, but it's just as significant that what Enlightenment humanity chose to do with its independence was to distract itself and play God, in the creation of creaky replica contraptions whose inferiority was only temporary—or so their inventors would claim. The automaton became the foremost creature of its time, a holotype or lectotype of humanity perfected—or as it wished to be perfected—free of infirmity, liberated from death.

To play with nature is to be a deiform child, a doll among dolls—and so it's understandable that the automation that matured into industrial machinery was first commercialized, or popularized, in toys. Jacques de Vaucanson's 1739 Digesting Duck gave the illusion of having an enginery metabolism, as if the grains it billed became the turd disburdened, though the duck had to be loaded with turd and the grains were collected for reuse in an adjacent compartment. The 1768–74 automata trinity of Swiss watchmaker Pierre Jaquet-Droz: The girl musician played an organ (five different melodies); the boy draftsman drew portraits (subjects included Louis XV, Cupid, and a dog); and the boy littérateur was able to write any text that didn't exceed forty characters (the text had to be coded onto a wheel one character at a time).

True automata demonstrated the mechanical's sophistication (and so, by extension, how much more sophisticated was the human creator—no automaton has yet created in and of itself). But it was the false automata that did more to excite curiosity about perception. The body, cut open and examined—modeled in plaster and wax for scale anatomical dummies whose removable vessels helped educate medical students in lieu of cadavers—laid bare humanity's most brute mechanics, its conduits of nerves, its systems of circulations and respiration, but a cross section of brain or a slice of outer eye or inner ear gave no evidence of an equivalent perceptual system. Instead, Wolfgang von Kempelen's 1770 chessplaying Turk beat the princes of Europe at the game of kings, though it was merely a shell, and crouched inside was its midget human director. Athanasius Kircher's Delphic Oracle, ca. 1651, was a statue whose movable mouth answered any questions posed. The voice, through a speaking tube, was Kircher's.

It was an impatience with the pedagogic substance of the *mille sescenti*—and too a skeptical regard for its style, with its propositions and lemmas and postulates and axioms all so foreign to the messy palimpsest of life—which led to its rejection by George Berkeley and David Hume. Rationalists had either ignored or been distressed by a strictly mental attention because for them all faculties of mind had to be physically or metaphysically locatable and this, whatever this was, remained the one semantic floater that refused to stay in its "organ" or "gland." Empiricists denied attention because for them all faculties of mind were themselves just mental conceptions—all things not merely sensations but conceptions of sensation.

Berkeley (1685–1753) would have denied the existence of this page, and asserted that it is only an idea in your mind, inexistent without being perceived. Hume (1711–76) would have noted that your perception is rather predicated on your drive to perceive this page, or just the idea or an idea of it, while your drive itself is only a matter of cost/benefit, to be settled either instinctively or by conditioning. The Empiricist idea that everything exists in your mind alone, or in your idea of mind, was just the secular transformation of the idea that everything exists in God's mind alone, or in His idea of mind, the wavering of either being the one thing inconceivable, or Apocalypse. This transformation being yet another instance of anthropomorphizing God by theomorphizing man—or else the other way around, with cause and effect counterpoised by perspective. Empiricism strips experience of all limbs not conceptual, and renders existence embryonic, life as a motile germinal "bundle"—Hume's word—of crudely interpreted sensations.

Étienne Bonnot de Condillac's 1754 *Treatise on the*

Sensations sought to prove that interpretation too was merely sensory, and accomplished this in a way that dramatized its reader along with its hero: a simulacrum or idol, a Dr. Frankenstein's monster—either the victim of a torture device like the bronze bull or iron maiden, or the device itself recast as a victim.

Condillac proposes a man, alive but imprisoned head to toe in marble. This carapace or exoskeleton prevents him from sensing, and his life will become reflexive or reflective only as the different panels—like heavy and shiny plates of knightly armor—are removed. First to go is the panel covering the nose, which then permits a sense of smell to the inmate. Condillac presents a rose; the olfactory sense is created but as the inmate has no sense of roses—of form, sound, color, or even of itself as a sensate being—he himself is created as smell; this smell being the sum of consciousness, he is this smell himself. Condillac then retracts the rose but the scent remains and even blooms in the inmate's memory (rather, the scent blooms to create his memory, to become his memory, and allows him to both attend and expect: the rose's retraction being the incipience of space-time). Other flowers are placed before the sniffing inmate, a violet, a jasmine, asafetida. The rose, being incomparable, had smelled neither good nor bad, but now, through memory, it can find its rank in the aromatic order, as the inmate determines his preferences. Memories, contrasted, become ideas. Comparison/contrast, or the attention to two or more ideas, gives rise to judgment, or discrimination. The sweetness of the rose and violet and jasmine, and the sourness of the asafetida, or the incarcerated man's memories or ideas of them, become abstracted into generalities of pleasure and pain. The incarcerated man himself, his sense of self, is nothing more than the concretization of such abstractions. Say taste and hearing and sight follow by a further removal of marble platelets. Tastes, sounds, and colors would join the smells perceived and the life of the prisoner would expectantly extend, broaden; yet the essential procedures comprising experience would remain. Colors, sounds, tastes, and smells would be mere sensations still, not yet referents to things external. To experience the external causes of sensation the prisoner must be allowed to touch, the tactile, or haptic, being the one sense that effectuates the ideas of size, density, and form in the development of his own conviction, or sense of being—a subject to himself and object to the universe.

8. THEATER, THE DIALECTIC
(OF THE INDIVIDUAL), THE FICTION
(OF SELFHOOD), TYPES OF TYPES

Our themes circle like model planets—like the automata of monks and Moors and Jews and Nativity livestock orbiting the faces of the astronomical clocks in Strasbourg, Dijon, Prague, Venice, Messina, and Bern, as death's skeleton—a japing *jacquemart* in cloaked disguise—tolls the bell to rouse the skull from its dreaming.

Or else—curtain up—consider the figures' themes: statuesque allegories for Beauty, Wisdom, Intellect, and Truth perched atop columns in the midst of a misty garden that might also be a cemetery. They're nude, or they aren't because they're not real, or they are real, just not cognizant of their nudity. Other figures are stilled toward the rear in a *tableau vivant*, still others painted onto, as, the backdrop: staffage. The cemetery is a set. This is a theater and you are an audience.

Music starts, a march for flute and drum, and dancers enter, in costumes immediately "read": merchants, farmers, shepherds—sheep. Others rush onstage as if refugees from war—this ruined cemetery must've been a battlefield. The dancers are survivors, dancing because they've survived, in historically accurate wardrobe and steps. They move before the statues in a mood that would've been propitiatory in Antiquity, but here is merely instructive—they're instructing their divinities.

In time, the statues are also moving: first an arm; then another arm; legs are uprooted from their pedestals; plaster turns to muscle; marble turns to the marbling of fat. Finally even the flesh-colored backdrop falls into flesh, and all the paintings come alive and join the living statues to twirl around and around like they're signing their autographs in air, while the pit orchestra decrescendos into a dirge.

It's always preferable to go to the theater than to discuss dialectics. Especially if the hope is to better understand "the individual," and if the boulevards outside the theaters have turned into proscenia themselves—theaters of rebellion, venues of debate over the authorization of rights (whether they're natural, or given by God, earned, or granted by state, whether they're transferable not just between France and America, for instance, but universally). Individuality has become the newest self, or the newest proxy for the self's understanding. If a thing cannot be looked at or listened to directly, other approaches have to be found: duction, analogy, metonymy (part for the whole/whole for the part), mimesis (incarnation in another).

Johann Gottlieb Fichte (1762–1814) defined the tripartite dialectic of thesis, antithesis, synthesis; the philosophical analogue of a systasis in the arts: in music, the sonata's "exposition" finding complication in the "development," only to resolve itself again in the home key, with the "recapitulation"; in painting, the X grid framing the resolutions of "length" and "width," whose intersection disturbs with a false appraisal of apex, or "depth"; while in drama, the three-act play—which introduces the protagonist, complicates his or her actions with the reactions of an antagonist, then leaves them both to their respective, comedic and tragic, conclusions—is too paltry a parody or satire of the structure of daily life to even consider as phenomenological. Editing Fichte, Georg Wilhelm Friedrich Hegel (1770–1831) shifted the weight of the antithesis from a counter-idea, or countervailing consciousness, to "reality"—the individual implicated in an empirically shared awareness. The world as it is would be the veritable development or depth of human experience—as the keys don't modulate but crash dissonantly; the counterpoint tangles into chordal knots; and with smeary Prussian blues the dewy plot of a *fête galante* dims into the *dämmerung*.

Hegel regarded history as the progress of a person becoming himself by dint of testing his theses, or self, against reality's antitheses, or everything that wasn't the self, which process would force both to revise their beings toward greater, or higher, or otherwise tralatitious synthesis. However, only the self can be conscious that every grouping to which it belongs is experiencing this same process, symbiotically: the nation-state, the empire. Russia strains to become more Russian; Germany to be better at being German.[8]

Each individual, in what he chooses to see and hear, in what he consumes, opposes himself to all the forces not himself and hopefully profits from the bargain. Life, then, can become a measure or frame, an event of self-composition, or curation. The mind can be a *Wunderkammer*, a museum of the self, where the exhibits

8. The development of a political entity recapitulates the development of its citizens, of humanity. This concept of Hegel's friend Friedrich von Schelling (1775–1854) was inverted and transposed into biological terms by Ernst Haeckel (1834–1919): "Ontogeny recapitulates phylogeny"; the development of an individual organism recapitulates the development of its species. Haeckel's biologizing was taken as evidence that every recapitulation was directed toward betterment or perfection. Subsequently humanity would convince itself it was able to manipulate the process: By practicing grafting and pedigree breeding, on itself, each improvement would mean more glory for the Volk.

change by the whim or the visitor. Which is also to suggest, in depressing terms, that when you become an individual, you risk becoming more or less than an individual: a parochial citizen, a nationalist, or just a mobile advertisement for your own "personality."

Hegel intuited an absolutism to be sought in the synthesis of subjective experience and objective world. It was left to Mozart and Watteau to attain it. Goethe and Voltaire tried their bests. Ideals like the subjective and objective, the true and false, as conceptions distinct from "fiction"—all were better dealt with in concerti (the piano or violin resisting integration into the reality of the orchestra), or portraiture (the figure either actually Pierrot, or just an actor playing Pierrot), or in the ductive and empirical languages of philosophy.

Instead, eighteenth-century literature was best concerned with identities—which might be defined, in a Hegelian sense, as the thoughts by which a person opposes knowledge. Such is the plot of the coming-of-age novel, in which a handsome young man typically spurned by a handsome young woman who's opted for marrying another, or death—sets out to find alternate meaning in life, which means, of course, himself. The *Bildungsroman* is often a closeted *Künstlerroman* or artist's novel, as its protagonists are often the narrators (first person), and the narration frequently proceeds by letters addressed to friends or diary entries strictly for self, all of whom are metafictional proxies for the reader. Metafiction, literature conscious of its own literariness, is the belated sibling to canon and fugue, and mirror-play *mise en abyme*. But unlike in music or painting, autoawareness in literature must be accomplished

596

in words, and so is not just acknowledged but also critiqued. Characters assume their own lives, quite apart from the stated intentions of their authors, and assume to comment on authorial plans and offer alternative prospects; their behaviors—obreptions, subreptions, editing peer characters (even if due only to the opportunities of epistolary structure), and passing among texts (Tobias Smollett's Roderick Random, and Samuel Richardson's Pamela, appearing as guests at a ball in John Kidgell's *The Card*, 1755)—none are difficult to read as drafts of equivalent liberties in life.

If Enlightenment existence took on many of the qualities of a book, or of the theater, misconduct in life had more immediate, social if not legal, consequences. The Church had told you how to live, feudalism told you how to live. You were a lord, good for you. You were a vassal, too bad; now go take a stroll in the Tiergarten (formerly the hunting ground of the Electors of Brandenburg, opened to the public in 1742), or in the Tuileries (formerly the private garden of the Medicis, a public park in 1792), money in the pocket.

Now you were liberated. An inhabitant of the British Empire had to settle for being an alternate definition of "subject," while the French *individuel*, between the Thirty Years' War and Napoleon, went from meaning "indivisible," as in numerically singular, to "separateness," or "distinction." You were a parishioner, an employee, and perhaps even a citizen too, if you were lucky enough to be French or an American Caucasian. You were lost. Not you specifically but also you specifically. That was the point. You were a character protesting that you were an author protesting that you were only you, ink and paper or of materials equally fragile. "Individualism" struggles into English in 1840, courtesy of the translation of the second volume of Alexis de Tocqueville's *Democracy in America*. De Tocqueville contrasts *Individualisme* with *Égoïsme*—the former a "mature," "calm" severance, the latter "a passionate and exaggerated love of self."[9] The book's first translator, Henry Reeve, appends a note to this new term—individualistically: "I adopt the expression of the original, however strange it may seem to the English ear, partly because it illustrates the remark on the introduction of general terms into democratic language which was made in a preceding chapter, and partly because I know of no English word exactly equivalent to the expression. The chapter itself defines the meaning attached to it by the author."

Attention is not just what you consider, but who you consider yourself to be. The defining feature of democracy is not the poetry of its liberties; rather, it's that such liberties encourage people to live as though the heroes of novels, the novels of their lives. But not everyone can be a Young Werther, let alone a Goethe. Few deserve to be even Eckermanns. The majority of every age is just a head at the rear of a mob, intact though disconcerted, between the execution of Charles I (1649) and the

9. De Tocqueville writes, in his first translation: "Egotism originates in blind instinct: individualism proceeds from erroneous judgment more than from depraved feelings; it originates as much in the deficiencies of the mind as in the perversity of the heart. Egotism blights the germ of all virtue; individualism, at first, only saps the virtues of public life; but, in the long run, it attacks and destroys all others, and is at length absorbed in downright egotism. Egotism is a vice as old as the world, which does not belong to one form of society more than to another: individualism is of democratic origin, and it threatens to spread in the same ratio as the equality of conditions."

guillotine slaughter of *la Terreur* (1793–94).

Within that span, London and Paris especially became as crowded as their fictions—as supporting characters and their descendants rushed to divert service from a lord or God to the Lord our God of capital; as they apprenticed themselves to masters, joined guilds, and escaped their births; as they died and were buried by a different demographic than the one by which they were raised. Society required an abridgement for this—an abbreviatory technique that communicated the essence of a person with the efficiency of the antiquated sumptuary decrees (in Elizabethan England only the royal family could wear "any silk of the color of purple," and only knights and barons could wear "spurs, swords, rapiers, daggers, skeans, woodknives or hangers, buckles or girdles"; while the color yellow—used in hats and badges—identified Jews in the German cities and throughout Austro-Hungary, until it was retired by Joseph II only in 1781).

With the collapse of feudalism, fixed rank determined by heredity became changeable position determined by commerce—each position to its persuasion. How much you had was who you were and how much you were both. Your politics, to say nothing of your free speech, would follow.

The ancient estates would be machined into "classes," and though by the time of Karl Marx (1818–83) they'd manifested as credible gradations, typing everyone from bourgeois burgher to proletarian, their origins weren't in industry, but in literary efficiency: in David Ricardo (1772–1823), a Sephardic Jew turned British economist, applying the abstract notion of "labor" to the humanity that made concrete, steel, and textiles.

Individuality, by contrast, was a private matter: You

might be an individual to your spouse, or family, or intimate correspondents, but in public you were subsumed. What followed was a reengagement of typology.

In the theater of Antiquity, masks denoted the roles. Aristophanes developed the boastful *alazon*, his ironic sidekick the *eiron*, and the fool, the *bomolochos*. Theophrastus's *The Characters* lists thirty varieties of character: Lalia, the Talkative; Logopoiia, the Fabricator; Authadeia, the Unsociable; Anaisthesia, the Absent-Minded. Menander wrote plays predicated on types: *The Heiress*, *The Misogynist*. Plautus's depictions of miserliness and lechery—his clever slave, *servus callidus*; foolish slave, *servus stultus*; and swaggart soldier, *Miles Gloriosus*—developed into the Pierrots and Harlequins (the servants, or *zanni*), the Pantaloni and Dottori (the elderly masters, or *vecchi*), the bounding Capitani and young innamorati, of the Commedia dell'Arte. Giovanni Boccaccio (ca. 1350) and Geoffrey Chaucer (ca. 1390) furthered this typification through political parody or satire. Christopher Marlowe (1564–93) and William Shakespeare (1564–1616) found individuality more readily, writing stock roles but for a recurring cast that would—typically—subvert them. The figure of the *alazon/Miles Gloriosus* reappeared after Waterloo as the fictional Napoleonic soldier Nicolas Chauvin, patriarch of "chauvinism," a French patriot before a partisan of gender. The courtesans of Antiquity and the Commedia took positions as ingénues and soubrettes in the music hall and opera, their roles essentially puppetry—trite marionettes, strings timeworn but still attached.

Meanwhile, "scientific" characterization—"typology"—comprises an altogether more sinister literature. Throughout Antiquity, literary and scientific systems of type were patently the same. With genotype inconceivable, phenotype was all, including personality. Hippocrates codified personality as being influenced by fluids, or "humors": blood, yellow and black bile, phlegm. Galen split the human temperaments into hot/cold and dry/wet, based on interpolations of the elements: Earth, Water, Air, Fire. Choleric men have broad jaws, sharp noses, compact builds; ambitious, active, dominant, they become politicians, generals, murderers. Melancholic men have square or rectangular heads, thin lips, lean physiques; passive, submissive, they're independent but fragile, artists to a fault. Phlegmatic men are stout, dimpled, florid; kind, affectionate, but weak and shy, they can be trained into wonderful husbands. But sanguine men might be the most desirable: their heads oval, builds moderate, hands strong but delicate, hair ample; they're sensitive, sociable, though easily distracted, and at risk of becoming alcoholics and smokers.

Combining rationalist science with superstition, Erasmus Darwin (1731–1802) suggested that animals could bequeath to their descendants the abilities they'd individually acquired, thereby improving the species. Jean-Baptiste Lamarck (1744–1829) adapted himself to this position and applied it to his theory of "transmutation," a term he inherited from alchemy. One of Darwin's grandsons, Charles (1809–82), never explicitly denied the inheritance of acquired traits, but chose to address himself instead to the processes of natural selection. It was left to another of Darwin's grandsons, Francis Galton, to apply Lamarckism to humanity, in the hopes of ascertaining whether genius could be nurtured into nature and passed along, while insanity and debility eradicated. In founding his science of eugenics, in 1883, Galton compiled genealogies of accomplished families, including his own. He studied twins sundered and raised in different environments, and experimented with graphology, phrenology, anthropometry, directed fertility, and succeeded in identifying, by superimposition of photographs, the composite or "average" "criminal," "tubercular," "cripple," and "Jew." Physician John Hunter (1728–93) believed Africans—"negroids"—were white at birth, but became blistered by the desert. Physician Benjamin Rush (1746–1813) believed "negroidism" to be a form of benign but heritable leprosy. Ethnologist Georges Cuvier (1769–1832) identified three races; James Pritchard (1786–1848) seven; Charles Pickering (1805–78) eleven, and Louis Agassiz (1807–73) twelve. Georges-Louis Leclerc, Comte of Buffon (1707–88), prophesied evolution if only by promulgating its opposite: a theory of devolution, which posited blackness as the degenerate result of poor diet and housing.

While racists charted pigmentation, a more superficial skin was being retailored. From 1801, fashion was produced by a machine that, after it was threaded, didn't require much humanity of any color for its operation. Joseph Marie Charles *dit* Jacquard's programmable loom, which encoded textile patterns by perforations on cards, was the warp and weft of Charles Babbage's Analytical Engine (described 1837), a contraption that allowed data to be encrypted on cards, and calculated. Babbage's machine, in turn, was the prototype of the Hollerith Tabulator, the human loom or punch-card machine that made its debut with the 1890 United States census. Because its inventor, Herman Hollerith (1860–1929), had been allocated the use of Treasury Department boxes, he commissioned cards the same size as paper bills (3.25 by 7.375 inches, at the time). Each person was allotted a card, and each card was marked as that person was marked; holes punched, keyed, to clarify every miscegenation: "mulatto, quadroon, octoroon," "crippled, maimed, deformed." Hollerith censuses followed in Canada, Russia, Austria, and Germany. By the first Nazi census of 1933, the textile industry had stitched its last brown shirt, and by the second of 1939, it was producing red armbands with black swastikas and white armbands with blue stars. The yellow-star breast patches followed. The Tabulator went on to schedule the rail deportations east into Poland, in a strange rearrival at origins: Hollerith claimed his device had been inspired by a trip he took through the American West, by the train conductors validating their passengers' tickets. The first hole the point of departure, the last just a pit, a mass grave.

I. DOUBLES, LAVATER, REDOUBLED DOUBLES, MAREY

Even art was affected by typing, not just by the distinctions between media but by the distinctions within them too, with paintings especially ranked by degree of achievement—which determination was informed as much by technical difficulty as by a work's institutional utility and social prestige—in hierarchies derived from the Renaissance but formally bolstered by eighteenth-century art salons and academies: Historical paintings were superior (but within that distinction, religious or mythological works were superior to renderings of more contemporary history); followed by portrait and genre or domestic-scene painting; followed by landscapes and still lifes. The less the painting depicted the human, the less it was respected; Italianate concerns for *imitare,* or the revelation of essential character, trumping *ritrarre,* or rote engrossment of the still and lifeless. It might be remembered, however, that the Renaissance developed this hierarchy only to put painting on an equal footing with the most inhuman and most static of art forms, architecture, in every column of which a sculpture resided.

According to Pliny the Elder, the Greek painters Zeuxis and Parrhasius once held a contest to decide which of them was the master of realistic or naturalistic painting. Zeuxis painted grapes, which birds mistook for real and ripe and flocked to them, to peck. Parrahasius's entry was apparently concealed behind a curtain, which Zeuxis demanded be tugged aside to finalize his victory, but the cloth was just whatever the Greek term is for trompe l'oeil.

Ovid's myth of Pygmalion, retold throughout the

Enlightenment, unites two valiant if vainglorious desires: Pygmalion's desire to bring his statue to womanly life is traditionally treated as climactic, but it's his penultimate desire that remains the more relatable—the desire to make a statue of an ideal, an apparition of perfection (there's no reason to work so hard for anything less than perfection).

Another Ovidian myth: A man notices his reflection, falls in love with it, reaches for it, and upon merging with the water becomes a solipsist. To contemporize, turn the water into a mirror, which preserves an essential symmetry but reverses the clockface's hands. The first contemporary Narcissus, the Narcissus of the cities: the double.

The double is a paradoxical artwork: superior, inferior—an unreal and unnatural replica of you who is also more real and more natural than you simultaneously. The double poses a singular threat: You don't have to fear the fall into solipsism (your double overturns the conviction of your singularity), but you don't have to be scared of narcissism either (whatever you admire in yourself, you detest in your double); the danger does not lie with you anymore, but is rather completely out of your control. Your double can do what it wants, when and where it wants, leaving you only the choice of attempting to kill it or yourself (murder as suicide v. suicide as murder). Or another option would be to become othered yet again; to change your name and domicile, your family and friends and face, and become a third-party alterity by dint of guilt; because—as in the best double literature of the nineteenth century—your second self was not encountered in the reflection of an emporium window or in a carriage passing by but was willed, projected: Your double is your own fault, utterly.

You've occasioned a rift with your supposedly unitary soul, perhaps with the help of a drug or intoxicant; your double, nurtured by that cleavage, escapes through that cleavage to explore its source and returns—if each of you is strong enough to survive without the other—to a reconciliation of moral and ethical duality (Robert Louis Stevenson's *Strange Case of Dr. Jekyll and Mr. Hyde*, 1886). Or perhaps you've engendered a double only to inhabit a socioeconomic class you the original cannot (Mark Twain's *The Prince and the Pauper*, 1881); or to have a career you cannot due to timidity or ineptitude (Fyodor Dostoyevsky's *The Double*, 1846); or because of legal strictures or a general propriety (Edgar Allan Poe's *William Wilson*, 1839). The generation of doubles—your resurrection of apersonality that wandered into your life from the fogged woods of folklore only to wander out again in flashier clothing and whistling, spending money and time neither of you have, checking into grand hotels in every European capital under the alias of the *doppelgänger*, or *sosie*—is the conscious admission that every book's protagonist is also its antagonist, an unconscious transference of every literate person's suspicion of themselves.

Before the age of twenty-five, there was nothing I would've found more improbable than that I would make even the slightest inquiry into, let alone that I would write a book about, physiognomy. At the time I was neither inclined to read about, nor even make the even vaguest observations on, the subject. The extreme sensitivity of my nerves caused me, however, to experience certain emotions upon encountering certain faces, which emotions remained even when the faces had departed. I, frequently, formed an intuitive judgment according

to these first impressions, and was laughed at, ashamed, abashed, and became cautious. Years passed before I again dared, impelled by similar impressions, to venture similar opinions. In the meantime, I occasionally sketched the face of a friend, whom by chance I'd been observing. I had from my earliest youth a strong propensity for drawing, especially for drawing portraits, although I had but meager talent and drive. By this practice, however, my latent feelings were gradually revealed. The various proportions, features, similitudes, and varieties, of the human countenance, became increasingly apparent to me. It happened that, on two successive days, I sketched two faces, the features of which bore a remarkable resemblance. This awakened my attention, and my wonder increased when I obtained certain proofs that these p ersons were as similar in character as in feature.
(From Johann Kaspar Lavater's 1775–78 *Essays on Physiognomy*)

You are not just interior structures—your biochemistry—you are also your exterior forms. Not eidola, auras, phantoms, or specters just yet but your nose, your chin, your skull in its ancestral guises. This was the determination of Aristotle, revived by Renaissance art and again by Enlightenment philosophy, which translated the conceit into "hylomorphism": the doctrine that things and even people exist primarily as the shapes by which they're encountered; appearances not just predicative but predictive, fateful.

The eighteenth century twinned this science of surfaces: The study of the individual by gesture and voice timbre, and by facial expressions, was pathognomy; the study of the unexpressed face, the resting visage deprived of its aspiration and disciplined training—which

607

lets inalienable nature communicate unimpeded—was physiognomy, whose master was a Swiss poet, Lavater.

Above are two plates from *Essays on Physiognomy*. In the plate at bottom right—following silhouettes, or "shades," of Moses Mendelssohn, Georg Ludwig Spalding, Christoph Friedrich Nicolai, and Friedrich Eberhard von Rochow—Lavater, as if he's exhausted famous friends, has left a record of himself.

He writes:

> This shade, though imperfect, is readily known. It must pass without comment, or rather the commentary is before the world, is in this book. Let that speak. I am silent.

But then to his shade's immediate left is another, unlabeled, and the anonymity is not a typo.

Of this figure Lavater observes only:

> One of the generally pleasing masculine profiles. Conceal the underside of the chin and a chance at greatness would be perceptible, except that greater variation in the entire outline is lacking, especially in the nose and forehead. The choleric and phlegmatic man is visible in the whole— especially in the eyebrows, nose, lower chin—as also are integrity, fidelity, goodness, and complaisance.

Upon being called to attend to this unidentified figure, you wonder if this man—possessed of such "integrity, fidelity, goodness, and complaisance"—might be the friend Lavater wrote about in the paragraph originally quoted, "whom by chance I'd been observing." But this just reinforces your confusion as to why Lavater chose to abandon his account of this man with whom he'd recovered his predilection for physiognomy in favor of an account of two sketches whose subjects might have borne a "remarkable resemblance," but whose common character is similarly left without description—blank.

The double is the duplicated self, the progenitor of mass production. If all products of a certain use resemble one another, it's because all means of production resemble one another, because all consumers are essentially disseminations of a single consumer, a phantasmagoria manufactured by advertisement in order that demand can manage supply.

The double—even as vampire or werewolf—is humanized capital, an entity that before being taken as a

609

demographic symbol by business represented a human straining against time; a way for its mortal original to work more, play more, produce more, consume more, without resorting to slavery or serfdom.

In this sense the double becomes a fantasy of attention; the lawless or recklessly improper copy the personification of notoriety, which only an original can appreciate as fame. The press carries exploits not yours, but yours; reputation is protected by a mask, or by a totally ulterior alter ego whose chivalry or charity justifies any societal latitude or erotic indulgence: Baroness Emma Orczy's *The Scarlet Pimpernel* (1903) being the first book to turn an anonymous or second identity into a prerequisite of true heroism.

To double yourself is to become a franchise, a genre, and it is no coincidence that the literature of doubles so seamlessly sequels itself, between the developments of photography (1820s) and film (1880s)—to the point of integration or a resingularity, with manipulated doubling or the sequencing of pictures bearing minute discrepancies being the very essence of the moving-picture medium. Germany produced much of this celluloid, though more credit might go to the French reaction: the appearance, between 1890 and 1900, of the paramnesiac terms *déjà vu* and *déjà entendu*, "already seen," "already heard." Painting, drawing—as in the physical drawing out of an inner persona—was paraphrase; but photography and film were quotation.

Chronophotography of Facial Expression—With the camera we used, although it has only one purpose, a subject can be photographed at a near distance, and show no alteration in perspective, no matter the duration of the photographic series. At present, it is the only type capable of affording a series of photographs that shows in every detail the changes in facial expression, the various movements of the hands, and the different positions of the feet in walking. It would be interesting to follow in this way all the transitions between a scarcely perceptible smile and a hearty laugh, and to still the characteristic expressions of surprise, anger, and other emotions. The great difficulty is to find a subject capable of performing these various expressions in a perfectly natural manner. Most people would produce only a grin or grimace. Clever actors would no doubt be more successful in assuming the various emotional expressions, and the method might even be useful to them in their own work. But what chronophotography renders most perfectly is the movement that accompanies the act of articulation.

[...]

Now from an artistic point of view. What is to be the outcome of this new method of reproducing the movements of speech?

Painters, to date, have apparently paid no attention to the subject. In the most animated scenes, it is the general expression of the features that conveys an idea of what the individuals are supposed to be saying, and the same holds true in sculpture. Rude [see below] has twice attempted to represent, if not actual words, at least a cry of imprecation or command.

We wanted very much to know what sort of expression a man's features would assume when he uttered a loud exclamation. The attendant at the Physiological Station was the subject of our experiment. He was placed in front of the apparatus, and told to yell at us several times in succession at the top of his voice. The series of photographs thus obtained showed the periodic repetition of facial expression, but the muscles of expression were so curiously

611

contracted that the appearance was rather that of an ugly grimace—and yet simply to watch him there was nothing extraordinary in the man's expression. The peculiarity of the photographs was due to the fact that they stilled exceedingly fleeting expressions of the face—movements essentially of gradual transition, none of which were seen as isolated expressions.

Let us place the series of photographs in a zoetrope and watch them as they pass in succession before the eyes, with the instrument turning at a convenient speed. All the strangeness suddenly disappears, and all we see is a man articulating in a perfectly natural manner. What does this fact imply? Is it not that the ugly is only the unknown, and that truth seen for the first time offends the eye?

(From Étienne-Jules Marey's *Movement*, 1894)

Before French physiologist Marey developed chronophotography, images depicting consecutive thoroughgoing motions could be presented only discretely, in strips of stills that would be motioned—would restore their subjects to motion—through their attachment to a wheel that could be spun both in and against narrative order (fast-forward, rewind), to the edification of both scholarly and recreational squinting (the zoetrope, 1833; the phenakistoscope and stroboscope, both 1841; the praxinoscope, 1877).

Marey's chronophotography ventured to record various stages of movement on a single photographic surface (inspiring Eadweard Muybridge's celebrated 1870s' stop-motions, which proved Marey's assertion that galloping horses spend intervals during which all four of their hooves are off the ground). Marey took his best photo trophies with an 1882 camera of his own design, equipped to take up to twelve frames per second in a single exposure. The lens itself was mounted between a butt and a sight barrel; the film was chambered up top; a trigger below—"a photogun," as Marey called it—stilling a copy of motion whose life continued, flying, swimming, fluent, phaseless and unfazed.

Motion provides attentional context; so too does proximity. What appears still from far away is far from still up close; emotional expression varies culturally, linguistically, generationally.

For example, Rude. In the excerpt quoted above, Marey mentions François Rude (1784–1885), a sculptor celebrated for his *La Marseillaise*, also called *Departure of the Volunteers of 1792*, a relief completed between 1833 and 1836 that adorns the Arc de Triomphe, on the side facing the Champs Élysées (opposite Corot's *The Triumph of Napoleon*). The sculpture depicts French citizens half stripped to the buff, half in Classical armor, being led into battle by the Roman personification of war, Bellona, and it's her expression that Marey might be citing as "a cry of imprecation or command."

Taken in situ, passing through, passing under the arch—that might be the effect of Rude's heightened immobile attempt at mobilization. But pried from context, isolated and brought nearer as bust, the sense you get is one of unalloyed shock—of a sexless witness about to be stabbed or shot, about to be or already violated.

10. *DUCTUS INTERRUPTUS*, TYPE-WRITE AND TYPEWRITE, WAVE-PARTICLE THEORY OF LANGUAGE, REACTION TIME (*WRITING B*)

Ductus, in the sense understood by the Church copyists, means "flow"—the stylization of language on the page and in time. This flow, of the font of the hand, of its genic rhythms and ranges of motion, was interrupted by the font—by types, typefaces.

Between handwriting and printing there can be no ligature—no connecting swoop or jot. Once hand-compositing—the manual ordering of printed texts, by the letter—gave way to mechanical means, and once the serif—the small upturns and downturns at the extremities of letters, a natural feature of handwriting, artificially reproduced in early printing—gave way to the sans serif, the ligatures went too: *æ* and *oe*, once conveniences, had become singularly distracting.

While in Renaissance Europe, the hand conditioned the press, in Puritanical America the press conditioned the hand. The eighteenth century's foremost formal hand was called Copperplate (John Hancock's 55-degree-slanting calligraphy, as well as the relative cacographies of the Declaration of Independence's other signatories), named after the etched copper plates from which handwriting instruction "manuals" were made. The nineteenth-century methods of Platt Rogers Spencer (supple but intricate, based on leaf shapes, tree shapes) and Austin Palmer (spare and angular, based on utilitarian motions) were both intended to inculcate through rote practice good character by good penmanship. While Spencer's, which was taught in primary schools, sought to improve students by the highest moral and aesthetic criteria, and Palmer's, taught in commercial courses, sought to do the same for businesses, end-user results were the same: The democratic proliferation of standardizations precipitated the collapse of standardization, though mechanistic philosophies continued in technological iterations.[10]

Modern text is typically typed when it should be "laced" or "plaited": Latin's *texo* means "to weave." Though the typewriter was invented by journalist Christopher Sholes, printer Samuel Soule, and lawyer (and inventor of the mechanical plow) Carlos Glidden in 1868, it's not a coincidence that the only entity with the ability to mass manufacture the product was the sewing-machine division of Remington & Sons, who made the best rifles to ever target the West (a fact straight out of dime-fiction).

Before word processing was for women it was for the disabled: Hans Rasmus Johann Malling-Hansen (1835–90), a pastor and head of an institute for deaf-mutes in Copenhagen, invented a *skrivekugle*, or "writing ball," with the hope that his patients might be able to express themselves faster with fingers on buttons than with fingers in air (sign language), though his interest shifted toward commerce when the Nordic Telegraphy Company purchased a few units (including one equipped for Morse code). Its geodesic keyboard—the keys arranged in a dome of staggered rows—was supposed to allow the blind to type by touch alone (considerably

10. John Pemberton, a druggist from Georgia, invented a nonalcoholic brand of coca wine in 1886. The accountant for the Pemberton Chemical Company, Frank Robinson, trained in Spencer, labeled the ledgers for this product *Coca-Cola*, which at the time and until it acquired its ®, read as exceedingly direct, even plain.

more difficult on a flat keyboard).

The mostly blind, syphilitic Friedrich Nietzsche bought a Malling Hansen writing ball, for 375 reichsmarks (plus shipping and handling), in 1882. One of the first texts he produced was a poem:

> *SCHREIBKUGEL IST EIN DING GLEICH MIR:*
> *VON EISEN*
> *UND DOCH LEICHT ZU VERDREHN ZUMAL AUF*
> *REISEN. GEDULD UND TAKT MUSS REICHLICH*
> *MAN BESITZEN UND FEINE FINGERCHEN, UNS ZU*
> *BENUETZEN.*

> *THE WRITING BALL IS A THING LIKE ME:*
> *OF IRON*
> *YET EASILY TWISTED WHILE TRAVELING.*
> *AMPLE PATIENCE AND TACT ARE REQUIRED*
> *IN ADDITION TO FINE FINGERING, FOR OUR USE.*

Nietzsche believed that this new way of writing influenced the writing itself: "Our writing tools are also working on our thoughts." As his syphilis worsened, so did his hand, degenerating into a spiky hermetic script, which caused him to rely on the writing ball exclusively. Nietzsche's style became retooled, aphoristically—stop—with a *Takt* (the word also means "stroke" or "tempo") reminiscent of telegraphy. The writing ball received his thoughts, and transmitted them too—From: the messiness of mind To: a product as neutral in appearance as a form letter. Fit for the files. Archivable. Immediately posthumous.

The mind had lined the page (slab, tablet)—or the stilus did, ruling, creating rules, replaced by the lead plummet, replaced by ink—until 1770, when John Tetlow,

British, patented a ruling machine, and thereafter paper was manufactured preruled. In 1844, Charles Fenerty, Canadian, and Friedrich Gottlob Keller, German, independently succeeded in making cheaper paper from pulped wood. Businesses that produced paper went on to diversify margins and line quantity/spacing, even while businesses that consumed paper advocated for standards. Characters were to be contained between two lines of uniform height, unless the paper was to be used in handwriting instruction, in which case there might be an additional line, at middle, indicating where to dot an "i" or cross a "t."

But the typewriter marked a return to purity (assaulted by noisy clickery). The page was a place not just to express but to set, typeset, yourself—freedom in fictility; each sitting a concrete poem:

MERKE — SPÜREN, VERNEHMEN

AUFMERKEN — SICH HINWENDEN ZU, DABEIBLE
IBEN, GESPANNT WARTEN, LAUERN

BE-MERKEN — VORBLICKEN–ÜBERSICHT, »FREI«

AB-MERKEN → MAL FESTNEHMEN

SICH MERKEN ← MERKMAL BEHALTEN, AUFBE
WAHREN, VERZEICHNEN,
VERMERKEN

VERMERKEN — IN MAL FESTHALTEN

BEMERKBAR MACHEN — KUND GEBEN.

TO NOTICE — TO SENSE, TO PERCEIVE

TO ATTEND TO — TO TURN TOWARD, TO STAY WITH,
ANXIOUS WAITING, LURKING

TO NOTE — *TO PREVIEW–OVERVIEW, "FREE"*

TO DE-NOTE → TO PREHEND FIRMLY AS SIGN

TO RETAIN ← TO KEEP TRACK, STORE, REGISTER,
NOTE DOWN

TO MARK DOWN — TO FIX AS A SIGN

TO MAKE NOTICEABLE — TO MAKE KNOWN.

Above are Martin Heidegger's notes for a 1939 lecture on the language-development theories of Johann Gottfried Herder (*Vom Wesen der Sprache, On the Essence of Language*). Their presentation is inextricable from the process of their creation; they could only have been created on a typewriter; they could only have been published as typed; only Heidegger could have typed them, and interpreted the mnemonic of their formatting. Each line marked an idea to be expanded upon, to be expended in breath.

Heidegger had spent WWI typing meteorological reports and censoring mail for the Wehrmacht. He spent WWII—the war of the *Schreibtischmörder*, the "desk-murderer," whose brief was to kill by typewriter alone, with deportation lists and Zyklon B orders—as a Nazified professor at the University of Freiburg, pondering the comparatively trivial effects of technology. In

1942–43, he delivered *Parmenides*, a lecture on the Eleatics that deals peripherally with the "hand," and how it discloses itself in the "act" (which includes the act of writing): "Man acts [*handelt*] through the hand [*Hand*], as the hand is, together with the word, the fundamental distinction of man." To Heidegger, the hand is humanity's basic greeting, farewell, and unspoken "word," which shakes to seal a vow or oath, and shapes the tools that, as if to return the clasp, shape humanity. By 1949, though, in *The Question Concerning Technology*, the hand has been converted to its use-value, five fingers' worth of labor. *The thing* that effectuates this conversion is the typewriter—a novelty halfway between a "tool" (handheld) and a "machine" (powered). The typewriter reframes the hand by concealing both the hand-as-script (handwriting), and the hand-as-word (speech), behind a black ribbon of inhuman uniformity.

Technology, to Heidegger, is whatever directs existence toward utility. Its expression is solely in its "enframing" (*Ge-Stell*), or the way by which technology recontextualizes all objects and even subjects by function: stones enframed as cutters of stones, rocks as producers of fire—a painting framed as a material asset, music measured only to rally morale or seduce (reproduced images, and recorded music, popularized these intentions). It follows, logically, that all frames are reversible, and might be hung upside-down: A man makes a thing, until the thing remakes the man. For Heidegger, the only way out of these co-instrumentalizing binds is *Gelassenheit*—"releasement"—to accept technology's outward convenience, but refuse its inward reconfiguration. How to do this, however, he never explains.

The typewriters used by Heidegger and Nietzsche

were not quite the same. Nietzsche's ball keyboard was positioned atop the paper, obscuring synchronic visual confirmation of the strokes. Text was checked on the Remington only by lifting its shutters. It was the Underwood of 1897 that made text visible the moment it was typed—turning writing into reading, or editing—but not even that provided a substitute *ductus*. Angelo Beyerlen, first typewriter dealer in Germany: "The spot where the sign to be written *occurs*," is "precisely what ... *cannot* be seen."

With the typewriter, handedness was outsourced/downsized to the fingers, which cramped less easily, or dispersed the cramping—the thumb that opposes man and ape, the forefinger that accuses, the middle that gestures rudely, the ring that betroths, the pinkie almost vestigial, useless. The self would be turned into a secretary, and secretary into a job. Mark Twain's *Life on the Mississippi*, 1883, might be profitably read not just as fictionalized autobiography, written for money in a rush, but also as the first work delivered to a publisher in "typescript"—though Twain left its typing to an amanuensis.

Life, then, existed in multiple forms, in multiple locations: Twain's own handwritten manuscript (a fictionalized autobio of the final bound product), the typed copy made by his secretary, Harry Clarke (the first man to type in what would become an almost totally female sector), Twain's hand corrections to the copy, which Clarke either retyped or sent straight to the publisher, James Osgood & Co., which set it. Galley proofs sloughed through the post, for further corrections. The text was reset. The book, at last, was published.

Though it might be stressed what setting, and resetting, meant: the laborious arrangement of text by the character, by the cast-metal sort—by hand. This process had been aided by the *cliché*, metal sorts containing commonplace phrases, "for instance," "for example," "as it were," "for that matter"—rather, their translated equivalents, as the cliché was first defined in France. The sound made when a phrase was cast, when the hot hackneyed metal words were dumped from their matrix into water to cool, was said to be, in French, *cliché—clich, clich, cliché*. That steaming onomatopoeia had acquired sense by 1890, with the introduction of the linotype machine, which allowed compositors to enter the text to be printed on a ninety-character keyboard. The typed characters would be retrieved, assembled into lines—"line o'type"— that were then cast to produce the "slug," capable of making nearly half a million imprints—"stereotypes," "multiple impressions"—before dulling. The larger the print run, the more useful the clichés: Steel was used for more widely reproduced periodicals (for ads and syndicated columns especially), lead/antimony/tin for lit.

Twain's books would benefit from this innovation, never Twain himself. He'd invested $300,000 of his royalties and wife's inheritance in the linotype's rival, the Paige Compositor, which—though it operated on a similar keying principle (except that the keys didn't release the sorts, rather directed a mechanical hand to pick them)—wasn't designed to cast type, only to arrange and set it. Though the Compositor printed 60 percent faster, and wasted no metal, James Paige was a relentless tinkerer, and by the time his invention was ready in 1894, the linotype had prevailed—the printing industry had stopped recycling foundry type and started casting anew for each job. Twain went bankrupt; Paige went flat broke into an unmarked grave.

Life on the Mississippi and the linotype are the beginning and end of a line—the carriage bell ringing on the mechanization of authorship. A book that took an author a year, or months, to write, and took a secretary just a week to type, could take a proficient linotype compositor only a single day to set, and though the book would exist in bound form for the public, and the typescript might be retained for posterity, the metal lines, if the book didn't sell, could always be melted down to be cast again for another author's attempt.

The compositor's great struggle was between accuracy and velocity. Words per minute (WpM) was an invention of shorthand. Proficient writers of Pitman, a phonetic system of single strokes for consonants and single dots for vowels, developed by Isaac Pitman (1813–97), were capable of transcribing up to 300 WpM. The average longhand of the time wrote approx. 30 WpM of memorized text, approx. 22 WpM of copied text, which was also the range of the average telegraph speed, the dots—and dashes—that communicated text neither strictly memorized, nor strictly copied, rather loosely both. In the 1890s, with telegraphy just starting its tap through the radio waves, CpM (characters per minute) became the standard rubric—the conversion rate between C and M commonly taken as 5:1. Speed typists vied for championships to publicize their courses. 123 WpM and 590 CpM were claimed as world records, simultaneously. But such feats were unsustainable beyond the minute mark. Consistency became the distinction, if not in competition then in business.

The emphasis, in courses, was on inculcating blindness—another debility the keyboard had been developed to ameliorate: A true typist would ignore the hands, and produce by touch alone. Early typewriters obscured the paper, but the mastering of later models required a shield over the keys. The focus was to be on the paper, or on nothing: "There are a few operators who can do this," according to the *National Stenographer*, 1892, "and I believe the number would be largely increased if they would learn to operate on a machine with a Blank Keyboard, that is, with no letters or signs on the keys."

The QWERTY keyboard—named for the first five characters of its top lettered row—was set by the Sholes-Soule-Glidden typewriter and popularized by the Remington No. 2, 1878. In America to popularize was to standardize, and the typewriter made this layout, and this principle, mandatory. The QWERTY keyboard, a 1:1 map of characters to the physical placement of the typebars they controlled, was arranged to prevent the bars from crashing into one another, from sticking—jammmming—smutting the page. This is why "w" and "h," "q" and "u," common diagraphs or syllabic couplings in English, are separated at such distance. But other languages favor different companions, and even require diacritics—āe, dž, eû, øy—not to mention umlauts, which are diagraphs themselves: As a refugee in California, Theodor Adorno (1903–69) used an American Underwood that turned his *Ästhetik* to *aesthetic* every time. As all German nouns, not just proper nouns, require capitalization, German typists have to make more shifts to and from the shift key—another introduction of the Remington No. 2, before which all typewriters wrote in all CAPS. Depending on the model, shift either lifted the bar "basket," or dropped the back-and-forthing, rolling "carriage," allowing the bar to meet the platen, and so the page, across more of its surface. This doubled each bar's capacity: minuscules were added under Majuscules; the 3 key, when shifted, produced the # sign. In Nazi Germany, G. F. Grosser typewriters shifted the 3 to the 𐊠𐊠 rune, while Seidel & Naumann models assigned that same function to the 5 key, which on American typewriters reproduces %.

Electric typewriters, in which pressure on the keys didn't control the levers that raised the bars, but rather triggered a motor to accomplish that task, were intended to reduce fatigue. Later this triggering was accomplished by a dedicated button or switch, which took even less effort to depress. The 1961 IBM Selectric completed the circle: The stationary bar basket was replaced with a ball containing every character—a successor *kugel*, turned from input mechanism (the writing ball's round keyboard) to output, and made to rotate and move laterally with the carriage. This innovation freed the typewriter from jamming, and allowed each language to reconfigure the keyboard's layout for itself. But all the major movements in this direction—whether seeking a better universal layout than QWERTY, or a better autochthonal layout attuned, say, to word formation across Latin alphabet language groups (pan-Iberian and pan-Slavic keyboards), or within one single Latin alphabet language (Turkish)—proved failures.[11]

Songs could be recorded and subsequently notated

11. Even the Cyrillic cultures based keyboards on the American design, establishing phonological or morphological correspondences between their languages' characters and Latin's. Arabic and Hebrew mapped their characters in QWERTY's reverse, mirror images especially pronounced in dual-use—L-to-R language/R-to-L language—keyboards. The history of the keyboard—of the typewriter too—in the logographic systems of Asia (hanzi, kanji, hangul) is a heroic exception to this rule, far exceeding the scope of a footnote, not least because it would have to be written in columns.

for sheet music; movies could be filmed and subsequently photographed for P.R. stills, but inefficient habit is not so easily back-engineered. Typewriting practice was as difficult to erase as type itself, and instead of a fresh sheet, corrections abounded. "QWERTY": an adjective meaning "irreplaceable but obsolete." "QWERTY": a contronym to be corroborated by computers.

William James served as his own typist. 1896, the first typewritten letter to his brother: "Dear Henry, I hope you will not be too offended at this typewritten letter to read it." "Dear Henry" preferred dictation. On his deathbed, in 1916, he deliriously dictated letters *as Napoleon*, and, following his death, his secretary, Theodora Bosanquet, claimed that not only was she was still receiving James's words, but also that Thomas Hardy, George Meredith, and John Galsworthy—though likewise deceased—were nonetheless vying for her stenographic assistance. In the Jameses' milieu: Point size of fonts was shrinking; space between words ("tracking"), and lines ("leading") of text, shrinking; more words were fit on the page, which wasn't the only reason why books were getting shorter: The three-volume Victorian novel was going out of fashion, becoming two volumes, becoming one.

Between 1890, when Henry published *The Tragic Muse*, and 1910, when William died, the number of books published in the United States nearly tripled (from 4,559 to 13,470). Journalism matched that growth. Quarterlies became monthlies became weeklies due to circulation demand and advertising revenue, while the linotype caused the number of daily newspapers to nearly triple as well (from approx. 1,000 to approx. 2,600, both in morning and evening editions). But expansion for industry was, in terms of individual publications, contraction of readership. There was too much to read, in too many forms (illustrated magazine, Sunday supplement), and by 1900 a new notice was appearing at the bottom of items, "continued on the next page"; the purpose of this "skip," or "jump," being to accommodate as many "headlines" as might fit on the "frontpage," the most pressing "above the fold." A concerned citizen's only hope was to read faster. To skim, scan, cluster, chunk. Utterly stripped of religion's preoccupation with quality, nineteenth-century attention was concerned with quantity, and while in literature the criterion considered was duration—girls musing out windows, boys contemplating the heath—in science it was capacity: how much of what can be handled.

The exclusively literary rhythms of the past—poetic meter, euphuistic and periodic prose—were reconceived as scientific phenomena. To George Eliot, novelistic form was a reckoning between the brevity of important events and the length between the events—the spells of subsidiary action, or introspection—that imparted their importance. While to her companion, George Henry Lewes (1817–78), this flow—whether artificial in book-time, or natural in lifetime—was to be experienced in "waves":

> We may compare Consciousness to a mass of stationary waves. If the surface of a lake be set in motion each wave diffuses itself over the whole surface, and finally reaches the shores, whence it is reflected back towards the center of the lake. This reflected wave is met by fresh incoming waves, there is a blending of the waves, and their product is a pattern on the surface. This pattern of stationary waves is a fluctuating pattern, because of the incessant

arrival of fresh waves, incoming and reflected. Whenever
a fresh stream enters the lakes (i.e., new sensation is
excited from without), its waves will at first pass over the
pattern, neither disturbing it nor being disturbed by it;
but after reaching the shore the waves will be reflected
back toward the center, and these will more or less modify
the pattern.

That quote is from the second volume of Lewes's unfinished *Problems of Life and Mind*. In the third volume, he
first floated the idea of a "stream of consciousness":

There is thus a Stream of Consciousness formed out of
the rivulets of excitation, and this stream has its waves
and groundswell: the curves are continuous and blend
insensibly; there is no breach or pause.

Though light and sound had been described as being
transmitted *like* "waves" since Antiquity (Vitruvius),
and as transmitting *in* "waves" since at least the sixteenth
century for sound (Galileo Galilei), and the seventeenth
century for light (Robert Hooke, Christiaan Huygens),
the eighteenth century abandoned the wave for Isaac
Newton's particles and his theory that both light and
sound traveled piecemeal, in lines of discrete "corpuscules." Newton's theory held until the nineteenth
century identified matter's true particles—molecules
and atoms (1803–08)—and James Maxwell proposed a
series of equations (1861–62) that demonstrated that not
only did magnetism and electricity travel in waves, but
also that light was merely their disturbance. It was with
electromagnetism that waves resurged as an analogy for
awareness.[12]

But while Lewes managed to contain this totalizing analogy of water, or fluidity, other writers were less elementally "focused" (visual), or "attuned" (aural). This "diffraction" or "refraction," "diffusion" or "dissipation," has been the case in every age, in every language, but was especially prevalent in nineteenth-century English, whose vast social literature ratified an equivalently social physiology (the science of physical function), and psychology (of mental function), and whose concern with class transferred its divisions to the cognitive. Attention, then, was not strictly physical—it could be "fixed" and "directed," "located" and "spanned"—or strictly mental—it could be both "ideated" and "idealized," simultaneously. It was also mechanical: attention could be "riveted"; and supernatural: attention could be "channeled"; it was pedagogical: to be "trained," or "disciplined"; economic: to be "paid" and "repaid"; and noticeably sexual: its "desire" could be "attracted," "aroused," "seduced," and even "stimulated"—it could also be "excited," a term that, as Descartes's *excitare*, was applied to the summoning of animal spirits, and, in its English translation, was used by a host of ocular and

12. Study of the 1887 photoelectric effect, which showed electrons being emitted from matter as a consequence of light absorption, inaugurated a partial reconsideration of particulateism, from 1896. Experimentation suggested a particle-like nature in the wave principle (electrons being transmitted in proportion to frequency and so in measurable quanta), and a wavelike nature in the particle principle (the motion of electrons). This would result in the proposal of a paradoxical wave-particle duality to describe both the properties of light (the proportional transference of electrons explained by their absorption of Albert Einstein's "photons," ca. 1905) and of all matter (initially the motion of electrons and later their energy spectra demonstrated as conforming to Maxwell's equations, ca. 1924).

auricular theorists to describe how sensations excited the "aether."

Just like light and sound were merely matters of this "disturbance," or "deviance," so too was attention. A disruption in the electromagnetic field became a perturbation of the cognitive field, and even a negligible differencing could comprise the totality of being. For Scottish physiologist Alexander Bain, "change of impression is essential to consciousness in every form"— his 1865 "Law of Relativity," which preceded the at least slightly verifiable theories of physics by half a century.

Humans attend to a feeling or thought, only because "its intensity is in a precisely inverse relation to its *extensity*," William Carpenter, *Principles of Mental Physiology*, 1874. "There are in us many changes, which are slight, or even *nil*, so far as pleasure or pain is concerned, but which are important as transitions, that is to say, as differences," Théodule Ribot, *English Psychology*, 1870.

Both of the above quotations point out the textual conundrum—too many words mean one thing (the intensity of a concept is denied by the extensity of its expression), and too many things are meant by one word (the differences between concepts register as slight, or even *nil*). "Attention" is all over Herbert Spencer's *Principles of Psychology*, 1855, but for every use of it in a distinct physiological or psychological sense, there's another placeholder, space-waster, usage: "let us confine our attention to the example," "but confining our attention to the elements with which we have immediately to deal," "in the last chapter we directed our attention mainly to a certain contingent class," "due attention having been paid to this fact."

The tension between attention the extensive proper name (addressing "the subject" of attention), and attention the intensive common name (addressing "the reader as subject" who is reading about attention): The Pragmatists, though practical in their expression, were less guilty of bisemous usage than their physiologist and psychologist peers (less guilty, perhaps, because their only laboratory was style). Charles Sanders Peirce, 1878: "In this pedantic age, when the general mob of writers attend so much more to words than to things." F.C.S. Schiller, 1912: "Formal logic is constrained by its chosen standpoint to confound together *verbal* and *real* ambiguity, and so it diverts attention from real and serious failures to convey meaning to mere diversities of usage which an intelligent mind has no difficulty in understanding."

The valorization of word over thing, the confusion of "verbal" and "real" ambiguity—not just verbal or real doubts about academic pedantry or analytic thought, but philosophy's attempts to forestall the dominance of science both by claiming it (the materiality of things) and criticizing it (ambiguity in the application to language of mathematical rigor). Meanwhile, France and Germany preferred to write their attention in numbers.

Data were better mirrors than prose, but better still was a mirror. Physiologist and ophthalmologist Louis-Émile Javal, professor at the Sorbonne in Paris, was reading silently—unfortunately, which book isn't recorded—with a mirror laid over the facing page. He noticed that his reading was not continuous but rather discrete, each line broken by pauses ("fixations") and sudden leaps ("saccades," after the abrupt jerking of a horse, or of a sail in the wind). Reading, it transpired, was nervous, neurotic, but naturally so—even in 1878. According to Javal, the average reader breaks the average line into sections of approx. fifteen to eighteen letters, each that, once fixed into view, are rapidly jumped from—comprehension as a wave, but particulate in its "fluctuations" and "rivulets," reading as the sine to the cosine of text.

Javal's eye was for the eye; Heinrich Obersteiner kept his ear to the ear. In 1874, he and his colleague at the University of Vienna, Sigmund Exner, built a "psychodometer":

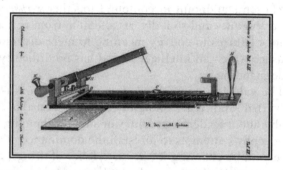

The handle (H) tugs a glass strip covered in soot (T), until the catch (G) releases the spring (F), creating a tone. With the spring's vibration, the needle or pin attached to its end scribbles sinuses in the soot of the strip—a timeline skipping through the ashes. The subject is instructed to depress the button (K) immediately upon hearing the tone, thereby lifting the needle or pin from the strip, and so recoiling the spring, and so ending the tone. The inscription remaining would be white on black, as if an inversion of text. Though it was Dutch ophthalmologist Franciscus Donders who first experimented with temporally measurable response, or "mental chronometry," in 1868, it was Exner who provided the gauge of *Reaktionsdauer*, "reaction time"—the number authenticated by an otherwise indecipherable signature.

Psychometrics—the timing of cognitive processes —was pioneered in 1879 in Leipzig, at the first psychological laboratory, administered by Wilhelm Wundt, who'd developed a theory that the basic unit of language was the "clause," or "sentence" (German's *Satz* means both), and that such mensurations of cognition represented "the willful structuring of a total conception into units that stand in logical relationship to one another." The timing of such units would not measure "perception"—for which it was sufficient to test by light/sound—but "apperception"—the ability to comprehend.

At Leipzig, Wundt's assistant, the American James McKeen Cattell, constructed the "gravity chronometer":

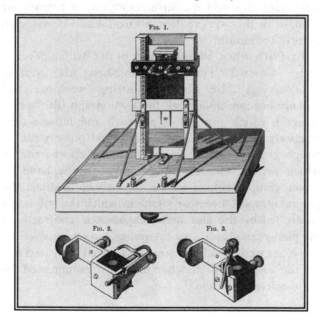

Fig. 1.

Fig. 2.   Fig. 3.

An electromagnetized white "screen," suspended between two brass stanchions, is suddenly released to fall—by a mechanism resembling a telegraph key—at a predetermined speed (adjustable up to 1σ, or 1/1,000th of a second), to reveal, in its place, a black pasteboard bearing a single word supported by clips (g and g). As the screen's fall is arrested—by the spring (f) and rubber supports (c and c)—the di-pronged copper wire (w) attached to its bottom makes contact with two bored basins filled with mercury connected to the binding screws (h and h), which start the ticking of the timing apparatus (a version of Matthäus Hipp's 1847 chronoscope, an infinitesimally accurate stopwatch, not pictured). This timing apparatus is stopped only when the subject pronounces the word into a mouthpiece (not pictured). The time elapsed would measure cognition, or literacy, or both, or neither—regardless, all would also be made an issue of the mouth.

By 1909, when Wundt's student the British psychologist Edward Titchener published his *Textbook of Psychology*, the new monitoring machines had already become historical: the kymograph (lit. "wave-writer"), which put blood pressure and muscle contraction onto paper; the sphygmograph ("pulse-writer"), which graphed pulse; the ergograph ("effort-writer"), which texted muscle strength through the hand or finger compressing a spring to activate a stilus; the pneumograph ("breath-writer," in which the stilus was controlled by the abdomen's expansion/ contraction); the plethysmograph ("excess-writer," in which swelling was measured by submerging the affected body part in a jar, the water of which, when displaced, compressed the air to activate a stilus).[13]

The new attention writing and so the new attention had developed its own "semiosis" (the word is Charles Sanders Peirce's):

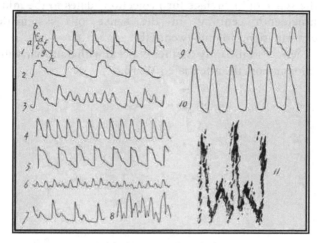

(*sphygmograph, pulses*)

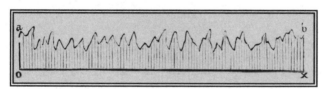

(*dynamograph of a carriage drawn by a horse*)

13. "Involuntary movement," Titchener writes, "is registered by the automatograph, a form of planchette or ouija board which still figures largely in spiritistic séances. A board is slung from the ceiling, so that it lies horizontally just over the surface of a table; a pointed glass rod stands vertically in a hole pierced at its forward end. On the table, under the point of the rod, is spread a sheet of smoked paper. If the arm is laid carefully on the board, and left to itself, the glass point traces on the paper the record of its involuntary movements."

The screens of the future wouldn't fall to expose a stimulus and trip the clock, they'd only—in the word's original Anglo-Saxon meaning—*screen* (the word in the sense of "a surface for projection" dates to the mid-nineteenth century, in the sense of "systematic examination," to mid-twentieth).

Screens would only further conceal with data, bar with information, the attenuated Word.

K. CASE STUDIES 1

CASE STUDY (CA. 1914): *MODERNISM*

You're unhappy, and it's debilitating to realize how unhappy you are, given that you're neither a woman nor a person of color, nor a public nor private homosexual. Your mother was "hypochondriacal," and "neurasthenic"; your father's "depression" expressed itself "psychosomatically." You yourself appear to be concealing something, to others, you suspect, but also to yourself, though you're not sure what that something might be: "delusional" (ca. 1870).

You own a factory. You have money but no time. Two newspapers come daily; you keep up with the industry through weekly trade magazines, and twice monthly you go to concerts and operas and museums and galleries. But the music you've been hearing lately sounds inappropriate or like two types being played both at once; or rather it's that lately you've detected an irony within music, in its juxtaposition of consonance/dissonance; or in its reference to a popular song with a bawdy lyric; or, perhaps, in its orchestration, which features uncommon combinations of instruments, like bassoons, tubas, a soprano saxophone, and a muted piccolo trumpet, accompanied by gongs and "vibraphone"; and the tune you thought you'd recognized not only isn't popular anymore, but isn't the tune you thought you'd recognized, which means the obscenity of the lyrics is all in your head, and your daughter has been clamoring for a radio; whereas the paintings you've recently seen either remind you of how much you like photographs, or look to you like incompetent photographs, like there had been a scratch on the lens or the tripod was missing a limb and the exposure was too much or not enough; or else you're not sure if that's supposed to be an apple or a bleeding abscess; or how far or close to stand from or to the canvas, whether far enough so that the grass can be viewed as grass or close enough so that it can be viewed as a swirl of green dots but then there are also scatterings of brown and yellow.

You feel as if you've seen and heard too much, but also nothing. Even going to the theater ruins your mood.

You're late, driving your automobile against the hoof traffic from Washington Square. But you can't be late because the theater issues only one ticket: one audience member per performance. The play begins at a strange time, five minutes after the hour, and ends at a strange time, five minutes before the hour, so that the audience members of consecutive performances never meet one another, and you wonder what the cast does during the ten-minute intermissions and why they can't shift their performance/appointment schedules, so that the audience members can come and go on the hour exactly, and when you get to the theater (42nd and Broadway), you ask the box-office woman about it and she answers, "Research has shown that the hour is intimidating," and you ask the usher girl and she drags you inside and answers, "Science has become skeptical of the natural numbers," but you don't pursue it further because now you've gone all the way down the empty aisle and up the stairs to the stage, set like a snug office with a smug Oriental rug and an armchair, in which the entire cast sits—one man, a doctor.

He clears his throat, as if expecting you to speak. But you don't know your lines. You didn't even know you had lines. You have to lie down. The doctor directs you to an angled settee such as you'd nuzzle your wife on.

You sit. Out in the audience is—your wife? being nuzzled? (The sitting itself is the cure.)

Even the doctor's face has an accent—Austro-Hungary: "Ridiculous, this war."

CASE STUDY (CA. 1904): *SEXISM*

a.) You are a woman working as the sole typist at a factory. You work on the office floor above the production floor. Last week you'd typed an interoffice memo from the owner to the manager telling him to "prepare a report on the suitability of employing women in our workplace," but then this week you typed an interoffice memo from the manager to the production chiefs telling them to "prepare reports on the effect on our workplace of employing women," which implied, to you at least, that a decision had been made, that female workers would be hired. You are conflicted. You are confused.

b.) The reports are submitted, handwritten, and you type them up. No consensus is achieved. One notes that approx. 20 percent of the U.S. workforce is women;

another notes that approx. 20 percent of U.S. women work. Labor statistics, phys/psych studies, are cited: "melancholy," "morbidity," "hysteria," "neuroses." Eighty percent of all typists share your gender. Other data are anecdotal, or polemical—political pamphlets for and against. One report insists that an increase in working women led to an increase in profits; another insists to a decrease; another insists to a decrease, but in agriculture. The only datum you can establish definitively is that between the censuses of 1890 and 1900 the State of Iowa lost two people, one to a head wound from a horse newly shod (your father), the other to tuberculosis (your mother). Council Bluffs, from where you escaped. Even the Sioux had gotten out of there.

c.) You live on Greenwich Lane with another typist (at another firm). Loves suffrage, hates temperance. Irish Catholic but an orphan too and so a sister nonetheless. Her father collapsed in the Park Avenue Tunnel, her mother to the Russian grippe. She'll try to get you out dancing tonight, to celebrate her new schedule: from working six days per week, to working five. Still eight hours per day, now forty per week. Her Friday nights are now free. Saturdays too. You suspect this has to do with the unions, or socialists, or communists, the Jews. But you can't go out dancing tonight, because you're still working six days. You're not disappointed however. You suspect that with her newly weekly bookkeeping sessions on Mondays, and her newly weekly training sessions on Wednesdays, designed to familiarize her with the new comptometer calculating machines under the tutelage of their new sales representative, your roommate's total work time, despite the Saturday reprieves, will actually *increase*.

"The weekend." You go to work on Saturday just when your roommate's coming back, babbling about the sales rep—"built like the Fuller Building"—who goes to a gymnasium where he walks on a rubber path that goes nowhere and bicycles in place. You take the subway, though as your office is on 46th Street you're never sure which stop, 42nd or 50th. Your home stop is as far away as 14th Street, but you don't mind the walk. Strange times when you can trust the Wright Brothers over a cruise on the *General Slocum*. You come back from work on Saturday and your roommate is gone, and you stay up waiting for her, reading the comptometer manual.

d.) On Sunday you shut all the doors and windows, from embarrassment. You go to your wardrobe, set aside the folded waists, reach below the automobile bonnet, but above the fleecy nullifiers. The typewriter you pinched and skimped for. A device of your own, to use at home, alone, this is what embarrasses you. As Sunday turns, you complete the reports, with stricter concentration than at the office. No ticktacky stock jottings. No bell-ringing cold candlesticks. But you've never worked this late before. You've never even stayed up this late before. Your roommate still hasn't come back. You doubt that she's at mass.

You consider the conclusions: Female employment should be confined to the office; should be confined to the unmarried population only ("widows and spinsters included"). "A dainty danger." "Spare perilous distraction." "Manual labor dulls the feminine." "Women make excellent typists, but the manual dexterity and concentrative capacities peculiar to the typewriter do not transfer to the production floor." The manager who'd asked you out to Coney Island a season ago and

641

is still waiting for an answer: "Women are naturally less productive than are men. Though it is our policy to pay weekly wages, if women are to be hired it is recommended to pay them instead on the basis of piecework. To pay them a wage equal to a man's, for work in no way equal to a man's, is unjust. To pay them per piece is to recognize women's unique maladies, enabling them to moderate their health, and us to moderate our payroll. It might also serve to foster a sense of competition that would accrue to mutual benefit." Two cents per page.

CASE STUDY (CA. 1894): *MIGRATION*

In 1849, in Königsberg, Hermann von Helmholtz calculated the speed of nerve conduction, or the rate at which an impulse travels along a nerve fiber. His tools were a galvanometer, a device named after Luigi Galvani, which measured electrical current, and Galvani's preferred creature, a frog. By stimulating the sciatic nerve fiber at regular distance intervals from the frog's gastrocnemius or calf muscle, von Helmholtz determined that the closer the stimulus, the faster the reaction. By subtracting the reaction times from one another, he determined that nerve impulses traveled surprisingly slowly—approx. 90 feet/27.4 meters per second; certainly slower than any electric or electromagnetic conductions; approx. twelve times slower than the speed of sound in air; approx. fifty-three times slower than the speed of sound in water; approx. twelve million times slower than the speed of light in a vacuum.

a.) Sensation is not simultaneous with stimulant. Rather, it's a matter of distance and duration, which are also the rudimentary quarantines of steerage. Yours was the Hamburg American Line, Hamburg–Southhampton–

New York, a deck below the waterline on the SS *Germania*, steaming. Germany is approx. six thousand kilometers, three thousand nautical miles, in the past, behind you.

b.) You work in a factory in Manhattan. You work on the line. You have, had, an accident. Everything you know you know from memory. Not from your own. From others'. Your memory is a broken line. You see, saw, the sparks before you hear, heard, the bang. You are aware of that now. You were aware of that then. You smelled and tasted the smoke of the mitrailleuse before you felt the burn or else you're dead—elementary stuff to a veteran of Gravelotte and Mars-la-Tour, the Franco-Prussian War (a conflict sparked by telegram).

A gasket is among the most material and so most fatal armaments of class warfare (especially given lack of safety protocols in the workplace). Steam, coefficient with the scalding pressure that powered your ship, builds up in another type of engine—the boiler. The boiler's gasket is weak and blows. The gasket hits you in the back. You fall forward, over the line, are pulled forward, by the belt, are pulled backward by your co-workers by your belt, but your belt breaks, the belt lurches, you fall, your feet get tangled in the ropes, are mangled by the pulleys, as the line slows from lack of steam, grinds the toes, itself, to a halt. Prussian honor is not at stake. You cry, pass out. The conveyance of your consciousness. Stops.

c.) You're returned to your senses, your tenement. Metzmann at one arm, a newly arrived Berliner at the other. Even the Berliner knows not to call a doctor. "Metsman" knows a nurse. She comes, cleans and

dresses your back and feet, and presses both her palms
to your fever. A pill, you don't recall, a tincture, extra
charge. The day foreman comes by, gives you two shifts
off. The night foreman comes by, gives you one shift.
Or the same foreman. Says different things. You've been
working double. Light and sound pass through the air,
through bodies that change their course, and you think
that the same might obtain for you, when you attempt to
project your thoughts deep into the future, or deep into
the past—that they might lose their potency or become
scrambled by materials unknown to you. You've been
worked double. You can't feel your feet. Your legs to the
knees. Your shoes by the bed. In tatters.

d.) No union equals no sick pay, no insurance. Yes
union equals maybe sick pay, maybe insurance, if
you can afford the premiums, separate from the dues.
$5/$6/week, $18/$20/month. Houston Street to work
takes twelve minutes on the streetcar, work to Houston,
twelve minutes too. The track arrives at its destination, perpetually, regardless of the cars. The Elevated,
the gutter. The Landsmannschaft should offer union
insurance, the party should offer Landsmannschaft insurance. For when you can't afford the plans or if your
benefits are cut. The nurse comes again, extra charge.
A different nurse, you don't recall. Too much muscle
traffic. Too much elbow in the needle. Try to borrow,
get lent at interest, die on credit, get buried in debt. It's
not just the Italians and Spanish who gamble. Though
it's pleasant to tour the reservoir they're draining for the
library (both before and after shifts), unless you forget
to avert your face as you pass the man amputated of legs
but rubbing at the air they occupied—his sign, propped
against his wheelchair: ANTIETAM.

644

e.) The line at work had once been lines. Each worker his own factory, with a table to himself, assembling his parts into a completed product. But then the manager decided it would be better to arrange the tables into a single line and have each worker contribute their special completory part to the product in its turn, a dedicated packer, a dedicated shipping supervisor in brakeman's overalls over sailor's stripes. Once each worker had been a generalist, capable and employable widely. But then the specialties narrowed. None were also friends. You'd been up for swing-shift foreman until the other foremen blocked you—cut your line—by arguing how liked you were, how kindly. How much you're liked, how kindly, can be assessed by how many visitors you've had in convalescence. Szentman. Erbnil. *Die Bildung ist für die enorme Mehrzahl die Heranbildung zur Maschine, Die Bildung ist die Heranbildung, Bildung Heranbildung, Bildungheranbildung.* "Repetition is, for the enormous majority, an anesthetic that pays a wage." (Hallucinating.)

f.) Humanity emigrates, labor immigrates. A part becomes a product sometime, someplace, between being modified by another part and completion. A German becomes an American after approx. a year in New York. Approx. another year and you're a German American. A lineworker is promoted to foreman within four years or remains a lineworker. A foreman is promoted to manager within six years or remains a foreman. A manager marries the owner's daughter within a decade or never owns a factory. Whether you've emigrated or immigrated depends on where and when life's best. Prussia, Alsace-Lorraine, the Ostbahn line to Russia: Berlin, Cüstrin, Landsberg, Kreuz, Bromberg, Dirschau, Elbing, Königsberg, Insterburg, Eydtkuhnen—the only things farther were Moscow and St. Petersburg, horse bone and disembodied cuirass. (Delirious.)

g.) Telegraphy (electricity through a field) moves faster than ordnance (mass across a spattered field), which itself moves faster than sensation. Distance is duration, between stimulation and a twitch, between an agony's signal and its acute cerebration. Manhattan's nerve grid is so long and wide, America hasn't felt its wound yet. But it will—sooner if it's warmer, later if it's colder.

Amid the span of Second Avenue, a billboard: vital-restorative, $2, intended to recover—the rest obscured by streetcar. The snuff and rush of gas. Stomach rumbles, clangs. But nothing can ever be recovered, no one is restored. The Landsmannschaft gives Bibles. The party pays a visit with stub cigars and schnapps.

h.) A fly digs in at shoulder. Just atop your old bullet scar, the chassepot lead that's skipped around under your skin like a toad, ever since the siege of Metz. A slight twinge, turns into a scathing tickle. You're an American German, not a machine. The morphine wearing off. Your stomach sweats. The fibers of your back bandage sweating loose. Your insulation. Your cladding. A seal. A gasket. Blow.

WARNING—DO NOT REMOVE COVER UNTIL CIRCUIT HAS BEEN ISOLATED ELSEWHERE

CASE STUDY (CA. 1884): *RACISM*

In 1860, in Leipzig, Gustav Fechner proposed to measure the intensity of sensation, not objectively for all people, but rather —as everyone has different thresholds—subjectively, for the self, whose feelings can bear no relation or comparison to anyone's. Fechner's Law, expressed in words, states: "In order that the intensity of a sensation may increase in arithmetical progression, the stimulus must increase in geometrical progression." Its expression as an equation is $S = K \log (I)$, where S is sensation, I the intensity (numerically estimated), and K the result of Ernst Weber's Fraction of 1846, which standardized units of intensity by defining the smallest detectable difference between a primary and secondary intensity of stimulus. Weber's Fraction was $\Delta I / I = K$, where I is the primary intensity, ΔI the increase/ decrease required for a difference to be perceived, rendering K the increment itself, signifying that the proportion of intensity gain/loss remains constant with each and every variance of intensity.

You should be dismantling that Liberty monument they're putting up. That statue. That's all you'll ever need. They're putting in so many telephones and so much electric and all that sister's just wire. Should just try and get a lock off her. They're all getting rid of gas, but where all that gas goes you're not clear. Hissing up into the air like spirits. Or collected for her torch to keep the dump lit.

You go out to the dump and then around the tinkeries and smithies that make the pots and pans and scrounge. The Pole trades money for what you haul, melts it down and puts around it better clothes than you have, and it's wire. Copper. Mine the bags.

You strip what you can. You lift something enough

you get to feel the certain weight. The more you lift the same something it feels lighter and only more weight feels the same. Your hands and arms get used to it. Like men. The more rods, the less they hurt. The more the whip, the pain lessens. You brought a kettle and got a certain amount but then you bring the same model kettle and get less because the Pole says now they're putting in it less copper than before.

You're not saying you can't tell the difference between then and now. You're saying that slavery is not being allowed to tell the difference. You're sure it's either crazier now than ever before or that every generation increases its limit as the crazy increases so the level is always maintained. You miss the old tools and if you find them you keep them because the old tools aren't made of copper. Adze, scythe, sickle. Your husband used them but you never did. You tell everyone at the roominghouse your husband's a prospector, a Creole lumberjack, Canadian. Staked out west to claim his acres. Anything but lynched. He would've voted Blaine. A Democrat in the house will send you back to chains. New Jersey's wrapped in the scraps of chains, mostly rusted, mostly useless. You notice things if you can.

Some are good for the field; some are good for the house. Saturday the white folks clean; Sunday the white folks throw out.

The elders told of the elderland where when you died you could come back again as a child. Some of the elders said this was good and some of the elders said this was bad, because you could come back only by taking over the body of a child and getting rid of its soul and the soul would just wander around. (Vodou.)

In the elderland if you craved another person's husband, or luck, or fortune, or power, you'd just put the powder around them or sprinkle them with drops and everything was yours for the taking and they'd become just a body—a body lost its soul.

The elders said the lost souls were trapped in bottles or jars, rendering the bodies too as empty vessels. A body whose soul had been trapped just lay around like a moldy sack. The body would just sit propped against a gate not moving or talking or anything until the man who had her soul would tell the body how to do and then she'd do it. Fetch and thatch, mend and tend, do how Polish tells you.

Some of the elders said that was bad but others said it was bad only if the spell wasn't wanted. You yourself have known folks to just give their souls away. Have known folks who just wanted to be bodies. They signed their X, forever. But you yourself don't believe in any of the spells or drops or powders. You believe in dumps, fair skies, life after Newark. Copper. You would not be like Liberty and let others into your head. Not for nothing. But not for everything neither.

12. CASE STUDIES B

CASE STUDY (*FREUD*)

Vienna, Berggasse—what are your associations? and why? His office ceiling is unpeeling and white—which is nice, as it's basically the only thing that you, the patient, the analysand, have on which to focus. White like that can't help but hypnotize. You can't decide whether a fan would help the effect or hinder. Freud gestures you toward the settee, whose angle supports you not quite sitting, but not quite lying either. You wonder why Freud insists on this settee and why he sits behind you, definitively sits, in a chair. His inaccessibility is both because he's uncomfortable listening while you speak, and because you're uncomfortable speaking while he listens, eye contact. While the angle of your recline can be explained as mediating between a sleep or dream state, and waking attentivity. Also it will be believed: R-handed people use more of their L brain when standing—the position most requiring logical thought—and more of their R brain when sitting and lying, positions most associated with—associative thought.

You inspect the office and muse to yourself that the decoration of an analyst's office tells you everything you need to know about the analyst, or perhaps it tells you nothing you need to know because the analyst too must know this and must decorate accordingly, which, if that's the case, tells you everything.

You are a train (Freud tells you). Proceed "metaphorically," a transitory word. *Metaphora*, in Latin and Greek, "to bear," "to bring," "to carry over." "Your mind is like or as a train," a simile—*similis*, "similar," *simila*, "to sift grain" (for similarity)—stimulus "to resemble." "Train!"

the imperative metonymy.

You are to do just this: Recline at the window of your train and think, or remark, on whatever passes by. "Act as though, for instance, you were a traveler sitting next to the window of a train car and describing to someone inside the car the changing views you see outside," Freud, *On Beginning the Treatment*.

This double transference—from the sensorimotor to the conceptual, from conceptual to verbal—comprises your *train of thought*, which does translate to German.

Even if Freud is not your analyst, he will try to ride along. It might be that his whole method can be explained entirely by his relief that this journey is just a function of language.

Freud was afraid of trains; scared of the challenges they presented, of the challenges his conception of them represented, rendering his use of train metonymy to explain his science an act of either neutralization or confrontation. The phallic symbol stops at the vaginal station, everyone gets off. Freud was a lineman, a switchman, of words; associating *Bahnhof*, "station," with *Friedhof*, "cemetery," letting him off at *Vorhof*, a "lobby" or "forecourt," but an anatomical term too, for the vulva's hole. From when he was a child leaving Moravia for Leipzig he recalled the station's gas lamps, "souls torched in hell"; later, on a journey from Leipzig to Vienna, he shared a compartment with his mother, who undressed in front of him—hairy. When new tracks were built from Vienna, just before Freud's birth, they bypassed his birthplace, Freiberg in Mähren, essentially bankrupting its burghers, among them his father—trains ruined fathers too.

Throughout his life Freud was traumatized by missing trains, and so showed up to stations early; missing a train was to miss an opportunity, for business or intercourse, an appointment with death; he dreaded the prospect of changing carriages, and even trains, while sleeping, though he'd never suffered from somnambulism; he had a phobia of accidents too and on vacations traveled separately from his family, whom he preferred not to witness his panic; he noted the mechanical excitation of trains, their sexual locomotival jolt; stops on the way to the spa were the Stations of the Cross; trains united and divided Jewry from gentiles, Jewry eastern and western; the class differences of a train, first and second class, based on nothing but purchasing power, both liberated and oppressed; the train carriage was a breeding stall of crisis, in which you the passenger sat stationary atop the border of public and private—exposed, neurotic about exposure, concealed, neurotic about concealment, compartmentalized, helpless.

Freud's problem was problematization: what/what not to problematize, how/why to problematize, attributing to everything its own pathology if not its own religion.

It's shocking that he never wrote anything about cars, for example, besides noting a case in which *automobil*, the word alone, called to mind another: *autoerotik*.

CASE STUDY (*MILITARY*)

a.) You're halfway through a war. You're the pilot of a bomber and your target is Hamburg. The Americans bomb by day. You, British, bomb by night. But all the lights in Hamburg are off. The gaßes and straßes are so black they're the Elbe and the Elbe's so black it's the sea. The North Sea. Though around Hamburg there are lights so bright that you find yourself believing it's Hamburg itself down there and so doubting your coordinates. After the war you're informed: The Nazis just set out a series of generators in the middle of a field, a pasture of floodlights, arc lamps, burning. This was supposed to distract you. To create the impression of a city. Of your target. The people you were about to destroy were elsewhere, playing dead in blackness.

b.) You're the captain of an American destroyer escort. Your ship is equipped with sonar. You transmit a ping, wait for the echo, ping and wait for the echo. Though whenever you ping a U-boat, by the time its echo is received, by the time its echo is processed, the U-boat's in another place, but then you're in another place as well, nearer, or farther, because the U-boat's also pinging you, and you echo, you can't help it. All sonar can detect is the past. The future floats between predictions. The U-boat might maneuver you astray, in a countermeasure obscuring the angles of your search, and so keeping concealed the second boat that would sink you. Though you might sink the first boat first.

c.) You return from the war. Intact and with enough medals to camouflage your trauma. The researchers have not yet returned to their universities, but remain in their clandestine barracks, having been ordered to experiment. On you.

You're a radar operator and they want to determine how many elements you can detect on a single or multiple screen(s). You operate a telephone switchboard and they want to determine how many calls you can handle at once. You're asked to search for letters, digits, figures. Letters/digits are spaced equidistantly, with no semantic content. No denotata, no conotata, nothing. Except one element, only one, will be different/wrong, a letter upside down, a digit backward. You're asked to identify which and timed. You're asked to identify between two tones, which lower, which higher, and then to find, within a cluster of tones, their sum. Count, enumerate, subitize, guesstimate.

On the switchboard, you're given two telephones, each broadcasting its own conversation, and are asked to type up transcripts of both, or even to memorize both, "to the best of your ability" (you're weary of that phrase). This is called divided, or dichotic, listening (if you're listening). The conversations are conducted in two different languages. They are about two different things. They are about the same thing and are, in fact, so boring and lacking in style, but so accurately boring and so accurately lacking in style, that you can't tell which is the original and which the translation.

On the radar screen(s), you're asked to react—to press a button—whenever a new blip appears. Blips appear at random intervals of space and time, both proximal and not. All the blips are a single color. All the blips are different colors. You're asked to react to a certain color only, (in)correct. You're asked to react to a certain color when and only when it's accompanied by a certain sound, (mis)taken. You're asked to follow one blip and your eye motions are monitored as other blips are added and still others subtracted—interference. You're told to "be selective," "the Central Intelligence Agency certainly is." Selectivity, though, is a general matter, or a specific matter, and lack of agreement leads precisely to tests. Semblance or stimulus, choose one. It's easier to focus on a certain blip if it's solid and the other blips are blinking. It's easier to focus on a certain blip if it's blinking and the other blips are solid. 1.) True or False: It's easier to focus when greenA is accompanied by sound. 2.) T or F: It's easier to focus when redB is not accompanied by sound.

d.) One war's airplane cockpit maintained a separate gauge for each function. Another war's airplane cockpit grouped the various functions—altimeter and speedometer, wind speed and direction—assigning each group its own gauge. You, a pilot, are asked to recall: Which best describes how you perceived your targets? As individual displays, or as multipurpose indicators whose dysfunction cried out en masse (weapons always get their own buttons)?

The surface vessels you commanded towed decoys behind them, which emitted a homing frequency to lure torpedoes, or a signal that honed the torpedoes' own, deflecting them toward an alternate target, even to the vessels of their launching. The submarines ejected zeppelins too, underwater blimps. Rapidly inflated bladders of air or just these intense bursts of bubble that approximated propeller cavitation. You, a captain, are asked to recall: How did you and/or your crew refer to these subaqueous bursts? ("Clouds.")

CASE STUDY (*INDUSTRIAL*)

You work in an office. An office automated to capacity. Or approaching capacity as you're a human and still employed. But even once everything human has been automated, choices must yet be made. Your position—you—will be either terminated, or retained, based on whether your expertise includes the servicing and repair of these information machines when, not if, they malfunction. It is, no doubt, one of these information machines that will make the choice whether to terminate or retain you (your position).

b.) Thankfully, your expertise militates against termination. You don't theorize, or program, you facilitate. You're an engineer, a technician. Your work is to keep everything working, including the thing that is yourself. When a machine breaks, you find out why, you gather information. But while a scarcity of information compels attention, an excess of information compels distraction, and so yet another economy is described. Information loses value when its quantity exceeds the capacity of your attention, and so attention is converted to commodity. Conversely, attention loses value when its quality results in ignorance of a more efficient/more expeditious solution. Worth is directly proportional to use. Relevancy is to be fought for like officing and grants.

c.) The machines in your lab have become the models for your own machine, your brain—both "a processor" ("machine," singular), and "a network" ("machines," plural). It occurs to you that every model of cognition you've ever encountered has integrated the models of every machine you've ever encountered, at least of its power controls: the large, noisy vacuum tube you began with shattered into the quieter, smaller transistor, which switched electricity on and off and amplified the current, while the transistor, in turn, you yourself have managed to incorporate into the (nearly) silent, (nearly) invisible circuit, which limits initial electricity flow through "a resistor," selectively limits flow according to preset conditions through "a diode," and stores and disburses single strong blasts through "a capacitor."

If you can regard current as currency—the present around you—it follows that potential is defined by control. When currency exceeds your ability to control it, you overload and fail. As a circuit, you can either "resist," and impede the initial flow of irrelevant data, diodically "decide," and select among the data for relevance, or merely "capacitate," which is to react—instinctively, reflexively.

d.) Such are the general schematics of attention, and it's the middle selectivity, that diodic quality, that interests. (To be clear: That's only because you've selected that interest.) To begin with, you don't impede irrelevancies (you're convinced of this). The very fact that you've considered that you might in fact impede serves as proof. Further, not only are you susceptible, you're often willingly submissive. In repairwork, it's often the perceived irrelevancies that prove crucial. This too can be explained neurologically. This too cannot be helped.

You are working to fix a component when a co-worker visits your cube. This co-worker is but another component, though he does not require fixing. He is, you're conscious of this, a superior. A scientist. A mind. But he's also irrelevant to your fixing. Still you hear him, you see him; he cannot be blocked. Even if he weren't a superior, but an inferior, he'd be unblockable, given his proximity and frequency, that flushed circle face and circuitous chatter. Rather, you ignore him; rather, you can only choose to ignore him. Though in that choice itself there's still enough proximity and frequency for you to become aware that he's chatting with someone else in some other cube who has (you've been told), or might have (you suspect), new information about the layoffs.

e.) Your superior's unintentional interruption has not been preattentively "filtered," but postattentively "attenuated." These are words for breaks; these words are breaks themselves. "Filter" makes you think of a tea bag, or a paper coffee cone, leaching the leaves or grounds for flavor, not for texture, keeping the water unhachured and pure. "Attenuation" makes you think of weakness, loss, fade, extinction. The wanelife of the unemployed. Volume turned down, color dulled.

According to attenuation theory—a theory of attention (selective, or perpendicular/intersecting with intent) within attention (total, or in parallel with stimuli)—irrelevancies are inhibited, until they exhibit as relevant. You don't need a job, until you don't have a job, unless you want one (or another). This most recent conception of attention suggests to you the most recent machine you've been working to fix—a machine that, in fact, has never worked, so, in fact, has never been broken. It's a machine used in business now intended for use in the home. (You yourself, throughout your career, had always been employed by universities, funded by governments—this current position has been your only experience in business.)

f.) "Computers" are not dedicated machines, not unitasked units; rather they're templates, platforms, capable of executing polyvalent tasks, synarchic "programs." Human programs that load immediately, simultaneously, are either innate or acquired (self-programmed). These include breathing (innate), stress/tension (acquired). Computer programming is currently strictly "innate," though there's a hope in the lab that computers might one day be programmed to "acquire"—to learn from users, teach themselves. There's even the dream that one day computers might become capable of processing the greatest of human programs, those involving apperception, or appreciation of the self, programs so demanding—involving ethics, morality, appetites, drives—that humans must still load them serially, with deliberate dedication.

g.) Execute the following programs: Explain how you didn't notice that your superior was addressing you; explain how you didn't register that he was letting you go; explain how it's not your fault that you've been inattentive lately; explain how the 5150's recent memory malfunctions haven't been because of you; explain why you weren't able to find your car in the parkinglot; explain why you suddenly found it; explain your feeling that you don't deserve your car; explain how you got lost on your way home; explain your lateness without mentioning getting lost and explain your earliness without mentioning job loss; explain how you're going to explain all this loss to your wife.

h.) Redundanated. Fired. Misfired. Laid off. You sprawl on the loveseat with your wife. IF how much, THEN moreover what, information is required? And why?

CASE STUDY (*SOVIET*)

You're a Russian poet, on a train journey from Moscow, fleeing one doomed love affair for another. Spying on your own life, your code name is "Boris Pasternak."

Your face—your "prominent" nose—is pressed against the window, which edits the landscape and then sequences it into frames. Subtitles, supertitles, enter (leap into) your head (your soul), in voiceover. Poetry, the overdub of life:

> stations flying from the train like
> stone butterflies/moths of rock

> the suffocating sun was borne along
> on innumerable striped divans

> Summer waved farewell to the wayside station. Thunder
> removed its cap to snap a hundred blinding photos.
> A bloom of lilac dimmed and thunder gathered sheaves
> of lightning exposing, from far fields, the stationmaster's
> hut.

> Wells hum like kobzas
> in the dust and wind,
> haystacks and poplars creak
> hurl themselves to earth.

> Stepping off the train, I tossed
> fresh paint on canvas
> for a willow grove
> where, again, I found you

Drafts—cold drafts whether winter or summer, or the hundred seasons Russia poses for between, interwar.

It chills you, how words used to promise more, at least to be more themselves, in the original: not in Russian, but before the words ever became Russian. (You'd believed that poetry, and even the prose of poets, existed prior to language: in spirit.)

But this regard for writing, once natural to you in the way that breathing continues to be natural (fogging the pane), turned absurd—attention shift, swerve, to another track—the very moment you associated it with "narration."

A bit of fence, a toppled chimney: There used to be a way of writing that was, at heart, still a way of being, a way of seeing and hearing things better, not worse, by writing them down. But then it changed, and this change was not akin to those rasputitsal mutations by which strangers become lovers, and lovers, strangers; neither was it related to any of those newer political or economic processes by which one thing is modified into another or gains and loses essence—like grain into bread, and bread into kvass, all of which are traded in the provinces, but bought and sold in the cities; or like tourism, which is a caricature of exile; or like space-time, whose mysteries have been obliterated by telecommunications and improvements of the post; or like calm, a virtue that's been condemned as laziness, idleness, decadence, parasitism.

This change was different because it changed not just your mind, but also your senses: smell and touch. Things lost their odors and textures, their tastes, which loss the poetry of your age felt the need to compensate for, vocabularily. The way words looked on the page, the way they sounded, declaimed.

CUT—The train is stalled just outside Kiev and is left like an unfurled banner whose propaganda can be read by the passengers only by marching alongside it. A stomping of barefoot pistons is the score.

CUT—[*to himself*] I should've switched at Kharkov.

You remember when you were separated from someone you wanted to write about—you couldn't get a picture of her in your mind, so you wrote to her requesting a photograph. Subsequently, that request was implicit in every line you wrote, not just of prose. You propped the photo against the telephone when you called her. You could not remember her voice. It was as if you were together only when there was something between you: glass, a fence, a guardrail. Or like when you open a package from Odessa that's been through customs, that's been through the censors, and though all its contents are received as they were sent, you're still able to sense that other presence.

That was the change—that intermediary presence felt in everything.

M. BEHAVIORISM AND GESTALT, NEUROACADEMIA, CONSUMPTION V. PROSUMPTION, BUDDHISMS

"The preceding two chapters will be followed by the two chapters that follow" (I read that in a textbook). The preceding two chapters dramatized, in sequence: Modernism in the arts; sexism and work; migration and the physiological experiments of von Helmholtz; racism and the psychophysics of Fechner and Weber; Freudian analysis and travel; the military-vigilance experiments of Norman Mackworth, along with the signal-detection research of David Green and John Swets (1954); industry and the filtration and attenuation theories of Donald Broadbent (1958), Jaroslav and Diana Deutsch (1963), and Anne Treisman (1964); and, finally, the mediation of experience through Soviet ideology.

I—first person—knew of no other way to do something I thought crucial: provide some perspective on how people of previous eras experienced and felt about attention. I've been in analysis and held bad jobs (though I've never been a white female secretary or a black female copper scavenger), and I've written this essay, for which I've read countless books, and what I find I'm still lacking is this: a true or just tractive account of how nonwriters, especially, attended. This, dear reader, is inevitable.

To wonder why so few memoirists and diarists wrote about attention at the turn of the twentieth century is to wonder why so few of them wrote about climate change, or genomics—either the topic hadn't yet occurred to them, or hadn't yet occurred. Perhaps they didn't regard their attention as being threatened; or perhaps

they didn't even regard their attention as being theirs—
as a property that others wanted (it could be taken), or as
a function that others wanted to make use of (it could be
manipulated). But whenever attention itself is stimulated
(addressed directly as attention), it responds as something else—in economic terms, the attention-property is
converted into a commodity, and the attention-function
is converted into a process of exchange.

That was the hypothesis of American psychologists
between the world wars, whose attempts at conditioning attention would capitalize—commercialize
—Behaviorism. Meanwhile, the Soviet Union had nationalized the attention of its comrade-citizens, so as to
redistribute it more equally, if more covertly, in bedroom cameras and water-closet mics. Only an animal
can read the name Pavlov without a reaction.

Ivan Petrovich Pavlov (1849–1936). His experimentation with animals conditioned him to zoomorphism,
a belief in his animal self. To Pavlov, animal life was
associative: a furry warren of innate and acquired re-
flexes, the former of which are instinctive (developed
by the species for survival, and heritable), the latter,
learned behaviors. The past teaches the future how to
respond; everything not a response is a stimulus to self,
while your own responses are merely stimuli to others—
especially in conditions of cost/benefit, or punishment/
reward (the system is nonexistent but rigged).

Behaviorism rejected volition in the sense of free
will, and so sought to deny the discriminatory, or prefer-
encing/privileging, aspects of attention (what to ignore,
the ordering of responses to simultaneous stimuli). It
accomplished this by contextualizing them socially: If
you believe you have volition, and you're surrounded
by others who believe they have volition, you might be

rewarded; however, if you believe you have volition, and you're surrounded by others who don't believe they have volition, you will be punished, for certain (Pavlov died the year of the great show trials and purges). For John Watson (1878–1958), speaking for Behaviorism, the school he established: "Attention is merely, then, with us, synonymous with the complete dominance of one habit system." Non-Behaviorist theorists of attention were misbehaving, in the words of Gilbert Ryle, by "misdescribing heed in the contemplative idiom" (*The Concepts of Mind*, 1949).

Gestalt psychology (Gestalt: "entirety of form," or "shape," "quiddity," "haecceity"), codified coevally with Pavlovian conditioning, appears to offer a middle ground: While some Gestaltists expressly denied attention, others just attempted to deprive the human of a choice in its control. Emerging from the laboratory experiments of Wundt, Gestalt sought the data to prove, in the definition of the discipline's principal founder, Max Wertheimer (1880–1943), that all physical and mental phenomena both were, and had to be perceived and conceived of as, "wholes [*Ganzen*], whose behavior is not determined by that of their individual parts [*Stücke*], conversely the behavior of the parts is determined by the structural laws [*Strukturgesetzen*] of the whole." To Gestalt, the wholeness of attention, then, had to consist of its response, and the constituent piecework—what neuropsychologists regarded as the discriminatory or preferencing/privileging capacities—was subordinated as features, or behaviors, of the stimulus itself. This demotion was merely an auxiliary purpose of Danish psychologist Edgar Rubin's *The Nonexistence of Attention*, 1921, Gestalt's extremest attention text—an attempt to disprove attentivity by proving that a person was unable to selectively focus on one specific reading of an optical illusion (either "the figure," or "the ground").

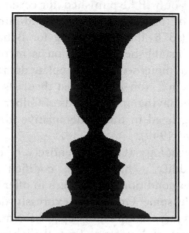

In illusions like "Rubin's Vase," a specific reading (of vase *or* faces) can result only in a reading of the whole (vase *and* faces), while a reading of the whole can result only in a reading of the specific (mentally, however, one can conceive of *either and both,* the specific *and* the whole).

Figure and ground constantly change, yet the differences between them, according to Rubin, "are essentially concrete"—"thus the use of the term 'attention' was rendered obsolete."

I've written this essay, I've written thus far, because I was interested in the subject. Which was: whether I was able to write about something I wasn't interested in, something I loathed. I needed the money. I was responding to pressure (social/professional), a blinking cursor (the computer's bell).

I'd always wanted to write an essay about nothing that was also an essay about everything, but the only thing I'd lacked was a subject, until.

It's a curious feature of science papers on attention—they're all much shorter, divided into much shorter sections, than anything I'm used to reading from the academic humanities. Also, they repeat too frequently—too frequently. In terms of structure, it's as if their researchers couldn't trust me, couldn't trust themselves, to pay attention throughout. Each begins with an Abstract, proceeds to an Introduction, moves to a Methodology, transitions to a Results, and ends with a Conclusion, yet at each stage reiterating a later, or earlier, stage, and so progressing and regressing both—*from the conclusiveness of the Abstract* ("We have examined the efficiency of attentional networks across age and after five days of attention training [experimental group] compared with different types of no training [control groups] in four-year-old and six-year-old children. Strong improvement in executive attention and intelligence was found from ages four to six years. Both four- and six-year-olds showed more mature performance after the training than did the control groups"), *to the results-expectancy of the Introduction* ("In this study, we explore how a specific educational intervention targeted at the executive attention network might influence its development. We explore training at ages four and six years so that we might compare influence of specific training at these two ages with general improvement due to development. The intervention we developed was designed to train attention in general, with a special focus on executive control in children of four years of age and older. We adopted a method used to prepare macaque monkeys for space travel and modified the various training modules to make them accessible and pleasant for young children. Before and after training, we assayed attention skills of the children by giving them the Child ANT [Attention Network Test, available @ sacklerinstitute.org/cornell/assays_and_tools]   while monitoring brain activity from 128 scalp electrodes. We also measured their intelligence. Their parents filled out a temperament questionnaire about the children as well"), *to the Methodology, which is attentivity itself, the very tautology being tested for* ("Electroencephalogram [EEG] Recording and Data Processing: [...] Forty of the forty-nine four-year-old participants and twenty-three of the twenty-four six-year-old participants agreed to wear the sensor net that allows acquiring EEG data. [...] Genotyping Procedure: Cheek swabs were collected from most of the six-year-olds [...] and genotyping of the DAT1 gene was performed. [...] Training Program: The first three exercises taught the children to track a cartoon cat on the computer screen by using the joystick. [...] The *anticipation exercises* involved teaching the children to anticipate the movement of a duck across a pond by moving the cat to where they thought the duck would emerge. [...] The *stimulus discrimination* exercises consisted of a series of trials in which the child was required to remember a multiattribute item (different cartoon portraits) to pick out of an array"), *to the introduction-memory of the Results*—Insert Charts—*then, again, the abstracted Conclusion*: The six-year-olds exhibited better executive attention than the four-year-olds, in the main, though the trained four-year-olds produced an EEG pattern similar to that of the untrained six-year-olds, while the trained six-year-olds evinced a more adult pattern, at midline frontal brain/electrode position Fz—though, too, genetics matter. Those with the homozygous long/

long allele had less difficulty resolving conflict than those with heterozygous long/short alleles. "We found that the long form of the DAT1 gene was associated with stronger effortful control and less surgency (extraversion). This finding suggests that the less outgoing and more controlled children may be less in need of attention training" (quotations from "Training, maturation, and genetic influences on the development of executive attention," M. R. Rueda, M. Rothbart, B. McCandliss, L. Saccomanno, M. Posner, *Proceedings of the United States National Academy of Sciences*, 2005).

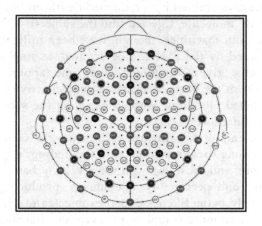

(*positioning of EEG electrodes on cerebral cortex; letters label lobes: [F] frontal, [T] temporal, [P] parietal, [O] occipital; odd numbers label left hemisphere, even to right; the closer to the midline, the smaller the number; "z" indicates electrode placement directly atop the midline*)

The experimental method, which once led with its theories or hypotheses, tested them, and then presented its conclusions, now leads with its conclusions (what follows, it follows, is conclusive as well). In cognitive neuroscience especially, different groups are subjected to the same or similar tests, though attention's traditional tempororubric of response time, RT, has been amplified by the spatiorubric of imaging: initially with MRI (magnetic resonance imaging, which uses a magnetic field to align the body's hydrogen atoms, emits radio frequencies that force the atoms out of alignment, then terminates the frequencies, as the energy expelled by the atoms as they automatically realign is converted into picture) and PET machines (positron emission tomography, which detects gamma rays emitted by a radionuclide tracer, bound to a glucose molecule, injected into the subject)—1970s to 2000. Both machines, though, have been millennially supplanted by the fMRI, a device that, as implied by the prefix, gives "functional," real-time (another RT) portraits of the brain, measuring neuron activity from oxygenated bloodflow without exposing the subject to undue radiation.[14]

In attention experiments, results must be compared from among these machines with the findings of genetic testing, and those too with the results of batteries of aptitude and personality assessments—producing, cumulatively, better likenesses of the subjects and scientists both, yet no more complete a concept of what attention

14. The fMRI reads all areas of the brain, while the EEG/MEG (electroencephalography/magnetoencephalography), which situates electrodes or magnetometers directly on the subject's scalp, reads more superficially, from the cortical surface. This gives the fMRI a spatial edge, though because hemodynamic response takes more time to measure than do electrical currents, EEG/MEG is considered temporally superior. The two, then, are regularly used in tandem, though the magnetic field of the fMRI can affect the electrical current, which effect must be calculated into the results.

is, moreover, of what it can be. Instead, what's obtained from the color blobs of the fMRI—kinetic fluoresced figurative Rorschachs—is not the idea of what's happening, only the idea that something's happening: somewhere, somewhen, somewhy. Technological impartiality can be a misnomer (that moldering bias effect by which the subject being scrutinized becomes cognizant of the scrutiny, and so behaves "atypically," and so scans "atypically"); brain activity can be misleading (the realization that all neuronal activity following a stimulus doesn't have to be stimulus-response)—though such problems pertain to attention only if attention is what is being examined, not just how machines and brains interact if given parallel, yet intersecting, tasks.

Neuroacademia, then, becomes split into lobes—complementary studies. A scanner stimulates the subjects as they complete a routine. The scientists monitor, attuned to whether all experimentally valid cues—like an expected light or sound—engage (for example) the dorsal frontoparietal regions (regarded as the primary network of "selective attention"), and all experimentally invalid cues—like an unexpected light or sound—engage that same dorsal region but in cooperation with (for example) a secondary ventral frontoparietal network (involved with interrupting "selective attention" and reorienting it toward evaluation of the relevance of new stimuli).

Note, then, that in one experiment alone, the attention being sought can be presented as both a property (the automatic concentration of mind) and a function, which doesn't just select (what to attend to), but also discriminates (as to how to attend), and is even capable of thought (in its differentiation between experimentally valid and invalid cues and between correct and incorrect responses).

"Attention," conclusively, must have "a basic static architecture," along with "a substrate processual structure," neither of which had been perceivable, until it was conceived, and so became "attention," at least in the wholeness of a part.

But if selectivity is to be admitted to attention, it must be selected among itself—with psychological distinctions admitted between "abience," the decision to attend to another thing based on a refusal of present attention; "adience," the decision to attend to the present thing based on a refusal of any and all other attention; "acturience," the decision to attend to a thing with the purpose of changing its nature; and "avoidance," the inability to decide on an alternate attention—and the methods of all must be tracked. Preferencing/privileging order is tested by instructing subjects to complete a series of tasks, in any order they choose, then to complete another related series in an illogical order—"related," and "illogical," defined by the experiment.

Neuroacademia discriminates most intensely among attention's discriminatory aspects: Not only can attention be "overt," "covert," "active/focused," "directed/voluntary," "split/divided," "distributed," "sustained," "restored/alternating," "shifting," "deconcentrated," "conditional," "phasic," "limbic," "cortical," but it can be all that and also "exogenous"—externally driven, stimulated from without, from the "bottom up"—or "endogenous"—internally driven, stimulated from within, from the "top down": "introspective," "retrospective." Neuroacademia relevates these designations to the nth degree—a thoroughgoing depth.

Following a stimulus, some neurons "fire"—respond —immediately, with "spikes," while others are constantly "chattering," or "babbling," emitting signals of increasing length in response to increasing stimulus amplitude/intensity. The territories of this verbose combat are divided into demi-hemi-spheres, by either attentive activity or type: one region "activates," "controls," "drives," or "executes"; another serves to "modulate," or "inflect." The first affects neurons directly, increasing or decreasing their synaptic activity; the second affects them indirectly (a third might integrate them with a fourth). The idea is that "executive" and "legislative" branches are separated, from each other, and within themselves, to make the best or at least most efficient use of prior information or memory (long and short: the "judiciary"), so as not to retain any information or intelligence previously registered—no duplicates. (Quotes in the paragraphs above are sourced from scholarly lit published since 2000.)

Ultimately, though, the major cleavage in the brain, and so in attention, obtains between its areas that receive the stimuli—the primary visual cortex (cerebral cortex, occipital lobe), and the primary auditory cortex (cerebral cortex, temporal lobe); along with the extrastriate cortices, bilocated adjacent to the primary visual, which aid in spatial and shape distinctions; and superior temporal area 22, bilocated adjacent to the primary auditory, which aids in pitch recognition on the R side, and word recognition on the L—and the areas that process it. The connections between such sensory receptors and the disparate sites of sense processing break down in the lab, under the scrutiny of technological receptors and processors, especially if the subjects themselves are already "broken." Which is the most enduring neuroirony: If attention is locatable, it is sensory; if it is measurable, it is processual; as both, as neither, it can be defined only by its absence—by a subject's inability to focus; an inability to decide on what to focus; an inability to switch focuses; an inability to resist switching focuses—and this absence is most noticeably present in subjects who are "diseased." They themselves become the flaw in the connection. In neuroacademia, positive evidence for attention deficit might be a lesion or tumor, but negative evidence remains deaf and blind. Anecdotal. Situational. It's the traumatized who set the average, and what are impairments to them can only be hypotheses to the rest.[15]

15. The temporoparietal junction (TPJ), according to Michael Posner (b. 1936), whose study was quoted above, "appears to be a very specialized region that plays a role in reorienting away from an attended location, irrespective of the direction of new stimuli" (*Cognitive Neuroscience of Attention*, Second Edition). The right TPJ remains the only brain region "activated by a shift of attention both when shifts are expected and when they are unexpected." Also, "whenever an expectation is breached." The rTPJ, then, acts as a "reset device," "activated by reorienting irrespective of whether cognitive control was exercised." However, the rTPJ "also appears to be the most frequently damaged brain area in patients who experience neglect."

   In September 2006, the journal *Nature* published an account of an experiment at University Hospital, Geneva, in which researchers treated a bedbound epilepsy patient by applying an electromagnetic current to her left TPJ. The patient immediately sensed the presence of another person—young, of indeterminate gender, but speechless, motionless, and mimicking her posture. She identified this person as being behind her, which would've been beneath her—within the bed itself. A second, more intense electromagnetic current, applied with the patient in a sitting position, her arms across her chest, resulted in her feeling another presence—this time a man, aggressively wrapping his arms around her. A third current, of less intensity, was applied with the patient still in the sitting position, but this time instructed to conduct a language test, with flash cards. This time the patient detected a man sitting behind and to her right. She

In the process of digging around in the prop trunk of punishment—stockades, pillories, cages, loops, hoops, and saddles—Michel Foucault (1926–84) exhumed Jeremy Bentham's 1791 panopticon, a prison-theater-in-the-round. What Bentham had proposed as a measure to rehabilitate criminals—immuring them in glassed cells situated around a central tower, from which a warden could observe them, without being observed himself—became, in Foucault's conception, an architectural paragon of postwar Europe. Within this prison's mortifying exposure, European citizens, bereft of the reciprocities of family and community, could at least count on the recognizance of the state.

Though concomitant with this governmental warden being able to see and hear, yet not be seen or heard—the panopticon was also always a panauricon—was the prisoners' paranoia that no such entity existed. The inmates became so accustomed to the idea of an audience, in a sense, that when they began to doubt its existence—Sovietism had been checked, and torture was never officially sanctioned in Western prisons—they began to reform into an audience themselves. This, at least, was the emendation of Thomas Mathiesen (b. 1933), who posited that Foucault's interpretation had been canceled by the fall of the Iron Curtain, but that the individual, far from being freed, had rather absorbed totalitarianism

... claimed he was attempting to interfere with the test: "He wants to take the card—he doesn't want me to read it." Experimentation continued in different poses, producing similar effects whenever the current applied to the ITPJ exceeded 10mA. The researchers speculated that the ITPJ was responsible for "self-image": interoception, proprioception/kinesthesia. When the ITPJ is disrupted, so too might be the sense of autopossession, or selfhood, projecting instead an exteroceptional *doppelgänger* whose pose mirrors that of its host.

bodily, psychologically, to culminate in a warding—or governance—of self. A self-monitoring, an autoregulation, would define life in the global capital synopticon/ synaurican. With the convicts converted to spectators, the "warden" became the ward—a force bestowing fame and craving capital. Where the few had engaged the many, now the many would engage the few—still not interacting personally, but through the walls of glass cells refurbished into voluntary vitrines, as transpicuous as prophylactics. Bentham's original template, drafted by architect Willey Reveley, resembled an amphitheater, a tiered stadium fit for bread and circuses, touchdown dances and brute gang-rape cheers (the fans incarnating the on-field teams, reenacting = the carnage), but also it resembled: a wraparound surveillant screen bank.

Circumperception—omniscience—was once a deferred dream of the mightier intelligence agencies. Now it is an index, and privacy is valorized in its every liquidity: It can represent secrets, hidden appetites, and desires (which can be satisfied, profitably, only through being revealed), or just vast reserves of "sensibility." It is time, though, that becomes the most covetable asset in *the attention economy*. (Alternately, it becomes the least recoverable resource in *the attention ecosystem*—the natural world continues to borrow its most salient terminology from the marketplace at preferential rates.)

Advertising is now the cost of free hosting. Celebrities get free clothing so noncelebrities buy same, or cheaper versions of same. Culture is given away gratis, to certain influentials—refluentials—in return for criticism (which at its most perceptive addresses the mechanisms of distribution and hype, and at its least perceptive becomes just another component of them itself). The price of content is nonnegotiable—it is content of your own. Worth is generated for businesses by non-employees, by the unemployed—freelance consumers, prosumers (producer-consumers). "Remediation," that anodyne trope casting each and every format iteration as a body/mind ghosted by the soul of the format it has supplanted—painting and sculpture remediated by photography; live music performance remediated by recordings; the typewriter remediated by computer; books remediated by ebooks; hardware and software remediated by network—has already managed to account for every technology besides the human, whose remanence—whose magnetic retention—has been on the wane for two millennia, and yet for whom the newest conception of a supersessionary infrastructure still promises immortality upon "a cloud."

Name the minimum amount of money you're willing to be paid to reread this book in return for recommending it to 1.) one "friend," 2.) two "followers," 3.) six "unique connections," and 4.) your "full circle" (four separate figures); name the minimum amount of money you're willing to be paid *not to reread this*, but just to recommend it to 1.) two "friends," 2.) four "followers," 3.) twelve "unique connections," and 4.) your "full circle" (four separate figures); name the minimum amount you're willing to be paid to reread this book, all over again, from start to finish, in an electronic edition (regardless if that's how you've read it already), while being 1.) optically tracked, 2.) tested via a skin reactance/conductance interface, to measure patience/impatience, resistance/submission, while 3.) you yourself are reading it, 4.) listening to my own reading of it (audio version), 5.) while you're stuck in traffic, 6.) midday of a Friday in a, 7.) major city in, 8.) Asia (how many primary solutions? how many secondary?).

Determine how irked you'd be if you'd mentioned this book *positively*, in a msg you sent via your preferred msging service (no endorsements), and your msging service offered to sell you another copy; determine how irked you'd be if you'd mentioned this book *negatively*, in a msg you sent via your preferred msging service (no endorsements not considered), and your msging service offered to sell you another copy; rank the objects of your irk in each situation, from most to least (irksome): the msging service; yourself; the partnering online retailer, if a subsidiary of your msging service; the partnering online retailer, if not a subsidiary of your msging service; me; determine, if someone in your circle mentioned this book *positively*, and you received a msg that informed you that you were currently two miles away from a bookstore—believe it or not—a chain bookstore—that sold this book, and that if you acted within two minutes and bought this book in person, you'd receive 20 percent off, though if you acted remotely, and bought this book virtually, you'd receive only 10 percent, what you'd do; determine, if someone in your circle mentioned this book *negatively*, and you received a msg that informed you that you were currently two miles away from a bookstore—believe it or not—an independent bookstore—that sold this book, and other books, and that if you acted within two minutes and bought this book, or any book, in person, you'd receive 20 percent off, though if you acted remotely, and bought this book, or any book, virtually, you'd receive only 10 percent, what you'd do; compute your respective objects and levels of vexation; determine, because you'd enjoyed, or at least reviewed (****), a number (10) of your msging service's GPS/temporosensitive incentivizing offers in the past, whether you'll opt out of future notifications, whether you're capable of opting out of future notifications; determine whether you'd be more or less likely to purchase a second copy and/or edition of this book if an advertising msg featuring the book had interrupted, as an "interstitial," or "pop-up," a primary task (active: writing/reading email); or a secondary task (passive interactional: alternate promotional game [please specify]; or just clicking through the sites [please specify]); determine whether your willingness to pay for this book if it were being offered by an online biblio-retailer whose ad causes an *uncontrollable/incongruent* interruption of a primary task is higher or lower than your willingness to pay for this same book if it were being offered *by another online biblio-retailer* whose ads never cause such interruption (other factors being equal: the retailer's politics, diversity hiring practices, zero-tolerance harassment policies, fair wages, salaries, and benefits packages); determine whether your willingness to pay for this book if it were being offered by an online biblio-retailer whose ad causes a *controllable/congruent* interruption of a primary task is higher or lower than your willingness to pay for this same book if it were being offered *by the same biblio-retailer* whose ad causes an *uncontrollable/incongruent* interruption of a primary task.

Determine "whether interactivity promotes stickiness"; determine what that sticky substance is on your keyboard; determine to what degree your *enhanced voluntary attention*, gained through this book's PR/marketing campaign, initially came in the form of attention directed toward the book's design or executional elements (its cover), or toward its conceptual property (its "copy," or the publisher's explanation of what the book is about); determine to what degree your *enhanced involuntary attention*, gained through this book's PR/marketing campaign, initially came in the form of attention directed not toward the book but toward the campaign itself; gauge your interest in what have been called "interrupt rights"—a scheme by which I would pay you for the opportunity of interrupting you, so that I might read you, in person or over the phone, the corrections to the first edition of this volume, line by line, with your time appraised according to your earnings, or alternate metric of socioeconomic position (a fame rating, like the "Q score," Marketing Evaluations, Inc.'s quotient of name-brand/brandname recognition);[16] gauge whether you'd be more or less interested in what has been called an "attention bond"—a plan by which I would make an escrow payment representing the guarantee that my communication, my reading you this edition's corrections, won't waste your time; your cashing out the bond would cancel the contact and stop me from contacting you ever again, but your leaving the money in the bank would represent the hope for further interaction—meanwhile, for the duration of our info-relationship, we'd split the interest earned by the escrow (though my publisher, and agent, will have to take their percentages—strictly from my half, I assure you).[17]

16. Scott Fahlman, "Selling interrupt rights: a way to control unwanted e-mail and telephone calls," *IBM Systems Journal*, 2002. Another interruption: In a Carnegie Mellon University message-board post of 1982, Fahlman invented the smiley and frowny emoticons: :-) and :-(.

17. Thede Loder, Marshall Van Alstyne, Rick Wash, "An Economic Response to Unsolicited Communication," *Advances in Economic Analysis & Policy*, 2006. Another bond: Prior to pricing the time of information, Van Alstyne, along with Geoffrey Parker, depriced the templates of its delivery, in "Information Complements, Substitutes, and Strategic Product Design," Proceedings of the 21st International Conference on Information

Determine the quanta of respect, bummed cigarettes, and cadged drinks I will get from friends—true friends—for giving them free copies of this book; square that with the quantum of capital—cash money—I will earn from the sale of this book (to lesser friends, least acquaintances, strangers); determine the dimensions of my cell (currently twelve feet by twelve feet); pronounce the length of my sentence (on this essay alone: 186 writing days, 10 hours, 8 minutes, 4 seconds).

But this is not the way it has to be, and this is not the way it is. I offer as proof, Asia. Attention (in the sense of its lack) might be an interpellative first-world problem, a telemediated problem, a late-stage capitalist problem—it is not, or not yet, an Asian problem, and it might be difficult to find a country more first world than Japan, more telemediated than Korea, more late-stage capitalist than China.

That the closest equivalents to "attention," in all the Sino-Tibetan and Japonic languages and Korean, are totally static, or spiritually contemplative, translates the Western regard for the concept's utility into a condition bordering on mania. A deficit of attention is, perhaps, just a surplus of fearmongering. Now the West's might be the closed economy—creating an artificial resource, only to create an artificial scarcity: a scare, a run on the bank of attention.

To Buddhism, Taoism, and Confucianism, Western

··· Systems, 2000: "A firm can rationally invest in a product it intends to give away [free] in perpetuity even in the absence of competition." This was enabled by "a complementary goods market": businesses distributing a format or platform at no cost to customers, in order to profit from the sale of media itself.

perceptions can only be linking devices, connections between, and conditioned by, life's myriad disparities. Attention, in the West, is the very essence of this disparity, as it's neither a principle of conduct, nor a self-development discipline; neither a religious practice, nor tenet; instead, it is an addiction, a delusion. Founded in sequence and lost in rupture, attention is incapable of anything but a perpetual reprioritizing, becoming not the arbiter of experience, but experience itself—a substitute, a sham. True present—being—is set in competition with unsatisfiable drives, the pursuit of which is pleasureless, or resembles the recouping of an investment. To attend to stimuli, regardless of their source, is either to reinforce by compensation, or to compensate by reinforcement. To merely recognize the existence of a stimulus is to fail to transcend it—to lose not nothing, but nonexistence.

Buddhism's analogues of attention are not fixations on the discrete and linear, but contemplations of an integrative cycle. Its great turning dynastic wheels serve as calendars, chronometers, paradigms of reincarnation, and emblems of memory. The human too must become this wheel, whose turning must be ceaseless. Meditation within this motion—spiritual stasis in material motion—is the only way to attain both contentment and Nirvana. This practice is neither a compelled reaction (there is no compulsion), nor a willed response (there is no will)—just a receptivity.

In Sanskrit, the receptive faculties are called *samadhi*, which mark three circuits of Buddha's Eightfold Path: "right effort/diligence," "right mindfulness," "right concentration," constelling a class that Mahayana Buddhism has defined as the third of the Trainings (the Eightfold Path is itself a stop along the way of the

Four Truths, the first of Buddha's teachings after his enlightenment). "Right effort/diligence" is a ridding of physical baseness; "right mindfulness" a ridding of mental baseness; while "right concentration" is the meditative practice itself—ideally as imperturbable in light as in darkness, in noise as in silence, and in my own ignorance of the languages of Buddhism as in the obscurities of translation. Meditation is a blankness (of blankness), unless it is trained on a concept (thing/image) or mantra (word/sound), on your breath alone, or an object retrieved from Theravada Buddhism's *karmasthana*, or "workplace," a mental space of forty essential substances, beginning with earth, water, fire, and air—the *krtsna* or "substances that can be conceived of directly"—and proceeding through the "foulnesses" (corpses swollen, festering, dismembered), through to the virtues, only to end, though never ending, in paradox: "infinite nihility," "neither perception nor nonperception."

Historically, Theravada Buddhism emphasized *samadhi*, while Mahayana's Zen emphasized *prajna*, or "wisdom" ("discernment," "understanding"). To the other, older Buddhist schools, *prajna* was the first training of the Eightfold Path—whose circuits were "attitude" and "intention"—but to Zen, in China, Korea, and Japan, such divisions only frustrated the spirit of the very "attitudes" they were "intended" to inculcate. "Sudden" insight—not lasting attainment—was the Zen epiphany, while, between the seizures, "gradual" cultivation might continue, if not in life then in parable:

Once when Master Bankei [19–90 Edo] was preaching to his followers, he was interrupted by a Shin monk who espoused a belief in miracles, and would not be silent about how their power might be attained by the repetition of holy words. Master Bankei's followers were distracted, and, as he was unable to proceed, he ceded his time to the monk:

"The founder of my sect," the monk said, "stood on one bank of a river with a writing brush in his hand, and had his disciple stand on the other, holding a sheet of paper. The founder waved the brush in the air, and across the river the sacred name of Amitabha [Amida Buddha] was written. Tell me, Master—are you capable of anything so miraculous?"

Master Bankei shook his head.

"Alas, my miracles are of a lesser variety," he said. "When I'm hungry, I eat. When I'm thirsty, I drink. When I'm insulted, I forgive."

14. TRANSITIVE/TRANSACTIONAL, SPEED, COMPUTERS ON SPEED, SURVEILLANCE DREAMING

Chirography, typography, and the printing press inscribe a malleable surface. In such technologies the page, which does not flicker, is struck and imbued with markings. This process is analogous to the making of money. A coin is minted by mold, metal is poured into it, and an image is stamped on the surface. Given that nickels are only 25 percent nickel, it's the image that coins the worth: glyphs of gods and portraits of kings, now kitschy graphics of livestock and wheat. Bills are likewise receptive to scripting—paper authenticated by the reproduced signatures of presidents or prime ministers, treasurers, reserve-chiefs. Pecuniary inscription is a residuum of the regent's seal or signet, the guarantor of authorship and so, of "authority." Sphragides, sigilia, specie, and fiat currencies, printing's movable type screwed to pages, all recorded writing systems to date—in each instance an arbitrary materiality is forcibly impressed with transitory value.

Enter the computer—ENTER or RETURN—a device by and on which no mark is made, no enslaving gashes or incisions. With the digital the finger definitively gives way to the *digit*, turning the writing eminently editable, deletable. The wit of Benjamin Disraeli—no hyperlink, you'll have to search him out yourself—can now be incorporated into my own with nothing more than a negligent click: "Plagiarists, at least, have the merit of preservation."

But with the recently enabled immortality of data—through server autonomia, and the clouding of storage—preservation has become a type of nonpreservation:

Just because information is stored, safe and secure, doesn't mean it exists or has value.

Instead, computationally, existence is founded in value, and value is founded in motion—transclusing principles that themselves transcluse the information and attention economies. If "it" is moving, "it" has worth; if "it" has worth, "it" *exists*—until, that is, the motion's stilled, and the screenwork's printed, leaving only a text, a page, whose meaning has been borrowed from the screen in a travesty of the way that folding cash and change borrow from governance and bullion. Increasingly, the meaning that's borrowed is charity.

The computer "is a brain," according to scientists; the computer "is not a brain," according to scientists. I have read both claims on a computer. A program is "a rule"; a program is "a law." Data, "a case." A firewall: a barrier or screen designed to limit the spread of fire in a structure, and/or to mitigate a burning structure's collapse. Firewall 2.0: a metonymic construct within each society, a conceptual barrier or screen separating security (institutional) from privacy (individual). Section 255 of the U.S. Telecommunications Act (1996) protects American citizens from technology and from themselves: Websites must be made operable for those with little or no color perception; those with little or no hearing; "touchscreen and touch-operated controls shall be operable without requiring body contact or close body proximity"—meaning: for users without hands.

Web advertising ("webvertising") regards as prime placement the top-left banner, in L to R languages, and the top-right banner, in R to L languages—the starting points of end-user reading. Our vergence is tracked, our strokes, logged. The best passwords are produced stochastically, aleatorically—by flinging our digits at the keyboard uncapped, CAPPING the keyboard and flinging again, or, if numbers were chanced in the inaugural fling, shifting and flinging for symbols—as9f, &Q:Y.

The average TK (nationality) spent TK (metric, hours) per TK (metric, day) at the computer in TK (year), and TK (metric, $, £, €) per TK (metric, month) online in TK (year). TK (metric, number) sites have been accessed in the writing of this essay. TK (metric, number) facts have been assimilated. TK, a hold, a reserve—a journalistic abbreviation meaning material "to come," and a purposeful mistake by compositors, who noted that no English words begin with those letters.

These letters too have been typed, not formed, my ductus a cursor (when unblinking), a caret (when blinking). They came into being—they began—as manifestations of light, beamed at a screen TK (60x) per TK (second). Since using the computer, since going online, it's as if my mind itself has evanesced—with my mental ligatures, my tropes and types, now not leading my own words so much as following the sentences of others; now not linked to what I mean so much as to what others have meant, and so to what I could or should mean also; linking lucific. On the computer, with all its connectivity and access, "writing"—word processing, text generating—can only be a contendent app, yet another task among tasks, scheduled to a catenated beta, to be checked into, to be checked and responded to. "Distraction" has become too pervasive to require wording, to even be wordable. I would be better off describing to you your own face.

The "commodification" (approx. 2,430,000 Google.com hits as of 12/31/17) or "commoditization" (approx. 633,000 Google.com hits as of 12/31/17) of communication is as old as communication itself, and as young as its next product. An artifact or interaction offline has more utility when on—where it becomes transitive, transactional. The cultural artifact especially, in its reproduction, reproduces not just its producer—as it always has—but its consumer too, whose every interaction becomes an artifact, the new remains of civilization: the numeronymic remnants of a comment of chat. The first book I didn't write on paper—the first book I wouldn't have been able to write on paper—is now storaged, both on my computer and on multiple servers in multiple hemispheres (though the exact numbers and locations, my provider assures me, are better kept confidential), where it's searchable by stratum, by shard.

What had been a dialogue with a page is now a polylogue with that least demanding, and so most diverting, of audiences—information. The opportunity, to be read, advantages the impulse, to write. Meanwhile, the second self who reads my writing has options of his own to consider. Farewell my *tu*, my *du*. My interests, purchasing habits, age, and geochronographical stats, most of which have strained most of the relationships I've had, constitute the totality of my relationships to advertisers. False models result, which, in turn, condition future relationships: "You might like this person," but I don't; "you might like this book," but I don't like myself. (This, parenthetically, was why I decided on "attention." Once again I'd become reliant on a mind that didn't seem to need or even want me, who seemed perfect despite me. Every thing I'd search, I'd find. Except "attention." It wanted, needed, would be perfected by, mine. But: Wherever I searched, it wasn't, and just when I was sure it was found, it was gone.)

ADHD. The pharmaceutical industry might be the chief cause of this disorder so communicable I can't even type it without suffering its effects, in quotes: "attention deficit hyperactivity disorder," a generic term for three comorbid (some say), noncomorbid (others say), syndromes—ADHD predominantly hyperactive-impulsive, ADHD predominantly inattentive, and ADHD combined (hyperactive-impulsive *and* inattentive)—none of which may exist "off-label."

ADHD's diagnosis is by exclusion; there are only symptoms, not consistent signs, and there are no tests not biased by conceptions of appropriate behavior—"appropriate" defined both developmentally and socially. The nominal neurological evidence: Patients diagnosed with ADHD have evinced, under imaging and autopsy, not just subnormal functioning but also subnormal surface areas and/or thicknesses of frontostriatal structures, including dorsolateral prefrontal cortex (associated with organization, planning), dorsal anterior cingulate cortex (response selection, error detection), caudate, putamen, globus pallidus (the basal ganglia: working memory, response inhibition). "Nominal": a name for a thing that exists in name only.

Dyslexia, for example, has been claimed to express fairly locally, in a dysfunctional arrangement of smaller neurons (cells) and axons (fibers), in the thalamus and, developed ectopically, in the cerebral cortex. Autism too has been claimed as relatively locatable: in a supernormal number of neurons/axon bundles in the medial prefrontal cortex. But neither observations can be called cause or effect—for now, they're merely aberrancies in common. The sheer range of structures found reduced in the brains of patients diagnosed with ADHD suggests: The reduction is the result of other factors (drugs or alcohol in utero), or ADHD is a "global perturbation." Alternatively, homeopathically, the range of neurological evidence must stand for another range: a behavioral "dimensionality," or "spectrum," one extreme of which just won't shut up, while the other extreme just—slumps.

ADHD's descriptions—"won't sit still," "won't sit down," "antisocial-greedy," "social-overgenerous"—are so divergent as to serve as etiology: Pharmaceuticals aside (profit motive), blame has been placed with genetics (anomalies in the dopamine genes); environmental (organophosphate pesticides); diet (the preservative sodium benzoate, present in almost all packaged foods, and artificial food colorings including "sunset yellow," "Red #40"); lack of exercise (exertion elevates dopamine); increased television consumption (5 percent of American children are diagnosed with ADHD); increased number of cuts in television programming, especially cartoons (30–60 percent of diagnosed American children report symptoms persisting into adulthood). Anthropologists have offered an evolutionary solution, associating hyperactivity with the "hunter-gatherer," or "nomadic," characteristics of pretelevisual/preagricultural society. Meanwhile, psychoanalysis refuses to let neurology forget that juvenile attention-seeking is caused by overparenting and underparenting both. It's the confusion of the craving of attention for the inability to pay attention that is the contemporary deficiency. The contemporary disease.

But there are treatments to treat ourselves to. There are ways to heal yourself. While researching this essay, to aid in researching this essay, I've had to acquaint myself with psychostimulants both legal (amphetamine salts, obtained from a shrink in Manhattan who asked me the most rudimentary of checklist questions pertaining to depression until, when the topic turned to sex, I interrupted and asked for a prescription, which he promptly scribbled, so ending the exam), and illegal ("speed," obtained from a perky Turk in Berlin, who delivered throughout Kreuzberg/Neukölln reliably and punctually).

At the time I lived in Berlin, Freud's favorite substance, cocaine, was expensive, but speed was cheap and easy to obtain—it was even cheaper and easier to obtain than aspirin. Speed was peddled in parks and on corners and out of the backs of *Spätis* (delis), whereas aspirin was exclusively available at *Apotheken* (pharmacies).

"Aspirin" was once proprietary, registered to the German drugmaker Bayer Pharmaceuticals, which lost its international trademarks in the Treaty of Versailles (Part X, Chapter V, Section IV, "property, rights, and interests"). The year of that treaty, 1919, also marked the synthesis of crystallized methamphetamine—a compression of methyl-alpha-methylphenethylamine—though the drug wasn't commercialized until the verge of the next war, 1938, when Temmler Werke, in Berlin, packaged it as Pervitin. In Berlin the streetname for speed is "Perv," and the majority of foreigners in the city assume that it's related to "perversion," though a true speedfreak would know that any sex requiring an erection is unthinkable while binging: Amphetamines are vasoconstrictors, which cause blood-vessel walls to contract. The Nazis subsidized Pervitin, and issued three-milligram daily doses to the Wehrmacht (approx. one-third the daily dose administered to the average ADHD child), while the Americans and British supplied their troops with their own nationally sensitive uppers—the Americans, like the Germans, preferring theirs in pill form, the British preferring theirs in the form of tinctures and inhalants.

Meth's parent substance, amphetamine—alphameth-ylphenethylamine—was developed in Berlin too, in 1887, by chemist Lazăr Edeleanu of Friedrich-Wilhelms-Universität (now Humboldt-Universität), who also invented the process of refining crude oil. Amphetamine was and still is a more responsible, if more costly, business/pleasure choice than meth, whose double methylation was an attempt to enhance the drug's delivery system—in essence, to boost its potency. The progenitor of all phenethylamine-class psychostimulants is the organic compound ephedrine, which was first isolated in 1885 from plants of the *Ephedra* genus, though according to the notes I took on a rainy weekend night at the library of Humboldt-Universität, extracts of *Ephedra sinica*—joint-pine or joint-fir?—have been used in traditional Japanese and Chinese medicines to treat asthma and bronchitis—since when? The Zoroastrians made entheogenic use of the *Ephedraceae* too? Neanderthals buried themselves in it, in Kurdistan? My notes are spotty, contradictory. The library is closed on weekend nights. Is memory loss from amphetamine abuse recoverable? Have I searched that up before?

Each book is myriad, is books—what was conveyed to you, what I hoped to convey, your life as you were reading, my life as I was writing—and all the links between them, unlike links online, have to be so embedded and tightly tucked away that they're unnoticeable; whatever rumples the covers has to be tautened, smoothed.

Back at my apartment—my "flat"—K was on the edge.

He was in the midst of a binge and pacing around his bed, which was just a mattress: no blankets, no sheets, sleepless.

K (that is seriously his initial) was my roommate in Berlin. He used to work for Google. He was hired young and cashed out young, at +/-$600/share. His room was trashed with computers, programming manuals (bindered paper, as if to prove his cred), American snacks ordered online (he missed California). Full ashtrays, empty bottles.

He took another of my pills and broke off half of it for me.

We swallowed dry.

A legal pill, an illegal pill—a pill legal (in America) illegally obtained (in Germany), a pill illegal (in Germany) legally obtained (in America)—whichever: They have the same effect. With other sources, however, you have to equalize the doses. One thirty-milligram pharmaceutical-grade pill is not always equal to one thirty-milligram street-grade pill, due to the street's tendency to cut: with flour, baking soda, baking powder, rodenticide (if you invest in scales and purity testing kits, you're done for).

I'm alert; the mind gets fast, fastens. I'm attached to a thought, but then I forget it, but then I remember it, but it's not the thought I'd had. I don't think it is, at least. A day passes and if the dosage isn't upped, the brain scatters like grains across the trackpad. If another day passes and the dosage isn't upped—until, after sleeplessness, a crash.

K was pacing, babbling about clocks. About clock rates. Upclocking, overclocking. Increasing operating speed through dynascaling, therming.

Computers had gotten too slow.

He'd had this idea, he said. Rather, he said he had *a concept*.

He wanted to give a computer drugs. He wanted to program a computer not to process the neurological effect of amphetamine, rather to *experience the effect itself*.

He was already tossing the room, assembling our experiment.

We would compare the effects of amphetamine on a computer with the effects of amphetamine on ourselves—to determine how our processing differed and whether there might be a way of improving computer function without purging memory or performing system upgrades. But as the human brain and the computer were mere analogies for each other, we had to synthesize an amphetamine especially for the computer.

This led to a discussion of methodology.

From the start, the idea of analyzing amphetamine effect on humans—on ourselves—and using that data to create a program to affect our computer in a similar way was rejected, for the reasons that: 1.) human drug experience is never reliable, because humans on drugs are never reliable, and the two of us were now especially untrustworthy, and 2.) computers aren't capable of consciousness. Rather, even if a computer could be programmed to be aware that it was on drugs, it could never be programmed with that uniquely human admixture of acceptance/denial that both acknowledges the altered state, yet repeatedly proclaims, "I'm OK," or "I'm perfectly fine to drive." At the time of our experiment, at least, programming neurosis was beyond K's—beyond anyone's—ability.

So we discussed and peer-reviewed, and finally a single approach was decided upon: The first step was to analogize the brain, the second to analogize the substance.

Firstly we'd analyze the way in which amphetamine

694

affected the different areas of our brains, as a means to identifying analogous areas within the computer's central processing unit (CPU).

Secondly we'd analyze the human amphetamine, or *humphetamine*, as we called it, in order to find a way to directly translate it to computer amphetamine, or *comphetamine*, as we called it, by coding their chemico-constituents—the isomers levo and dextro, the hydrogen, NH_2, and CH_3—into their computational equivalents.

So we went ahead, began analogizing brain structure: Memories short-term and long-term became issues of storage (humphetamine having slight impact on long-term main memory or disk, the comphetamine equivalent would have to focus on affecting the short-term or random access/cache); primary visual and auditory cortices became the computer's instruction pointer, which receives and keeps track of the order of programmed instruction; the mesolimbic and mesocortical "reinforcement pathways," which control responses of satisfaction or pleasure at the completion of each task, became the write-back connection located between the instruction pointer and the register file (which stores the memory of each executed instruction: operands/results); the dopamine, serotonin, and glutamate neurotransmitters, and their respective transporter proteins, were found in the internal clock, the crystal oscillator, and their connections (all of which determine and conduit rate of processing).

As for the drug, the comphetamine itself: It was coded with supplemental l-and-d enantiomers, which, in context, were instructions to the processor to: 1.) buffer or ignore—levo—any auxiliary program we attempted to run during the running of the initial program, if that auxiliary program was larger or took longer to load, and

2.) reinforce that buffering or ignorance by preventing—dextro—the pointer from sending the execution for write-back—essentially telling the computer not to store any record of its activity in the cache. Lastly, the hydrogen, the binding essence of the molecule, was the primary instruction to the computer's internal clock—to continually and steadily increase its speed for the duration of the experiment.

Then we had to choose the initial program. We chose something medium-sized. Nothing with video or audio. Word processing.

We loaded our word processer, ran the comphetamine master. We dosed the computer, full strength.

The computer began processing, radiating heat; the cooling fan whirred (K had decided that the computer would not be allowed any supplementary cooling elements).

Throughout the processing, as I typed—or rather flung my digits at the keys: jrfivytnggggggghh10pz,.—K floated over me, interrupting my flinging with attempts to run the auxiliary programs: regular checking of processor speed, irregular searches of cache for memory of executions the computer had been instructed to buffer or ignore, a file (huge) of *Scarface*, these bit.torrents (huge) of a complete season of a German reality show I didn't recognize—*Frauentausch*—the translation would be *Wife Exchange*? *Wife Swap*?

The intention was that the intervals between K's running of these programs would decrease in direct proportion to the increase in clock rate—but we weren't so organized, or unimpaired.

Error msgs. Fails.

It got so that I was typing into void: Stuff I'd typed seconds ago, one two three four seconds ago, still hadn't appeared onscreen.

The flicker was mutual; the hum was in my hands.

I was still typing when it crashed.

A fantasy, a dream—or whatever you call a dream when you're not sleeping. Such are the moments—the moments just before sleep when you're occupied by a notion you'd like to accompany you into your proper somatic oneiric peace; and it will if you try, or only if you don't try, though if it does, you might not remember that it has, or you might not yet remember that it did, meaning that it's stored but accessible only to a future computer that can read everything stored but not humanly retrievable (you've never been the user approved); or else it might be accessible, perhaps, but only under the influence of a future medication that would remove such limitations within yourself (repression/suppression, senescence); or else it might be accessible, perhaps, but only to a future computer that must be administered its own version of this future medication to compensate for your initial storage or transmission having been faulty, degraded.

The idyll, the reverie. Our attentions have only as much in common as our dreams do.

Science has proposed attention as the purview of an enormous organ, an organon—a system with functions of reflection, projection, and even reasoning; while philosophy has proposed attention as a metonymic presumption whose evolution has conditioned scientists—in an age in which attention has been declared endangered, or nearly extinct—to use the term to link more than any analogy can "handle": the visual, auditory, olfactory, gustatory, and tactile perception of objects, and the

697

apperception of everyone's favorite nodding subject, the self. The most pressing concern is not that such things aren't connected—no one would claim that they weren't—neither is it that they shouldn't be—no one would claim that either—rather it's that their connection will lead to further medications and technologies that will mediate us and our mutual experience.

It should be no consolation that though we can never become conscious of our own attention, we can become conscious of each other's. Science's model of a totally integrated attention system enduringly monitoring and tracking, remembering, and expecting is as much a description of our hopes for ourselves as it is of our anxieties about the vigilant global sensorium surrounding.

TEST

1. According to her own diary, had Alice James (1848–92), sister of William and Henry, and victim of "hysteria," contemplated: a.) parricide, b.) suicide, c.) parricide *and* suicide, or, d.) fratricide, parricide, *and* suicide?

b. If Deuteronomy 25:19 instructs us to "blot out the remembrance of [the people] Amalek," why does it also instruct us: "thou shalt not forget it," or even mention Amalek in the first place?

3. Jesus is mentioned as writing only once, in John 8:6: "He stooped down, and with his finger wrote on the ground." Below, paraphrase his message.

d. Avicenna (ca. 980–1037) claimed the existence of five internal senses, to complement the five external senses of sight, hearing, smell, taste, and touch. Below, match the five internals to their functions:

Collects the attention   *Vis cogitans*

Memory of attention   *Vis memoralis*

Collects the intentiona   *Vis aestimationis*

Memory of intentions   *Imaginatio*

Compounds/divides the   *Fantasia/Sensus*
attention/intentions   *communis*

5. "Homer" mentions writing only once, in *The Iliad*.

Bellerophon, son of Glaucus, is exiled from Ephyra for having killed—possibly his brother, possibly his own shadow. He arrives in the Argives, dominion of King Proteus, where the queen, Antea, offers to have sex with him. He, being honorable, refuses—only to be accused by her of attempted rape. But Proteus is honorable too, at least in context, and refuses to kill his guest. Instead, he dispatches Bellerophon to his father-in-law, King Iobates of Lycia, bearing a sealed message the hero does not open. Bellerophon is banqueted by night; the next morning King Iobates asks to read the message from his son-in-law. King Iobates, despite being convinced by the message that Bellerophon is a rapist, is also reluctant to murder a guest—once again, violence deferred, or deflected. The king sends the hero to slay the goat-bodied, lion-headed, snake-tailed, fire-breathing, and female, Chimera. Bellerophon is successful at this, as he is at every test that follows: the conquering of the Solymi, and of the Amazons (helped along by his pet project, the horse Pegasus), and this success indicates to the king that Bellerophon is an offspring of the gods. With this intelligence, the content of the concealed message is nullified, and the king even offers Bellerophon his daughter in marriage. Concealed messages become important plot devices in subsequent—written—literature. Give another example of a communication that is never disclosed, and yet another of a text that contains no subtext.

f. Explain the Cartesian theater and/or the entertainment preferences of the homunculus.

7. Demonstrate *Sitzfleisch*.

h. Fill in the blanks: Contrary to the evolutionary monogenism of _____ _____, the creationary polygenism of American ethnographer _____ _____ _____ and Swiss paleontologist and glaciologist _____ _____ posited the different races of humans as separately created species. But the theories of German biologist and naturalist _____ _____, derived from the ideas of German, Proto-Indo-European linguist _____ _____, accommodated their polygenism within an evolutionary system. _____ proposed that several diverse language families had emerged, separately, from speechless prehominid *Urmenschen*, who were, themselves, the direct descendants of simians. It was those languages that effected the transition from animal to human, as each language family, under the influence of its tongue, evolved its respective race traits—with the languages with the largest vocabularies forming the races, the species, with the greatest economic/political/cultural/military might.

Arrange those languages, according to the schema of _____, in order from most to least evolved: Semitic/Indo-Germanic/Greco-Roman/Berber/Jewish/German.

9. Average shot length in Hollywood movies: 1930 (advent of "talkies")–60 approx. 9.5 seconds; 1960–70 approx. 7.5 seconds; 1970–80 approx. 6.5 seconds; 1980–90 approx. 5.5 seconds; 1990–2000 approx. 5 seconds; 2000–10 approx. 4 seconds.

At the average rate of acceleration, calculate the expected average shot length in films of the present decade.

j. Graphology, the study of the individual stamp in handwriting, involves having a person write freely, then subjecting that sample—in content and appearance—to analyses both objective (how large or small are the letterforms?) and subjective (how schizoid or angry is this word shape?). The laws of graphology are the rules of writing: There aren't any. Being foremost a margin of interpretation: Is this writing rushed or leisurely? Dominant or submissive? Graphology exercises taste, not diagnosis, and the graphologist must always entertain the suspicion that the writer is disguising his hand.

Shakespeare's plays and poems have survived; their manuscripts have not. The only specimens of his writing are signatures, of which six exist. One is appended to Will's will, his final testament of 1616, in which he left his second-best bed as his sole bequest to his wife. All the signatures are somewhat different in appearance, and even somewhat differently spelled—disparities that have ludicrously encouraged the Shakespeare Did Not Write Shakespeare Industry. The signature is the writer's outer expression or face (tellingly, there is only one confirmed likeness of Shakespeare), and it remains—from job applications to credit-card receipts—the primary representation of human authenticity, even with the availability of retinal/thumbprint scanners and other biometric devices. Graphology's junk science was ultimately mooted not by collaborative cloud .docs, but by what Microsoft Word calls "Properties": the function that tracks which user created, and subsequently altered, which document, when and even where, imparting to writing a total accountability. At the time of Shakespeare's death, common law held that a testator's signature was not vital to the validity of a will, nor were signatures required, or even admissible, on business contracts and marriage agreements—a provision due to both pervasive illiteracy and ease of forgery (there being, of course, no incentive to regularize a signature). Only in 1677, when English Parliament passed an Act for the Prevention of Frauds and Perjuries (also called the Statute of Frauds), did the signature become the official formal gesture, though it was popularly regarded as flawed.

Perhaps the most infamous failure of graphology was the case of Captain Alfred Dreyfus (1859–1935). The handwriting on a confidential dispatch, a *bordereau*, offering to pass French military intel to Germany was found to have matched a snatch of writing willingly provided by a detained Dreyfus, despite the fact that his slanted, modified Copperplate script was taught and required at every *lycée* and *école*. Lieutenant Colonel Armand Mercier du Paty de Clam, lead investigator into *l'affaire*, and an amateur graphologist (preferable to a professional), testified to a general staff tribunal that the two writing samples were identical, and Dreyfus, convicted by his own hand as much as by dint of his race, was branded a traitor to France.

Identify whether the writing below is Dreyfus's, or that of the forgery that convicted him. Analyze it, separately, as both.

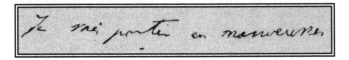

11. Can the margin, fringe, and focus model of sight be reconciled with the focal (fovea)/ambient (peripheral) model? If no, is this because the former doesn't distinguish between object distinction and orientation? The

two photoreceptors of the eye are rods and cones, and each of the three types of cone is geared to a different range of light. Pick one best description of trichromacy and explain your selection: Red, Green-Yellow, Blue (the human application), or Cyan, Magenta, Yellow (the standard of digital printing). Since a single type of cone isn't capable of perceiving the full spectrum, the cones interact to signal the primary visual cortex, which effectually mixes them to determine intensity/color. Rods, though, are achromatic, and don't allow us to distinguish poisonous berries, or blushing. Explain the nostalgia inherent in black-and-white media. Explain that innate sentimentality physiologically. Finally, why is the musical scale called "chromatic"? Is synaesthesia purely psychological? Why is it that Western pigments have many names, but Western sounds no more than twelve, given well-tempered tuning? If black noise is equally silent at all frequencies, and white noise equally loud at all frequencies, what is gray noise: the psychoacoustic experience of a sound's equality of silence or loudness at all frequencies, or both black noise and white noise inexperienced, tickling the ear hairs at inaccessible frequencies?

l. Explain why humans don't have lidded auricles (ears). How might we acquire them? Shut your eyes, consider "blue," note whatever substance you conceive of. Would you judge yourself by it?

13. The American psychologist Julian Jaynes (1920–97) proposed a split in the brains of primitive man: a preliterate bicamerality. The dominant L practical hemisphere of the brain dealt with the subsistence tasks of early civilization. When a trickier circumstance

arose that did not elicit an immediate response, the recessive R creative hemisphere would activate, sending strange messages that were not understood and so attributed to higher, or lower, forces—God, or demons.

Refute this.

n. Confirm/deny both statements: To become conscious of attention is to create attention. To become conscious of attention is to destroy attention.

(Short) Notes on A (SHORT) HISTORY

Texts originally in English are presented as written. All translations, however, are my own, especially their faults. A list of books consulted would be a book unto itself. Of the texts not cited or hopefully evident, there's one in particular I'd like to mention as being free of charge, universally available, and indispensable: "The Prehistory of the Concept of 'Attention,'" Ciarán McMahon, doctoral thesis, University College, Dublin, 2007, books.google.com/ books/about/ The_Prehistory_of_the_Concept_of_Attenti. html?id=83dMREnwWB8C.

Acknowledgments are due to Sam Frank and Alexander Provan, editors at *Triple Canopy* (canopycanopycanopy.com), where an excerpt of this essay first appeared, in different form.

But then even my gratitude first appeared in different form:

> Two studies examined the role of self-focused attention on gratitude and indebtedness. In Study 1, higher dispositional levels of indebtedness were associated with lower dispositional levels of gratitude. Moreover, individuals prone to greater public self-consciousness and social anxiety reported more indebtedness and, to a lesser extent, less gratitude. Social anxiety and public self-consciousness were unique predictors of indebtedness, though only social anxiety was a unique predictor of gratitude. In Study 2, we induced self-focus via the presence of a mirror. Under high self-focus conditions, people reported more indebtedness when recalling a recent benefit; gratitude was not significantly affected by the self-focus induction. Thus, the findings from these studies suggest that self-focused attention can play an important role in how people recall benefits received. ("Looking at me, appreciating you: Self-focused attention

distinguishes between gratitude and indebtedness,"

M. Mathews, J. Green, *Cognition & Emotion*, Vol. 24, Issue 4, 2010.)

Image credits

Fitzcarraldo Editions
243 Knightsbridge
London, SW7 1DN
United Kingdom

ISBN 978-1-910695-74-6

Design by Ray O'Meara
Typeset in Fitzcarraldo
Printed and bound by TJ International

fitzcarraldoeditions.com

Fitzcarraldo Editions